GAZA

The series in Comparative Politics and International Studies

Series editor, Christophe Jaffrelot

This series consists of translations of noteworthy manuscripts and publications in the social sciences emanating from the foremost French researchers at Sciences Po, Paris.

The focus of the series is the transformation of politics and society by transnational and domestic factors—globalisation, migration and the post-bipolar balance of power on the one hand, and ethnicity and religion on the other. States are more permeable to external influence than ever before and this phenomenon is accelerating processes of social and political change the world over. In seeking to understand and interpret these transformations, this series gives priority to social trends from below as much as to the interventions of state and non-state actors.

JEAN-PIERRE FILIU

Gaza

A History

Translated by
John King

HURST & COMPANY LONDON

The book was first published in French as Histoire de Gaza, by Fayard in 2012.

First published in the United Kingdom in 2014 by
C. Hurst & Co. (Publishers) Ltd.,
41 Great Russell Street, London, WC1B 3PL
© Jean-Pierre Filiu, 2014
All rights reserved.

A Cataloguing-in-Publication data record for this book is available from the British Library.

ISBN: 978-1-84904-401-1

www.hurstpublishers.com

This book is printed on paper from registered sustainable and managed sources.

To the memory of the thousands anonymous
Who died in Gaza before their time
Though they had a life to live
En famille and in peace

CONTENTS

CONTENTS

True it was a long time ago
But now I read in this book

A sad history book
The tale of a people fighting to live

True all this is still sounding
In my grandfather's heart

True it was a long time ago
But life keeps flowing

Hope stays vibrant
Like an echo in the loneliness

Looking through this book
I found the following dates

Page 22, the mandate on Palestine
Page 47, the partition plan

Page 48, the rivers of the refugees' tears
Page 67, the Six-Day war

Palestinian Rapperz (PR), Gaza, 2006

FOREWORD

The word 'Gaza' arouses passions and emotions whenever it is uttered. In this small territory of 360 square kilometres, wedged between Israel, Egypt and the Mediterranean Sea, more than 1.6 million souls live out their daily lives in what has been described as 'the largest open air prison in the world'.[1] Although thirty-eight years of physical occupation came to an end with the Israeli withdrawal of September 2005—and though the settlements that had appropriated a quarter of this limited space have now been dismantled—Gaza has remained cut off, first 'sealed' and then besieged, while the rivalries between the Palestinian factions have grown ever more embittered.

In June 2007 the supporters of Fatah and Hamas became embroiled in a civil war. Hamas, which emerged as the victor, subsequently established an Islamist administration in Gaza whose intransigence contrasted with the more moderate stance of the Palestinian Authority in the West Bank, where negotiation continued to be the preferred option in relations with the State of Israel. Israel responded with a military onslaught against the new administration in Gaza in the closing days of 2008. But this had little effect on Hamas's resolve, despite the intensity of the violence—in those dark times, one inhabitant of Gaza in a thousand lost his or her life in the fighting: never had the territory undergone such destruction, much of which has yet to be repaired due to the subsequent Israeli blockade.

Considering the appalling reality of life in contemporary Gaza, a broader view of the current situation can only be taken from the perspective of history, with an attempt to set aside the disorientation, the horror and the hatred that the present situation has engendered. The 'Gaza Strip', as it is today, is not so much a geographical entity as the product of the tormented and tragic history of a territory where the majority of the population is made up of refugees who have already attempted to escape other torments, and other tragedies. Gaza's borders have closed in on those who have fled there: the refugees born within the territory have been destined to remain confined within it, a fate they also share with all of those who have dreamed of leaving it. Neither Israel nor Egypt wanted the 'Strip' to exist: it is a territorial entity 'by default'.

The intensity of the situation in Gaza enabled Palestinian nationalism to come into existence. It was here, a place without any particular symbolic significance, from which the Palestinian fedayin, and then in 1987 the 'intifada', emerged. The intifada, the so-called 'revolt of the stones', was the first step in a process that culminated in Israel's recognition of the PLO (Palestine Liberation Organisation) and the latter's recognition of the State of Israel. This was the first act in an ongoing peace process that has failed to result in peace. The participants in the process, the Palestinian Authority and the Israeli Labour Party, initially aimed to transform the territory of Gaza into the Hong Kong of the Middle East, a goal which appeared to be realistic enough at the time. Yet such an outcome now seems so distant as to be beyond reach.

It is therefore necessary to re-examine Gaza's history in order to open a vista beyond today's devastation and grief and to bring into view a new horizon for the future. This will not only benefit Gaza; as part of the world's destiny is unfolding in symbolic terms within this small scrap of land, we all stand to gain from a better understanding of the territory's long and complex history.

The act of writing a history of Gaza involves many difficulties and methodological problems, the first of which pertain to the local archives. In many cases parts of the archives have been destroyed in the course of successive conflicts, while other sections have been moved out of the territory by successive administrations and are today the object of wrangling between Fatah and Hamas, each of which claims to be the sole legitimate Palestinian Authority. In November 2010 I sought to overcome this deficiency with regard to local information by conducting a series of interviews, and I also succeeded in assembling a substantial repertoire of

FOREWORD

unpublished documents. The security constraints which prevailed in the territory, where certain zones remain off limits to research, presented a further problem. When the appropriate moment arrives, it would consequently be beneficial to go further into the various aspects of Gaza's history that cannot be explored at present in order to enrich a Palestinian historiography that is still unduly centred on Jerusalem and the West Bank.

A further constraint that a historian encounters when researching contemporary Gaza concerns Hamas's policy of promulgating an 'official history'. Since taking power in 2007, the publications that have appeared in Gaza under Hamas's auspices spuriously credit the Muslim Brotherhood with a continuous existence in a position of pre-eminence over the last seventy years, which suggests that the Brothers had always been in the vanguard and at the heart of the Palestinian nationalist struggle.[2] Claims such as these naturally tend to withhold credit from the other Palestinian factions, and in particular from Fatah, which constitutes the current Palestinian Authority in Ramallah. The perspective of history provides the ability to reinterpret these often tenuous and biased accounts of Gaza's history; and as Hamas's intention is to reinforce its dominant position now and in the longer term, much is at stake.

The completion of this book would not have been possible without the help of a number of individuals, and I would like to express my sincere gratitude to all of those whose support was essential for undertaking this task. These include, from the French diplomatic service, Frédéric Desagneaux, France's consul-general in Jerusalem, and his colleagues in Gaza, Jean Mathiot and Majdy Shakoura; Christophe Bigot, the French ambassador in Tel Aviv, Alexis Lecour-Grandmaison, deputy director for the Middle East at the French Ministry of Foreign Affairs, and Dominique Vondrus-Dreissner, keeper of the diplomatic archives. In Gaza I would like to acknowledge the assistance of Sami Abdel Shafi, Freih Abu Middain, Sahba Barbari, Towfik Bseisso, René Elter, Ayman Mghamis, Rabah Mohanna, Issa Saba, Moussa Saba, Misbah Saqr, Jason Shawa, Rawya Shawa, Ghazi Sourani, Intissar al-Wazir, and of the late Mustafa Abdel Shafi and Eyad al-Sarraj; in Jerusalem, Mordechai Bar-On, Charles Enderlin and Jean-Baptiste Humbert. I would also like to acknowledge the assistance I received in Paris from Tewfik Aclimandos, Hassan Balawi,

FOREWORD

Marc Etienne, Henry Laurens and Elias Sanbar. I am also grateful for the help of the staff of UNRWA, Anne Le More and Richard Cook in New York, and Amani Shaltout in Gaza.

My thanks go to Jean-François Legrain, Benjamin Barthe and Alexis Tadié, all of whom generously gave up their time to read the manuscript. Maurice Sartre, from his base in Damascus, generously agreed to guide my footsteps through the topic of ancient Gaza. I am grateful to those academics who have allowed me to give papers on my ongoing research within their institutions. These include Rashid Khalidi, Peter Awn and Astrid Benedek at the University of Columbia in New York, and Luz Gomez Garcia and Ana Planet at the Universidad Autonóma de Madrid. I also wish to thank the staff of the libraries in which I worked, at the school for doctoral research at Sciences Po in Paris, at the Moshe Dayan Centre at the University of Tel Aviv, and at Columbia University. Finally, this book could not have appeared without the confidence and support lavished on me by Olivier Nora and Sandrine Palussière at my French publisher, Fayard, along with Michael Dwyer, at Hurst & Co.

J.-P. Filiu

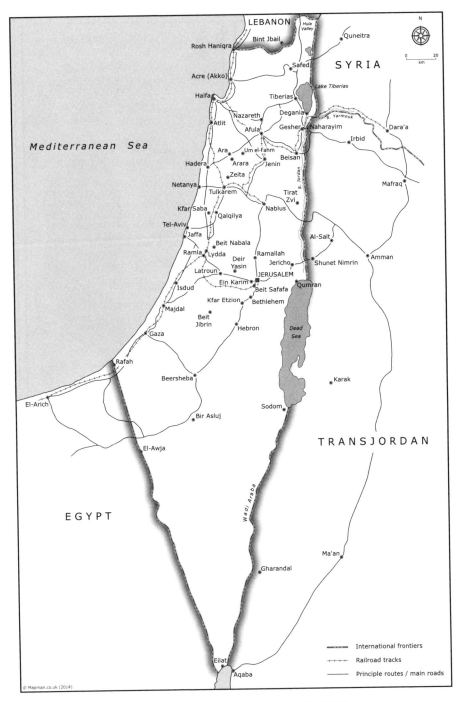

Map 1: Mandatory Palestine, 1922-1948

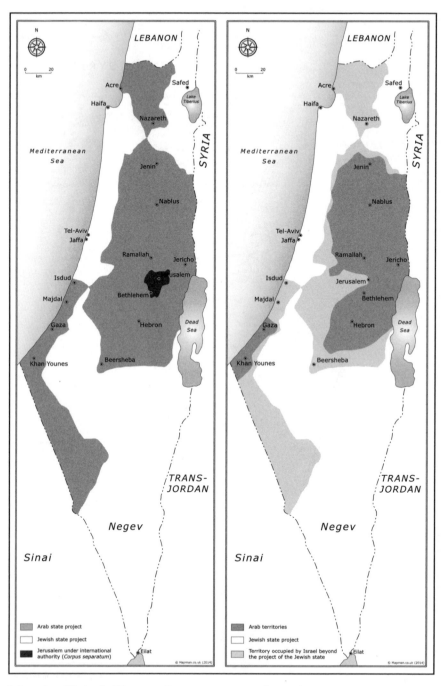

Map 2a: United Nations Partition
Resolution 181, 1947

Map 2b: 1949 Armistice Agreements
and Demarcation Lines

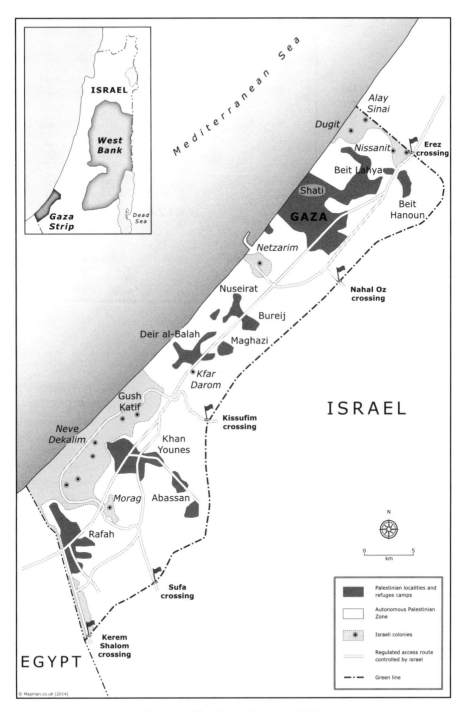

Map 3: The Gaza Strip in 2000

Map 4: The Gaza Strip in 2009

GAZA BEFORE THE STRIP

1

THE CROSSROADS OF EMPIRES

Travellers who have visited Gaza over the centuries have often remarked on the fecundity of its vegetation and the diversity of its agriculture, both of which are the products of its underground waters and the gentle nature of the prevailing climate. The Gaza Valley (Wadi Ghazza), which runs down into the sea to the south of the modern city, offers a welcome refuge to migrant birds and small animals; the coolness and shade of this coastal oasis contrast with the dusty tracks nearby that lead towards the Negev. Gaza is the endpoint of the Levant coastline, the last haven before the inhospitable desert. Mastery of Gaza has therefore been a key issue in the rivalry between the powers that have established themselves in the Nile Valley and the Middle East. Whereas it was impossible to conquer Egypt from the eastern Mediterranean without relying on Gaza, Gaza was also an indispensable bridgehead for any invasion of the Levant from Sinai. As a result, ownership of Gaza has often been transferred from one empire to another. According to the Book of Genesis, its original Semitic population had links to the people of Canaan, of which Gaza was at the southern edge.[1]

The Hyksos established themselves in the Middle East in the eighteenth century BC, where they created forts 8 kilometres to the south of Gaza around Tall al-Ajjul, including the fort in Sharuhan, sometimes known as 'southern Tall al-Ajjul', the site of which lies in what is today the Israeli Negev. The Hyksos used these forts as a base for their conquest of Egypt.[2] They founded their own dynasty of pharaohs, the fifteenth dynasty, before

3

gradually losing their hold over Egypt under the onslaught of the rulers of Thebes. After being hounded out of the Nile Valley they entrenched themselves in the southern part of the present-day Gaza Strip. The Theban Pharaoh Ahmose I, the first of the eighteenth dynasty, was only able to capture Sharuhan after a three-year siege, with the enemy stronghold finally being razed around 1530 BC. By the time of the reign of the third pharaoh of the eighteenth dynasty, Thutmose I, Gaza had come under the rule of the Egyptian pharaohs.

Gaza Between Egypt and the Orient

Thutmose III, the sixth pharaoh of the eighteenth dynasty and one of the great architects of Egypt's territorial expansion, carried out a series of campaigns against Syria. In around 1457 BC he took personal command of his troops in the advance up the 'Horus Road', as the littoral route towards the north was known in the era of the pharaohs. Following the celebrations for the twenty-third anniversary of his accession to the throne in Gaza,[3] an army of 20,000 men went into action in the territory of Canaan.[4] It was at this time that Gaza, sited slightly inland from the shoreline and adjacent to a natural harbour that was perfectly suited to coastal navigation, began to develop as a city.

As the principal residence of the region's Egyptian governor, Gaza assumed the role of an administrative and commercial centre, with its neighbouring trading posts, such as Rafah and Deir al-Balah, sharing in its prosperity.[5] Canaanite sarcophagi from this period, in human shape, found at Deir al-Balah and once owned by Moshe Dayan, can be seen in the Israel Museum.[6]

Yet as different rulers succeeded each other, Egypt's control over Gaza gradually became looser until Pharaoh Sethi I sought to bolster his authority with an expedition towards the east in 1294 BC, soon after he had ascended the throne of Thebes. Friezes at the Temple of Karnak commemorate this successful campaign against the Mediterranean cities.[7] Sethi I's successor, Ramses II, successfully mobilised the Egyptian garrison in Gaza to check the new threat from the north: the Hittites. Gaza thus remained vital for maintaining control of the Egyptian territory of

Canaan[8]—no less than sixteen pharaohs are said to have resided in Gaza during the course of their reigns.[9]

In the twelfth century BC the so-called 'Sea Peoples' irrupted into the Levant. Archaeologists are divided as to whether the latter were of Asiatic, Mediterranean or even European origins. Yet it was their arrival, and the ensuing turmoil it created, that sounded the death-knell for the Hittite Empire. In contrast, Pharaoh Ramses III was able to preserve the inviolability of Egypt as a result of his land and sea victories over the invaders, even though he was obliged to cede to them part of the so-called Horus Road. The Philistines, the most powerful of the Sea Peoples, were subsequently able to establish themselves on the threshold of Sinai and the Negev, where, through force and assimilation, they transformed this part of south-west Canaan into 'Philistia', a name of unknown origin from which the name 'Palestine' is derived. Philistia was organised as a 'pentapolis': a federation of five city-states in which Gaza joined with Ascalon (modern Ashkelon), Isdud (which lay close to modern Ashdod), Ekron and Gath.

The Philistines gradually came into conflict with the Jewish tribes of the interior because they impeded the latter's access to the sea. It was the persistence of this confrontation which gave rise to two of the most famous biblical stories: the legend of Samson, and the story of David and Goliath. In the Old Testament, the Angel of God proclaims the birth of Samson, destined to 'deliver Israel out of the hand of the Philistines', though this was on the condition that his hair would never be cut.[10] A brave fighter of Herculean strength, Samson repeatedly challenged the Philistines until he was betrayed by the crafty Delilah, who had his head shaved as he slept. After being delivered into the hands of his enemies, with his eyes put out, Samson was dragged in chains to the prison at Gaza where he was put to turning a mill. It was also in Gaza, with his hair grown once more and his strength regained, that he took his vengeance by pulling down the pillars of the pagan temple of the Philistine deity Dagon upon his oppressors, a story that has inspired dramatists over subsequent centuries, from Milton's *Samson Agonistes* (1671) to Cecil B. DeMille's film *Samson and Delilah* (1949). The conflict between the Philistines and the Jews is similarly reflected in the story of David, who was still a boy when he was said to have brought down the Philistine champion Goliath before unifying the kingdoms of Judah and Israel.

In the second half of the tenth century BC, Pharaoh Sheshonk I, the founder of the twenty-second dynasty, embarked once more on the conquest of Canaan. This military campaign was launched from the Nile Delta and began with the occupation of Gaza, the stepping-stone of operations directed at the Levant, as had been the case with earlier Egyptian efforts to conquer Canaan. But the rule of Sheshonk I, or 'Shishak', as he is referred to in the Bible, was not to last. While Gaza was in practice obliged to pay periodical tribute to Jerusalem under the reigns of Solomon[11] and Hezekiah,[12] it remained a Philistine city until the eighth century BC, which brought down upon it the maledictions of the Prophet Amos.[13]

During this period the pendulum of imperial domination oscillated between Assyria and Egypt. Hanun, the king of Gaza, tried to play one off against the other until the sacking of his city by Assyrian invaders in 734 BC obliged him to concede his fealty to Nineveh. He sought to shake off the Assyrian yoke twelve years later, but he underestimated the violence of the ensuing counter attack. Egyptian reinforcements were blocked at Rafia (present-day Rafah), south of Gaza, where Hanun fell into the hands of his adversaries and was sent in chains to Nineveh. Gaza offered no challenge to the domination of the Assyrians over the course of the following century, and its autonomy was recognised by the Assyrians in return. This situation lasted until the fall of Nineveh in 612 BC and the collapse of the Assyrian Empire in 609 BC, when Gaza again fell into the Egyptian sphere. But this was only to remain the case for less than a decade due to Egypt's capitulation to the new Babylonian Empire of Nebuchadnezzar II, when Gaza became Babylon's western front line: an advance post at the gateway of Egypt, Babylon's vassal state.

Gaza retained this role as a front-line garrison when Babylon was subjugated by Cyrus the Great, the founder of the Persian Empire who had already conquered Lydia and Ionia in Asia Minor, in 539 BC. A battle-hardened contingent of Greek mercenaries supported the Persian officers who now replaced their Babylonian predecessors. In the ensuing two centuries of Persian rule, Gaza flourished as a commercial crossroads between Egypt and the Levant and as a maritime terminus for the caravans from 'Arabia Felix', as Yemen was known, the source of spices and precious stones.[14] In return, Gaza spread Attic pottery around the region, as well as

Athenian money, which was eventually struck in Gaza's own mints.[15] In around 450 BC Herodotus likened Gaza (which he called Cadytis) to the largest urban centres in Asia Minor, and described it as being under the control of the 'Syrians of Palestine'.[16] As a fortified and prosperous city, it was the natural base for the Persian attacks against Egypt in 343 BC, although the absence of exploitable forests nearby ultimately prevented Gaza from developing its own fleet and becoming a maritime rival to such Phoenician cities as Tyre, Sidon and Byblos.

The Wrath of the Two Alexanders

Alexander of Macedon's assumption of power and his conquest of Alexandria in 333 BC was the source of anxiety in Gaza, which was now Persian in its heart as well as for reasons of state. The population closed ranks around the garrison, backed up by Arab mercenaries,[17] under the leadership of a redoubtable commander, Batis, who was known as the 'King of Gaza'.[18] Alexander surrounded the city in 332 BC and anticipated a swift victory, despite the fact that he had recently been obliged to besiege Tyre for months before it was eventually taken. In the event the siege of Gaza involved 100 days of fruitless attacks and tunnelling. This is the first historical reference to the loose subsoil of Gaza, with the construction of tunnels and counter-tunnels prefiguring the current tunnels into the modern-day Gaza Strip. Alexander, who was wounded in the course of a counter-attack by the besieged force, was suffused with a vengeful rage when Gaza ultimately fell. All of those suspected of having fought were slaughtered, while their families were sold into slavery. Batis, who refused to kneel before the conqueror, was bound to Alexander's chariot after having his legs broken, and his body was then dragged in agony below the ramparts of the defeated city. The sack of Gaza filled six ships with booty to be sent back to Macedon.[19]

In the aftermath of this military catastrophe Gaza was rebuilt by the Greek colonists, as well as by the inhabitants of the region who became thoroughly Hellenised. However, after Alexander's death in 323 BC, Gaza again found itself disputed among different powers as his heirs fought over control of his empire: this time the confrontation was between Egypt,

Ptolemy's fief, and the Seleucid Empire in the east, the creation of Alexander's erstwhile satrap in Babylon, Seleucus, whose capital was originally close to the site of present-day Baghdad. Despite their rivalry, Ptolemy and Seleucus shared a common enemy, Antigonus Monophthalmus (the One Eyed), whose armies, under the leadership of his son Demetrius, were finally crushed outside Gaza in 312 BC. It was this victory which allowed Ptolemy to consolidate his hold over Palestine, while Seleucus entrenched himself in the north of Syria and transferred his capital to Antioch. This situation persisted until around 200 BC, a period in which Gaza developed into one of the most active ports in the region and remained the preferred destination of the caravan route from the Arabian Peninsula through which trade took place with the more distant Orient. A representative of the Ptolemaic dynasty was specifically charged with oversight of the incense trade through Gaza, the extent of which did not diminish following the establishment of the Egyptian port of Alexandria.[20]

As the second century BC began, the equilibrium between the empires swung once more towards the east. After a number of failed attempts, the Seleucids took control of Gaza along with the whole southern part of greater Syria. But this change of ruler did not affect Gaza's development nor its appeal as a commercial centre. The worship of Zeus Marnas (in Aramaic: 'Our Lord'), the god of rain and corn, seems to have been connected with the Philistine cult of Dagon, the leading figure of their pantheon.[21]

Yet the power of the Seleucids was destined to wane. Following the resounding defeat of Antiochus III, who went as far as to challenge the power of Rome, even in Greece itself, for which he paid the price with a treaty in 188 BC recognising his defeat, the Seleucid Empire was truncated and henceforth compelled to pay Rome a heavy tribute. A lengthy dispute over the succession began after the death of Antiochus V in which the rival contenders sought external help, with Rome's eventual involvement in the issue of the Seleucid secession leading to a growth in its influence in the region. Gaza was also affected by the local rebellion of the Jews of Judaea in 168 BC, led by the Maccabee family, who refused to worship what they viewed as pagan gods. The rebellious Jews attacked Gaza eight years after their uprising began, burning the surrounding orchards and making camp under its walls. The city yielded to their demands and sent the sons of its notable citizens as hostages to Jerusalem. As is recorded in the Bible:

[Jonathan] went to Gaza, lest they of Gaza shut him out; wherefore he laid siege unto it, and burned the suburbs thereof with fire, and spoiled them. Afterwards, when they of Gaza made supplication unto Jonathan, he made peace with them, and took the sons of their chief men for hostages, and sent them to Jerusalem ...[22]

Gaza subsequently enjoyed half a century of calm. Seleucid suzerainty was maintained, but on a looser and more intermittent basis. The Jewish rebels were engaged in a more or less open conflict with the Seleucids, which eventually caused them to withdraw from Jerusalem. The Hasmoneans, who succeeded the Maccabees, set up a de facto independent kingdom in 152 BC, whose expansionist policy resulted in the occupation of a part of the coast. Gaza was aware that it was more vulnerable to this expansionist drive by Jerusalem than it was to the edicts issued in Antioch. Business nevertheless continued to flourish within this restricted environment. All of the camel trains that made the two-month journey from Yemen passed through the Nabatean kingdom of Petra, and Gaza's hope was that its close relations with such Arab centres of power would protect it from the ambitions of the Jews. However, when the Hasmonean ruler Alexander Jannai made a move against Gaza in 97 BC, appeals for help from Apollodotus, the governor of Gaza, to the Nabatean King Aretas II went unheeded.

The Hasmonean siege of Gaza continued for a year and only came to an end with the murder of Apollodotus by his own brother. This may be indicative of the struggles between pro-Nabatean and pro-Hasmonean factions that divided the city. This act of treason threw the city open to attackers who massacred the members of the Council (the Boulè, as it was known in Ancient Greek), some of them within the Temple of Apollo.[23] Like Alexander the Great before him, Alexander Jannai carried out reprisals against the population of Gaza for having held out for too long against him. Whereas the sacking of the city and the massacres of 332 BC had led to the exile of the population, the slaughter and devastation of 96 BC preceded a policy of voluntary Judaisation which had a severe effect on the indigenous communities. This was an era of desolation: 'Gaza deserta'.[24] The new masters neglected the ruined city, preferring to inhabit and develop the port of Maiumas, close by.[25]

Pax Romana

It fell to the great Roman General Pompey to draw the Levant into Rome's orbit. The conquest of Jerusalem in 63 BC brought an end to the Hasmonean domination of Gaza,[26] in recognition of which the inhabitants symbolically declared a 'Pompeian Era' where Year 1 represented the commencement of the reconstruction of their city. This immensely complicated task, which was carried out under the supervision of the Roman governor of the Province of Syria, was rendered yet more so by the persistent struggles for power that dictated the fate of Gaza. In 40 BC, Herod, the king of Judaea, was granted control of Gaza along with other territories after subduing the last of the Hasmoneans. In 36 BC, Marcus Antonius, then the ruler of Egypt, reconquered Gaza in order to offer it as a gift to his wife, Cleopatra. But in 31 BC Gaza was again restored to Herod's kingdom following the defeat of the armies of Marcus Antonius and Cleopatra.[27]

Gaza had always been proud of the status of 'city' (the Greek *polis*) that it had gained under Alexander the Great and maintained under the Seleucids. However, on the threshold of the modern era the city of Gaza was designated part of the Roman province of Syria, with privileges and institutions that it was to retain through the six centuries that followed. The so-called 'Horus Road', the coastal road from Egypt to Palestine with Gaza as its key point, was Latinised as the 'Via Maris', underlining its unaltered strategic value. Gaza, once more a prosperous centre of commerce, enhanced its access to the sea with the development of the port of Anthedon, in what is now the Balakhiya area of Gaza. Gaza's wealth at this time was indicated in the extravagance of the Temple of Zeus Marnas; other manifestations of Zeus were also revered, and Apollo, Hecate, Aphrodite and Helios all had their own temples or sanctuaries. Such ostentation aroused the wrath of the Jewish zealots, who sacked Gaza in the course of their revolt in AD 66. But the cults continued—a marble statue representing Zeus Marnas dating from the second century AD, discovered in 1880 at Tell al-Ajjul, for instance, is displayed in the Archaeological Museum in Istanbul.[28] After the suppression of the Bar Kokhba rebellion of AD 132–5, Emperor Hadrian, who had visited Gaza in AD 130, granted its inhabitants permission to take vengeance by selling the Jewish prisoners taken during the revolt as slaves. A much-diminished Jewish community nevertheless continued to live in the coastal area of Maiumas, where they rubbed shoulders with other minorities, including Samaritans, Zoroastrians and Christians.

The city, already established as a commercial crossroads, now began to develop orchards, fields and vines. Plutarch is said to have described Gaza as *aromatophora*—the dispenser of perfumes—in reference to its crucial position on the incense and aromatics trade route from Yemen and the Indian Ocean.[29] Gaza's amphorae were exported in large quantities to Alexandria and to Beirut.[30] The city boasted a hippodrome, a gymnasium and a theatre, as well as a stadium where Olympic-style sports contests were held every four years. Each year a *panegyris* to Hadrian, a festival in the emperor's honour, was held to commemorate his visit. Gaza was also proud of its schools of rhetoric and philosophy in which Hellenic sophistry was cultivated. Once Gaza's fiscal resources were secured, Rome refrained from further interference in the city's internal affairs.

Yet everything changed with the arrival of Constantine as Roman emperor. In AD 313, Constantine placed Christianity on an equal footing with Rome's former religions, and on his deathbed, in 337, he was himself baptised. The Hellenised aristocracy of Gaza were intensely prejudiced against the teachings of Christianity and had supported the persecution launched by Constantine's predecessor, Diocletian. On the other hand, the merchants and tradesmen of Maiumas, many of whom were of Egyptian origin and therefore relegated to an inferior legal status, used the new creed to challenge the domination that Gaza exercised[31] by appealing to the emperor for recognition as an independent city. Their request was approved, and Maiumas was authorised to name itself Constantia.

The ensuing confrontation between Christian Constantia and Gaza, which remained faithful to Zeus Marnas, continued for the remainder of the fourth century. Above and beyond the issue of religion, the elite of Gaza were determined to recover the city's outlet to the sea. They finally achieved their goal during the reign of Emperor Flavius Claudius Julianus (AD 361–3), known as Julian the Apostate, who reintroduced Rome's former pagan religion while purporting to reform it. Julian also released those who had been responsible for anti-Christian riots in Gaza. As a result of these measures Julian endorsed a kind of exemption from official

Christianity for the city of Gaza, one which it continued to enjoy under his successors, though these were more disapproving of the worship of the pagan Roman deities. The growth of Maiumas's population did not present a challenge to Gaza's official commitment to its pagan gods. However, by rejecting reunification with Gaza, the Christians perpetuated a painful separation between the relatively prosperous church in Maiumas and that in Gaza, which was isolated and represented only a tiny minority.[32]

Hermits and Sophists

Bishop Porphyrius (Saint Porphyry of Gaza) assumed his post as bishop of Gaza in AD 395,[33] the very year the Roman Empire split in two, dividing itself into the Empire of the East and the Empire of the West. The new bishop quickly took stock of the limited size of his small congregation of 280 members. He was later able to increase it by making several dozen conversions when, after a night of fervent prayer, the appearance of rain put an end to a crushing drought.[34] The Christians of Gaza were nevertheless harassed by their fellow citizens and continued to be excluded from the Council (the Boulè). Porphyry persuaded his superior, the archbishop of Caesarea, to accompany him to Constantinople, where Empress Eudoxia, a pious Christian, put their case for the suppression of the pagan religions to her husband, Emperor Arcadius. But the emperor was reluctant to risk the significant contributions from the worshippers of the pagan deities in Gaza, whom he referred to as 'such good taxpayers',[35] and refused to consider even dismissing the pagans from their civic positions unless they were accused of financial malpractice.

Porphyry would not admit defeat and contrived, together with the empress, an ingenious legal ploy. The newborn son of Arcadius and Eudoxia, the future Emperor Theodosius II, had been accorded the imperial title of Augustus, and the bishop of Gaza was authorised to present his petition to him, which was deemed to have been approved when the infant gave a nod of his head.[36] Arcadius thus endorsed the suppression of the worship of the pagan deities in Gaza by the future emperor, who was not in fact to succeed him for a further six years. Porphyry returned to Maiumas in triumph before entering Gaza at the head of a mob of

Christians bent on vengeance, while the imperial officials immediately proceeded to demolish the shrine of Zeus Marnas and the other temples in the city.[37] Ten days of looting and maltreatment of the pagans followed, which were vindicated as a purge of the city and its buildings of all trace of the pagan deities.[38] Conversions abounded, though the bishop had few illusions as to their sincerity.

To mark the inauguration of the new era a monumental new church on a cruciform plan was built on the ruins of the Temple of Zeus Marnas. The church, which was consecrated on 14 April 407,[39] Easter Sunday, was named Eudoxiana in honour of the patroness of Bishop Porphyry, who himself became a member of the city's ruling establishment. Although the worshippers of the pagan gods did not wholly disappear, they kept a low profile in the face of the triumphalism of pious Christianity. The games of the Roman circus and the traditional Greek contests were henceforth prohibited in Gaza as they were too closely associated with the pagan gods. But dramatic performances continued, as well as the annual *panegyria*, now in a Christian form and much changed from the festival that had been identified with Hadrian.[40] A Jewish community also remained active in Maiumas, whose presence in the region is evidenced by a mosaic representing King David playing the lyre, taken from the floor of the ancient synagogue in Gaza, which is displayed in the Israel Museum in Jerusalem.[41] Yet as the authoritative rabbis of late antiquity did not regard Gaza as part of the Land of Israel, the community did not pay tithes to the Jewish temple nor was it obliged to practise the Jewish custom of leaving the land fallow every seventh year.[42]

None of the subsequent holders of the bishopric of Gaza, which continued to be subordinate to Caesarea within the hierarchy of the Church, was able to rival the political acumen of Porphyry (d.AD 420), to whom a church was dedicated in 442. In contrast, however, Gaza was important in Palestinian monasticism, since the region rivalled the Judaean desert in its attraction for those with monastic vocations. The fashion can be traced to the pioneer effort of Hilarion (AD 291–371), born into a wealthy family in Gaza, who was initiated by the anchorite Antony in Alexandria and founded a monastic community close to his native city. Hilarion died in Cyprus after resuming his spiritual pilgrimage. His remains, which were brought back to

Gaza, became the object of popular veneration, encouraged by the instructive biography of him written by St Jerome in around 390. Today, Hilarion's tomb is at the monastery of Umm al-Amr, on the edge of the Nuseirat refugee camp, some 13 kilometres to the south of Gaza. The French research expedition which has worked there for many years has brought to light a site that was active from the fourth to the eighth century. In around AD 440, Prince Peter, nicknamed the Iberian (signifying 'from the Caucasus'), a Georgian hostage brought up at the Court in Constantinople, was drawn to Gaza by the example of Hilarion and became a monk in an institution that had been richly endowed by Jerusalem.

The controversy over the nature of Christ, and the question as to whether he was divine, human or both, tore the Eastern Church apart in the mid-fifth century. In AD 451 the Council of Chalcedon decided in favour of the dual nature of the Son of God, which in turn led to an uprising in support of the Monophysite position regarding the principle of the singularity of the nature of Christ. Peter the Iberian was one of the spiritual leaders of this revolt, as a supporter of which he became bishop of Maiumas.[43] However, the ousting of this dissident prelate by the Imperial Army in AD 453 consigned Peter the Iberian to twenty years of a nomadic and ascetic existence. Though he returned to Gaza in AD 486, he lived there as a recluse until his death five years later, without deviating from his Monophysite beliefs, which had come to represent the majority creed in Egypt.[44] His teaching was the inspiration for a community in the monastery at Maiumas who were expelled to Egypt in AD 519. The Emperor Justin I thus re-established the authority of the official Church in Palestine at the precise moment when the rejection of the Council of Chalcedon was laying the foundation of the dissident Coptic Church in Egypt. Gaza, pulled towards both the Levant and Egypt, was once again left swinging from one to the other.

It was important to the restored orthodoxy to establish its active occupation of the symbolic ground of Gaza. A monastic community was established to the south of the city on the site of present-day Umm al-Amr,[45] first under the leadership of Abbot Seridos and then of his successor Aelianos.[46] The monastery became sufficiently wealthy to support some 400 monks in addition to a large number of pilgrims—no complex of greater size existed in the Byzantine Near East closer than that of Saint Simeon, in the north of Syria. The expansion of this community enabled it to obtain favourable treatment from the government in Palestine, and it also prompted the adherence of the sons of good families. Among the most prominent of these were Dorotheos and Dositheos: the 'Instructions' of the former and the 'Life' of the latter serve as a benchmark of the spirituality of their time.[47] Bishop Marcian, a native of Gaza, where he presided from AD 530 to 549, oversaw ambitious works in the Church of Saint Sergius, which he is credited as having built. He also instigated the construction of the churches of Saint Stephen and Saint John.[48] His architectural ambition left its mark on the sixth-century mosaics of Palestine, excavated at the Jordanian sites of Madaba, Umm-Rassas and Ma'in, all of which accord a central position to Gaza and its churches.

The sophist Choricios, who composed the encomia for Bishop Marcian, is in the direct tradition of Gaza's Hellenistic school, where philosophers and rhetoricians simply needed to profess their adherence to Christianity in order to continue their writing and dialogues, simultaneously active in Old Testament exegeses and classical apologists. It is thus noteworthy that Choricios praises Marcian's membership of the elite of Gaza, which he shares, while placing less emphasis on his episcopal qualities.[49] Such intellectual conceits, couched in Greek between men of good society, were inaccessible to most people in Gaza, who spoke Aramaic. The lack of written sources or other materials means that the reality of ordinary people's lives in the port and around the markets can only be guessed at—they were of little interest to the solitary monks or the sophists.

Under the Byzantine Empire Christian Gaza enjoyed a level of prosperity that seems to have been equivalent to that of the pre-Christian pagan city at the time of the Pax Romana. But this was to change from the middle of the sixth century onwards when Byzantine Syria suffered constant harassment from the Persian Sassanid Empire. In 614 the Persian ruler Khosroe finally took Jerusalem, and by 618 he had captured the whole of Palestine. In the ten years that followed, Gaza was isolated from the other Byzantine provinces until it was recaptured by Heraclius in 629. For the first time in its long history Gaza was now the prize in a clash between two vast oriental empires, rather than being the object of the centuries-old regional rivalry between the Levant and Egypt. Now firmly seen as part of Palestine, Gaza was on the eve of the most lasting of its historical mutations, namely the new faith that was to be imported by way of the same caravan route that had nurtured its opulent past.

2

THE ISLAMIC ERA

Cosmopolitan Gaza had been home to a substantial Arab population since the days of antiquity. It was a largely Arab garrison that had defended the city against Alexander the Great,[1] and the city had been one of the preferred destinations for Arab merchants from the Nabatean kingdom of Petra or from the Arabian Peninsula itself. Furthermore, the fate of two particular Meccan caravan leaders was already bound up with Gaza even before their later association with the glory of Islam.

The first of these, Hashem ibn Abd Manaf, a notable of the tribe of Quraysh who dominated the oasis of Mecca, regulated the pilgrimage to the sanctuary of the Kaaba and controlled its access routes in the Arabian Desert. Hashem, born around 500,[2] enjoyed the distinguished responsibility of providing food and water for the pilgrims. For that purpose he led two caravans each year to Syria and Palestine, which were provided with a certificate of safe-conduct issued by the Byzantine authorities.[3] It was during one of these expeditions that he died in Gaza at the age of twenty-five.[4] He was survived by his sons, one of whom, Abd al-Muttalib, lived in Medina, where he fathered six daughters and six sons. One of these sons, Abdullah, married a wife named Amina—it was from their union that the Prophet of Islam, Muhammad, was born in around 570.

Muslim tradition presents Hashem, the great-grandfather of the Prophet, as a descendant of Abraham through his son Ishmael, the symbolic ancestor of all Arabs.[5] Their descent from such a distinguished fore-

17

bear places the Hashemites, one of the three great clans within the Quraysh, on a par with the Abbasids and the Alids. A Hashemite dynasty, which drew its authority from its prestigious ancestor, was able to rule over Mecca for a millennium before establishing itself on the throne of Jordan in the twentieth century. In Islamic literature, Gaza is clearly designated 'Hashem's Gaza' (Ghazzatu Hashem), though the veneration of this ancestor of the Prophet came later.

The second of these two Meccan merchants who was destined for greatness was Umar ibn Khattab. A skilful, wise and experienced man of business from the tribe of Quraysh, his success in commerce came to outweigh his relatively lowly birth. The caravans he sent to Gaza laid the foundation of his fortune,[6] which enabled him to take his place within the elite of Mecca. Like many of his fellow merchants, he initially rejected Muhammad's message, the strict monotheism of which seemed to him to pose a threat to Mecca's pagan pilgrimage. But this was to change following his conversion in 618, when he became one of the Prophet's most ardent believers. In 622 Umar Ibn Khattab accompanied the Prophet on his 'hijra' to Medina and later became the second caliph.

Caliphates

The Byzantine and Persian Empires were too preoccupied with their own rivalry to pay attention to the emergent power of Islam's warriors in the heart of Arabia, and although Muhammad wrote to Heraclius and Khosroe to threaten them with jihad if they failed to convert to the newly revealed faith, it was not until after the Prophet's death in 632 and the succession of Abu Bakr, who became the Prophet's first khalifa, or caliph (literally, 'follower'), that the first expeditions were mounted outside the Arabian Peninsula. During one of these raids, in February 634, the Byzantine defenders of Gaza suffered a serious defeat some kilometres from the city. The battle served as notice of the threat represented by what Thomas the Presbyter, a chronicler writing in about 640, called 'the nomads of Muhammad',[7] who did not on this occasion press home their advantage. The goal of spreading Islam by force of arms became altogether more serious when the Caliphate passed from Abu Bakr to Umar ibn Khattab in

August 634. Having left the days of his caravans from Mecca to Gaza far behind, Umar went down in history as the 'caliph of jihad', bound to defeat the two great Empires.

The Muslim armies first attacked the Christian territories of the north. The decisive battle was on the Yarmuk River in August 636, when the Byzantine forces were routed. Caliph Umar, eager to turn his attention to the Persian Empire, delegated the western front to the intrepid Amr ibn al-As. In June or July 637 Gaza was taken by storm and its garrison massacred, but its population was spared. Amr then used Gaza as a base from which to press on into Egypt. While the church of Saint Eudoxia, which had been built on the ruins of the temple of Zeus, was transformed into a mosque, (which was to be dedicated to Caliph Umar after the latter's death), the neighbouring church of Saint Porphyry was allowed to remain open for Christian worship. The population of the city appears to have accepted Islam with an enthusiasm that contrasted with the resistance that pagan Gaza had put up against Christianity.[8] On the other hand, the surrounding countryside seemed more reluctant to convert, as was evidenced by the persistence of the cultivation of vineyards despite the Islamic prohibition of alcohol. In general, the Near East was to remain largely Christian for up to two centuries after the Islamic conquest.

Gaza was part of the military district (*jund*) of Palestine which was administered from the central point of Ramla during the Umayyad period (from 661 to 750). Following the advent of the Abbasids a decision was made to relocate the seat of the Caliphate to Iraq, which resulted in the distancing of Gaza from the centre of the Islamic government. But this did not prevent Gaza from developing a reputation as a place of intellectual importance. The city was the birthplace in 767 of the Imam Shafi'i, the celebrated founder of the Shafi'i school of religious law (*madhhab*), one of the four juridical schools of Sunni Islam—though he left the city in his early youth to complete his education, the tomb of Imam Shafii's daughter, together with that of one of his close associates, can still be found in the Muslim cemetery in Gaza's Zeitoun district. In the more worldly sphere, commerce of every kind continued to flourish in the port of Maiumas, which came to be known around this time as Mimas. Travellers and writers stress the city's prosperity and note the burgeoning orchards and farmlands surrounding it. The Gaza Valley (Wadi Ghazza), which opens into the Mediterranean to the south of the city, was only rivalled in the flow of its water and the luxuriance of its vegetation by the Jordan Valley.

The 'Pax Islamica' was to last for more than a century and a half, until geopolitical tensions between the Middle East and Egypt once more darkened Gaza's horizons. Between 899 and 905 the Abbasid caliphs of Baghdad, who were no longer prepared to tolerate the dissidence of the Nile Valley, despatched expeditions through Gaza to bring Egypt to heel. At the same time, as Hamadani, a chronicler of Persian origin has recorded, there was jostling between Iraq and Syria over the possession of Islam's most attractive lands. By this stage Palestine was regarded as part of Syria, the *bilad al-Sham* (as greater Syria was known), with Syria's eulogists boasting of the land's 'two brides in this world, Gaza and Ascalon'.[9]

Yet in 969 Egypt was conquered by new masters who came from the west: the Ismaili Shi'ite Fatimid dynasty, who spread their messianic doctrine from their base in Tunis. The new rulers of the Nile Valley also laid claim to the position of the Caliphate and founded a capital whose very name rang out like a challenge, Al-Qahira (literally, 'the Victorious'), which we know today as Cairo. The Fatimids immediately moved to take hold of Gaza, the necessary point of transit for their offensive against Jerusalem. The representatives of Cairo made no attempt to proselytise in Gaza, which remained staunchly faithful to Sunni orthodoxy.

The contention between Baghdad and Cairo was of an entirely strategic nature, and hence bore no resemblance to the internecine conflicts of the Eastern Church in the fifth century. At the close of the tenth century the chronicler Al-Muqadissi describes Gaza as one of the largest cites in Palestine, to which only Ramla, the current capital, could be compared.[10] His contemporary Ibn Hawqal described Gaza as 'a fine city and very prosperous'.[11] Fatimid rule did not disrupt the regular passage of the caravans from Egypt to the Levant and vice versa, and the mosque of Umar continued to be much frequented by the merchants, who, according to Al-Muqadissi, were attracted by the echoes of their distant forerunner Umar, who had made his fortune in Gaza even before his conversion to Islam.[12]

THE ISLAMIC ERA

Crusaders and Mongols

In 1071 the Fatimids lost Jerusalem to Baghdad, where, however, the caliphs now exercised only the semblance of power. In fact, the Turkish Seljuk sultans governed in their name, with brutality often taking the place of piety. Jerusalem was bitterly disputed between the Fatimids and the Seljuks and the city changed hands several times over the space of a generation before finally falling under Cairo's control. These military upheavals and the religious polemics that accompanied them seriously impeded the Christian pilgrimage to Jerusalem, and it was this issue which Pope Urban II used to justify his crusade for the liberation of the Holy Sepulchre in 1095. Jerusalem was stormed four years later, and after the surrender of its garrison, when the Egyptians took flight, a blood bath among the city's population ensued.

The carnage the crusaders inflicted spread terror throughout Palestine. In Gaza, the inhabitants fled ahead of the invaders, who took the city without conflict. The mosque of Umar became a church once more, in an act of posthumous vengeance for Eudoxia and Porphyry. To control the southward route to Egypt, the crusaders built the fort at Darum, on the site of present-day Deir al-Balah. When Gaza was absorbed into the Frankish Kingdom, the Fatimid defenders of Jerusalem fell back to Ascalon, on the coast, which had remained a Muslim enclave. These two coastal cities, some 15 kilometres apart, which had been lined together from the days of ancient Philistia, were now separated by the front line of the confrontation between the Cross and the Crescent.

In 1149, angered by continuing Muslim raids from Ascalon, King Baldwin III of Jerusalem instructed the Knights Templar to make Gaza their stronghold and impose peace on the coastal region. Before long, a new crusader castle loomed over the outskirts of Gaza, threatening the defenders of the nearby Fatimid redoubt. The church that had been built on the foundations of the mosque of Umar was enlarged to become a cathedral of the Latin rite, which was dedicated to Saint John the Baptist. In 1153 Ascalon surrendered after a seven-month siege and was transformed by the occupying crusaders into a bridgehead for projected maritime expeditions against Egypt. Gaza, which was no longer in the forefront of the conflict, lost much of its strategic value. But its role as a mercantile crossroads continued to ensure that it was relatively prosperous, something attested to by the Arab geographer Al-Idrissi: 'Gaza is a modest city whose market is nevertheless renowned.'[13]

The Islamic re-conquest was the achievement of Kurdish General Salah ad-Din, who was still fighting on behalf of the Fatimids. In 1170 his forces took possession of Darum (Deir al-Balah) and made forays as far as the walls of the crusader castle at Gaza. In 1171 Salah ad-Din abolished the Fatimid Caliphate and founded the Ayyubid Sultanate, thereby uniting Damascus and Cairo under his military rule, which enabled him to defeat the crusaders in a pincer movement. In 1187 he annihilated the crusader armies at a battle near Lake Tiberias, putting an end to the Frankish Kingdom of Jerusalem. The Knights Templar abandoned Gaza to the Islamic forces, but the reaction when Jerusalem itself was lost enabled the king of England, Richard Coeur de Lion, to raise a new crusade. In 1191 Richard's troops took Gaza before pressing on to Ascalon. However, the resurgence of the Christian knights was of short duration; Salah ad-Din soon regained the initiative on all fronts, obliging the crusaders to agree to the surrender of Gaza and Ascalon and to the destruction of their fortifications.

Gaza was left defenceless and was therefore as easy to take as to lose, which in turn meant that it was to pay a high price for the military comings and goings of the thirteenth century. Initially, Gaza came under the control of the descendants of Salah ad-Din, the Ayyubid sultans in Cairo. Yet in the treaty signed in 1229 between Al-Kamil, the fifth Ayyubid sultan, who was Salah ad-Din's nephew, and Frederick II, the king of Sicily who was also the holy Roman emperor, Gaza was again handed over to the crusaders. Ten years later the Christian armies went on the offensive again, led by Theobald, count of Champagne and king of Navarre.[14] This time they were defeated at Beit Hanoun, near Gaza, by the troops of Shuja al-Din Uthman al-Kurdi, who died during the battle. In 1244 an ephemeral coalition of Turkish and Egyptian military leaders seized Gaza and expelled the crusaders, who retreated to Ascalon, which served as a refuge for the Knights Hospitaller for three further years. In 1250, the Ayyubid Sultanate in Egypt was overthrown by the Mamluk generals, and these liberated slaves, often of Caucasian origin, again raised the flag of jihad against the last bastions of the crusaders.

However, everything was to change once more due to the advent of a much more powerful enemy in the Middle East in 1258. In that year Baghdad fell to the Mongol hordes from the East, led by their all-conquering general, Hulagu, a grandson of Genghis Khan. After defeating their opponents, and committing massacres throughout the region in the process, the invaders from the Central Asian steppes were soon able to conquer Palestine, where they reached Gaza in 1260. Hulagu himself then left the Middle East, returning to Mongolia to stake his claim in an unsuccessful struggle for succession to the position of great khan within the Mongol Empire (his brother, Kublai Khan, eventually assumed this position). In the meantime the Egyptian Mamluk Sultan Qutuz brought together a powerful army that was able to reconquer the city of Gaza. In September 1260 the Mamluk General Baybars, who was soon to displace Qutuz after the battle, won a decisive victory at Ain Jalout, near Nablus, which led to the withdrawal of the Mongol armies from the Levant.

The Golden Age of the Mamluks

Gaza was the westernmost point of the Mongol advance, just as it had been the southernmost point of the Frankish Kingdom of Jerusalem. Due to the extreme violence of these turbulent days and the damage and destruction that the city incurred, Gaza's traditional mercantile connections were left in ruins and its position as a commercial port was comprised. Yet during the Mamluk period from 1260 onwards, once the chaos had been brought to an end and the city had been rebuilt, Gaza and its hinterland experienced a golden age. After his victory at Ain Jalout, Baybars made himself sultan and Gaza regained its past prosperity. The city was soon replete with impressive buildings and Baybars built a new mosque dedicated to Caliph Umar in Gaza, on the site of the Latin Cathedral, where the former mosque had stood, endowing it with a library of more than 20,000 books. This new Mosque of Umar (the Umari mosque), together with the 'Pasha's Palace', the seat of the governor, or *wali*, remain to the present day the two principal buildings in Gaza, close to the area of Shujahiya, where the local elite have lived since the Mamluk era. On the other side, the central square extends from the commercial area of Zeytoun, with the Samara Hammam (bath house), restored in 1297. Gaza's place names still show the influence of Salah al-Din and the Ayyubid dynasty (1170–250), though this has left few architectural traces. Thus the Shujahiya area is named for the general Shuja al-Din, who died in 1239 fighting the crusaders at Beit Hanoun, while the street that marks the boundary of this area from the town centre proper is Salah al-Din Street.

The successors of Baybars on the Mamluk throne in Cairo continued to exercise their power over Damascus and the Bilad al-Sham, as Greater Syria was known. Once more, the road north through Gaza was crucial. Named the 'Horus Road' by the Pharaohs, and the Via Maris by the Roman Empire, the road was now known as the Sultan's Road (*al-darb al-sultani*), linking Egypt with Palestine by way of the coast. Gaza became the seat of one of the governorates (*wilayat*) of the Mamluk Sultanate, normally administered from Damascus. Gaza was occasionally promoted to the status of an autonomous province, as for example in 1291, when the Mamluk authorities marked its elevation by adding a further minaret to the Mosque of Umar.

The emergence of Sufi brotherhoods during the medieval Islamic period also affected Gaza, which was no exception to the spread of this deeply rooted mystical and social movement. Sultan Baybars himself professed particular veneration for the Moroccan Sufi sheikh, Ahmad Badawi (1200–76), who grew up in Mecca and had been trained by the great Sufi masters of Iraq. Based in the Nile Delta, at the town of Tanta, Badawi spent his life in asceticism and preaching, and at the time of his death he was regarded as the virtual patron saint of Egypt. His devotees banded together into the Ahmadiyya order (*tariqa*, literally 'Way'), and built a network of Sufi religious houses (*zawiya*), which served both as centres for prayer and as places of residence for the order's disciples. Gaza, which had fallen under the sway of Mamluk and Egyptian culture, flourished as a centre for the Ahmadiyya, whose *zawiya*, close to the governor's palace, was opened in 1331 and remains active up to the present day. Another mystic of Moroccan origin, Sheikh Ali Ibn Marwan, chose to base himself in Gaza where he died in 1316. The mosque adjacent to his mausoleum, restored and extended in 1370, was dedicated to his memory.

In 1348 an epidemic of plague which ravaged the entire region is said to have resulted in the deaths of 22,000 people in the province of Gaza alone.[15] The celebrated traveller Ibn Battuta, who made his third visit to Gaza in that year, found the city 'deserted' and estimated that 1,000 people fell victim to the plague every day.[16] Gaza eventually overcame the aftermath of the epidemic and was able to resume its normal commercial activities with support from the Mamluk authorities, which encouraged the re-emergence of the market with the construction of a fortified caravanserai half way between Gaza and Rafah. This khan, which served both mercantile and military purposes, was inaugurated in 1387 by Emir Yunis al-Nawruzi. Located close to quarries and to abundant wells, it was the site of a postal relay, an essential facility on the road from Cairo to Damascus. The protection provided by this 'Khan Yunis', as the place became known, gradually attracted an ever larger local population, leading it to develop into a proper town that was soon in competition with Rafah to be regarded as the second city of the Gaza region. In all, there were five such postal relays in the region in the Mamluk period, at Rafah, Khan Yunis, Al-Silqa, Darum (Deir al-Balah) and Gaza. North of Gaza, the preferred commercial route went on to Damascus via Ramla, but two other itineraries were also possible, namely towards Kerak via Beit Jibrin, or to Aqaba via Asluj.[17] The fortified style in which such structures were built indicates the magnitude of the threat posed by the Bedouin tribes from the Negev and the Sinaï.[18]

In 1438 plague struck again, this time causing 12,000 deaths.[19] However, as during the previous plague crisis, Gaza was able to count on the concern of the Mamluk government. Sultan Sayf ed-Din Inal (1453–61), who had formerly been governor of Gaza, was especially helpful. In this period, the *madrasa* (school) of Emir Bardabak in the Shuhajiyya area of the city was built, where the traditional teaching role of the *madrasa* was combined with that of an Islamic court, or *mahkama*. The overwhelming majority of the population at this time were Sunni Muslims who followed the Shafi'i school of law, which had been laid down six centuries earlier by an imam who had been born in Gaza. Yet the Christian communities, who followed the Orthodox rite, were also able to practise their faith in the heart of the city. In addition, Rabbi Meshullam of Volterra, who passed through Gaza in 1481 on his travels, counted sixty Jewish families in the city, together with four Samaritans.[20]

Far from Istanbul

In 1453 the Ottoman sultans, already the masters of Anatolia, captured the capital of the Byzantine Empire, transforming the erstwhile Constantinople into Istanbul, which they in turn made their capital. However, as their attention was focused on Europe and the West, it was two generations before they consolidated their hold over the Middle East. Turning eastwards at last, Sultan Selim I (1467–1520) went on the offensive, first against the Persian Empire, where the Ottomans emerged victorious from the Battle of Chaldiran in 1514, and then against the Mamluk armies in the Levant, whom the Ottomans vanquished in August 1516 at the Battle of Marj Dabiq in northern Syria. This opened the gates of Greater Syria to the Ottoman forces, who took Aleppo, Damascus and Jerusalem. Their next objective was to take Cairo itself and bring about the downfall of the Mamluk regime. Khan Yunis was taken by storm, but only a small contingent was sent to Gaza, which was regarded as of lesser military value.

The notables of Gaza, more so than its ordinary population, were initially confident that the Mamluk government could hold its own, seeing their destiny as linked to that of Cairo, even though Palestine, immediately to the north, had already fallen under Ottoman domination. Rumours circulated in Gaza that Selim I had been defeated on the road to Egypt, causing the city to rise up in revolt, slaughtering the Ottoman garrison. This led the sultan, who had in fact been victorious both in Egypt and in Mecca, to return to the rebellious city in a rage, carrying out massacres there that were only too appropriate for his nickname 'The Grim' (Yavuz). The four subsequent centuries of the Ottoman presence in Gaza were consequently inaugurated by an act of pitiless butchery. By 1525 the population had fallen to less than 1,000 families.[21]

Gaza, humiliated by the vengeance of the Sublime Porte, as the Ottoman government was known, discovered that its strategic position as a link between north and south was of no value within the new empire, whose grip over Egypt was as firm as its hold over Greater Syria. The days of playing the Levant off against the Nile Valley were at an end under the Ottoman dispensation. To this difficulty was added the development of the sea route by way of the Cape of Good Hope, which diverted many of the trade routes that had formerly reached the Mediterranean by way of Gaza. The make-up of the city's population also began to change during this period. According to tax registers, religious minorities came to make up at least a fifth and perhaps a quarter of the people of Gaza. The registers were of course most precise in relation to the so-called 'People of the Book', effectively the Jews and the Christians, who were subjected to a specific tax regime.[22] The decline of the city was palpable throughout the sixteenth century, but later the growing independence of one of Gaza's governing families, the Radwan, led to the reversal of this tendency. In 1570 Radwan Pasha was granted the hereditary governorship of Gaza, which then passed for three generations from father to son, first to Ahmed Pasha (1572–1600), then to Hassan Pasha (1600–44) and finally to Hussein Pasha (1644–62).

In the reign of Louis XIV, France, which was seeking to develop its influence in the ports of the Levant, offered its assistance to Gaza and support to its governor, Hussein Pasha. Hussein enjoyed a significant amount of local popularity for having re-established order throughout the region, suppressing the Bedouin tribes and the assorted footpads who preyed upon the highways.[23] According to Laurent d'Arvieux, who travelled to Gaza in 1659 with the French consul appointed to serve in Saida, Hussein Pasha took on the role of the protector of the 'Fathers of the Holy Land',[24] allowing them to settle in Gaza on the supposed site of the temple pulled down by Samson, and even guaranteeing their supplies of fish during Lent.[25] Laurent d'Arvieux described Gaza as 'a very cheerful and agreeable place', adding that there were 'no walls but only quite high earthen ramparts that were constantly thickened with night soil that was deposited upon them, though this caused no harm to the quality of the air because of Gaza's advantageous situation with winds that drove off any bad odours'.[26] He compared the bazaars of Gaza to Parisian fairs, and noted 'the constant passing through of caravans from Syria to Egypt and from Egypt to Syria'.[27]

Hussein Pasha was to pay dearly for his special relationship with the Christians. He became a victim of the intrigues of the Turkish Court, and in 1662, accused of treason, he was executed in the citadel in Damascus. The Radwan family recovered from the setback, however, and contrived to placate the Ottoman authorities. In 1662, Musa Pasha Radwan succeeded his late brother as governor of Gaza (1662–79), but the Radwan family had now lost some of its local influence due to the bad reputation Hussein had acquired. Disputes between the leaders of Muslim factions were observed minutely and with trepidation by the Greek Orthodox and Armenian Christian minorities, who feared the consequences of those quarrels on their own fate.[28]

The small Jewish community, meanwhile, made up of around 100 families, was concerned by other issues. In 1663 a rabbi named Nathan Ashkenazi left Jerusalem and settled with his wife's family in Gaza. He began to assert that he was receiving Messianic visions, linking the salvation of the Jewish people to the career of a notorious Kabbalist from Smyrna, Sabbatai Zvi. From 1665, Nathan of Gaza began to campaign publicly in favour of Sabbatai Zvi, embarking on preaching missions to his co-religionists. In reaction to the furore aroused in Jerusalem by his prophetic pretensions, he proclaimed Gaza to be the new holy city for modern times, declaring that the new messiah would in due course physically take possession of the crown of the sultan himself in Istanbul. In 1666, however, when Sabbatai Zvi presented himself to Sultan Mehmet IV, he made a public conversion to Islam. This volte-face took the wind out of the sails of the messianic movement but failed to change the mind of Nathan of Gaza, who continued to make heretical proclamations abroad, roaming between Italy and the Balkans until his death in 1680. In Gaza, the Jewish community made a show of proclaiming its loyalty to the sultan in the hope of erasing the memory of a rabbi whose actions had been so provocative.

Ahmed Pasha, Musa's son and the nephew of Hussein, was the final member of the Radwan family to govern Gaza, ruling from 1679 to 1690. The Sublime Porte thereafter withheld its support from such local dynasties. By this point Gaza was no more than a minor element in the plans of the Ottoman Empire, whose officials now prioritised the security and continuity of the overextended empire's financial resources. Care was taken to secure the 'Sultan's Road', between Palestine and Egypt, by way of Gaza, Khan Yunis and Rafah. The pilgrimage route from Damascus to Mecca, however, continued to be harassed by brigands. In 1754 the Ottoman caravan to the Hajj was pillaged by these irrepressible rebels, who, adding insult to injury, set about selling their booty in the market in Gaza.[29] Punitive expeditions and brutal suppression had no lasting impact on such chronic instability at the margins of the empire.

Although Gaza was gradually supplanted by the port of Acre as the preferred maritime outlet for the province[30] it was nevertheless situated in what the Ottoman bureaucrats classified as 'useful territory', and in the eyes of Ottoman officialdom it remained of critical value as a staging post on the route to Egypt. In a confidential report sent to the Sublime Porte in around 1769,[31] Jazzar Pasha stressed the importance of Gaza as a stepping stone for any operation to re-establish control over Egypt and thence over the Nile Valley. He estimated that an expeditionary force would need just twenty-four hours to reach Cairo from Gaza, with the key proviso that a supply of water for that period would need to be made available for the transit of Sinai.[32] Gaza was inevitably centrally involved in such advance dispositions. Yet Jazzar Pasha, who would be made governor of Saida in 1775, was never to put his plans into practice. Worse still, the same plan was effectively turned against him when Napoleon Bonaparte followed his invasion of Egypt in 1798 with a campaign against Palestine. On 18 February 1799 the Ottoman garrison at El-Arish surrendered to Bonaparte's troops after a siege of just ten days. Gaza capitulated without a fight on 24 February, and the French general spent the night in the 'Pasha's Palace', which had been abandoned by its defenders.

Farewell to Bonaparte

The French troops did not linger in Gaza, though they were responsible for significant destruction there, presumably in order to cover their rear.[33] General Bonaparte advanced up the Sultan's Road, capturing Jaffa by force of arms before cooling his heels in front of Acre, where Jazzar Pasha withstood his siege. The general, frustrated in his Syrian ambitions, was obliged to retrace his steps. He returned, ingloriously, through Gaza, left a French garrison behind at El-Arish, and left Egypt for France in August 1799. In January 1800 Gaza became the assembly point for the Ottoman contingent that would drive the French out of Egypt. Among them was a wily commander, Muhammad Ali Pasha, in charge of a contingent of recruits who like himself were of Albanian origin. El-Arish was soon retaken; the French interlude in Egypt came to an end in 1801, leaving the Mamluks, the Ottoman troops and the Albanian mercenaries to joust for power in Egypt.

Muhammad Ali, who emerged as the victor from this civil strife, gained the Sublime Porte's recognition for his status as governor of Egypt, with de facto autonomous power, in 1803. For a time the Nile Valley satisfied his ambitions, but in 1831 he delegated his son Ibrahim to undertake the conquest of Syria. Gaza was occupied without a struggle as he made his way up the 'Sultan's Road'. The city was to remain under Egyptian control for eight years, during which time compulsory conscription was introduced despite the opposition of Gaza's population who had hitherto been accustomed to being observers of the region's military conflicts. However, the citizens of Gaza, with their more relaxed political attitudes, did not join the uprising that shook Palestine, Negev and Galilee in 1834.[34] By that time, Gaza, together with Jerusalem, Nablus and Acre, was one of the four most populous cities in Palestine.[35]

Ottoman rule was restored across the Levant in 1840 under pressure from the great powers. After the withdrawal of French support, Muhammad Ali was obliged to abandon Syria and Palestine in exchange for Ottoman recognition of his family's hereditary rule in Egypt. Egyptian troops thus passed once more through Gaza, this time on the way back towards Egypt. Although Gaza's inhabitants were subsequently angered to find that the Ottomans intended to resume military conscription, Gaza benefited from the Ottoman refurbishment of the city, including a nod to piety with the construction in 1855 of a mosque on the site of the mausoleum dedicated to Hashem, the Prophet's great-grandfather. In accordance with its usual style of rule, the Sublime Porte appointed a Sunni mufti of the Hanafi school (*madhhab*), who represented the majority in Turkey, while the population of Gaza continued to adhere to the Shafi'i school.

In 1847 French diplomats estimated that the population of Gaza and the surrounding district comprised 40,000 Muslims, together with 500 Christians.[36] Other sources, consistent with this estimate, report that the number of inhabitants of Gaza proper remained somewhere between 15,000 and 19,000 during the entire second half of the nineteenth century.[37] The principal change during this period was in fact less demographic than social, due to the adoption of a new property law in 1858 that tended to favour wealthy landlords over a population of peasants that was becoming increasingly proletarian. In Gaza, this process, in which landholding became concentrated in fewer hands, particularly benefited the Shawa, a Gaza family that had historic links with the Arab clan known as the 'Kulayb', who had become the principal landowners throughout Palestine.[38]

The active cultivation of crops for export, especially barley, contributed to the Shawa family's prosperity. The French author Pierre Loti, who travelled across Sinai to Gaza in March 1894, noted that he had arrived 'in the fields of Canaan … in the midst of vast fields of barley all clothed in green'.[39] Others among the wealthier clans also benefited, including the Bseisso family, the Souranis, the Radwan[40] and the Husseinis (the latter of which have no connection with the Jerusalem family of the same name). The genealogies of these families can be found in Mustafa Tabaa's history of Gaza.[41] Such notables, each of whom patronised their own clientele of sharecroppers, day-labourers and others who were indebted to them, enjoyed the Ottoman title of 'effendi' and in due course they would all find seats in the municipal council of Gaza that was established in 1893. The prestigious religious positions of imam, mufti or judge (*qadi*) were often occupied by members of these families and they themselves vied to be the most generous in the provision of mosques and religious bequests (*waqf*, plural *awqaf*). Their prosperous landholdings were no longer under threat from the Bedouin of the Negev, who had become increasingly sedentary since the establishment of the city of Beersheba in 1889. Said Shawa, by far the region's richest man, became mayor of Gaza in 1907, and during his ten years in office he opened the municipal hospital and two secondary schools.

In 1882 Britain consolidated its hold over Egypt, and in the same year the British Church Missionary Society (CMS) opened a dispensary in Gaza, which in 1908 became a hospital that also treated patients from El-Arish and Beersheba. The United Kingdom had a consular representative in Gaza, as did Greece and Italy. The Greek Orthodox remained in the majority among the Christian population, with their Church of St Porphyry in the city centre, but the Catholics and the Anglicans also had their own parishes—a 'Latin' church was opened by an Austrian preacher in 1879, with a Protestant church following four years later.[42] The Catholic Church also maintained a girls' school in Gaza, attached to a similar institution at Beit Jala, close to Jerusalem. In 1906, an agreement signed at Rafah formalised the 'administrative border' between the Ottoman province and Egypt under

British tutelage. It was agreed with the British that the line should go through Rafah, so as to control the exit point from Sinai. However, it was also agreed that the Bedouin tribes should continue to be able to move freely across the frontier line, which was seen as largely artificial.[43]

Despite its small size in Gaza, the Jewish community had its own synagogue in addition to a school run by the 'Alliance Israélite Universelle' (AIU), a Paris-based international Jewish organisation. There were also two Jewish institutions outside Gaza, at Gedara and Qastina, both situated in the countryside north of Gaza City. Foreign visitors were impressed by the charm and diplomacy of a leading local figure, Eleazar Isaac Shapira, a Jew from California who had converted to Anglicanism, whom the Zionist activists mistrusted as an 'apostate'.[44] Such personal issues, exacerbated by uncertainty as to whether Gaza in fact formed part of the 'Land of Israel', meant that the region was omitted from the colonisation movement that Theodor Herzl and his supporters launched in the early years of the twentieth century. Moreover, the presence and involvement of Gaza's landowners obstructed the kind of deals that the Zionist agents had been able to make with the absentee landowners in central Palestine.

The Arab conquest of 637 was accompanied by the conversion of the population of Gaza to Islam, which took place in stages but was swiftly accomplished. 'Hashem's Gaza' oscillated between the authority of various Muslim governments in the Middle East and Egypt during the thirteen centuries that followed. The crusader interlude of the eleventh century, with the attachment of Gaza to the Frankish Kingdom in Jerusalem, linked to the crusaders' access from the sea, appears with hindsight to have been an anomalous episode in Gaza's historic evolution. The fate of the Templar castle, erected in 1149 and destroyed in 1193, was symbolic of the inability of the crusaders to put down roots in Gaza, though it was not until 1244 that the fluctuating coalition of Islamic forces was permanently able to fend off the crusader threat.

By contrast, the Mamluk period came to be recalled in Gaza as a golden age, so much benefit was the city able to extract from the special position accorded by the sultans in Egypt to their satellite city in Palestine. Khan Yunis, a caravanserai transformed into a settlement in its own right, remains the best illustration of this prosperity. The rise to power of the Ottoman Empire in the Levant in 1517 seemed to be a backward step in many respects, mitigated in Gaza in the seventeenth century only as the result of the growing autonomy of the Radwan family, the local governing dynasty. As regards the brief French intervention in Gaza in 1798–9, it is hard not to compare the frustration of Napoleon's goals, and his inglorious arrival and departure, with the ephemeral character of the Mongol occupation of Gaza in 1260 that resulted from the Mongol push towards the west.

In the first half of the nineteenth century there was a confrontation between the Khedives of Egypt and the Ottoman Empire over control of Gaza in which the Sublime Porte ultimately prevailed. The restoration of Ottoman authority in Gaza was symbolised by the construction of the new mosque of Hashem, on the spot where the remains of the Prophet's great-grandfather were reputed to lie. 'Hashem's Gaza' enjoyed a privileged position within the Palestine of that era. The local notables, who had grown wealthy on the profits derived from exporting cash crops, were able to extend their influence. Great Britain, the hegemonic power in neighbouring Egypt, also reached out towards Gaza, but without intending to challenge Ottoman rule directly. It was not until the outbreak of the worldwide conflagration in 1914 that the line drawn by the British and the Ottomans through Rafah in 1906 would at last be breached.

3

THE BRITISH MANDATE

On 2 August 1914 the Ottoman Empire concluded a secret alliance with Germany. The Ottoman commitment to support the Central Powers in World War I resulted from the diplomatic manoeuvres of a triumvirate of senior military men and politicians, Enver Pasha, Talaat Pasha and Djemal Pasha, each identified with the Committee for Union and Progress (the so-called Young Turks), who imposed their Turkish nationalism during World War I under the façade of defending the Ottoman Sultanate and the Caliphate. Lobbying on the part of Berlin also played a role in Sultan Mehmet V's decision to declare a 'jihad' against Britain, France and Russia three months later. Yet despite the fact that the sultan was also the caliph and hence the nominal head of the global Islamic community, his declaration failed to arouse the Muslim populations of these three colonial empires. Under the British protectorate established in 1914 Egypt remained inactive, and in the early days of February 1915, Djemal Pasha, based in Jerusalem, moved his forces into Sinai and threw them into an attack on the Suez Canal. The action failed and the Ottoman troops retreated into Sinai. Two months later, French ships bombarded Turkish positions in Gaza in an operation that had no sequel. The front lines remained fixed, despite frequent skirmishes.

The Battles of Gaza

After Djemal Pasha's defeat at Suez, the British took the initiative. From March 1916 onwards, the Egyptian Expeditionary Force, under the command of General Sir Archibald Murray with substantial contingents of Australian and New Zealand troops, began the re-conquest of Sinai. A second front was opened against the Turks in June 1916, when the governor of Mecca, the Sherif Hussein, with British assistance, embarked on his 'Arab Revolt' and seized the port of Jedda. London had promised the rebels that an 'Arab Kingdom' would be established in a Middle East free from Ottoman rule. This was the outcome desired by Hussein and his Hashemite dynasty, named in honour of Hashem, the ancestor of the Prophet Muhammad whose tomb, it will be remembered, lies in Gaza. In December 1916 the British contingent occupied the oasis of El-Arish before going on to take Rafah and then Khan Yunis. Gaza, the unavoidable crossing point, once again appeared to block the way to Palestine and it would be many months before the British army was able to dislodge the Turks who were under the command of a German officer, Colonel Friedrich Kress von Kressenstein.

At dawn on 26 March 1917 General Murray began his attack on the city of Gaza, which was defended by a Turkish force 4,000 strong. However, the German–Turkish garrison in Beersheba was able to repel the attackers due to serious lapses in the conduct of the operation, including a misdirected artillery barrage, thereby obliging the British forces to retreat to their original positions. It was an unambiguous defeat for the Egyptian Expeditionary Force, which lost 4,000 men, as against 2,500 losses for the Turks.[1] General Murray, who had concealed the scale of the failure from his superiors, was ordered to consolidate his positions to the south of the Gaza Valley with a view to launching an immediate attack on the city. The railway painstakingly constructed by the British troops from the Suez Canal was ready to bring up the reinforcements and supplies required for this imminent breakthrough. Meanwhile, an aqueduct crossed the desert from Suez to replenish the reservoirs of Khan Yunis, where Murray established his headquarters.

But the attack Murray launched on 17 April was no more successful than the previous one. The defenders of Gaza had used the intervening weeks to fortify their bunkers and trenches, while their artillery, skilfully guided from the air, inflicted considerable losses on the attacking force. The British lost half the force that attempted to capture Tell al-Muntar, the hill overlooking the road into Gaza, but to no avail.[2] At the end of three days of fighting, Murray called off the attack with casualties that were even higher than in the previous month—6,500 of his men in contrast to 2,000 for Gaza's defenders.[3] A static war subsequently developed, with both sides stepping up their rail facilities. German planes twice bombed the aqueduct from Suez, and in fact only a miniscule proportion of the water pumped from Egypt reached the expeditionary force. To raise the morale of the British troops, the chaplains stressed the religious imperative of the 'liberation' of the Holy Land, even referring to Samson's sacrifice of himself in Gaza.[4]

In June 1917 Murray was replaced by General Sir Edmund Allenby, who had recently emerged as the victor from the Battle of Arras in France. The new commander brought with him a significant amount of extra equipment, including some sixty aircraft, and his troops made contact with the Arab insurgents loyal to Sherif Hussein, after their capture of Aqaba. Allenby carefully planned a joint action against Beersheba and Gaza, preceded by a massive artillery bombardment, together with air attacks and shelling by naval guns. The bombardment of Gaza began on 27 October and continued until the morning of 31 October when the ground attack began. Beersheba fell on 1 November, allowing the attackers access to its precious water resources. It was not until 7 November, however, that Tell al-Muntar was finally taken, opening Gaza to the British troops. Djemal Pasha's forces fell back in good order, leaving behind a devastated city strewn with shell-holes where many of the buildings that had escaped destruction had been pulled down to construct the now abandoned Turkish fortifications.

The Military Government

General Allenby entered Gaza on 9 November 1917. Emptied of its inhabitants after the bombardment, the city served as Allenby's gateway into Palestine, a role it had played in the past for conquerors from Thutmose III to Bonaparte. Like his illustrious predecessors, Allenby marched on to Jerusalem to drive the Ottoman forces further back towards the north. On the day Allenby arrived in Gaza, the British press published a letter that had been sent to the Zionist leadership from the British Foreign Secretary Arthur Balfour a week earlier, on 2 November. The 'Balfour Declaration', as it became known, affirmed that 'His Majesty's government view with favour the establishment in Palestine of a national home for the Jewish people.'[5]

This public British commitment to the Zionist project gave rise to hostile comment in Cairo, Damascus and Istanbul. But in Gaza the population was too occupied with their cautious return to the homes from which they had fled at the height of the battle. The British expeditionary force busied itself with the northward extension of the railway line that ended at Deir al-Balah. Another major enterprise, which resulted directly from the scale of the recent conflict, was the construction of two military cemeteries to accommodate the remains of the British soldiers who had died in Palestine. The British military cemetery in Gaza, the larger of the two, which was in use until March 1919, would ultimately contain 3,000 graves. The other cemetery, in Deir al-Balah, served as the last resting place for some 700 bodies.

The British conquest of Palestine was completed in a month, after which a military administration was set up in the occupied territories. Palestine became the southern section of the OETA (Occupied Enemy Territory Administration), of which the western section was the territory now occupied by Lebanon, the north was Syria, and the east consisted of Transjordan. This system continued until June 1920 when the Near East was divided between the French and British Mandates.[6] Britain was careful to distinguish this chain of command from the hierarchy already in place in Egypt in order to avoid being accused of entertaining any ambition to annex Palestine. However, once the system had been put in place, it enabled London to defer the fulfilment of the promises it had made to its various partners until the conclusion of the war. France was thus frustrated in its plans to share the government of Palestine: Paris had been keen to take on the administration of the districts of Jaffa and Jerusalem, while those of Hebron and Gaza would be left to Britain.[7] The Arab revolutionaries, in a similar manoeuvre, were confined to the eastern bank of the River Jordan, while the implementation of the Balfour Declaration was also delayed until such time as the military regime might be terminated.

On 11 December 1917 General Allenby made a solemn entry into Jerusalem where the imposition of martial law was proclaimed in English,

Arabic, Hebrew, Greek and Italian. The victorious general received the keys of the city and the formal surrender of Hussein al-Husseini, the Palestinian mayor who had been appointed by the Ottomans. The mayor, who passed away shortly afterwards, was succeeded by his brother, Musa Kazim al-Husseini. Despite the new international dispensation, such administrative posts continued to be shared out locally among the members of a handful of powerful families in the larger cities of Palestine, whose position rested on their prestige and whose standing was frequently reinforced by their status as wealthy landowners. Like the Ottomans before them, the new British masters played one family off against another in order to divide and rule. Thus the traditional rivals of the Husseini family, the Nashashibis, regained the mayoralty of Jerusalem in 1920 when the position was taken by Ragheb Nashashibi. His promotion by the occupation authorities led the Husseini clan to espouse the nationalist position.

A similar 'politics of the notables', to use historian Albert Hourani's expression, applied in Gaza, where the military governor alternated between arbitrary rule and paternalism in order to control the principal families and counteract their influence. The deposed mayor, Said Shawa, was briefly incarcerated in the prison at Ramla before being granted a personal pardon.[8] However, the centralisation of the British administration in Jerusalem, to a degree unknown in Ottoman times, had an effect on the occupying power's treatment of Gaza, where close attention was paid to political developments in the Holy City. In the end, the rivalry between the Shawas and the Souranis began to mirror that between the Nashashibis and the Husseinis, with each family vying in the fervour of their nationalist rhetoric in order to boost their popularity. There were other concerns in Gaza in 1920, however. The town had not yet been fully rebuilt,[9] and more effort undoubtedly went into the process of repairing the damage done during the ravages of 1917 than was expended on the intrigues of politics.

Said Shawa personally oversaw the reconstruction of the minaret of the Mosque of Umar, and his successor in the mayor's office, Mahmud Abu Khadra, also kept a low profile, restricting himself to administration. In addition, Gaza was less subjected than the rest of Palestine to the turbulent consequences of Zionist activities, which were mainly located in the centre of the country. In general, in the south, British officials relied for support on the Bedouin tribes that had taken part in the Arab revolt of 1916. In 1920, for instance, Sheikh Freih Abu Middain became a member of the newly appointed British-sponsored Majlis al-Shura (Consultative Council) and in 1922 he became mayor of Beersheba. After some hesitation, the British divided Palestine into six districts (based on the Ottoman *liwa*), and the district of Gaza was itself divided into two sub-districts (based on the Ottoman *qadha*). Gaza, by far the most populous, included the coastline from Isdud to Rafah, while Beersheba was very much marked by the Bedouin character of the Negev desert. The *mukhtars*, literally the 'chosen ones' (in practice the customary chiefs of villages, areas or tribes) continued to occupy the same administrative and mediatory positions they had enjoyed in the Ottoman era.

Husseinis in Jerusalem and Gaza

Military government in Palestine continued until July 1920 when the first high commissioner, Sir Herbert Samuel, was appointed to head a civil administration. Negotiations at the League of Nations were nevertheless to occupy another two laborious years before the formal announcement of a British Mandate over Palestine, incorporating the Balfour Declaration and its reference to a 'jewish national home'. The Zionist inclination of the Mandate was accentuated by the personal sympathies of Sir Herbert Samuel, which prompted militant Arab circles to reject the very principle of the Mandate. The Muslim–Christian Associations, (which organised nationalist activities), appointed an Arab Executive.[10] In July 1922 it issued a reaction to the declaration of the British Mandate demanding a Palestine that would be 'Arab, free and autonomous.'[11]

The Arab Executive was headed by Musa Kazim al-Husseini, whose secretary was his cousin Jamal al-Husseini. Jamal al-Husseini was an ardent advocate for Palestinian ideas at the international conferences of the post-war period. He rejected a British proposal according to which he would be put in charge of an Arab Agency, which would be the counterpart of the Jewish Agency. In more general terms, the Arab Executive called for a boycott of the Mandate's institutions and compelled the British authorities to cancel the elections it had planned for June 1923. In Gaza, where a

Muslim–Christian Association had been in place since 1920, nationalist views divided the leading families. The mayor, Mahmud Abu Khadra, decided to wash his hands of the issue. He agreed to join the Consultative Council instituted by the British when new members were appointed, in which he represented southern Palestine, together with Sheikh Abu Middain who was re-appointed.

Another cousin of the president of the Arab Executive, hitherto a secular Arab nationalist, Amin al-Husseini, who bore the title of Hajj as an honorific after his return from the pilgrimage to Mecca, became a religious official in 1921 when he succeeded his half-brother Kamil as 'grand mufti' of Jerusalem. The Husseini family had in fact largely monopolised the position of mufti of Jerusalem since the end of the eighteenth century. The epithet 'grand', incidentally, he owed to the British, who intended thus to reinforce the prestige they wished to attach to Jerusalem as part of their centralisation of the administration of Palestine. He combined his responsible religious position with the presidency of the Higher Muslim Council, which managed schools, orphanages and above all the administration of religious bequests (*waqf*). In 1923 Hajj Amin embarked on an ambitious restoration of the esplanade of the Jerusalem Mosques (the 'Haram al-Sharif'), with an international fundraising campaign.[12] In Gaza, he initiated the restoration of the mausoleum of Hashem. The former mayor of Gaza, Said Shawa, represented the city at the Higher Muslim Council, jointly with Sheikh Muhyeddin Abdel Shafi, a cleric educated at the Egyptian University of Al-Azhar, who was at the time Gaza's *qadi* (a religious judge). The Abdel Shafi family had been Muslim dignitaries for seven generations.[13]

In Gaza as elsewhere in Palestine, the anniversary of the Balfour Declaration on 2 November was marked each year by a strike of merchants and officials, and there was also widespread action of the same kind when Lord Balfour visited Palestine in March 1925.[14] In reaction to the political activism of the Husseinis, echoed in Gaza by the new mayor, Umar Sourani and his brother Musa, the Nashashibi family sought local support in Gaza from the Shawa family, and from Sheikh Abdel Shafi. Due to the nationalist boycott of the administrative machinery of the Mandate, the Higher Muslim Council became the stage where these rivalries were acted out. The mufti's supporters declared themselves to be pro-Council (*majlisiyun*) while those backed by the Nashashibi represented themselves as the opposition (*mu'aridun*).

A dissident minority, however, refused to follow the factional strife of the notables and rebuked the traditional ruling class in its entirety for what the critics alleged was simply playing the colonialists' game. Among the leaders of this militant group was Hamdi al-Husseini, a Gaza schoolteacher (a member of the Gaza Husseini family which was not connected to the celebrated Husseini family of Jerusalem).[15] Hamdi al-Husseini, who made no secret of his communist sympathies, was a member of the Anti-Imperialist League, sponsored by the Comintern. Despite this, his anti-British stance led him to collaborate with avowed Islamists, such as Sheikh Ezzeddin al-Qassam, the *qadi* of Haifa.[16] Hamdi al-Husseini was soon dividing his time between Gaza and Jaffa, where he organised branches of the Young Muslims Association, placing the stress on working-class solidarity.[17] Gaza, normally a placid city, was occasionally capable of violent outbreaks, as was the case in April 1928 when a demonstration against proselytisation by Christian missionaries was put down by the police, though without serious casualties.[18]

The disturbances that broke out in September 1928 at the Western Wall in Jerusalem during the celebration of Yom Kippur, when Muslims objected to the erection of temporary screens next to the Wall by Jewish worshippers, led to the mufti's decision to undertake major works next to and above the Wall. According to Muslim tradition this is the place where Muhammad tethered his magical steed Buraq at the time of his night voyage from Mecca to Jerusalem, referred to by the first verse of sura 17 of the Quran, 'The Journey by Night'. Tension mounted in the area of the sacred site until violence broke out in August 1929, extending across the whole of Jerusalem as well as Hebron, Safed and Haifa. These unprecedented riots inflicted equal suffering on both communities, with 135 Jews dead and 136 Arabs.[19] The disturbances reached Gaza, where the tiny Jewish community, which counted only fifty-four persons in 1922,[20] was protected from a lynch mob by neighbourhood solidarity and the intervention of the former mayor, Said Shawa, and the Shawa family.[21] Though there were no fatalities, the episode was so terrifying that the Jewish inhabitants of Gaza, the inheritors of a centuries-old tradition, left the city for ever. Hamdi al-Husseini, accused of having fomented the inter-communal tension in Gaza, was sentenced to a year of house arrest in Nazareth. Three Arabs who had been involved in the disturbances were executed in Gaza. From 31 August to 9 September 1929, a squadron of thirty-five RAF aircrafts was stationed in Gaza to carry out reconnaissance operations in southern Palestine, but their deployment was also partly intended to dissuade militants from neighbouring Arabia from crossing the frontier into Negev.

In May 1928, Fahmi al-Husseini (who was also unrelated to the celebrated Husseini family, and indeed was a political ally of their rivals, the Nashashibis), became mayor of Gaza after the demise of Umar Sourani. A lawyer by training, he soon began to make a reputation by launching a monthly magazine, followed by a daily newspaper, *Sawt al-Haqq* (The Voice of Truth). He embarked on a programme of urban improvements, including a new municipal hospital (with the former hospital becoming the new town hall), and also extended the city limits as far as the sea. The opening of the zone next to the beach for building enabled the construction of the smart modern suburb of Rimal (The Sands). Fahmi al-Husseini also transformed a stretch of land he owned into a public park, whose popularity was all the greater because it contained a well. In 1931, Omar al-Mukhtar, the leader of the anti-Italian resistance in Libya, was executed, and the mayor commemorated him, and underlined his nationalist commitment, by re-naming the main street from the centre of Gaza to the sea in his honour, despite protests from the Italian consulate in Jerusalem.[22]

In 1932 the *Guide Bleu*, the French tourist handbook, spoke of the 'bustling bazaars' of Gaza, whose population was cited as numbering 17,480 inhabitants, as against 3,890 in Khan Yunis, 916 in Deir al-Balah and 600 at Rafah. The *Guide* added that the 'most significant' mosque was that dedicated to 'Hashem, the ancestor of Muhammad', and that there was a Roman Catholic mission as well as an Anglican mission and a Greek Orthodox church.[23] Gaza's communications were also good, the handbook remarked, situated as it was at the half-way point of the railway line linking Haifa to the Suez Canal along the coastal route, with a daily train in each direction. Gaza could also at this point be reached by a service bus from Beersheba to the south and Hebron to the east.

The Great Revolt

While Gaza built up its infrastructure, in Jerusalem Hajj Amin al-Husseini was consolidating his stature as a nationalist leader, not only in Palestine but in the wider Muslim world. He particularly sought to cultivate his contacts in Egypt. The grand mufti visited Cairo on a number of occasions, each time passing through Gaza. In the Egyptian capital he developed a relationship with King Farouk, as well as with the Wafd Party which dominated the political scene, and the Muslim Brotherhood, which had recently been founded by Hassan al-Banna.

Hajj Amin's efforts were rewarded in December 1931 when an Islamic Congress, which attracted delegates from across the Muslim world, was held in Jerusalem. The Wafd was represented by Abdurrahman Azzam, and other leading Arab and Muslim nationalist figures were also present, including Lebanon's Riyad al-Solh, and Muhammad Iqbal from India. Hamdi al-Husseini, militant as ever, upset the apple cart on the second day of the Congress when he accused 'British imperialism' of encouraging the pan-Islamic movement in order to create divisions between nationalists.[24] He succeeded in persuading the Congress to issue a formal condemnation of 'imperialism'. In 1932 he took his radical approach even further when he joined the pan-Arab Istiqlal (Independence) party, resuming his contacts with Ezzedin al-Qassam, the militant sheikh of Haifa.

In Geneva, Victor Jacobson, the representative of the World Zionist Organisation in the League of Nations, presented a plan motivated by the rise of anti-Semitism in Europe. According to his plan, Palestine would be divided into a Jewish state and an Arab state, into which more than 100,000 Arabs should be transferred, in return for financial compensation. Gaza would play a key role in this plan, since it would be the only coastal sector that would remain under Arab control. The future Arab entity would be empowered to enter into a confederation with the Hashemite Kingdom of Transjordan.[25] However, the nationalist Arabs were less alarmed by such Zionist projects than by the inflation in Jewish immigration, accelerated by the rise to power of the Nazis in Germany. There were 61,854 Jewish immigrants in 1935, as against 42,359 in 1934, 30,327 in 1933 and only 9,533 in 1932.[26]

Ezzedin al-Qassam was determined to mount a revolutionary jihad against the British and the Zionists. He suggested to Hajj Amin al-Husseini that the two should cooperate in organising an uprising, and that he should take charge of activities in the north of Palestine.[27] Although the mufti of Jerusalem rejected the proposal, he granted permission to some of those in his circle, and in particular Abdelkader al-Husseini, to organise into cells that would launch the 'holy jihad' (al-jihad al-muqaddas) when the moment came. The discovery that arms were being delivered to the Jewish Haganah militia gave fresh impetus to the secret preparations that were being undertaken in Arab circles. Ezzedin al-Qassam was the first to go into action, leading a guerrilla force of a dozen men before being killed in an ambush set by British troops in November 1935.

On 15 April 1936 the supporters of the late sheikh (now known as al-shahid, the 'Martyr') took their vengeance when they halted a bus and killed three Jewish passengers. The Haganah reprisals that followed led to further Arab violence in Tel-Aviv and Jaffa. This time the mufti of Jerusalem led the movement, and on 25 April he accepted the presidency of a newly established Arab Higher Committee in a demonstration of national unity embracing the Nashashibis. Hajj Amin al-Husseini called for a 'Holy National Jihad' (al-jihad al-watani al-muqqadas).[28] Though there was no official representative of Gaza on the Arab Higher Committee, the general strike it called took effect as strongly in southern Palestine as elsewhere in the country. This was the onset of the Arab Revolt in Palestine, which the Palestinian nationalists began to call a 'revolution' (thawra).

The Gaza strike committee brought together the supporters of the grand mufti, including Musa Sourani and Asim Bseisso, together with the allies of the Nashashibi, such as the brothers Adel and Rushdi Shawa.[29] In the Jerusalem region, Abdelkader al-Husseini fought as part of a guerrilla group and clashes multiplied through the summer. In Egypt, the Muslim Brotherhood launched a campaign in solidarity with the Palestinian uprising, though the mufti, anxious to maintain the national character of the movement he led, refused to accept foreign volunteers. Hassan al-Banna accepted the mufti's ruling, but a minority of activists in Egypt, led by Ahmad Rifaat, went to fight in Palestine. Ironically, Rifaat was suspected of being a double agent or a British spy and was executed by the very

Palestinians he had gone to help.[30] Anti-British activities intensified in the early autumn as the nationalist and revolutionary aspect of the uprising intensified. This revitalised the antagonism between the Husseinis and the Nashashibis, whose supporters in Gaza, anxious at the sight of their harvests of barley and citrus fruit rotting without being gathered in, began to ask for the strike to be suspended.[31]

The human costs quickly mounted for the Palestinians, whose death toll by mid-October was 1,000, by comparison with eighty Jews and thirty-seven British who had lost their lives.[32] The Arab Higher Committee was obliged to declare a halt to the general strike and therefore also to civil protest, though the guerrilla forces continued their operations, which, in Gaza, were directed mainly at the railways and the telegraph lines. A total of 20,000 British troops were deployed in Palestine against some 2,000 insurgents.[33] In April 1937, the mayor of Gaza, Fahmi al-Husseini, warned the British authorities against any suggestion that the country could be partitioned in order to establish a Jewish state. As he put it: 'It would be better for the British government to consign the inhabitants of Palestine to death and destruction, or even to envelop them with poison gas, than to inflict upon them any such plan.'[34]

In May 1937, Ezzedin Shawa, who was an administrator for the Mandate authorities in Jenin, though he privately supported the rebellion, was officially reprimanded and went into exile in Syria to organise the transport of arms for the insurrection.[35] The British plan for the partition of Palestine, published in July 1937, led to a fresh outbreak of the nationalist uprising. In Gaza, where one of the local leaders of the rebellion was a Christian, Butros Sayegh, only the intervention of Father Elias Rishawi, the leader of the Greek Orthodox community, saved Muslims convicted of participation from being hanged.[36] Three months later, Hajj Amine al-Husseini escaped arrest by fleeing to Lebanon, following which the rebellion, besieged on all sides, set up its headquarters in Damascus.

The British mobilised some 6,000 Jewish auxiliaries, mostly recruited from the Haganah, who were encouraged to build fortified settlements along strategic axes. These were built in salient positions, even in southern Palestine, in both the Negev and in the Gaza region. They formed part of Britain's strategy to secure their access routes to Sinai and to the Suez

Canal, an obsession of the British leadership. In the summer of 1938, the Arab insurrection seemed to get a second wind but the operations to crush it were ferociously effective. In Gaza, the grand mufti's faction lost its leadership with the imprisonment of Musa Sourani and Asim Bseisso. Even Fahmi al-Husseini, the mayor, was not spared. He was arrested shortly after he had overseen the installation of electricity in the city, putting a sudden end to his ten years at the head of the municipality. He was interned at Sarafand and then in Acre before being exiled to Lebanon in early 1940. He was allowed to return to Gaza but died there from a heart attack in December 1940.

The British authorities initially considered replacing him as mayor with Adel Shawa, who was strongly identified with the Nashashibi family. However, in January 1939, they appointed his brother Rushdi Shawa, a less controversial figure. Thus the mayoralty of Gaza reverted to the Shawa family, whose patriarch, Said Shawa, had held the position at the close of the Ottoman period. Three other sons of Said Shawa (Ezzedin, Saadi and Rashad) remained in exile due to their links with the rebellion. The British army did not hesitate to impose collective punishments to crush the last outposts of resistance. In July 1939, for example, the mayor of Khan Yunis and his deputies were imprisoned for the sabotage of telephone lines in the areas under their administration.[37] The 'Great Revolt', launched in 1936, had by now effectively been bled to death. In three years, 3,000 men had been lost from the Palestinian population of less than a million people.[38] Gaza had not suffered as much as the towns in central Palestine, but its trade was at a semi-standstill and a string of Jewish settlements had made their appearance on its near horizons.

The Allies Against the Axis

The outbreak of the Second World War on 1 September 1939 intensified the iron grip in which Mandate Palestine was already held. After two years of exile in Lebanon, Hajj Amin al-Husseini fled to Iraq, where his opposition to the British led him to link up with the pro-German camp, taking him far astray from the politics of Palestine. The former mufti was in Baghdad when he first opened a dialogue with the Führer in January 1941.

47

The defeat of the Iraqi nationalists by the British four months later led the mufti to seek refuge in Germany, to which he travelled via Iran, Turkey and Italy. In November 1941, he proposed to Adolf Hitler that he should raise an 'Arab Legion', which would fight in the Middle East alongside the Nazis, and he also made inflammatory broadcasts on Axis radio stations calling for 'jihad' against the Allies.[39]

This 'jihad' in German interests was no more effective in 1942, however, than it had been in 1914. The fascist war machine might broadcast the exhortations of the mufti of Jerusalem, just as the Central Powers had publicised those of the Ottoman sultan, but they found little response in the Arab world. The Nazi armed forces recruited only 6,300 auxiliaries of Arab origin, of whom only 1,300 came from Palestine, Syria or Iraq.[40] By way of comparison, across the entire course of the conflict, 7,578 Arabs enlisted in the British army in Palestine alongside 10,483 Jewish volunteers.[41]

In the spring of 1941, the defeat of the supporters of Vichy France in Syria and Lebanon completed the British victory over pro-German forces in Iraq. Mandate Palestine found itself at the heart of a Middle East under Allied control. The loss of momentum of the Nazi invasion of the Soviet Union and the entry of the United States into the war reinforced Britain's confidence. The colonial authorities were determined to halt clandestine Jewish immigration into Palestine. Meanwhile, Gaza remained on the margin of developments on the world stage. Australian troops were stationed there and British officers sat on a so-called security committee, alongside the mayor, Rushdi Shawa, and other local personalities. In the event of an air raid, for example, and without any proper equipment to raise the alarm, it was agreed that Gaza's muezzins would give the alarm from the minarets of the city's mosques.[42]

There were in fact few Axis bombing raids on the Gaza region, and those that did take place failed to cause any civilian casualties. On 8 September 1941, four bombs were dropped on Deir Suneid and Beit Hanoun, and on 3 March 1942 several bombs were dropped on Gaza itself. World War II seemed at the time to be relatively merciful to a population that had undergone the ravages of World War I. The presence of British and colonial troops brought with it employment, and the wartime economy was a stimulus for local businesses. The population of the city doubled in a decade, reaching almost 35,000.[43] However, the German offensives in the summer of 1942 led to the withdrawal towards the eastern part of the British administration in Cairo and to the arrival of some middle-class Egyptians. Gaza held its breath until the Allied victory at El Alamein and the strategic reversal of November 1942. The Axis forces were gradually pushed back as far as Tunisia, where they were caught in a pincer movement by the American landings in North Africa.

This is when information started to filter, it became known that the Nazis had exterminated at least 2 million Jews.[44] The consequence was the reinvigoration, especially in the United States, of the Zionist campaign to open Palestine to Jewish immigration. In December 1942, Rushdi Shawa and Gaza's municipal council made known their opposition to the pro-Zionist sympathies of the United States. A strike by merchants of Gaza was followed by another, in the same cause, in Khan Yunis.[45] However, the Gaza region did not appear to have occupied a prominent position in the plans of the Zionists, and the Jewish population had long since vanished from the towns after the riots of 1929. Nevertheless, new settlements were regularly established in the region, with a marked increase in the number of Jewish inhabitants, of whom there were 1,070 in 1941 and 2,174 in 1942.[46] By 1944, there were 2,890 Jews, as against 132,500 Muslims and 1,250 Christians.[47]

In 1944, between Gaza and Majdal, Polish immigrants of left-wing socialist sympathies set up the Kibbutz Yad Mordechai, named after Mordechai Anielewicz, one of the heroes of the resistance in the Warsaw ghetto. By 1945, 4 per cent of the land in the Gaza region was owned by Zionists (who only comprised 2 per cent of the population), as against 75 per cent of the land that was owned by Palestinian individuals and 21 per cent belonging to the public domain.[48] In contrast to those who had come before them, the recently arrived settlers made no attempt to cultivate relations with their Arab neighbours.[49] This was all that was needed to spur the notables of Gaza to turn for support to Saudi Arabia,[50] whose founding sovereign Ibn Saud had refused to make any compromise with Zionism.[51]

The Palestinian political class, decimated in the course of the suppression of the rebellion of 1936–9, generally kept a low profile, torn as they were between their wish to dissociate themselves from the mufti's pro-Nazi stance and the impossibility of replacing him with an alternative leader of national stature. Local intrigues broke out involving notables of a variety of allegiances, which were accentuated by the ill health of the mayor, Rushdi Shawa, who suffered two heart attacks in 1944. The British administration was also preoccupied by the recurrent vendettas between the larger clans, who were in addition often involved in various smuggling enterprises across the frontier with Egypt.[52] A deceptive feeling of detachment between Gaza and the outside world developed, one which was to persist after the German surrender in May 1945.

The Egyptian Muslim Brotherhood had by this time taken shape as a mass movement. Some fifteen years after its foundation, it had half a million determined and disciplined members.[53] Hassan al-Banna, who had been obliged to remain passive during the Palestinian uprising, was on this occasion determined to take an active part in the jihad in the Holy Land. In October 1945, he sent his son-in-law Said Ramadan to Jerusalem to set up a Palestinian branch of the Brotherhood. Sections of the movement were subsequently established in the main towns, and in Gaza two respected older men in their sixties took charge of the local group. Its president was Sheikh Omar Sawan, a retired judge, who had been a religious judge in Yemen and had then risen through the ranks of the judicial hierarchy in Gaza. He was backed up by Sheikh Abdullah al-Qayshawi, a Quranic scholar who did not shrink from public controversy with missionaries and Western orientalists.

The Muslim Brotherhood launched its Gaza section with a founding conference at the Samer Cinema on the occasion of the Islamic New Year, which in 1946 fell on 25 November. The mainstay of the operation in Gaza was the Brotherhood's local secretary general, Zafer Shawa, whose background was in the Muslim boy scouts and in sporting clubs and was distantly related to Said Shawa, though the latter's sons refused to accept him as a family member.[54] The Palestinian Muslim Brotherhood was closely linked to the Egyptian structure. The 'Central Committee of the Administrative Office', which controlled the Palestinian organisation, contained seventeen members, two each from the sections in Jerusalem, Haifa, Jaffa, Nablus and Gaza, who sat alongside seven delegates from the management of the Muslim Brotherhood in Cairo.[55]

The proximity of Egypt led to frequent visits by the leadership of the Brotherhood to Gaza, where the Brotherhood's organisation was even more under Egyptian influence than in the rest of Palestine. During this same period, 1945–6, the country also witnessed the development of a more indigenous organisation known as the Najjada (literally, 'The Reinforcements') which incorporated ideas drawn from the boy scout movement and from sporting associations. Members wore uniforms, conducted parades and undertook physical training sessions to prepare for militant activities or even armed operations.[56] The youth branch of Al-Najjada, known as Al-Futuwwa (The Youth), a name linked to the mystical and political brotherhoods of medieval Islam, enjoyed considerable popularity in the Gaza Strip, though clashes of personality hampered its recruitment programme.

Gaza was spared the wave of Jewish terrorism that rocked Palestine at the end of World War II, in which the Haganah as well as the more extremist Irgun and the Stern Gang took part. The Irgun was a revisionist militia that had split from Haganah in 1931, and the followers of Avraham Stern later left the Irgun in 1940 to create the so-called Stern Gang, also known as Lehi. In May 1946, Gaza's preoccupation was the British commitment to withdraw from Egyptian territory and even its Suez Canal base. For the British command, Gaza once more played the part of an advanced base from which, this time, it would monitor the Suez Canal rather than the Nile Valley. In October 1946, the Jewish National Fund scored a major victory when it simultaneously opened eleven kibbutzim in Gaza and Beersheba. The settlement at Kfar Darom, close to Deir al-Balah, was attached to the Mizrahi movement, which had been founded in 1922 and differed from mainstream Zionism in its rejection of Marxism. This religious kibbutz was located on the strategic road linking Gaza to Rafah,[57] while the other Zionist settlements, attached to the Labour Party, were further to the east in the Negev. The British administration observed that these settlements were all built on the same pattern and were well protected, each containing around thirty young and highly motivated activists.[58] Attempts at Jewish immigration from Egypt were also reported.[59]

Hajj Amin al-Husseini, arrested in Germany in May 1945 by the French army, spent a year under house arrest in the outskirts of Paris before evading his captors and fleeing to Egypt with a borrowed passport.[60] On his arrival in Cairo he was granted political asylum and assumed his former position at the head of an enlarged Arab Higher Committee.[61] The former mufti's prestige enabled him to take control of the militant activities of the Muslim Brotherhood in Palestine, which formally acknowledged him as their leader.[62] Yet his authoritarian tendencies and his troubled record as an exile were both obstacles to Palestinian action, at a time when the international campaign for partition of the country was already under way. In the meantime there was internal dissent within the Arab League, which had been founded in 1945. The League was highly dependent on its host country, King Farouk's Egypt, and there was minimal cooperation between the member states. There was little sympathy between the two Hashemite monarchies of Iraq and Transjordan; Ibn Saud's Saudi Arabia was a case apart, sustained by its special relationship with the United States; and republican Syria was obsessed with its own regional ambitions.

In Gaza, as in the rest of Palestine, the year 1947 took on the character of a protracted calm before the storm. Jewish terrorism obliged British officials to barricade themselves into their positions, with the official in charge of Gaza scarcely leaving the fortified security of his headquarters.[63] On 4 February, the families of expatriates and 'non-essential civilians' were evacuated from Gaza, which aggravated the widespread feeling of instability and uncertainty.[64] A month did not pass without the foundation of a new Jewish settlement in the region, and the Zionist activists no longer hesitated to attack any Bedouin tribesmen who entered their territory. Violence was also in the air in Gaza. On 25 March, there was an attack on a Jewish merchant who was saved by the intervention of the British police, and on 19 August a Jewish bus passenger was lynched.

On 31 August the United Nations Special Committee on Palestine (UNSCOP) submitted a report in which it recommended the partition of Palestine into a Jewish entity and an Arab entity, possibly within a federal structure of the two states or alternatively in an economic union. The Arab Higher Committee rejected both options, and leading figures in Gaza who dared to think about partition, now that it seemed inevitable, were soon cowed into silence. Mustafa Abdul Shafi, a medical doctor, who took the view that a negotiated partition would be preferable to an imposed solution, for example, was detained because of his ideas. In October 1947, he withdrew himself from the situation and emigrated to Egypt to work on an anti-cholera campaign.[65] Zionist activists who supported the partition plan began to act as if the Mandate had already come to an end, while the Arab population could hardly comprehend the full range of consequences that would follow the British departure. As the local British administrator observed on 18 November 1947, 'Gaza has begun to grasp that Britain is about to leave the country, but Beersheba is yet to be convinced.'[66] It was only a matter of days, however, before war would break out.

1947–67

THE GENERATION OF MOURNING

4

THE CATASTROPHE

On 29 November 1947 the United Nations General Assembly passed Resolution 181, which endorsed the plan to partition Palestine by thirty-three votes to ten. A further thirteen states abstained, including Great Britain, the Mandatory power. The Zionist leadership, which had strained every sinew to get the resolution passed, celebrated their diplomatic victory. Only the ultra-extremists of the Irgun and the Stern Gang rejected the implied territorial compromise. Crucially, the resolution was supported by the United States, the Soviet Union and France. All of the Arab and Muslim member states of the United Nations had opposed it, whether because they repudiated the principle that 'Arab Palestine' could in any way be partitioned into a Jewish and an Arab state, or because of their perception of the injustice of the partition plan as it was being envisaged. But to no avail. A Jewish population that amounted to only a third of the population of Palestine was to gain more than half its territory, including the most fertile lands in the coastal plain next to Lake Tiberias, as well as the Negev Desert. The resolution deemed the city of Jerusalem a 'corpus separatum', a zone not forming part of either state to be administered directly by the United Nations on the basis of a special legal status.

From One War to Another

In the partition plan, the Gaza sub-district, was only partly to be attributed to the Arab state. It was to be separated from the Arab area to the north of the town of Isdud, some 30 kilometres south of Tel Aviv, by a corridor linking the coastal sector of the Jewish state to the Negev. This corridor, which included the Jewish settlement of Negba, separated the northern part of the Gaza sub-district, including Isdud and Majdal, from the Arab localities of Beit Affa and Faluja, though these were its close neighbours. The Zionist colonies in Gaza were enraged by the prospect of becoming part of the minuscule Jewish minority that would remain within the future Arab state (though Arabs were to comprise almost half the population of the future Jewish state).

The violence which erupted the day after the adoption of the partition plan occurred mainly in Jerusalem, Jaffa and Haifa. In the city of Gaza the situation remained calm as the Zionist leadership prioritised consolidating their control over the territory that had been allocated to them under the plan and deferred the task of securing the 'corridor' to the Negev to a later date. Arab militias were organised in the region, but here as elsewhere they suffered from a lack of coordination. This gave the advantage to the tightly organised nucleus of the Muslim Brotherhood, which had some 500 members and was closely linked to the Islamist leadership in Cairo.[1] In December 1947, a three-day general strike in protest against the partition plan was observed throughout the region, and in one month the British authorities registered the deaths of twenty-four Jews and seven Arabs, including the mukhtar of the village of Huj and his brother, both of whom were murdered for 'collaboration with the Jews' during a visit to Gaza City.[2] The Zionist activists based in isolated settlements in the Negev, who refused to contemplate the possibility of any kind of retreat, paid the highest price for these clashes.[3] It was against this background that the British government announced its intention to leave Palestine on 15 May 1948.

The National Committee, established in Gaza on the same pattern as in other towns in Palestine, comprised fifty-two members who represented all shades of local opinion. But the committee failed to install competent management. By this time security in the region depended on a variety of militias, some of which were under the National Committee's direction and some which were not, while the British now limited themselves to patrolling the zone and made no further attempt to involve themselves in its administration.[4] In this situation, the Islamist fighters and their Egyptian allies had the advantage. By February 1948, there were still less than 100 volunteers from Egypt,[5] but in the following month Cairo secretly sent officers to take charge of the activists that had been infiltrated. On 12 March 1948, a large Zionist convoy was attacked at Faluja by the village militias, with the loss of thirty-seven of their men as against seven Zionists.[6] The Haganah carried out a punitive operation on the same day, dynamiting a dozen buildings in Faluja, including the Town Hall and the post office.[7]

From 19 to 22 March 1948, Hassan al-Banna came in person to encourage the Muslim Brothers in the Gaza region, taking possession of the former British camp at Nuseirat for the Brotherhood's operational base.[8] During the month of April, Palestinian and Egyptian Muslim Brotherhood guerrillas began a campaign of attrition against the Jewish settlements in Gaza and in the Negev. In the early hours of 14 April, Mahmoud Labib, the Brotherhood's head of operations in Palestine,[9] headed a fruitless attack against Kfar Darom.[10] On 11 May, at dawn, a further attack was launched against the same kibbutz, this time led by an Egyptian officer.[11] The Islamists suffered heavy losses, but still failed to occupy Kfar Darom. However, they partly compensated for this defeat with a successful attack on a Jewish convoy. On 13 May, Zionist commandos of the Givati Brigade took the villages of Batani al-Sharq and Bureir to the north of the Gaza district.[12] There were less than 400 Arab fighters in the Gaza region facing the impressive efficiency of these organised units, and their dispersal throughout the region hampered their ability to organise. According to Muhammad al-Azaar, in May 1948 there were only 365 Arab fighters in Gaza: eighty were Muslim Brothers, and 209 belonged to local nationalist militias, including 109 for 'Holy Jihad' and 100 for the 'Army of Salvation', who were supplemented by seventy-six volunteers of various nationalities, including some Palestinians from elsewhere sent by the Arab Higher Committee.[13]

On 8 May 1948, the British high commissioner estimated that more than 10,000 refugees from Jaffa were already in Gaza, and proposed that they should receive supplies overland from Egypt rather than from Haifa by sea.[14] On Friday, 14 May, in a ceremony that began at four in the afternoon, local time, before the beginning of the Jewish Sabbath, in anticipation of the formal termination of the Mandate at midnight, the Zionist leader David Ben Gurion proclaimed the existence of the State of Israel, which was recognised in the same evening by the United States. The armies of the Arab states, which had thus far refrained from acting, launched what Israel calls the 'War of Independence', which is often also referred to as the 'First Arab–Israeli War'. Some historians prefer to use other expressions. Henry Laurens, in his book *La question de Palestine*, for example, distinguishes this conflict, which he calls the 'Palestine War', from the 'Palestinian Civil War', which continued from the announcement of the partition plan up to the proclamation of the State of Israel. Elias Sanbar, in *L'expulsion*, calls it the 'Second Palestinian War', distinguishing it from the 'First' such war which was waged from December 1947 to May 1948. Finally, Oxford University's Avi Shlaim and Eugene Rogan call it the 'War for Palestine'.[15] The various Arab forces that entered the conflict totalled some 20,000, and even with the addition of the thousands of local militia who had been committed to the struggle since December, their numbers were less than the 30,000 to 35,000 Zionist fighters.[16]

The Israeli army was brought into existence by grouping the other Zionist forces around the nucleus of the Haganah under the acronym Tsahal (which stands for Tsvai Haganah Le Israel: i.e. 'Forces for the Defence of Israel'). It lacked heavy weapons and the engagements it had been involved in over the preceding months had taken their toll, as against the still fresh Arab forces. On the other hand, it had a unified command and an operational coherence which were painfully lacking among the Arab forces, which consisted of the armies of six different states in addition to the various Palestinian militias. This absence of coordination was aggravated by a tacit contradiction between the war aims of the governments of Egypt and Transjordan as embodied in the orders given to what were the two principal contingents. Transjordan sent its Arab Legion into action to take control in its own interests of the central section of Palestine, which had been allocated to the Arab state under the partition plan: it took no interest in the fate of High Galilee, of Gaza or the Negev. Egypt, on the other hand, cast itself in the role of the spearhead of the anti-Zionist front, and on 6 May 1948, in addition to the regular Egyptian officers, who had been engaged since March, an Egyptian unit was set up to support the militias, mostly Islamists, who were fighting in southern Palestine. According to the historian Walid Khalidi, this lightly armed force with four officers and 124 men reached Gaza on 11 May.[17]

The rivalry between the dynasties of Transjordan's King Abdullah and King Farouk of Egypt exacerbated this strategic contradiction. Farouk had ordered his prime minister and a reluctant government to become involved in the war. At the same time, King Abdullah was engaged in secret negotiations with the Zionists. On 10 May 1948 he received a visit in Amman from Golda Meir, at the time the political director of the Jewish Agency, who reminded him of their 'long-standing friendship' and their 'mutual understanding' in the face of 'common enemies' such as the mufti of Jerusalem and his Egyptian protectors.[18]

Egypt's Intervention

From 15 May 1948 onwards, almost 10,000 Egyptian soldiers were to arrive in Palestine, facing fierce resistance from the Jewish settlements on the coastal strip which they frequently attempted to bypass.[19] The main body of the Egyptian troops worked their way up the route of the railway line to Tel Aviv, which served as a guide in the absence of reliable maps. Due to logistic failures it took ten days before the Egyptian contingent reached Isdud, 35 kilometres north of Gaza, but they failed to press further forward. The Egyptian force was therefore still within the territory allocated to the Arabs under the partition plan. While there, the Egyptians disarmed the local militia in Gaza, as elsewhere, in order to maintain Egyptian control over operations. In contrast, the units fighting on the Beersheba front, which included both regular troops and guerrillas, were much more aggressive and broke through the Zionist lines, advancing in less than a week as far as Hebron and then to Bethlehem, which was in the sector held by the Transjordanians.

Gamal Abdel Nasser, Egypt's future president, served with the staff of the Egyptian sixth infantry battalion, first at Rafah and then at Gaza, as a young Egyptian officer.[20] He was soon disillusioned. His fellow officers told him that there had been an attack on the Zionist position at Nirim, to the east of Khan Yunis, known as Dangour by the Arabs, which had been repulsed with heavy casualties, yet Egypt's propaganda machine had announced that this enemy bastion had fallen. Nasser spent the night of 19 May 1948 at the field hospital in Gaza, which was overflowing with soldiers injured in the attack on the Jewish settlement at Yad Mordechai (which the Arabs called Deir Suneid), and was once again shocked by the Egyptian leadership's fraudulent claims of victory.[21] On 24 May, Yad Mordechai was finally taken following a joint attack by the Egyptian army and the Muslim Brotherhood.[22] Meanwhile, Israeli units were systematically driving the Arab population out of the combat zone, even when their villages had offered no resistance to the advance of the Zionists. Thus on 31 May the inhabitants of Huj were driven out and their houses were looted and destroyed, even though they had always had good relations with their Jewish neighbours (indeed, their mukhtar had recently been assassinated due to his lack of patriotism).[23]

On 11 June 1948, a four-week truce was declared under the auspices of the United Nations. Nasser, by now stationed at Isdud, raged against what he called 'the myth of a political war' in which success was being claimed while Israel was consolidating its positions.[24] The Egyptian high command was not inactive, however, since the troops under its command had now increased to 18,000 men, including fighters of other nationalities who had come for the most part from Sudan and Saudi Arabia.[25] The future Egyptian president's experience in Palestine was similar to that of an entire generation of Egyptian officers, such as Muhammad Neguib, with whom Nasser would carry out the coup of 1952, and Abdelhakim Amer, who was Nasser's deputy until 1967. However, in 1948 it was Nasser who was the most vehement in his denunciation of the incompetence and disorganisation of the Egyptian command structure.[26] Nasser was all the more severe in his criticism because he was still a member of the Muslim Brotherhood, having been among those Brothers who had been clandestinely infiltrated into the army.

On 7 July King Farouk went to Gaza to inspect the Egyptian troops, where he praised their 'courage' and their 'sacrifice'.[27] The truce ended two days later and the settlement at Kfar Darom, which had been surrounded for two months, soon fell. During the 'ten days war' that was waged until 18 July, the Zionist command put its efforts into breaking the links that had been established on the southern front between the Egyptian and the

Jordanian forces. The Muslim Brothers counter-attacked at the village of Asluj, which they succeeded in taking.[28] By contrast, the Egyptian attacks on the settlements at Negba and Berot Yezhak were driven back.[29] These violent clashes were accompanied by the displacement of Arab populations, more towards Hebron than towards Gaza. The Israeli units massed around the key position of Negba, protecting it while also taking the neighbouring village of Beit Affa, before retreating prior to the arrival of the Egyptian forces. The inhabitants of Beit Affa, who had fled to neighbouring locations during the fighting, did not return to their homes due to their fears that the Egyptian occupation could be as short-lived as that of the Israelis.[30]

The United Nations Swedish mediator, Count Folke Bernadotte, was able to engineer a second truce. The Israeli government estimated at the time that less than 90,000 Arabs remained on the territory allocated to the Jewish state under the UN partition plan.[31] Bernadotte prioritised the rapid return of the Palestinian refugees, who already numbered hundreds of thousands. However, his murder in Jerusalem on 17 September 1948, by agents of the Stern Gang, precluded any further diplomatic effort in that direction. The Israeli–Arab stalemate left the field free for inter-Arab negotiations with Cairo promoting the establishment of a Palestinian entity under its influence, which would have obstructed Amman's ambitions in the West Bank. Jamal al-Husseini, the Palestinian secretary of the Arab Higher Committee, obtained the agreement in principle of the Arab states to this proposal, albeit with the exception of Transjordan.

'All Palestine'

In September 1947 the Arab League had rejected the establishment of a Palestinian government by the Arab Higher Committee, and it was to be a year before this decision was looked at again. Hajj Amin al-Husseini's arguments in favour of this solution had failed to garner support from the Arab states, who had little inclination to hand over the conduct of hostilities to a hypothetical Palestinian authority. In fact, no plan to put in place a Palestinian administration was embarked upon, either before or after Israel's declaration of independence. While this inaction can partly be explained due to a fear of appearing to endorse the partition plan, it was also the result of inter-Arab intrigue and of the reciprocal frustration between the Arab states regarding each other's ability to move.

The work of the Arab Higher Committee, confronted by a Zionist leadership entrenched in the territory of its choice, was severely undermined by the dispersion of its members and their exile from Palestine. Hajj Amin, based in Cairo since 1946, favoured the establishment of a Palestinian government in exile; in fact, only one member of the Arab Higher Committee was still resident in Palestine by 15 May 1948. This was Ahmed Hilmi Abdul Baqi, better known by the title of Ahmed Hilmi Pasha that had been conferred on him by the Hashemite monarchy. Ahmed Hilmi Pasha was the founder of the Arab Bank, and after his appointment as military governor of Jerusalem by King Abdullah he had remained in the Holy City throughout the fighting. Well entrenched in royal circles in Amman, he called in every favour he could in the hope of reaching a consensus, but in so doing he also became the focus of Hajj Amin's unwavering hostility.

Though Jamal al-Husseini was Hajj Amin's cousin, he could not but prefer Ahmed Hilmi as a personality around whom Arab support for a future government in Palestine could be rallied. Even the Egyptian secretary of the Arab League, Abdurrahman Azzam, gave private assurances that Hajj Amin would not leave Cairo, and that his influence would remain indirect.[32] In any case, inter-Arab diplomacy seemed to have been turned on its head, with Transjordan accusing Egypt of having shamefully acquiesced in the partition plan through its support for a Palestinian equivalent of the Israeli government. In order to counter what it regarded as an attack on its motives, and to justify its stance, the Egyptian government pressed for the installation of an All-Palestine Government (in Arabic, *hukumat 'umum filistin*).

On 6 September 1948, the Arab League endorsed the principle of such a government, announcing its formation two weeks later on the basis of Jamal al-Husseini's investigations. Gaza, as the only Palestinian town of any size under Egyptian control, was designated the seat of the All-Palestine Government, and the prospective ministers were taken there with Egyptian assistance. On 22 September, a cabinet of twelve members was established under the leadership of Ahmed Hilmi. Jamal al-Husseini was appointed foreign minister and the government also included other supporters of Hajj Amin. The notables of Jerusalem and Nablus dominated the All-Palestine Government, the first Palestinian government in history, in which nobody represented Gaza itself, which had become the stage on which the drama was enacted. The new prime minister declared his dedication to the total liberation of Palestine, and, in order to strengthen his claim to democratic legitimacy, called for a representative assembly to be convened in Gaza.

Of the 150 members of the National Council, whose mandate was to be a constituent assembly, only eighty-three succeeded in getting to Gaza, largely as a result of the restrictions imposed by the Hashemites in central Palestine.[33] Transjordan regarded the All-Palestine Government as a hostile tool of Egypt. These accusations only intensified after Hajj Amin, whose status as a political refugee in Cairo theoretically precluded him from leaving the city, contrived to enter Gaza on 27 September 1948, claiming to have slipped past Egyptian security in order to bring his eleven years of exile to an end. On his arrival in Gaza, his prestige as a nationalist figurehead was boosted by demonstrations that his supporters had organised. Meanwhile, the relaunch of his 'Army for the Holy Jihad' (*jaysh al-jihad al-muqaddas*) was intended to establish him as a protagonist in the conflicts to come. In Gaza, Hajj Amin took up residence in the house of Musa Sourani, the most dedicated of his followers, and commissioned Musa's nephew, Jamal Sourani, to lead the nationalist militia in the south of Palestine alongside an Iraqi volunteer, Abdulhaq al-Azzawi. For the time being, however, the truce with the Israelis continued, and the All-Palestine Government campaigned for international recognition and began to issue Palestinian passports. Some 14,000 travel documents were issued by the government, largely for the notables of Gaza and their clients.

The Palestinian National Council was convened on 30 September 1948, though it was unable to find any other venue in Gaza for its meetings than a partially closed school whose dilapidated surroundings added nothing to the solemnity of its proceedings. It was here that the Council appealed for the general mobilisation of all Palestinian men aged from eighteen to forty. Hajj Amin was unanimously elected president of the Council, which gave Ahmed Hilmi's government a vote of confidence by sixty-four votes to eleven. The Council also endorsed a declaration of the independence of Palestine, with Jerusalem as its capital, one of the provisions of which was the 'safeguard of the Holy Places, with a guarantee of freedom of worship for all faiths'.[34] At the same time, Egypt refused to consider the suspension of its administration, even in Gaza itself. Transjordan was also determined to block the nationalist impetus. On the same day as the meeting in Gaza, 30 September, a rival Palestinian Congress was convened in Amman where hundreds of participants swore allegiance to the Hashemite monarchy. The constitution of the All-Palestine Government was rejected on the basis of a rhetorical claim that no government could represent Palestine before the complete liberation of its territory, and that until such time it was appropriate for Transjordan to advocate the Palestinian cause instead.

The delegates who gathered in Gaza were certainly more earnest and less dependent than those in Amman, but there were fewer of them and they were more isolated. The call for a Palestinian army of liberation elicited an emotional response from the displaced populations, but it came painfully late in view of the multiple land-grabs already made by the Zionist forces, which went well beyond the boundaries provided for in the partition plan. The efforts of the All-Palestine Government were therefore concentrated in the diplomatic arena. On 12 October 1948, Egypt was the first state to offer it recognition, followed by Syria, Lebanon, Saudi Arabia and Yemen. Even Iraq, which had 1,500 troops in the Nablus sector, finally recognised Ahmed Hilmi Pasha's government after Jamal al-Husseini had promised Baghdad that the mufti would be permanently excluded from it.[35] In Beirut, the newly appointed foreign minister of the All-Palestine Government conveyed the same message to the prime minister of Transjordan in the hope of placating Amman's animosity.[36]

However, this did not lead King Abdullah of Transjordan to moderate his hostility to the government in Gaza, which he regarded as a major obstacle to the extension of his control over the West Bank. Amman had the full support of Britain on this issue, which perceived the partition of Palestine between Israel and Transjordan as the best way to secure its own interests in the region. A further consideration was that the British government had never excused the mufti for his collaboration with Nazi Germany. Indeed, as the British chargé d'affaires in Cairo declared to his

French colleague, in a 'furious and vindictive manner', 'Hajj Amin ought to have been hanged five years ago, and would have been if he had fallen into British hands in 1945.'[37] For its part, the Quai d'Orsay took the view that no valid consideration could lead France to 'take sides in a dispute that, since it opposes the Grand Mufti to King Abdullah, has divided the Arab League'.[38] However, the British position gained more support in Washington, where Hajj Amin and the All-Palestine Government attracted little by way of sympathy. French neutrality on the one hand, and the Anglo-Saxon veto on the other, both stood in the way of any gesture, no matter how small, in the direction of the Gaza government.

In mid-October, with the renewed outbreak of war between Israel and Egypt, the fate of the All-Palestine Government was sealed amid the chaos of the fighting. Hajj Amin, obliged to return to Cairo, was effectively placed under house arrest, and the deteriorating military situation also led to the departure of all the other Palestinian ministers from Gaza. The most disillusioned merely transited through Egypt before going on to Amman to swear their allegiance to King Abdullah. Jamal-al-Husseini went as far as to propose the transfer of the territory controlled by the All-Palestine Government to the Hashemite throne in the interests of the sacred principle of anti-Zionist unity.[39] Yet once the Palestinian government had departed from Gaza it was nothing but an empty shell, the administrative costs of which the Arab League was reluctant to pay. In addition, Transjordan had no further need of the belated endorsement of its former adversaries in order to achieve its annexationist goals. On 1 December 1948, the Second Palestinian Congress, assembled on this occasion in Jericho, formally recognised the authority of King Abdullah. Their public declaration of allegiance was rephrased by the king's supporters to emphasise its unconditional nature, and the proclamation was soon cited in justification of the official union of the two banks of the River Jordan in a Hashemite Kingdom of Jordan, re-founded on this basis.

The All-Palestine Government, which was no more than the shadow of its former self, was henceforth to vegetate in Cairo where it retained only minimal and occasional contact with Gaza. The Palestinian minister of defence, with no financial resources, was compelled to dissolve the last remaining nationalist militia units that were still active.[40] This disastrous experience of Arab bad faith and nationalist impotence weighed heavily in the collective memory, and more so in Gaza than elsewhere in Palestine. However, amid the general collapse of a country and a society, Gaza would still appear retrospectively as the only theatre where, for a few weeks, the Palestinians had assembled under their own flag, to defend their cause by their own efforts, before being defeated as much by their supposed Arab friends as by their Zionist enemies. But this was a brief parenthesis in a developing tragedy. For Gaza, the worst was yet to come.

A Sea of Humanity

On 15 October 1948, the second truce in what was referred to by the two sides respectively as either the 'War of Independence' or the 'Palestine War' was broken by Israel, which opened an anti-Egyptian front,[41] launching what came to be known as Operation Yoav. Forces commanded by Yigal Allon, commander of the southern front, pushed back the enemy lines and forced the Egyptian troops to fall back towards Gaza after fierce fighting. Artillery and aerial bombardments terrified the population in the most exposed Palestinian localities, while Gaza (on 17 October) and Majdal (on 21 October) were shelled by the Israeli naval forces.[42] Transjordan, meanwhile, remained aloof. Glubb Pasha, the commander-in-chief of the Arab Legion, wrote to his commanding officer on the ground that 'if the Jews want to fight a private war with the Egyptians and the government in Gaza, we don't want to be involved. The Gyppies and the Gaza government are almost as hostile to us as are the Jews.'[43] By now the Israeli forces had free access to the Negev and had laid siege to Beersheba, which surrendered on 21 October.

On 22 October 1948, a daring Israeli operation broke through the Egyptian lines, seizing the village of Beit Hanoun and thus cutting the rail and road link to Majdal, 20 kilometres north of Gaza. The Egyptian forces held on to a strip of territory on the coast, while Egyptian and Israeli ships engaged each other close to the shore.[44] But this situation was not tenable for the Egyptians, and, as a result, from 27 October the Egyptian command began to evacuate their troops, first from Isdud, and then from Majdal which fell without a fight on 5 November. The Israeli victories were accompanied by the exodus of tens of thousands of Palestinian civilians. Some abandoned their villages and their houses; others, who had already fled the fighting earlier in the conflict, were obliged to flee a second time. The invaders allowed a remnant of the Arab population to stay in Majdal, but they drove out the inhabitants of the neighbouring location of Al-Joura, as well as the 300 residents who had held on in Isdud despite the fighting.[45]

All of these displaced groups tended to gravitate towards the relative security provided by the Egyptian army in the region of Gaza. The population of the area, numbering some 80,000 people before the start of the hostilities, had already doubled thanks to the influx of refugees in the spring of 1948.[46] Almost all of the 7,000 inhabitants of Yibna, south of Ramla, had arrived in Gaza by June in order to escape the Israeli advance.[47] Operation Yoav alone prompted the flight of 75,000 terrified civilians to Gaza, where aid to the refugees, initially provided by the Egyptian army, was increasingly taken over by American Quakers, financed by the United Nations and operating under what was called the American Friends Service Committee (AFSC). On 1 December 1948, the United Nations set up an agency specifically to give assistance to Palestinian refugees, the United Nations Relief for Palestinian Refugees (UNRPR), under the leadership of the US ambassador in Egypt, Stanton Griffis. Meanwhile, in Egypt itself, the military disaster contributed to a profound political crisis. On 8 December Egypt's prime minister, Mahmoud Nuqrashi, banned the Muslim Brotherhood and confiscated its assets as part of a campaign to suppress militant Islamism. This policy extended to the Gaza Strip, where the fighting units of the Muslim Brotherhood were dismantled in Gaza prior to their transfer to internment centres in Sinai.[48] The Islamists took their revenge with the murder of Nuqrashi, who was shot in Cairo by an assassin disguised as a police officer on 28 December.

Amid the general collapse, Gaza became the last place the Zionist advance could be avoided. The paradoxical appearance that Gaza was a sanctuary became exaggerated in the closing days of 1948, while the Israeli forces were eliminating, with some difficulty, the Egyptian positions at Bir Asluj and Al-Awja. This provided access to Sinai, by-passing the Faluja pocket and surrounding it in order to neutralise it. It was here that Gamal Abdel Nasser was still fighting valiantly. Yigal Allon hoped to obtain total capitulation at Gaza, like that of Beersheba, and to that end he circled round the city and took Rafah from the rear by dispatching his commandos into the Egyptian desert. He failed, however, to reckon with the anger of the United States and Britain, who felt that such a humiliation for Egypt would only serve the interests of the Soviet Union. London and Washington therefore demanded Israel's withdrawal from Sinai, thus preserving the Gaza region from strangulation. On 7 January 1949 the ceasefire between Egypt and Israel brought an end to the first Arab–Israeli war.

The final military manoeuvres entailed the influx of a further 33,000 refugees into Gaza, whose population had almost tripled in less than a year, with the number of inhabitants in the City of Gaza itself rising from 35,000 to 170,000. Arlette Khoury-Tadié, the daughter of a senior Palestinian official in Gaza, describes her feelings as a child with regard to the displaced masses:

We saw thousands of people arrive, all looking exhausted. They didn't even ask for anything to eat or drink. When we offered them food, sometimes they refused it, sometimes they threw themselves on it as if starving. We had never seen anything like it. The streets, which were in general empty, suddenly pullulated with vast crowds who seemed to wander aimlessly; no-one knew where these people were going and from what or whom they were fleeing. The main street was packed with people going in both directions; some came by sea, arriving by boat down the coast from Jaffa, while others came on foot from places close by.[49]

The first wave of refugees from Jaffa and Ramla received a relatively warm welcome from the local population. Those with money were able to rent somewhere to live, while the more poverty stricken found footholds in the barracks, schools and mosques. But the available places to live were limited and later arrivals soon had to take their chances on the beaches, in orchards and on the pavements. The approach of winter exacerbated the situation since it had only been possible to distribute a few hundred tents, and the provision of flour was also problematic.

The International Committee of the Red Cross estimates that about ten children died each day from hunger, cold and the lack of care.[50] Mustafa Abdel Shafi, the only doctor practising in the entire region from the south of Gaza to the Egyptian frontier, lost count of the number of children who died of gastroenteritis or acute pneumonia.[51] A refugee from Beit Affa, who lost two of his eldest children when they were of a young age, tells how:

an epidemic of measles was declared, but there were no medicines and no heating. In our villages, we knew how to deal with children's ailments, but we were unable to do anything while we were in tents and in that situation. There was no doctor, no medicines, and most of the children who were still breast-feeding were carried off by the measles.[52]

These dreadful circumstances were not to improve until March 1949 with the delivery of 2,000 tents by the Turkish government, followed by the opening of temporary classes for some 16,000 refugee children. A methodical census enabled an assessment to be made of the demographic upheaval Gaza had experienced by the time the 'Palestine War' had come to an end.[53] The 80,000 inhabitants of this coastal strip of territory were joined by slightly more than 200,000 souls, cast adrift by history, two out of five of whom were from the central area of Palestine. A large proportion of the refugees were from the Gaza sub-district itself, of which forty-five out of fifty-six local centres of population had been emptied of their inhabitants by the Israeli occupation. These people, even more than the rest, were haunted by the desire to return to homes and lands that were sometimes within sight. These were mainly peasant families, or Bedouin. Two thirds of the adult men had no educational qualifications, while 90 per cent of the refugees as a whole were illiterate. Their organisation, according to their villages of origin, under the authority of their traditional chiefs, partly served to dull the pains of exile and brought at least some hope of an early return.

The Palestinians refer to the immeasurable loss of 1948 as the *nakba*, the 'Catastrophe', for which the mourning bell has sounded each 15 May since then. Gaza, submerged by waves of displaced persons, wedged between the sea, the desert and the Israeli troops, underwent a paroxysm of collective trauma. As the tragedy unfolded many inhabitants of Gaza, Khan Yunis and Rafah lost the lands, the outlets and the markets which had enabled them to live. Though not hounded from their homes, they shared with the mass of the refugees the same despondency and the same enforced deprivation, overwhelmed by the same incomprehension and the same bitterness.

Although this coastal strip represented only a little more than a hundredth of the area of Mandatory Palestine, it now provided a home for a quarter of Palestine's Arab population. Up to the present day, the inhabitants of Gaza take the view that their 'Strip' has become an involuntary 'Noah's Ark' for the former Palestine which disappeared in 1948. While it is true that many of the refugees originally came from the Gaza region, tens of thousands of them had fled from the central area of Palestine and even from as far afield as Galilee. For a few weeks in 1948, Gaza also served as the venue in which the whole of Palestine attempted to establish a government. But this was only an episode, and one which was swiftly forgotten.

5

REFUGEES AND FEDAYIN

The Gaza Strip, which emerged from the ruins of Palestine, is a territory of some 360 square kilometres, stretching along the Mediterranean with a coastline of around 40 kilometres. To the north of Gaza City the territory is no longer than 5 kilometres across, and it widens to no more than 13 kilometres on the Egyptian frontier. This is why it is referred to as a 'Strip'. The two urban centres of Gaza and Khan Yunis, as well as the villages of Jabalya, Deir al-Balah and Rafah, were now surrounded by significant concentrations of refugees, thereby endowing a region hitherto given over to meadows and orchards with an urban character.

At the time of the ceasefire this accidental territorial entity became the object of intense negotiations between the belligerents. On 12 January 1949, Ralph Bunche, the American UN mediator who had previously been Count Bernadotte's deputy and now succeeded him, convened a meeting of the Israeli and Egyptian negotiators on the island of Rhodes. Cairo rejected any form of political recognition of Israel. Bunche, however, in the unusual context of an indefinitely prolonged armistice agreement, and in the absence of a peace agreement (which was inconceivable at that point), contrived a diplomatic solution.[1] The Gaza Strip, delimited by the international frontier at Rafah and by the Israeli–Egyptian ceasefire lines elsewhere, would, de facto, be administered by Egypt. But this went too far for King Abdullah, who held a secret meeting in northern Transjordan with Moshe Dayan, then Israeli commander in East Jerusalem, on

73

16 January. Dayan was accompanied at the meeting by Eliyahu Sasson, a veteran of clandestine contacts with the Jordanians, first as head of Arab affairs in the Jewish Agency and then as head of the Department of Arab Affairs at the Israeli Foreign Ministry, a post he held from the creation of the State of Israel in May 1948 onwards. The Hashemite monarchy demanded that it be given sovereignty over Gaza in order to provide the country with access to the Mediterranean Sea, but also to rein in this hot-bed of Palestinian nationalism.[2]

However, the Israelis opted to give priority to the consolidation of their southern front. The armistice agreement signed with Egypt on 24 February at Rhodes provided for the establishment of a demilitarised zone at Al-Awja and for the evacuation of the Egyptian troops who were still surrounded at Faluja. On 5 March, David Ben Gurion initiated Operation Uvda ('Facts on the Ground') which secured the Negev as far south as the port of Eilat, which stood opposite the Transjordanian port of Aqaba. These final manoeuvrings of the first Arab–Israeli war resulted in new displacements of population, some of whom went to Gaza. According to the Rhodes Agreement: 'The Armistice Demarcation Line is not to be construed in any sense as a political or territorial boundary, and is delineated without preju-dice to rights, claims and positions of either Party to the Armistice as regards ultimate settlement of the Palestine question.'[3]

Israel's Annexation Plan

At the same time as some 200,000 refugees were enduring their first ter-rible winter in Gaza, the members of the United Nations were engaged in a bitter dispute over the fate of these uprooted people. On 11 December 1948, the UN General Assembly adopted Resolution 194, which estab-lished a UN 'Conciliation Commission' for Palestine and resolved that:

the refugees wishing to return to their homes and live at peace with their neighbours should be permitted to do so at the earliest practicable date, and that compensation should be paid for the property of those choosing not to return and for loss of or damage to property which, under principles of international law or in equity, should be made good by the Governments or authorities responsible.[4]

By announcing an official alternative between compensation and repa-triation, this text established the principle of the right of return for the

Palestinian refugees. Resolution 194 was badly received by Israel as it had equal weight in international law to that of Resolution 181 on the partition of Palestine, adopted a year earlier, which had established the legitimacy of the State of Israel.

The UN Conciliation Commission for Palestine (UNCCP), which the United States, France and Turkey were appointed to administer, began its work before the ensuing Egyptian–Israeli armistice. Lebanon and Transjordan quickly signed their own armistice conventions with Israel, with Transjordan re-designating itself the Hashemite Kingdom of Jordan on 3 April 1949 to mark its acquisition of the former territory of Palestine west of the Jordan river, which became known as the West Bank. The UNCCP subsequently persuaded the Arab states to agree to participate in a peace conference intended to implement the 'right of return of the refugees'.[5] On 18 April 1949, David Ben Gurion informed the UNCCP of his plan to annex the Gaza Strip, a territory over which Egypt had never asserted any claim of sovereignty.[6] The Israeli prime minister wanted to take the achievements resulting from Operation Facts on the Ground with regard to Israel's southern front to their logical conclusion. His hope was thus to obtain at the negotiating table what his armed forces had been unable to achieve in December 1948 due to the opposition of the United States and Britain. Ben Gurion also sought to avoid any transfer of the British base in Suez to Gaza, given his unease over the British military presence to the east of the River Jordan.

On 27 April 1949 the UNCCP convened a meeting of the delegations of Israel and the Arab states at Lausanne, without any independent representation for the Palestinians. On 11 May, the UN General Assembly formally admitted the State of Israel as a member, though with an explicit reminder of the content of Resolutions 181 and 194. Israel's admission to the UN enabled the Lausanne conference to proceed. On 20 May, the Israeli plenipotentiary made a formal proposal for the annexation of Gaza, which he presented as a contribution to the settlement of the refugee question. According to the proposal, the refugees could stay where they were and would thus become Israeli nationals on the condition that substantial international assistance was provided in view of their need for resettlement. It is notable that the Israelis believed the population of the Gaza Strip numbered 180,000, when the real figure was already 50 per cent more than this.[7]

The United States took the view that any such Israeli modification of the partition plan should be accompanied by territorial concessions of comparable extent elsewhere. On 28 May President Truman wrote to David Ben Gurion to that effect, warning him that there would be consequences if the Lausanne conference failed.[8] The Israeli diplomats, however, succeeded in convincing their American colleagues that their plan to annex Gaza could enable the stalemate at the peace conference to be overcome. The US State Department ultimately adopted the Israeli proposal on condition that it be accompanied by compensatory adjustments in the Negev, which would be defined in due course.

Washington was increasingly insistent in offering its 'good offices' to Cairo in order to challenge what it described as Egypt's 'negative' attitude.[9] The United Kingdom also backed the move, suggesting that the Israeli annexation of Gaza could form part of an overall plan under which Egypt would recover part of the Negev and would have at its disposal a land corridor to Jordan.[10] But Egypt refused to countenance these suggestions and, on 3 August, Israel announced that its final decision was to admit no more than 100,000 refugees into its territory—in other words less than half the number of refugees in the Gaza Strip alone.[11] On 15 September, after months of fruitless exchanges, the Lausanne conference broke up.

This diplomatic fiasco resulted in the temporary status of the region becoming permanent due to the impossibility of imposing a settlement on the parties involved. On 11 August 1949, the UN Security Council passed Resolution 74, which created the United Nations Truce Supervision Organisation (UNTSO), whose remit was to oversee the observance of the various armistices. On 8 December, the General Assembly replaced the former UNRPR (United Nations Relief for Palestinian Refugees) with UNRWA (the United Nations Relief and Works Agency) significantly adding 'works' to the initial 'relief'. The urgency of the winter of 1948–9 was superseded by an approach more suited to the longer run. A programme of major works was instituted that was intended to make the refugees more productive and to reduce their dependency on international aid. In the Gaza Strip, where more than two thirds of the population were refugees, this change of perspective was to have far-reaching consequences.

Egypt and The United Nations

Egypt found it extremely difficult to manage the internal repercussions stemming from the Palestinian tragedy. The Muslim Brotherhood, whose supreme guide, Hassan al-Banna, had been assassinated on 12 February 1949, accused the Egyptian government of having connived with the British to crush the jihad in Palestine.[12] The authorities took no risks. They maintained their censorship over news concerning the armistice negotiations with Israel and gave a hero's welcome to the returning combatants who had been evacuated from Faluja. Nor was there any question of allowing refugee camps on Egyptian soil: the 3,000 or so Palestinians from Jaffa who had ended up in the Cairo quarter of Al-Abbassiyya were transferred to the camp at Qantara on the east bank of the Suez Canal, all of whose residents were in turn sent towards Gaza a year later.[13] Egypt's refusal to issue work permits to Palestinian refugees meant that only the better-off or students with scholarships were able to live in Cairo.

The Gaza Strip was under the authority of an Egyptian military governor with the rank of general, whose administration took its powers from the state of emergency that had been in force since the onset of hostilities with Israel. The first governor, Ahmed Salem (whose Arabic title was *hakim*), recreated the provisions in force under the British Mandate, except where they clashed with Egyptian military law, issuing six ordinances to that effect ('*amr*, plural '*awamir*) in May and June 1948.[14]

This formal continuity placed the Egyptian governor in a position where he was the de facto head of the institutions that had been inherited from the Mandate and these were now re-established under his authority.[15] The system in which mayors represented the towns and 'mukhtars' headed the local areas and villages was reinstated. The governor also became the president of the Higher Islamic Council (HIC) with responsibility for appointing Islamic dignitaries such as judges and *waqf* administrators throughout the Gaza Strip.[16] Jamal Sourani, previously the leader of the short-lived militia in the south of Palestine, who was only the secretary of the HIC rather than its head, owed his appointment to the Egyptian military governor.[17] The governor's fifth ordinance, promulgated on 1 June 1948, established a 'national guard' of Palestinian auxiliaries under Egyptian military authority, and these were the only Palestinians who were entitled to bear arms.[18]

International aid was unloaded at Port Said and brought to Gaza via Sinai by train. Accounts agree as to the efficiency of the Egyptian army and its cooperation with the American Quakers in assisting the Palestinian refugees.[19] By February 1949, food rations were being distributed to around 260,000 people, but this figure was inflated by double registrations, the non-reporting of deaths and applications from existing Gaza residents who were poor but unregistered. By September 1949, the figure had been reduced to just over 200,000,[20] and a centralised monitoring system for registered refugees was also established. According to the definition UNRWA eventually adopted, the status of refugee was conceded to any person who had lived in Palestine for at least two years before the conflict of 1948 and had lost their home and their means of subsistence as a result of the fighting. Failure to resolve the Palestinian question resulted in this status being transmitted from one generation to the next, with the consequent inflation of the refugee population that has resulted from this. Meanwhile, alongside the historic hospital of the Anglican mission, which was now placed at the service of the refugees, two other hospitals were established by the Egyptian Red Crescent and the military authorities.

The extremely low educational level of the refugee population complicated the humanitarian agencies' ability to co-opt local volunteers and delegate responsibility.[21] In the spring of 1949, less than a third of the 65,000 refugee children of school age were in education, leading to the inauguration of crash courses for schoolteachers during the summer in Gaza and in Khan Yunis.[22] Weaving and carpentry workshops were opened, and an unfinished mosque in Gaza, which had been used as a food distribution centre, was equipped with running water and showers, enabling families, some of whom were living with ten people in a tent, to enjoy at least an elementary level of hygiene. Skin diseases, which had spread among the people during the previous year, gradually began to disappear.[23]

UNRWA established eight refugee camps in the Gaza Strip from 1950 onwards. Both the permanent habitations and the tented dwellings in these camps remained the property of the United Nations, which established the conditions under which the refugees were to live in the camps. Each group of four people was allowed an area of 33 square metres, including a bed-room of 9 square metres.[24] The largest of these camps was at Jabalya, the northernmost camp in the Strip, where there were 35,000 people. Next in order of size came Beach Camp (Al-Shati), where 33,000 of the most deprived refugees continued to live under canvas. The biting cold in these tents is documented extensively in the refugees' accounts of these early years. This camp was on the edge of Rimal, Gaza's seaside suburb. Gaza City proper contained around 13,000 refugees, and to the south side of the town there were the four camps of Nuseirat, Bureij, Deir al-Balah and Maghazi (in decreasing order of size), which together sheltered around 38,000 people.

The largest number of refugees was in Khan Yunis, where there were 25,000 residents of the fixed camp and 31,000 Bedouin living in tents. At the southernmost end of the territory, the Rafah Camp, adjacent to the town of Rafah, held 25,000 refugees.[25] UNRWA was the main provider of social services in the Gaza Strip, as well as the main employer, though the local municipal services that Egypt administered made efforts to provide jobs for some of the qualified refugees.[26] Economically productive activi-ties, whether agricultural, commercial or in small-scale industry, continued to be the preserve of the indigenous population.

In February 1950 Egypt submitted a modest proposal to the UN for the return of half the Palestinian refugees in Gaza to the territory allocated to the Arab entity under the provisions of the 1947 partition plan. This pro-posal became bogged down in the bureaucratic procedures of the UN special agencies.[27] But it also ran up against the implacable opposition of Israel, which only ever authorised one solitary exercise in repatriation from Gaza, relating to a group of 114 women and young children from the Jaffa region and Majdal[28]—in the period that followed, the gates of Gaza slammed shut on those who had been uprooted.

Despair and Infiltration

The majority of the Palestinian refugees from the Gaza Strip came from the villages neighbouring the Ottoman (*qadha*) of Gaza, which had remained an administrative sub-district under the British Mandate. The grave difficulty of overcoming the trauma of dispossession was exacerbated by the artificial nature of the lines of demarcation when the former dwellings and family lands of the refugees were so close at hand. The despair of enclosure was even worse for the Bedouin, who were accustomed to roaming in the southern desert but were now stuck in the outskirts of Khan Yunis. In June 1950, an Israeli intelligence report noted that the refugees in Gaza were 'condemned to utter extinction as the goods they brought with them are being used up bit by bit'.[29]

The traditional household now took on the semblance of a lost paradise in the tales of these uprooted people and in the upbringing of their children. Every day, hundreds of refugees braved the mines and border patrols to attempt to see what they still regarded as 'their' land,[30] though few succeeded and those who crossed the demarcation line could consider themselves lucky if all that happened to them was to be driven back into Gaza. The frontier kibbutzim punished such 'marauders' with the greatest severity. In the first six months of 1950, for example, the kibbutz of Erez, to the north of the Gaza Strip, caused the deaths of thirteen 'Arabs', eleven of whom were killed by mines.[31] Any Palestinian farmers who tried to cultivate what had formerly been their land in the no-man's land between the two sides would find themselves and their livestock targeted by Israeli military outposts.[32] The UN estimated that around 4,000 inhabitants of the villages of Beit Lahya, Beit Hanoun, Deir Suneid and Dimra lost access to their lands in the neutral zone.

Due to its fear of an uncontrollable escalation on the frontier, the Egyptian army did as much as it could to prevent such incursions across the line. A series of deadly incidents in October 1949 led to the re-demarcation of the armistice line, which had hitherto been signalled only by a line of empty jerry-cans. The Israeli troops reacted to incursions with increasing brutality in order to discourage any lingering hope of escape from Gaza. The level of violence occasionally led to vendettas between the families involved and Tsahal. In March 1950, for example, the killing of three young villagers, including two girls, who were also raped,[33] by Israeli soldiers was followed by the murder of five Israelis, including three soldiers who were killed by a mine.[34]

In June 1950, the *New York Times* revealed that 100 civilians who had attempted to infiltrate from Gaza and elsewhere had been abandoned in the desert and dozens of them had died of thirst and exhaustion.[35] However, Moshe Dayan, who was now the commander of the southern front, continued to maintain a tough stance. It was on his instructions that the inhabitants of Majdal, on the Israeli side of the armistice line, were driven out by stages into the Gaza Strip in the summer of 1950,[36] where they placed further pressure on refugee camps that were already over-crowded. The Israeli military were careful to confiscate the birth certificates of children born after 1948 in order to avoid any later dispute.[37] Just as Isdud had now been given the Hebrew name Ashdod, Majdal would later be known as Ashkelon (echoing the ancient Ascalon).

The 'border war', as the Israeli historian Benny Morris aptly described it, intensified in 1951. King Farouk's Egypt, governed by the Wafd party, was locked into its own confrontation with Britain, which was keeping 38,000 men in its base on the Suez Canal instead of the garrison of 10,000 agreed by the Anglo-Egyptian Treaty of 1946. David Ben Gurion feared that this British contingent could be sent into Gaza, a plan to which the Egyptians would agree but which would face an Israeli veto. In Gaza, the Shawa family schemed for the return of the British, arguing that it would bring a substantial amount of money into the territory. The mayor, Rushdi Shawa, spoke out in favour of a British return,[38] while his brother Rashad went even further, lobbying for it in articles in the Cairo press,[39] where he also castigated what he said was the incompetence and corruption of the Egyptian administration in Gaza.[40] The prosperity that the presence of Allied troops had created between 1940 and 1945 was thus recalled as something of a golden age.

The confrontation between Britain and Egypt led the Egyptian govern-ment to transfer part of the force it maintained in Gaza to the west bank of the Suez Canal. This dilution of the Egyptian presence in Gaza led to a resurgence of Palestinian incursions into Israel, which responded with a devastating raid on the eastern outskirts of Gaza City on 21 October 1951 that left dozens dead and twelve houses destroyed.[41] In reply to Egypt's claim that it was unable to seal off the Gaza Strip, the Israelis stated that the mass of the refugees should be transferred to the other side of Egypt and be placed in the desert adjacent to the Libyan frontier.[42] There were angry exchanges on this issue, and it received even shorter shrift after

23 July 1952 when the 'Free Officers', led by Muhammad Neguib and Gamal Abdel Nasser, overthrew the monarchy and took power in Cairo.

Militant Enthusiasm

Although the Muslim Brotherhood had no legal existence in Gaza between 1949 and 1952, as was also the case in Egypt, the Brothers were able to establish an organisation ostensibly restricted to educational and social activities, the 'Jami'yyat al-Tawhid' (Association of Unity),[43] named in reference to the 'Unity' of God, a central tenet of the Muslim faith. This organisation, led by Zafer Shawa, the former secretary-general of the Brotherhood in Gaza, spread throughout the newly established refugee camps. Its stated objective was to 'reconstruct the spirit of the Muslims through devotion, their intellect through knowledge and their physique through sport'.[44] As well as Qur'an studies and the exegesis of texts, members celebrated the high days of the Islamic calendar, which provided the opportunity to invite conferees from Cairo. Summer camps provided a further venue for the inculcation of militancy, where there were also night-time marches and even basic weapons training.[45]

The Brotherhood had ten sections, known as 'families' (*'usra*, plural, *'usar*), throughout the Gaza Strip, and in 1950 it could boast of more than 100 members in Nuseirat Camp alone.[46] Two young activists from the Muslim Brotherhood, Fathi Balawi and Salah Khalaf (later known as Abu Iyad), were granted permission to pursue their studies in Cairo: both of their families were from Gaza, though Khalaf had grown up in Jaffa, from which he had been expelled in 1948. At that time the General Union of Palestinian Students (GUPS) had been established in Egypt in order to promote the Palestinian cause and also to look after the interests of scholarship holders, who were under constant threat of losing the allowances they received from the Arab League. Fathi Balawi gained the support of leftist sympathisers and became secretary-general of the Union, while Salah Khalaf spent his time agitating against the Arab League and particularly against its Palestinian assistant secretary-general, Ahmed Shuqairy.

Khalaf found himself sentenced to six weeks in Cairo's Abdin prison as a result, yet upon his release he was able to link up with another young activist, none other than Yasser Arafat, who was at the time a Muslim Brotherhood sympathiser without being a member.[47] Arafat's full name was Muhammad Yasser Abdel Raouf Arafat al-Qudwa al-Husseini, and as an activist he also became known as Abu Ammar. Arafat's family, historically from Aleppo, had taken up residence in the Gaza Strip two centuries earlier.[48] His father was a merchant from Khan Yunis who had settled in Egypt, and Arafat himself was born in the Cairo suburb of Heliopolis in 1929.[49] After his mother's death he was brought up in Jerusalem from 1933 to 1937. The young Arafat then returned to Egypt for his school education and university studies. Although he was caught up in the general excitement of agitation against the British Mandate in Egypt, he only seems to have played a limited part in the fighting in Gaza, though both this and his contribution to arms smuggling for the Palestinian nationalists are mentioned in the biography given in his official Nobel Prize citation.[50] However, it does seem that Arafat later associated himself with the students who sought to fight the British forces on the Suez Canal. Fathi Balawi, on behalf of the Muslim Brotherhood, backed him for the presidency of the General Union of Palestinian Students, to which he was elected in September 1952 with the support of an Islamist–nationalist coalition.[51]

The Muslim Brothers were not the only group plotting militant intervention in the Gaza Strip. The communists were also part of the anti-imperialist tradition initiated in Gaza twenty years previously by the Association of Young Muslims and Hamdi al-Husseini, although the Palestinian communists had lost much of their support after they backed the partition plan of 1947. When an official communist party was established in Israel in 1948, a so-called 'League for National Liberation' recruited communist activists in the West Bank and Gaza. The Gaza branch was officially run from the head office in the West Bank but in practice it had a considerable degree of autonomy. Their condemnation of the 'Egyptian occupation'[52] and the accent they placed on 'national liberation' were the twin slogans used for recruiting the communists in the Gaza Strip, where the League for National Liberation was the only group to advocate an independent Palestinian state.[53]

The coup by the Free Officers in Cairo in July 1952 also had a significant impact on the political scene in Gaza. By this time few remembered Gamal

Abdel Nasser, though he had been a staff officer in Gaza in the spring of 1948, but General Neguib had been the Egyptian military governor of the Strip from December 1950 to December 1951. The Muslim Brotherhood backed the anti-monarchist revolution: they came out of hiding, and a delegation of Egyptian Muslim Brotherhood officials visited Gaza to consolidate their links with the Gaza branch.[54] Sheikh Umar Sawan, who had led the Islamist party in Gaza as early as 1946, was appointed mayor of Gaza by the Egyptian authorities to replace Rushdi Shawa, who paid the price for agitating in favour of the transfer of the British base from the Suez Canal. The Muslim Brotherhood instituted 'mercy trains' (*qitarat al-rahma*) to bring humanitarian aid from Egypt into Gaza, where this highly politicised aid was distributed by the organisation's activists.[55]

As a guarantee of their loyalty to the Free Officers, the Muslim Brothers suspended incursions by their commandos into Israel, to the great irritation of the hard-core Palestinian nationalists. Led by Khalil al-Wazir, who was soon joined by Kamal Adwan, these youthful activists finally persuaded the Brotherhood to allow them to set up the 'Justice Battalion' (*katibat al-haqq*),[56] though the Brotherhood made the proviso that their secret training would be carried out at the Egyptian oasis of El-Arish rather than in Gaza itself.[57] In similar secrecy, Salah Khalaf set up his own groupuscule, the 'Family of the Sacrifice' (*'usrat al-fida*), which also included two other resolute teenagers, Assad Saftawi and Salim Zaanoun. This group, which accomplished little, was later renamed the 'Battalion of Vengeance'.[58] In the meantime the League for National Liberation had been subjected to the full force of the Egyptian anti-communist crackdown of August 1952 and became dormant as far as its activities in Gaza were concerned.[59]

Incursions into Israel, often undertaken by tribal groups and sometimes even by individuals, continued while these various political evolutions took place. The brutal reprisals Israel launched in response were intended to be highly discouraging, such as the response at the end of January 1953 when five civilians including three children were killed in a Tsahal raid. According to the French consul-general in Jerusalem, 'a collective assassination of this type would have made a big impression had it taken pace on the Jordanian frontier. It is likely that what has happened in Gaza will have fewer repercussions, since the victims were Palestinian refugees for whom the Egyptians have very little concern.'[60]

Moshe Dayan, who was now head of operations in the Israeli general staff, assigned the task of carrying out clandestine strikes on sites from which incursions might originate to a young and ambitious officer, Ariel Sharon, who was then aged twenty-five.[61] On 28 August 1953, the first expedition on the part of what became known as Unit 101 was carried out on Bureij Camp, killing twenty civilians.[62] Israel denied all responsibility for the massacre, for which it officially blamed members of a maverick frontier kibbutz.[63] Tsahal had attached a military journalist to Sharon's commando units. This was Uri Dan, aged eighteen at the time, whose internally circulated reports were intended to boost morale.[64]

The Egyptian authorities' relative lack of concern over the fate of the Palestinian refugees contributed to an ominous tension that persisted throughout 1953. The Muslim Brotherhood was restrained by its loyalty to the Free Officers, though the Brothers were upset by the legalisation of the Baath Party, which professed an explicitly secular version of Arab socialism. The organising nucleus of the Baath in Gaza consisted of Misbah Saqr and Jamal Rayess, with Abdullah Hourani in Khan Yunis. In contrast, the former members of the League for National Liberation stepped up their opposition to the Egyptian administration and organised themselves into an independent 'Palestinian Communist Party of the Gaza Strip', which was not recognised by any outside body. Their leading figure, Muin Bseisso, who had experience of communist activism in Iraq, was especially active in the union of teachers working for UNRWA. The United Nations was by far the leading employer in Gaza and under the martial law in force in the territory only UNRWA staff had the right to join unions.

On 30 August 1953 Bseisso led a march through Gaza City in protest against the Israeli attack on Bureij. The Egyptian authorities responded with the arrest of thirty-four demonstrators who were accused of 'communism', though most of them were members of no political party.[65] Bseisso later revealed that Egypt and UNRWA had agreed in October 1953 to resettle between 50,000 and 60,000 refugees in the peripheral areas of Sinai that were scheduled to be irrigated.[66] The Gaza communists portrayed the proposed transfer as a betrayal of the Palestinian cause, which was prompted by the Israeli raids that were terrorising the refugees, and in 1954 they began to agitate against it, demanding the complete abandonment of any kind of resettlement plan.

The Muslim Brotherhood, which was represented among the UNRWA teachers by Fathi Balawi, also endeavoured to reinforce their position in the refugee camps. By 1954, the Brotherhood had 1,000 members in the Gaza Strip,[67] which contrasted with only a few dozen communist militants.[68] Nasser's rise to power in Egypt, where he had supplanted Neguib (the Brotherhood's preferred candidate), led to a deterioration of the situation in Gaza. In March 1954 the Islamists joined with the communists to demand that the people be armed. The Egyptian army had retained only one company of soldiers in the Gaza Strip and now depended on a locally recruited police force 700 strong, among whom the Muslim Brotherhood had many affiliates.[69] This 'Palestine Frontier Police', later known as 'Battalion 11 of the Palestine Frontier Guard', had been set up by an Egyptian Islamist named Abdelmoneim Abdelraouf, who facilitated the recruitment of Muslim Brothers.[70]

A cycle of incursions and reprisals now got under way across the armistice line, and on 26 April 1954 an artillery duel brought the Egyptian and Israeli military into direct conflict. On the night of 10–11 July, a commando unit of parachutists led by Ariel Sharon crossed over into Deir al-Balah where they killed a dozen Palestinian policemen and went home with two prisoners. Sabotage of the water supply of the frontier kibbutzim on 11 August was paid back with the destruction of Gaza's water tower four days later. The Egyptian military accused the Muslim Brothers of recommencing their raids into Israel 'with the intention of provoking a response'[71] and imposed a curfew from 5 p.m. to 6 a.m. across the most vulnerable sectors of the Gaza Strip.

In September 1954 some 200 Palestinians deemed liable to engage in incursions were interned,[72] including Khalil al-Wazir, who nevertheless managed to preserve the existence of his 'Justice Battalion'. In October, the arrest in Cairo of the supreme guide of the Muslim Brotherhood in Egypt, which was followed by an Islamist attempt to assassinate President Nasser, preceded a comprehensive crackdown on the Brothers. At the same time Nasser told the British he wanted to negotiate a lasting peace with Israel, but on the basis of the partition plan of 1947. In this context, he said he was ready to see the Gaza Strip given to Jordan, which would also receive the Negev as far as Beersheba.[73] In Gaza itself, Fathi Balawi and other

Islamist officials were briefly incarcerated. The Egyptian military intelligence, the redoubtable 'Mukhabarat' (*al-mukhabarat al-askariyya*), which answered to the Ministry of War, combed the territory, and their commander in Gaza, Colonel Mustafa Hafez, was constantly at the elbow of the governor, Abdullah Rifaat. There was also a political police force in Gaza, attached to the Interior Ministry, whose designation, *Al-mabahith al-'amma*, meant 'general investigators'. Between November 1954 and February 1955, seven Palestinians, three Israelis and one Egyptian were killed in various incidents around Gaza.

The Turning Point

On 23 February 1955 a guerrilla group from Gaza, possibly on an intelligence mission on behalf of Egypt, penetrated as far as the suburbs of Tel Aviv, where they murdered an Israeli civilian.[74] Ariel Sharon was ordered to undertake a reprisal raid against an Egyptian military barracks north of Gaza City. The operation, carried out on the night of 28 February by 120 men of Unit 101, was particularly bloody. Thirty-six Egyptian soldiers and two Palestinian civilians, including a child, were killed, together with eight Israeli soldiers. Sharon claimed that he had 'struck at the heart of the Egyptian military institution in Gaza'.[75] On the morning of 1 March violent demonstrations erupted across the Gaza Strip, where the population directed its anger against both Egypt and the United Nations.

Communist and Islamist activists forced the schools to close to protest against Nasser's 'dictatorship',[76] while, in the streets of Gaza, demonstrators shouted slogans against 'American agents'.[77] At the instigation of Yusuf al-Najjar,[78] a Muslim Brother from Rafah Camp, UNRWA's offices were stormed and the civilian personnel of the UN were evacuated. At least four demonstrators were shot dead in an attack on the office of the governor, Abdullah Rifaat. The rail link from Gaza to Port Said was suspended and Gaza was cut off from the outside world. In Cairo, Palestinian students, well trained by Salah Khalaf, protested with such fervour that they were eventually granted an audience with Nasser himself.[79] The governor of Gaza was compelled to concede to the organisers of the demonstrations, Muin Bseisso, speaking on behalf of the communists, and Fathi Balawi, for the Muslim Brothers, that all plans for the transfer of Palestinian refugees would now be abandoned.

The protestors presented this as a victory, though the technical feasibility of the proposed transfer to Sinai had in any case been highly doubtful. Yet the enthusiasm generated by the 'March uprising', which was designated by the Arabic expression 'intifada',[80] was of short duration. Hardly had calm been re-established than Abdullah Rifaat, the governor, arranged for Bseisso, Balawi, Najjar and sixty-five other activists to be imprisoned in Egypt. This convinced both the communists and the Islamists to refrain from pressing their advantage. The union of UNRWA teachers was dissolved and the right to strike and demonstrate was suspended.[81] One of Nasser's ministers was subsequently authorised to make a public statement of the proposition that had been put to the British five months earlier, when Egypt had stated that it was ready to transfer its authority over the Gaza Strip to Jordan, on condition that Israel reciprocated by conceding the southern part of the Negev to Jordan.[82]

This proposal, which Israel rejected out of hand,[83] enabled Egypt to assert that it entertained no territorial claim over Gaza. The Syrian leadership concluded that Egypt's main objective was in fact to absolve itself from responsibility for the refugees in the Gaza Strip.[84] It was in this context that Gamal Abdel Nasser went in person to Gaza on 29 March 1955, his first visit since 1948. His gesture was generally received favourably by the population. At the end of the visit, which had been given exhaustive media coverage, Nasser published his personal account of the first Arab Israeli war in the Cairo press. His message was clear: in 1948, just as in 1955, 'the [Egyptian] army was not responsible for the defeat in Palestine'. It was Israel and Israel alone that was responsible for the 'tragedy'.[85]

Canada's General Burns, the director of UNTSO, presided ex officio over the Israel–Egyptian Armistice Commission and initiated the endorsement by the Security Council of a plan to consolidate the ceasefire in four stages. First there were to be joint Israeli–Egyptian patrols; then the exclusion of all but regular forces; thirdly an effective closure of the Gaza Strip; and, fourthly, regular meetings between Egyptian and Israeli officers.[86] Cairo accepted these arrangements in principle, but Israel rejected the plan for joint patrols on the basis that it would bring Egyptian troops on to its territory.[87] On 3 April 1955, David Ben Gurion, who was minister of defence in Moshe Sharett's Labour government, once again suggested that Gaza should be subject to Israeli occupation, but he failed to get a majority of his cabinet colleagues to support the proposal. Moshe Sharett was strongly opposed and Ben Gurion was supported only by Golda Meir and two other ministers, with nine against and two abstentions. On the following day Ben Gurion also failed to get a majority for a proposal that Israel should unilaterally renounce its armistice with Egypt. On the ground, during the month of May, clashes between the Israelis and the Egyptians multiplied in the absence of any preventive mechanism. The French consul-general in Jerusalem alerted the Foreign Ministry in Paris regarding the tension that prevailed in Gaza: 'Discontent mounts constantly among the 200,000 refugees, with the Egyptian authorities controlling only with difficulty their hostility both to themselves and to the United Nations observers, who would be in a precarious situation were anything serious to occur.'[88]

On 11 May 1955, with the aim of formalising Gaza's legal status, Nasser promulgated the 'basic law of the region under the control of Egyptian forces in Palestine'.[89] This text, which was the first official document to use the expression 'Gaza Strip', defined the powers of its 'Administrative Governor General', who was to be responsible to the Egyptian Ministry of War. This basic legislative document led to little practical change but it did serve to emphasise the existence of a Palestinian reality that was prioritised by Egypt, which was an alternative to Jordan's 'Union of Both Banks'. Nasser received General Burns in early June, telling him that 'the laying of mines ... is not done by Egyptian regular troops: it is carried out by Palestinian refugees, driven by intense anger at having been expelled from their country and aided by a knowledge of the terrain that makes it difficult to control their movements'.[90]

The reality was more complex, since Colonel Mustafa Hafez's Mukhabarat were in fact training and leading the Palestinian commandos, and the Arab press often celebrated the heroism of these fedayin, an expression that had already been used to refer to irregular fighters in Palestine in 1948 and in the Suez Canal Zone in 1951–4. (The word literally refers to those ready to make a sacrifice, even of their lives.) Mustafa Hafez, who had been engaged for some months in frustrating Islamist activities within the border police, persuaded his commanders to allow him to set up a special unit, Battalion 141, whose absolute loyalty he was able to guarantee because of its judicious composition: its first 150 recruits comprised fifty men who had previously worked for him on intelligence missions into Israel, another fifty who were specially chosen for the mission and a further fifty who were on parole from sentences they had been given for infiltration into Israel[91] (wherever possible, Colonel Hafez preferred his recruits to be those released from the justice system rather than activists with an obscure past).[92]

The 'Justice Battalion', which was secretly established in 1952 by Khalil al-Wazir and Kamal Adwan under cover of the Muslim Brotherhood, now put itself at the service of the new Egyptian policy. The same was true for Salah Khalaf, who later denied all links to the Muslim Brotherhood and who re-named his 'Family of the Sacrifice' the 'Battalion of the Armed Revolutionary Struggle'.[93] The break with the Muslim Brotherhood was an essential condition for obtaining the support of Egyptian intelligence: something which these Palestinian activists, some of whom had been released from prison for this specific purpose,[94] accepted with little hesitation, so strong was their nationalist commitment. Khalil al-Wazir adopted the nom de guerre of Abu Jihad, while Salah Khalaf became Abu Iyad.

On 22 August 1955, the Egyptian army was again humiliated by another violent raid on the part of the Israeli army. Nasser responded by deploying the fedayin, with ten groups infiltrating into Israel from 27 August. Most of these commandos returned to Gaza after one or two nights in Israel, where between eleven and seventeen people were killed over several days.[95] The fedayin campaign was seen as a clear success by the Egyptian high command and was much appreciated by the population of Gaza. Yet in Israel it caused consternation, and Moshe Sharett, who was the caretaker prime minister while his rival David Ben Gurion was in the process of forming a new government, agreed to a major reprisal operation. On the night of 31 August/1 September 1955, two columns of parachutists entered the Gaza Strip. One of these, commanded by Rafael Eytan, took possession of an abandoned Egyptian position at Abassan. The other, led by Mordechai Gur, attacked the barracks at Khan Yunis and destroyed the houses around it.[96] Seventy-two Egyptians and Palestinians were killed, with the loss of just one Israeli.

The UN Security Council abstained from apportioning responsibility on this occasion in view of the immediately preceding fedayin attacks, though it had condemned Israel for its raid on Gaza of 28 February 1955. General Burns was aware that there could be no more joint patrols, but he attempted to ensure that the armistice line was at least designated with barbed wire. His Egyptian opposite number rejected this suggestion, arguing that he did not want to give Gaza 'the look of a concentration camp'.[97] The Egyptian Mukhabarat subsequently brought the fedayin campaign to a halt, though they were able to continue their incursions into Israel from Jordan and Syria, sometimes using Palestinian activists trained in Gaza. Nasser then played a trump card with an announcement on 27 September that a major arms deal had been concluded with Czechoslovakia. This move, which situated Egypt in the Soviet camp in the Cold War, aroused 'popular enthusiasm', according to Abu Iyad and other observers in Gaza.[98] By the end of 1955 forty-seven Israelis and 216 Arabs had been killed on the Israeli–Egyptian frontier (as against eight Israelis and eighteen Jordanians on the eastern border).[99]

The Countdown

The Egyptian clampdown brought a few months of calm. Even those Palestinians who had graduated from Egypt's military colleges observed that they had no freedom of action and that their Egyptian opposite numbers were given better equipment.[100] But the strict subordination of Palestinian action to Egyptian strategic planning did not prevent the outbreak of frontier incidents, which resumed at the beginning of April 1956. On 5 April, an artillery exchange left four dead among the Egyptian forces, who took their revenge on the neighbouring kibbutzim, forcing the inhabitants into their shelters. Moshe Dayan, the chief of the general staff, responded with a strike in the town centre of Gaza City.[101] The market and the hospital were bombarded by 120 mm mortars from just after 4 p.m. The United Nations established that the nearest military objective was more than a kilometre away.[102] Fifty-eight civilians were killed in this blind shelling, including thirty-three men, fifteen women and ten children. It was not clear whether Prime Minister David Ben Gurion had personally approved the operation, which Moshe Sharett, who had become the minister for foreign affairs, had no hesitation in describing as a 'crime'.[103]

Nasser reacted by restarting the fedayin attacks. From 7 to 12 April 1956, Palestinian commandos who had infiltrated into Israel from Gaza killed ten Israelis, mainly civilians. Yet sixteen of the commandos lost their lives during these missions due to the effectiveness of the preventive measures taken by the Israeli forces during the preceding months.[104] The personal intervention of the UN secretary-general, Dag Hammarskjöld, who went both to Cairo and Jerusalem, was a determining factor in preventing the crisis from escalating. From 18 April, a ceasefire between Israel and Egypt was formally re-established. But this failed to take account of the momentum of the vendetta that had taken shape as the result of months of incursions and reprisals in and around the Gaza Strip.

The kibbutz of Nahal Oz, set up in 1953 just 1 kilometre from the armistice line, already had a history of incidents involving Arab 'marauders'. The kibbutz's security officer, Ro'i Rothberg, had become the bête noire of the Palestinian guerrillas.[105] A group of infiltrators including an Egyptian policeman and a Palestinian farmer acted together to take revenge, and on 29 April 1956, without the knowledge of the Mukhabarat in Gaza, they ambushed Rothberg and killed him, carrying his body back across the frontier.[106] This grisly spectacle failed to impress the United Nations, whose observers restored the corpse to Nahal Oz. Emotions subsequently ran high in Israel, and on 19 April 1956 Dayan took it upon himself to give Rothberg's funeral obsequy. 'Let us not, today, cast blame on the murderers,' said the Israeli chief of staff:

What can we say against their terrible hatred of us? For eight years now, they have sat in the refugee camps of Gaza, and have watched how, before their very eyes, we have turned their lands and villages, where they and their forefathers dwelled, into our home. It is not among the Arabs in Gaza, but in our own midst that we must seek Ro'i's blood.[107]

It was in the same spirit that Ben Gurion agreed to regard the murder of Rothberg as an isolated incident that should not call into question the ceasefire between Israel and Egypt. On the other hand, the Israeli military intelligence services (known by the Hebrew acronym 'Aman') were determined to eliminate the Mukhabarat commander, Mustafa Hafez, whom they regarded, not unreasonably, as the driving force of the fedayin campaign. On 11 July 1956 an Israeli double agent delivered a booby-trapped parcel to Colonel Hafez, who was killed in the explosion. The Palestinians of Gaza celebrated the 'martyrdom' of this 'hero'—streets and squares were renamed for him,[108] while many newly born babies were named 'Mustafa Hafez'.[109] On 26 July, President Nasser himself paid his respects to Gaza's late intelligence chief in the historic speech in which he announced the nationalisation of the Suez Canal.

The Egyptian president's appropriation of the Suez Canal for Egypt enabled him to gain immense popularity across the Arab world. In the Gaza Strip it was now sacrilegious to criticise Nasser;[110] even the communists, who had excoriated the Egyptian leader as a dictator just eighteen months ago, began to fete Nasser for his nationalist stance, while activists such as Abu Iyad came to believe that 'everything was now possible, including the liberation of Palestine'.[111] The Muslim Brothers, on the other hand, kept an even lower profile than they had done previously. However, Nasser's announcement enabled Ben Gurion to reprise his earlier plans to counter Egypt's regional ambitions. Following Nasser's nationalisation of the Canal, Guy Mollet, France's socialist prime minister, who had never forgiven Egypt for supporting the Algerian revolutionaries, began to consider a joint Franco-Israeli offensive against Egypt. Britain, though more reserved over the question of whether to mount a military operation, was also unwilling to allow Nasser to go unpunished.

It was against this background that Israel began to increase its pressure on Egypt in Gaza. During the night of 16–17 August 1956, an Israeli patrol entered the Deir al-Balah sector where it killed three Egyptian soldiers. Shortly afterwards, an Israeli ambush at Rafah left six dead in an Egyptian ambulance. The United Nations protested to Israel, but this failed to halt the continuing deterioration of the situation, to the point where Dag Hammarskjöld made a depressing assessment of the probable consequences in a letter to Ben Gurion:

The situation is clear enough. You believe the threat of reprisals is a deterrent. I believe they are the cause of further isolated actions by the Arab forces, to a greater extent than the governments concerned are willing to admit. You believe that reprisals will avoid future incidents. I believe that they will provoke future incidents.[112]

What the UN secretary general had failed to realise was that the Israeli prime minister was indeed determined to escape from the cycle of reprisals against Gaza, but by stepping up the level of his actions rather than by de-escalation. Ben Gurion, who had by now side-lined the more reasonable Moshe Sharett, was able to rely on the belligerence of Moshe Dayan, who viewed a strike on the Egyptian regime as being the optimal way to destroy the Palestinian fedayin. On 8 October 1956, the Israeli high command secretly decided to launch what was known as Operation Kadesh, which provided for the conquest of Sinai in three phases (a parachute drop on the hills of the western desert, followed by the capture of El-Arish, followed by that of Sharm el-Sheikh), before taking control of the Gaza Strip.[113]

Despite the scale of their tragedy, the Palestinians who became refugees in the Gaza Strip in 1948–9 were far from passive in accepting their fate. The women struggled to bring a little cheer to the dwellings in which they found themselves, and the children, thanks to UNRWA, were enrolled in a school system that swiftly developed. An economy of sorts, based on services, developed around the agricultural exchanges and the small-scale industry that were native to Gaza. However, it was the hope of return to a land that was sometimes very close indeed that drove this community of undiscouraged exiles. Neither minefields nor violent repression halted that continual flow of infiltration into Israel.

Such an atmosphere prompted unprecedented cooperation between communists and Islamists. The transformation of the infiltrators into fedayin took place in two stages: first the phase of politicisation, through the dissidence, outside the Muslim Brotherhood, of a militant minority committed to the armed struggle among whom were the future founders of Fatah; and second, the phase of professionalisation, with the leadership and management of Palestinian incursions by Nasser's Egypt within the context of its confrontation with Israel. It was in Gaza that the fedayin were moulded, and the Hebrew State would soon make Gaza pay for it dearly.

6

THE FIRST OCCUPATION

During a secret meeting in the Parisian suburb of Sèvres on 24 October 1956 the leaders of France, Britain and Israel agreed to launch a coordinated offensive against Egypt.[1] The operation began with a series of Israeli attacks against Egyptian positions in Sinai in the late afternoon of 29 October. This was followed twenty-four hours later by a Franco-British ultimatum addressed to Israel and Egypt, which was designed to serve as a pretext for a joint Franco-British operation to 'protect' the Suez Canal. On 30 October, American and Soviet diplomats at the United Nations in New York demanded an immediate cessation of hostilities and the retreat of the Israeli forces to the armistice line, but a British and French veto at the Security Council obliged them to seek endorsement of their demand from the UN General Assembly, which voted for a ceasefire plan on 2 November. Britain and France ignored the UN demand and launched an airborne invasion of the Suez Canal Zone on 5 November. On 7 November the General Assembly passed a resolution demanding the withdrawal of the invading troops, which was approved by sixty-five votes to one (the vote of Israel itself) with the abstention of ten nations, including Britain and France.

Raids and Massacres

As the hostilities got under way, the French navy shelled Rafah on 31 October while British aircraft began to bomb Egypt's airfields. On

1 November the Israelis claimed to have captured Rafah and their artillery began to shell the Gaza Strip. By 2 November 1956, the Egyptian forces had virtually lost control of the Sinai Peninsula, and the United Nations evacuated its personnel from the Gaza Strip on board the vessels of the American 6th Fleet. The Israeli occupation of Tell al-Muntar, the high ground commanding the access to Gaza City, left the Egyptian governor, Fouad Dougawi, no choice other than to capitulate. His offer of surrender was conveyed to the Israeli military via the few UN observers still on the ground, who compelled the Egyptian command to accompany them to the last few centres of resistance in the town to confirm the order to cease fire.[2]

The speed of Rafah's fall had prevented the Egyptian forces from pulling out of Gaza, although many individual fedayin were able to escape into Egypt in small boats. It was in this way that Kamal Adwan was able to join Abu Jihad in Cairo.[3] Most Palestinian fighters opted to avoid Sinai, where the fighting was still going on, instead crossing the Israeli lines to head for Hebron and the West Bank, which had remained out of the conflict. A strict curfew was imposed in the Gaza Strip, where the population was warned by roving public address systems to surrender all arms in their possession. The new Israeli rulers installed themselves in the offices of the former Egyptian administration, where they summoned the notables of Gaza to persuade them not to leave. Israeli diplomats even informed the United Nations that they wished UNRWA to continue its mission among the refugees, though the movement of UNRWA officials would be strictly controlled.

Moshe Dayan attributed the Israeli victory to the fact that 'the [Egyptian] force in the Strip was split into small units dispersed in scores of separate outposts, none able to rush to the help of another and none capable of singly withstanding an attack by tanks or half-tracks'.[4] This operational fragmentation was an important factor in the swift occupation of Gaza City, but paradoxically it also explained the stubborn resistance of Khan Yunis, where Egypt's General Yusuf al-Agrudi refused to lay down his arms. Israel sent its air force into action there on 2 November 1956, inflicting heavy losses on the civilian population, which was also subjected to artillery shelling. On 3 November Israeli infantry and tanks entered Khan Yunis, whereupon hostilities ceased. The invaders combed the town for fighters, and executed on the spot many men suspected of having borne arms.[5]

While these executions were being carried out in the homes or work-places of the victims, all men over the age of fifteen were forcibly mustered. There were two massacres of civilians who had been seized in this way, one in the central square of Khan Yunis, with the execution by machine gun of victims lined up along the wall of the old Ottoman caravanserai, and the other in the refugee camp, where the victims were also shot. The corpses were left for hours, sometimes overnight, before the families were permitted to recover the bodies.[6] UNRWA later assembled a list it regarded as 'credible' of the names of 275 people who were executed on 3 November 1956, including 140 refugees.[7] Palestinian sources count 415 killed and fifty-seven disappeared.[8] Abdulaziz Rantissi, who became the leader of Hamas in 2004, was an eight-year-old child in the refugee camp at Khan Yunis when the massacres took place. He claims that 525 Palestinians were killed there by Tsahal 'in cold blood'.[9]

Israel's savage treatment of Khan Yunis may have been connected to the town's protracted resistance, though the massacres were in fact largely confined to the civilian population. The principal aim of the occupying army was to root out once and for all the presence of the fedayin in the Gaza Strip, which Israel estimated at some hundreds, in contrast to 4,000 Egyptian troops and Palestinian auxiliaries who were 'trapped' in the territory.[10] This at least was the justification given for the arrest of all males aged between fifteen and sixty. Roving vehicles with loudspeakers threatened death to anyone who attempted to escape the round-up. Long lines of men, with their hands in the air, were taken under military escort, with frequent warning shots, to various public buildings, school courtyards and social centres, where their identities were checked. The Israelis also destroyed four monuments that had been erected at various sites in the Gaza Strip in honour of the murdered intelligence chief, Mustafa Hafez.

The Israeli military was assisted by Shin Bet, the Israeli Security Service, which was also known by its Hebrew acronym 'Shabak'. Part of its remit was the surveillance of the Israeli Arab population, which was extended in 1956 to the Palestinians of the Occupied Territories. Shin Bet was initially attached to the Ministry of Defence (as was Aman, the military intelligence service) but was later placed directly under the authority of the prime minister (in the same way as Mossad, the service for external operations).

Together they worked from lists of fedayin whom they claimed to have identified, but it was sometimes sufficient to have a picture of Nasser on the wall, or to bear a name that resembled that of a suspect, or to be the victim of a simple misunderstanding, to become a target and to be incarcerated in the old Ottoman Serai in Gaza.[11] While these individual and collective interrogations were being carried out, Israeli units would search the houses of the suspects for weapons, hidden caches or concealed militia fighters. Children would sometimes be used as human shields when there was a danger of hidden snipers or booby traps.[12] Wilful damage and pilfering often occurred in the course of these operations.[13] Dayan himself concedes that his troops ransacked shops in Gaza, with the involvement of settlers from the local Jewish settlements.[14]

Collective rounding up of suspects also took place on 3 November 1956 in the refugee camp at Deir al-Balah and next day at the camp in Maghazi. The camp at Nuseirat was combed for suspects on 6 and 7 November, and many were rounded up and sent either to Gaza or to the Israeli prison at Atlit, in contravention of the Geneva Convention, which forbids the transfer of an inhabitant of an occupied territory to the territory of the occupying power. No information on these round-ups filtered abroad as almost all of the UN observers had left Gaza. In New York, the Security Council was still unable to act due to the threat of a French and British veto. As a result, it fell to the General Assembly to resolve in favour of creating an international force known as UNEF (United Nations Emergency Force), which was to be empowered to take charge of Sinai. But Israel could have evaded the obligation to evacuate Gaza on condition that it allowed the refugees that had been expelled in 1948 to re-enter its territory.[15] Through this stipulation, the objective of the UN's policy-makers was to resolve the thorny issue of the fedayin. At the same time, however, Israel had a plan to respond on the ground in an entirely different way.

On 10 November, after several days of random detentions and searches in the town, the population of Gaza City was woken at dawn by loudspeakers instructing all the men to gather in the main squares at 7 a.m. The men complied with heavy hearts, fearing for their safety, but also because rumours had begun to circulate that the occupying forces were raping women.[16] The interrogations and checks went on throughout the days in different locations. In the Zeitoun quarter, several dozen young men aged between eighteen and twenty-five were blindfolded and taken away to an unknown destination. Although different stories subsequently emerged regarding their fate, a common grave discovered after the Israeli withdrawal from Gaza proved to hold thirty-six bodies identified by a court doctor as those of the 'disappeared' of 10 November 1956.[17]

On 12 November Rafah Camp, with its population of 32,000 refugees, was the next to be subjected to an Israeli raid. The bloodiest incidents occurred when men were being mustered in one of the designated centres, the school run by UNRWA, which was situated at the end of Al-Bahr (Sea) Street, one of Rafah's main thoroughfares. The Israeli soldiers stationed along the street, which had been laid out in a straight line when the camp was built by the UN, did not restrict themselves to firing over the heads of the Palestinians travelling towards the school, but also used their weapons to wound or kill those who lagged behind, whom they accused of being fedayin. Further violence was perpetrated at the school after checks had been carried out for ten hours, during which any accusation brought by a collaborator could lead to summary execution. The suspects were despatched in buses to Atlit and the day ended with yet more brutality towards civilians. During the night, defying the curfew, families went to recover the bodies of the victims from Tell Zurub, to the west of Rafah.[18]

The massacre at Khan Yunis had been carried out while the war in Sinai was in full swing. But the massacre in Rafah took place several days after the Franco-British attack on the Suez Canal Zone had been suspended under the concerted pressure of the United States and the Soviet Union. The British and American press got hold of the story, with the *Times of London* reporting that '60 refugees were killed at Rafah'.[19] On 21 November, the UN secretary-general raised the issue with Golda Meir, the Israeli minister for foreign affairs. Moshe Dayan gave evidence regarding the events to the relevant Knesset committee two days later, and on 28 November Prime Minister David Ben Gurion, questioned by a communist Knesset member, produced the official version. According to him, rioters incited by the Egyptians had attacked the UNRWA buildings in Rafah. In Ben Gurion's words, '48 were killed, and many others were wounded, while inspections had enabled 250 Egyptian soldiers to be identified and a large quantity of arms to be discovered'.[20]

UNRWA denied there had been any military presence in the camp and published a list, described as 'trustworthy', of 111 people, of whom 103 were refugees, who had been killed at Rafah on 12 November 1956.[21] Palestinian sources, on the other hand, suggested that there were 197 dead and twenty-three who had disappeared.[22] The level of the response to the Rafah bloodbath, against the background of the general international disapprobation of the 'tripartite aggression' against Egypt, obliged Israel thenceforth to maintain at least some restraint in the Gaza Strip. Security sweeps continued in the refugee camps, particularly in Jabalya and Beach Camp, and summary executions continued. But large-scale slaughter like that which had occurred in Khan Yunis and Rafah did not happen again. The head of the UN observer mission took the view that such killings of Palestinians, far from being the result of individual misdemeanours, were never sanctioned by the Israeli military. His position was that they were consistent with Israel's intention to get rid of the major part of the refugee population of the Gaza Strip.[23]

Civil Resistance

On 4 November 1956 Moshe Dayan paid a brief visit of a few hours to the Gaza Strip. This was sufficient for him to begin to gestate large-scale plans for the territory which would involve exploiting its agricultural resources and for excavations to take place at archaeological sites. During the visit he claimed to have discovered a tomb from the Canaanite era, from around 1300 BC.[24] He appointed Lieutenant-Colonel Haim Gaon, who knew the region well from having represented Israel on the joint armistice commission with Egypt, to the position of administrator of the territory. A former representative of military intelligence in Paris, Gaon had maintained his connections within the French army, whose forces landed on 6 November at Port Said. On the same day, Colonel Gaon forced the mayor of Gaza, Munir Rayess, to make an appeal for calm and discipline among the population. Gaon also took a series of steps to reinforce Israel's long-term position in Gaza. A Bailey bridge was erected across Wadi Hasi, in the north of the region, and the visible signs of the demarcation line between Israel and the Gaza Strip were removed. On 3 December, the Israeli pound was decreed to be the only legal currency in the territory. An advantageous rate of exchange was put in place in order to sweep up the Egyptian pounds that were in circulation.

After a few days, privately run schools were allowed to reopen and the curfew was relaxed to permit a rudimentary level of economic activity to resume. Egyptian health officials were allowed to remain at their posts, under a special decree, in order not to jeopardise the functionality of the UNRWA clinics. Other Egyptian officials, on the other hand, were regarded as prisoners of war. The Egyptian prosecutor in Gaza, for example, was held at the Serai, then transferred for a month to Atlit, and was finally returned to Gaza before being released under the terms of an Israeli–Egyptian agreement.[25] The UNRWA schools in the refugee camps stayed shut for a long time, however, due to the insistence of the Israelis on checking the individual credentials of each teacher, numbering around 1,000 in total.[26] This was motivated by the occupation authorities' fundamental mistrust of UNRWA's teaching staff, many of whom retained a strong commitment to activism, eighteen months after the demonstrations against the plan to transfer the Palestinian refugees to Sinai.

The Gaza communists, who had been supporters of Nasser since his nationalisation of the Suez Canal, now wanted to place themselves in the forefront of resistance to the Israeli occupation and set up a 'National Front'. But they also wanted to cooperate with the Israeli communists, who similarly opposed the occupation of Gaza, which led to their being rebuffed by the other political factions whose anti-Zionism could not admit of any exception.[27] By December 1956, therefore, the Muslim Brotherhood and the Baathists came together without the communists to set up a 'Popular Resistance Front'. These two 'Fronts' were in agreement on the promotion of Gaza's Arab character and on a boycott of the occupation, in education and other spheres. The communists' objective was the declaration of an independent Palestinian state in a liberated Gaza Strip.[28] Pro-Nasser Arab nationalism was too strong for such an idea to materialise. In addition, the Egyptian Mukhabarat had infiltrated into the militant groups of Nasserists and other Arab nationalists in the Gaza Strip, with later reorganisation in view.[29]

By January 1957 the Israeli army believed it had eliminated the Palestinian fedayin in Gaza as well as the remaining Egyptian intelligence agents. Under the direction of the new military governor of Gaza, Colonel Mattityahu ('Matti') Peled (who became one of the leading figures in the Israeli peace movement from 1975 onwards), Israel aimed to stamp out civil disobedience. According to Peled, speaking at the time, Tsahal had uncovered Egyptian documents listing the names of 640 fedayin, of whom 300 were arrested. Peled was reticent, however, as to the fate of the other 340, though he declared that the fedayin threat had been 'eliminated'.[30] In the meantime a call by the 'National Front' for a general strike led to a roundup of suspects within the ranks of the communists.[31] Notables were no longer exempted, with those arrested including Rashad Shawa, Farouk al-Husseini (the son of Fahmi al-Husseini, who had been mayor during much of the British Mandate period) and Munir Rayess (despite a plea on his behalf from the 'mukhtars' of the Gaza Strip). Yet the detention of these figures only served to restore their credibility as nationalists, regardless of their initial reaction to the Israeli occupation. The unifying theme of a diverse movement of opposition to Israel's objectives became the demand for a return of Egyptian tutelage over Gaza. This was at a time when the international community, which had been too preoccupied with the Suez crisis itself to pay attention to Gaza, increasingly focused on the fate of the territory.

Eisenhower and Ben Gurion

Soon after being re-elected to the US presidency on 6 November 1956 Dwight D. Eisenhower called for an immediate halt to the Franco-British attack on the Suez Canal Zone. As Washington saw it, France and Britain had strayed into a military adventure more suited to a bygone age, and this calamitous resurrection of 'gunboat diplomacy' should cease without delay lest it open the door for Soviet influence in the region. For this reason, the United States and Canada devoted their efforts to the swift deployment of UNEF, the United Nations Emergency Force, whose emblematic 'blue helmets' were in reality American military headgear repainted for the occasion. First Britain, and then France, agreed to evacuate their troops to be replaced by UNEF from 22 December. However, from Nasser's perspective—although he had transmuted his military defeat into a political triumph thanks to the convergence of US and Soviet policy in his favour—

vengeance for the 'tripartite aggression' would not be complete until Egyptian control had been restored in the Gaza Strip.

In contrast to France and Britain, both of which accepted the withdrawal, Ben Gurion demanded that Israel should be able to continue to occupy Gaza, as well as Sharm el-Sheikh, in the south of Sinai, the key to maritime control over the Straits of Tiran, by way of compensation for the withdrawal of Israeli troops from Sinai. As the Americans stepped up their pressure on Israel to withdraw, the Israeli prime minister said he would be willing to evacuate Sharm el-Sheikh if freedom of navigation were to be explicitly guaranteed in the Gulf of Aqaba and in the Suez Canal. He remained obdurate, however, on the issue of Gaza, which he said Israel should be allowed to retain, though he conceded that the management of local affairs should be restored to the hands of the Palestinian population.[32] Israel's refusal either to allow Egypt to return to Gaza or to allow the deployment of UNEF there was reproved as an affront to the UN's authority at the General Assembly session of 24 January 1957.[33]

On 3 February 1957 Eisenhower wrote to demand an unconditional Israeli withdrawal from Gaza. Ben Gurion observed that this somewhat blunt correspondence coincided with the official visit to the United States by Ibn Saud, the ruler of Saudi Arabia, which was a pillar of the anti-Soviet bloc in the region. After three weeks of difficult exchanges with the United States, Israel ultimately agreed to the entry of UNEF into Gaza. Israeli diplomacy enlisted the support of France, Israel's partner in the anti-Egyptian expedition, for the principle that it should be able to intervene in Gaza in the event of the collapse of civil administration under the United Nations.[34]

It was in this context that Golda Meir confirmed to the UN General Assembly the imminence of Israel's retreat from Gaza on 1 March 1957. The US ambassador, however, chose this occasion to underline Egypt's right to exercise its authority over the entire territory, up to the armistice line including Gaza. The US declaration roused a stir in Israel, where on 2 March 1957, for the first time since 1948, the cabinet met on a Saturday (the Jewish Sabbath). Despite the risk of the collapse of his coalition government, Ben Gurion agreed to retreat from Gaza and to accept the guarantees offered by the United States. A key consideration in doing so was his belief that Israel's security was not necessarily enhanced by the direct occupation of the territory.[35] On 7 March, the Israeli army withdrew from the Gaza Strip and handed over authority to UNEF under its director, the Canadian General Burns, who had previously been in charge of the Israeli–Egyptian Armistice Commission.

The population of Gaza was overjoyed at the disappearance of the Israeli military in the space of a few hours. Activists of every stripe came out of hiding and threw themselves into the liberation of their comrades who had been imprisoned. The Serai of Gaza, which had become the symbol of the oppressive Israeli regime, was ransacked in a local re-enactment of the tak-ing of the Bastille, with no intervention on the part of the UN force.[36] The two Palestinian resistance 'Fronts' launched a general campaign for the restoration of the Egyptian administration, and against the 'internationali-sation conspiracy'.[37] Few leading figures were inclined to give the UN a chance to show what it could do; and few seemed concerned at the prospect of Palestinian identity being diluted within a broader Arab nationalism.[38]

The same communist militants who had been involved in the intifada (uprising) against Nasser in March 1955, who was then regarded as a 'dic-tator', now took the lead in a new intifada in favour of Egypt's return. While it is certainly the case that Egyptian agents went into Gaza to rouse up popular pro-Nasser feeling, there was also genuine support for Nasser and his regime. Demonstrations followed one upon the other, and UNEF was overtly defied to a growing extent. On 10 March 1957, the Danish contingent fired over the heads of a crowd that was trying to replace the UN flag with that of Egypt. A young Palestinian, wounded by a stray bul-let, died two days later. General Burns, who realised that the situation could spiral out of control, asked the UN secretary-general to obtain a promise from Egypt both to demilitarise Gaza and to ban the fedayin.[39] On 13 March Ralph Bunche held a meeting with President Nasser, who gave him his unreserved assurance on both points.

Having given the UN such guarantees as were required, nothing further stood in Nasser's way: he appointed a new military governor to run the territory and dispatched him to Gaza the following day. General Muhammad Hasan Abdellatif, Nasser's new representative, was met by an excited crowd whose anti-UN ardour he attempted to cool by making a plea for full cooperation with UNEF. Such promises of goodwill were appreciated at the UN headquarters in New York, where it was stressed that Abdellatif, in spite of his military rank, would head a civilian team of less than 100 officials. The key to Gaza's future stability, according to Burns, lay in the hands of around 400 Palestinians who made up the local police force, 'who were doing the same job before the Israeli occupation, and of whom a fair number had continued under the Israelis, while others who had quit the service had now returned to their posts'.[40] While Golda Meir threatened her French and American opposite numbers with the prospect of Israel reoccupying Gaza,[41] the Israeli episode now seemed to have come to an end.

With the attested deaths of between 930 and 1,200 people out of a population of 330,000[42]—Palestinian sources put the figure higher, with 1,231 dead and 215 disappeared[43]—the human cost of the four-month Israeli occupation of the Gaza Strip was alarmingly high. If the figures for those wounded, imprisoned and tortured are added to the number who lost their lives, it would seem that one inhabitant in 100 had been physically harmed by the violence of the invaders. The resulting feeling of abandonment and impotence was worse among the refugees, who, according to the director of UNRWA, were 'more conscious than ever of the precarious nature of their position; of the total uncertainty of their fate'.[44] The large-scale raids, the intrusions into private homes and the prolonged curfews were all aspects of the particularly harrowing nature of this period. The arbitrary brutality of the military, in Khan Yunis and elsewhere, united the townsfolk and the people of the refugee camps as they faced the same ordeal side by side.

In reaction to a period of such trauma, it is understandable that there was a swing towards Egypt due to its role in having 'preserved' Gaza from being overrun by the Israelis in 1948–9. Nevertheless, a unique opportunity to re-launch the Palestinian national project, on this occasion under the aegis of the United Nations, seemed to have been lost. The Gaza communists made little more than a gesture in the direction of an independent state, after which the outbreak of Nasserist enthusiasm inhibited the expression of an authentically Palestinian nationalism. Is there any doubt that the history of Gaza would have taken a different direction had a

Palestinian entity been established there, under UN protection, in defiance of Israel, while maintaining special ties with Egypt? Figures in Gaza with incontestable nationalist credentials today ask themselves this question.[45] Following the ephemeral All-Palestine Government of 1948, the abortive scheme of 1957 to place Gaza under international control only served once more to defer the affirmation of an independent Palestinian identity.

7

NASSER'S CHILDREN

'Egypt is our mother', was the message displayed on some of the posters put up in Gaza after Tsahal's retreat.[1] It was inevitable that Gamal Abdel Nasser should emerge as the protective father figure, basking as he was in the glory of having compelled the Israeli enemy to undertake a historic retreat. The explosion of celebration in honour of the Egyptian president that enveloped the broader region was at its most intense in Gaza, where it served to wipe out the traumas of the recent months of occupation. A fact of which few in Gaza were aware was that the Israeli retreat was also due to pressure from Ibn Saud, the king of Saudi Arabia. Saudi Arabia had become the Muslim Brotherhood's refuge from persecution in Egypt and it also served as a counterbalance to Cairo's hegemonic ambitions. The mood of the moment, however, was one of exclusive adulation of Nasser: those who did not participate were soon destined to suffer the consequences.

New Rules

Once he had finalised the details of his relationship with UNEF, General Abdellatif took up his position as governor of Gaza with full powers at his disposal. On his arrival he held an audience with around thirty Gaza notables and personalities, who came both to welcome him and in the process to reaffirm their allegiance to Egypt.[2] He selected a new municipal council for Gaza, some of whose members were appointed without having sought office,[3] and restored Munir Rayess to the position of mayor, removing Rushdi Shawa, who had headed the administration during the last three months of the Israeli occupation. Many Palestinian officials, whose loyalty had been cast into doubt owing to their having remained at their desks during the Israeli interlude, including those who were in purely technocratic positions, were removed in favour of Egyptians.

The most delicate issue was that of the security forces in Gaza. When Nasser extended the guarantees he gave to the United Nations he had envisaged the dissolution of the various 'Palestinian' units, whose officers were in any case still mostly Egyptian. But he was dissuaded from this course of action by Hajj Amin al-Husseini, who still sought to be an active player from his place of exile in Cairo.[4] Nevertheless, the Egyptian High Command would not allow the two battalions of 'Palestinian frontier guards' (numbering 319 and 320) to be stationed in Gaza. Instead, they were confined to barracks in Qantara on the eastern bank of the Suez Canal, giving rise to a growing problem of discipline among the Palestinian militiamen, who were furious at being exiled from their native land. In contrast to their fate, hundreds of former fedayin who had taken refuge in Jordan and had been disarmed during the occupation of Gaza were repatriated to the Gaza Strip via Syria. Once returned, they were quietly absorbed into the local police and were commissioned to observe Israel's activities and prevent Palestinian incursions.[5]

The Egyptian leadership's overwhelming priority was in fact to avert any provocation of Israel so that nothing would stand in the way of Nasser's retention of his post-Suez gains. Indeed, just as reformed traffickers often make the best customs officers, these ex-fedayin, selected for their unswerving loyalty to Egypt, were especially capable when it came to undermining groups of would-be infiltrators in a context where Palestinian patriots in Egyptian uniform would have been more difficult to manage. Meanwhile, Colonel Kamel Hussein, the head of the Mukhabarat in Gaza, kept a close eye on Palestinian dissidents from the Muslim Brotherhood for fear that they could resume their activities as commandos.

Most of those who had been part of the armed struggle for the liberation of Palestine had in fact already left Gaza for various destinations in the Gulf. Kamal al-Adwan and Yusuf al-Najjar, for example, went to Qatar.

Abu Jihad joined Yasser Arafat in Kuwait, where he made a passionate appeal to the Muslim Brothers, calling on them to commit themselves to the armed jihad for Palestine in the same spirit as they had done in 1948.[6] The Muslim Brotherhood had been put on the back foot by the ban on their legal front organisation, the Jam'iyyat al-Tawhid (Association of Unity). They decided not to answer the call to jihad but to embark instead on a long-term programme to re-Islamise society in Gaza. Fathi Balawi, an individual whom the Brotherhood had reservations about owing to his commitment to nationalism and even more so to his relationship with the communists, left the Muslim Brotherhood entirely and returned to his studies in Cairo.

Abu Iyad was the only member of the new generation of politicised fedayin to remain active in Gaza. A schoolteacher by profession, he was initially appointed to a girls' school in Gaza City, before being transferred to the refugee camp at Nuseirat. Due to his knowledge of clandestine techniques he succeeded in evading the surveillance of the Egyptian Mukhabarat and recruited a handful of activists, whom he organised into a 'chain', rather than a 'cell', where each member knew only his own superior within the organisation. Abu Iyad, characteristically, perhaps, of his past experience in the Muslim Brotherhood, demanded strict moral behaviour from his followers and imposed a total ban on alcohol. However, his group was able to achieve little more than the distribution of literature and did not claim to be capable of any serious cross-border infiltration. In the end, drained by the struggle, Abu Iyad also left Gaza and went to find Arafat in Kuwait. The Mukhabarat, which was aware of his intentions, took him in handcuffs to the airport.[7] This takes the story up to 1959, with the era of the fedayin in Gaza apparently over.

Arab Intrigues

The Egyptian administration had thus provided itself with the means to keep Palestinian activism strictly in check in order to avoid any unwanted entanglement with Israel. UNEF noted that observation of the ceasefire was much more effective than it had been before October 1956. However, Nasser's regional ambitions led him to use his relationship with Palestine, and therefore with Gaza, as a ploy in his game of power politics with the other Arab states. Cairo was also determined to discourage other Arab states from any ambition to exercise influence in the Gaza Strip. The first such confrontation of this kind involved Jordan, where Nasserists unsuccessfully tried to overthrow King Hussein in April 1957. After the failure of the Nasserist coup in Jordan, the Egyptian Mukhabarat in Gaza struck at the prestigious Shawa family, which had close and well-developed links with Amman.

Saadi Shawa had in fact visited King Hussein to exhort him not to abandon Gaza to its position as the exclusive fief of Egypt and to ask him to promote transport facilities and commerce between Gaza and the West Bank. On his return from Amman, he reported his conversation with the king to a number of individuals in Gaza. One of these, in order to curry favour with the Egyptian governor, made a note of what Shawa had said and passed it to the Mukhabarat. As a result Saadi Shawa was taken into custody, after which he was accused of a conspiracy endangering national security and condemned to death for high treason. His two brothers, Rushdi and Rashad Shawa, were also imprisoned and then transferred to an unknown destination inside Egypt.[8] In so doing the Egyptian military was settling old scores dating back to 1951–2 when Rushdi Shawa had been an advocate of the transfer to Gaza of the British garrison on the Suez Canal, while Rashad had railed against the corruption of the Egyptian governor and his subordinates. The ferocity directed against the Shawa, whose name was dragged through the mud by agitators of all persuasions, was meant to serve as a warning to Gaza's notables in general: only by backing Egypt could safety be found.

The affair also had consequences well beyond Gaza. The Voice of the Arabs (*Sawt al-Arab*), the Cairo radio station that was heard across the Arab world from the Maghreb to the Mashreq, broadcast the show trial of Saadi Shawa. Nasser received pleas for clemency in his case, from King Hussein, naturally, but also from Ibn Saud and from Syrian President Shukri al-Quwatli.

The Syrian intervention proved to be opportune, since Nasser, who was anxious to spite the Hashemite monarchs in Jordan and Iraq, was already drawn to the idea of a union between the republics of Syria and Egypt.

Saadi Shawa was pardoned as a gesture of good will towards Damascus on Cairo's part, although he continued to be banned from Gaza and was obliged to live in exile in Egypt. Rushdi and Rashad Shawa were also released from military gaol in Cairo, where they had been held in degrading conditions. The Shawa family thus survived their ordeal, despite being very chastened by the experience. Their punishment had its effects on other personalities in Gaza, who drew the lesson that no purpose was to be served by challenging Egypt's hegemony.

The formation of the United Arab Republic (UAR), the union between Egypt and Syria, was proclaimed on 1 February 1958. This gesture was greeted with a surge of enthusiasm in both Cairo and Damascus, as well as in Gaza. Hajj Amin al-Husseini seized on the occasion to call for the establishment of a Palestinian government in Gaza on the basis of which Palestine would then join the UAR.[9] Nasser swiftly dismissed this idea, and instead installed a 'Legislative Council' in Gaza as prescribed by the 'Fundamental Law' of 1955. This body, composed of thirty members—twenty of them Palestinian and ten Egyptian—was to play only a consultative role. In contrast, the Arab Nationalist Movement (ANM), a militantly Nasserist group set up in Lebanon by a group of Arab nationalists including two Palestinians, George Habash and Wadih Haddad, was allowed to operate openly in Gaza. The ANM even received discreet encouragement from the Mukhabarat, who found it preferable to the Baathists and the communists.[10]

On 14 July 1958 the Iraqi Hashemite monarchy was overthrown in a bloody military coup. Iraq's new rulers, Abdelkarim Qassem and Abdessalam Arif, appeared to be sympathetic to the UAR. In order to counter the possible spread of an apparent Nasserist contagion the United States and the United Kingdom took action, the former in Lebanon and the latter in Jordan. In due course, however, Qassem took a different direction. He ousted Arif and sought support from the Iraqi Communist Party, well entrenched among the Kurds and the Shi'ites, in order to counterbalance the Arab Nationalists which had put down stronger roots in the Sunni community. This volte-face resulted in a rapid decline in relations between Cairo and Baghdad, with an escalation of accusations and propaganda campaigns between the two regimes and their clients. In March 1959, the point of no return was reached when the UAR explicitly backed a military uprising in Mosul, which Qassem's communist militia mercilessly crushed.

In this highly tense situation, any sympathy shown towards the Iraqi regime by an individual in Gaza would have severe consequences for the person concerned. Musa Saba, for instance, a militant respected for his Arab nationalist credentials (for which he had been detained throughout the Israeli occupation of 1956–7), was denounced as pro-Iraqi and spent a year in Cairo's Abbassiyya jail.[11] Muin Bseisso was also arrested in a round-up of communist activists. After interrogation in the Gaza Serai, which the Israelis had also used as a prison during their occupation, suspects were routinely transferred to detention centres in Egypt, often to be tortured.[12]

It was during this period that Ernesto 'Che' Guevara came to Gaza, bearing on his shoulders the mantle of Cuba's successful revolution. His brief stay in July 1959 was arranged by Egypt, where Che Guevara was paying a visit in the context of a lengthy international tour on which he had been sent by Fidel Castro a few months after his takeover.[13] Guevara said little during his Palestinian stopover, even during his tour of the refugee camps, though he did not give the impression of sympathising with the Egyptian authorities.[14] Nasser's anti-communism, virulently expressed in Egyptian propaganda of the time, can have done little to smooth the diplomatic exchanges between the guest and his hosts.

The Competition for Palestine

Nasser's overweening personality continued to inhibit any expression within Gaza of the idea of an independent Palestine. But pressure in this direction was becoming increasingly strong outside the territory. In August 1959, Hajj Amin al-Husseini once again raised the idea of a Palestinian government, which had been ruled out by Egypt eighteen months earlier. He no longer referred to the short-lived All-Palestine Government of 1948, which had briefly existed in Gaza, but instead put forward the model of the Algerian GPRA (Gouvernement Provisoire de la République Algérienne—'Provisional Government of the Algerian Republic'), which had been formed by the Algerian nationalists who were struggling for their freedom from France.

In October 1959 Yasser Arafat secretly founded the Palestinian Liberation Movement (*harakat al-tahrir al filastini*) in Kuwait under the name of its reversed acronym, 'Fatah'. The word *fatah* also refers to the Islamic idea of 'conquest' or 'victory', in a conscious reference to the victory over Mecca by the Prophet Muhammad in AD 630 and to Saladin's capture of Jerusalem in 1187. Abu Jihad, Abu Iyad, Kamal Adwan and Yusuf al-Najjar, who were initiated into the armed struggle in Gaza, thus diverging from the path chosen by the Muslim Brotherhood, all took part in the launch. Fatah had soon attracted a few hundred supporters among the Palestinian diaspora, and a month after its launch acquired a public voice with the launch of its publication, *Filastînuna* (Our Palestine), which appeared in Beirut.

One of Fatah's officials, Mahmoud Abbas, known as Abu Mazen, maintained contact with its sympathisers inside Gaza under cover of journeys to the territory ostensibly undertaken on behalf of the Qatari Ministry of Education.[15] Selim Zaanoun, a former companion of Abu Iyad in his clandestine years, left his position with the courts in Gaza to join up with Fatah in Kuwait.[16]

On 15 December 1959, Iraq's President Qassem accused what he described as 'three gangsters' of dividing up the remains of Palestine, placing Egypt and Jordan on the same plane as Israel. As he put it, 'the Palestinians were capable of administering their own affairs',[17] and he subsequently established a 'regiment for the liberation of Palestine' in Iraq. Hajj Amin al-Hussein left Cairo at this point to take up residence in Beirut, where he could work directly with Qassem. Nasser responded to this direct challenge by sending back to Gaza the battalions of Palestinian frontier guards whom he had confined to the Suez Canal Zone, declaring somewhat pompously that they constituted the 'Palestinian Army'. A local militia for 'popular resistance' was also set up in Gaza to counter Iraq's propaganda.[18] In the same spirit of revitalisation of the Palestinian cause, Egypt took a number of steps that undermined UNRWA. On 17 February 1961, the Egyptian governor of Gaza announced to the governmental press agency MENA that 'UNRWA's policy towards the refugees is a demonstration that there is a definite plan to starve and impoverish them.' An official leaflet published soon afterwards emphasised Egypt's efforts to enable the refugees in Gaza to avoid 'taking UNRWA's charity'.[19]

However, in the event, the major blow to Nasser's regional designs came from Damascus rather than Baghdad. Syria seceded from the UAR on

28 September 1961 following a military coup, thereby regaining its independence in a move supported by Jordan and Saudi Arabia. During the three and a half years of the UAR, the Egyptian military had treated Syria almost as though it was an outlying province of Egypt, which had transformed the erstwhile pan-Arab dream into a nightmare. No faction in Damascus emerged to defend the UAR. Egypt was humiliated by Syria's decision and continued to call itself the UAR after the split. Nasser drew from the experience a new determination to highlight the Palestinian nature of Gaza in order to continue to give a broader Arab dimension to what had otherwise become, in effect, the 'United Republic' of the Nile Valley.

On 5 March 1962, Nasser promulgated a 'constitutional status for the Gaza Strip'[20] to take the place of the 'Basic Law' of 1955. This proclaimed 'the Gaza Strip to be an inalienable part of the territory of Palestine', with the Palestinian people themselves being a part of the Arab nation in the wider sense (the *umma*). This subordination of Palestinian aspirations to Arab nationalism, as defined by Nasser, was given expression by the creation of a 'National Union' (*ittihad qawmi*) in Gaza, which, following the Egyptian model, assigned executive powers to the governor. The military governor presided over an 'Executive Council' of ten members, who were in practice the heads of the various local administrations, as well as a 'Legislative Council' of forty-two members, of whom only twenty-two were elected. This gave Gaza a basic level of internal autonomy, at least ostensibly, which, fourteen years after Egypt's first involvement, finally enabled the inhabitants of Gaza to manage their own affairs, at least at the municipal level.

This somewhat deceptive apparatus once again gave prominence to such nationalist personalities in Gaza as Haydar Abdel Shafi, the former director of Gaza's health services, and Farouk al-Husseini, a lawyer imprisoned by the Israelis in 1957. However, in practice the Egyptian governor retained all significant powers, and the elected Palestinian officials were hardly more than a front.[21] Both the General Union of Palestinian Students (GUPS) and the General Union of Palestinian Workers (GUPW) retained their headquarters in Cairo, despite their increased activities in Gaza. Over the course of the previous decade Nasser's regime had taken control of the student organisation, which had once been so militant when it was headed by Yasser Arafat and Abu Iyad. Nasser also sought to ensure that workers' unions remained firmly under his control.

Egypt was now less inclined than ever to relax its control because it had become embroiled in an 'Arab Cold War' with Saudi Arabia, to use the expression coined by the American political scientist Malcolm Kerr.[22] The two countries had become the Middle East proxies of the Soviet Union and the United States respectively, confronting each other in Yemen and levelling mutual accusations against each other of betraying the Palestinian cause. In this confrontation, which took many forms, Nasser won a symbolic victory in 1963 when he recruited to his side the Saudi ambassador to the United Nations, Ahmed Shuqayri, a naturalised Saudi citizen of Palestinian origin.

Shuqayri had been the assistant secretary-general of the Arab League before becoming a national diplomat, first for Syria and then for Saudi Arabia. In September 1963 he returned to the Arab League headquarters in Cairo to be the Palestinian representative. In November 1963, at Nasser's behest, Shuqayri headed a Palestinian delegation invited to New York to attend the UN General Assembly's annual debate on the Palestinian refugees. The make-up of the fourteen-member delegation, which was the result of onerous inter-Arab negotiations, included three personalities from Gaza, including the mayor, Munir Rayess. It was not empowered to speak at the debate in New York, except to provide information, and was not recognised as having any representative status. In Gaza itself, the 'Executive Council', whose powers continued to dwindle, was asked to endorse the increasing involvement of Egyptian forces in Yemen.[23]

The First PLO

Although Abdelkarim Qassem's disappearance from Iraq's political scene was welcomed in Cairo, the Baath Party with its 'Arab socialism' had since taken power in Syria, and following the suppression of Qassem's sympathisers in Gaza it was now the turn of the militant Baathists to face persecution. Abdullah Hourani was forced to leave Khan Yunis and went into exile in Dubai,[24] and Misbah Saqr had to prove he had broken with the Baath Party in order to resume his career as an officer in the Frontier

Guard.[25] Syria's increasing involvement with Palestine, and its support for the position of Yasser Arafat and Fatah, had again left Egypt on the defensive. Nasser was aware that he could not fight on every front, and he thus sought to be reconciled with King Hussein of Jordan. It was in this context that he convened the first Arab Summit under the auspices of the Arab League in January 1964.

The various heads of state agreed that Shuqayri should be put in charge of the Palestinian question. A relentless schemer, Shuqayri soon went well beyond his formal mandate. In May 1964, under the aegis of King Hussein, he convened a 'Palestinian National Council' (PNC), which ended with the official inauguration of the 'Palestine Liberation Organisation' (PLO). The PLO was to be run by a fifteen-member executive committee, headed by Shuqayri, among whose members were five personalities from Gaza, including Haydar Abdel Shafi and Farouk al-Husseini. The second Arab Summit, which was held in Alexandria in September 1964, endorsed the measures taken by Shuqayri's PNC, including the imminent formation of a Palestine Liberation Army (PLA), whose leader, it was announced, would be the Palestinian commander of the emir of Kuwait's personal guard, Wajih al-Madani, to be assisted by Qusai al-Abadla, a judge born in Khan Yunis who was president of Gaza's Arbitration Tribunal but who was also a graduate of the military academy in Cairo.

During the Summit, Nasser made an undertaking to his Arab colleagues 'to place Sinai and the Gaza Strip at the disposition of the PLO for the training of its army'.[26] But this was simply a ruse designed to rule out any initiative on Syria's part. Egypt was unwilling to cede any control over Gaza's security, especially in view of the Mukhabarat's concern over the wish of the fedayin to return to the territory. In the autumn of 1964, Yasser Arafat's Fatah, after years of caution, began to organise itself in Gaza[27] in order not to leave the field free for the PLO, which was seen as Nasser's creature. Fatah, encouraged by the Syrian Baath, set up an armed wing, Al-Asifa (The Tempest), to be led by Yusuf al-Najjar.[28] In the early days of January 1965 there were a series of more or less successful incursions by Fatah commandos in the north of Israel. An attempt to mount an initiative of the same kind from Gaza was undermined by the Egyptian Mukhabarat.[29] Egyptian propaganda was immediately launched against Arafat and Fatah, who were accused of being Muslim Brothers and of serving the ends of American imperialism.[30]

At the time the governor of Gaza was General Yusuf al-Agrudi, who had distinguished himself in November 1956 as commander of Khan Yunis by his refusal to bow to Israel's attack. With such credentials, Agrudi was able to obtain the endorsement of the Legislative Council in Gaza for a statute in March 1965 institutionalising obligatory military service for the male Palestinian inhabitants of the territory. His objective was to outflank the fedayin by channelling the popular enthusiasm that had been aroused by their early operations for Egypt's benefit. In practice, the Egyptian authorities enrolled only 3,500 new recruits in the Gaza Strip, enough to enable Egypt to announce the re-launch of what it called the campaign of 'popular resistance'. In reality, no more concrete steps were taken than in 1959.[31] Despite Shuqayri's protestations of loyalty, the Egyptian High Command continued with its strict supervision of the PLA's activities, restricting the arms to which it was given access and circumscribing its development.

When Nasser declared that the PLO was the representative of the Palestinian people in May 1965, his support was primarily intended to obstruct the activities of Fatah rather than to reinforce Shuqayri. Arafat was aware of his movement's relative lack of strength and its incapacity to muster a credible force to match that of Israel. The premise of his strategy was to spark an escalation of attacks and responses through fedayin raids that would draw one or more Arab states into confrontation with Israel. The expression Fatah commonly used for this strategy was the 'war of entanglement' (*harb al-tawrit*). It was precisely this kind of involvement which was most feared in Egypt, and it is hence from this which sprang the implacable character of the antagonism between Nasser and Arafat.

Cairo's obsession with operational control impelled it to keep the PLA in check, so that by 1965 the PLA had only seven battalions of frontier guards (of which, since 1960, two were based in Gaza), all of which were sparsely armed and under Egyptian command.[32] The real intention was to give the impression of Egyptian support for the Palestinian cause, symbolic capital from which Nasser's regime intended to benefit. The PNC, which served as the PLO's parliament, met in May 1966 in Gaza, which was the place of origin of thirty-five of its 150 members. Shuqayri took the opportunity to announce that there were 17,000 members of the PLO in Gaza, including 2,000 women,[33] and pressed for the adoption of resolutions hostile to Jordan.

This verbal escalation was consonant with the re-launch of the 'Arab Cold War' between Nasser's Egypt and Saudi Arabia, now under the rule of King Faysal, with which King Hussein of Jordan had opted to align himself. The ANM, whose Palestinian branch was led by George Habash, had promoted Egyptian policy in Yemen among other places, and in return it enjoyed more freedom of action in Gaza than any other political grouping. Thus the first internal election within the PLO resulted in a large majority for the ANM candidate in Gaza, Yusuf al-Jaru, against Haydar Abdel Shafi, who paid a price for his independence. In April 1966, owing to the hostility between Jordan and the PLO, Gaza was the only region where it was possible to hold elections to the PLO's newly formed and ephemeral democratic body, the Popular Palestinian Organisation. The latter organisation held its first meeting in Gaza in September, but it was immediately suspended when Haydar Abdel Shafi protested against the presence of Egyptian Mukhabarat in the room. The ANM sent some of its activists for military training within the PLA, but in October 1966 it was from Jordanian territory that Arab nationalists of ANM launched their first cross-border attacks into Israel, carried out by their 'Heroes of Return' militia, specially constituted for the occasion.[34]

The Egyptians continued to ban any fedayin activity in the Gaza Strip. The leadership of the ANM nevertheless succeeded in creating a clandestine structure in Gaza City, known as Sarim (Inflexible), which was able to avoid being mopped up by Egyptian security because of its strict compartmentalisation and its elitist recruitment policy.[35] In contrast, the Baath were highly disadvantaged by the security measures to which they were subjected, and the communist activists, already split into a number of ideological factions, were weakened by the departure of Muin Bseisso to Beirut in January 1966.[36]

Although the Muslim Brotherhood continued to keep a low profile, their retreat into social activity did not exempt them from a new campaign of repression in the autumn of 1965 which coincided with the retention in prison of their Egyptian ideological leader Sayyid Qutb, who was eventually executed in Cairo in August 1966. On the ground, Hani Bseisso, who had been sent from Kuwait to head up the Brotherhood in Gaza, was locked up.[37] This was also the fate of one of the Brotherhood's sternest moralisers, Ahmed Yassin. In December 1956, this pious twenty-nine year old teacher was secretly held for a month in Gaza's central prison, before being released after challenging his detention over legal technicalities. The experience gave Yassin an implacable hatred for the Egyptian regime and the Arab nationalism that supported it.[38]

Gaza's Shop-Window

From 1957 onwards Egypt sought to integrate Gaza into its own economy. The port of Gaza grew in importance as a 'free port', with a developed network of more or less legal commercial links with Egypt by way of Sinai.[39] Its 'free zone' status encouraged visits by small-scale Egyptian businessmen, with the construction along the seafront of hotels appropriate for the new clientele.[40] Congestion was eased in Gaza City's town centre with the opening of Al-Wahda (Unity) Street, a new thoroughfare parallel to Omar al-Mukhtar Street. The construction of this new urban axis was carried out with scant regard for the existing Islamic monuments of the neighbourhood, which were often damaged or destroyed entirely.[41]

A series of export agreements between Egypt and the countries of the Eastern bloc, especially Yugoslavia and Czechoslovakia, provided a guaranteed market for Gaza's citrus crop, whose cultivated area multiplied tenfold.[42] Such growth profited Gaza's large-scale landowners: thirty notable families continued to own almost a third of the fertile land[43] while the restrictions on union activity kept salaries for agricultural day-labourers very low. The average annual income per capita in 1966 was only 80 dollars in the Gaza Strip,[44] half of that in Egypt. UNRWA assistance, together with remittances from migrant workers in the Gulf, continued to be essential resources for the Palestinian refugees. In 1966, UNRWA contributed around a fifth of the Gaza Strip's GDP.[45] The Gaza Strip was UNRWA's sole field of operation where, in 1966 it was still making a general distribution of clothing and blankets.[46]

Egypt remained keen to use Gaza in its own public relations. Whereas Ernesto 'Che' Guevara had been taken to Gaza in 1959, in 1967 it was the turn of the 'first couple' of French philosophy, Jean-Paul Sartre and Simone de Beauvoir, to be welcomed there as part of a two-week trip to Egypt from 23 February to 13 March arranged by Nasser in reaction to an invitation they had received from the left-wing Zionist Mapam party to visit Israel. Muhammad Hassanein Heikal went to Gaza with the French couple as President Nasser's representative. Sartre visited three refugee camps, but he restricted his comments to compassionate observations about the humanitarian plight of the displaced persons, whereas his Egyptian hosts may well have hoped for criticism of Israel.[47] According to a press conference Sartre gave in Tel Aviv on 29 March 1967, his conversations with the PLO in Gaza had given him a desire to go on to Israel, if only to meet the Arab population there.[48] In general, Sartre spoke solely about his experience in Gaza in the most neutral terms, a reticence he maintained even in private. Sartre said to Meir Yaari, of Mapam, which had invited him to Israel for the visit he undertook from 16 to 30 March 1967, that 'the refugee camps I have seen will be a heavy burden on Israel's future'.[49] Sartre's invitation to Gaza was brokered by the magazine *New Outlook*, which supported Jewish–Arab reconciliation. A number of Palestinians bitterly reproached Sartre for his relatively low-key stance.[50]

Back in March 1957, David Ben Gurion had stuck to his guns in defiance of the Israeli 'hawks', with Golda Meir at their head, who wanted Israel to reoccupy the Gaza Strip in order to prevent the re-establishment of Egypt there. Ben Gurion, in contrast, took the view that Nasser would do a better job of crushing any resistance on the part of Gaza's population than an Israeli occupying army.[51] The reality of the decade from 1957 to 1967 seemed to bear out Ben Gurion's intuitions. It was true that the Gaza Strip had been the regular target of Israeli raids, invariably portrayed as legitimate however disproportionate they might be. On the other hand, even Tsahal conceded there had been far less tension on Israel's frontier with Gaza than on Israel's armistice lines with Syria, Lebanon and, of course, Jordan. A great part of this relative tranquillity sprang from Fatah's inability to operate from Gaza.

By early 1967 the PLA still numbered only 5,000 men, backed up by 4,000 frontier guards, and it remained under the control of the Egyptian military command in Sinai which alone had access to heavy armaments.[52]

Nasser continued to respect the undertakings he had given to the United Nations ten years earlier regarding the neutral status of Gaza. The 5,000 PLA troops were flamboyantly dubbed the 'Ain Jalout' brigade, a name which referred to the victory of Egypt's Mamluk regime over the invading Mongols near Nablus in 1260. The other PLA brigades, which formed part of the armies of their host countries, were as portentously named. The brigade based in Syria was the Hittine brigade, named for Saladin's victory over the crusaders in 1187; that in Iraq was the Qadissiyya brigade, for the defeat by the Muslims of the Persian Empire in 636; and the brigade in Jordan was dubbed the Badr brigade for the Prophet Muhammad's first victory over his enemies in 624. The disparity between such bellicose rhetoric and the operational reality was yet another cruel deception.

On 7 April 1967 the Israeli air force shot down six Syrian aircraft in the course of an action over Damascus. Saudi Arabia and Jordan, who were both on Fatah's side for once, accused Egypt of hiding behind the troops of UNEF rather than coming to the aid of its Arab ally. Rival Arab propaganda raged for a month. Nasser, who could no longer continue to justify his policy of 'wait-and-see', demanded the withdrawal of UNEF from the Egypt–Israel frontier on 16 May. However, he asked for it to remain in the Gaza Strip and at Sharm el-Sheikh, the two focal points of the Israeli withdrawal of March 1957. The UN secretary-general, U Thant, rejected the very idea of a partial withdrawal of UNEF, and in the same all or nothing spirit Nasser responded with a demand for the total withdrawal of UNEF to be carried out by 19 May.

The Egyptian president was emboldened by the surge in his popularity across the Arab world that resulted from this gesture. On 26 May 1967, he threatened Israel with 'total war' in the event of any Israeli aggression against Egypt or Syria.[53] Shuqayri did what he could to fan the flames, reiterating aggressive statements, but Nasser told him that conflict with Israel was still not an immediate prospect.[54] The principal objective of these grandiose manoeuvres was in fact to cow Egypt's Arab rivals, and the level of pressure Nasser brought to bear on Jordan brought swift results. On 30 May, King Hussein flew to Cairo to bury the hatchet with Egypt, where he signed a mutual defence treaty with Nasser which placed his kingdom under Egyptian protection. Saudi Arabia held out against Nasser's pressure, but the radicals in Syria were obliged to fall into line. Nasser could boast that he had won the 'Arab Cold War', while Gaza came to believe it was safe from harm within Nasser's paternalist embrace.

1967–87

THE GENERATION OF DISPOSSESSION

8

THE FOUR YEARS WAR

On 1 June 1967, with Israel surrounded by hostile forces, a national unity government was formed: the Labour prime minister, Levi Eshkol, invited Menachem Begin, the head of Herut, the main right-wing party, to join his government as minister without portfolio. However, the most significant appointment was that of Moshe Dayan to the position of defence minister. The chief of staff, Yitzhak Rabin, was not best pleased to find himself overseen by the man who had been chief of staff at the time of the Suez adventure of 1956. He was determined not to amend the plan for a pre-emptive strike against Egypt that had already been decided upon. Yet Dayan, on the basis of his own experience, did not want to see a new occupation of Gaza: his preference was to bypass the territory in order to concentrate on the Egyptian forces in Sinai.[1] In the event, Rabin got his way and the Gaza Strip became an objective, though secondary, of the war that was in preparation.

At first light on 5 June 1967, Israel launched a surprise attack on Egypt's military airfields, destroying most of Egypt's aircraft on the ground. At 8.30 a.m., Tsahal's French-built Fouga Magister aircraft bombed the road from Khan Yunis to Rafah in preparation for the deployment of the tanks of the 7th Brigade, massed at Nahal Oz. The Israeli tanks met strong resistance from Palestinian units stationed outside Khan Yunis which destroyed seven M48 Patton tanks during the first hour of the invasion.[2] The Israeli tanks then went on towards Rafah, where the Egyptian defences were caught in a pincer movement by the simultaneous attack of Colonel Rafael Eytan's parachutists. Israel's air force pounded the Egyptian units, who were cut off at the rear, while Tsahal took control of the southern sector of the Gaza Strip during the afternoon. At least 1,500 Egyptian soldiers were killed in the battles that took place along the 60 kilometres of road between Khan Yunis and El-Arish.[3] The same evening, under an artillery barrage, Tsahal took Tell al-Muntar, which overlooked Gaza City, but lost eight AMX13 tanks in the battle.[4]

On 6 June 1967, at the break of day, Israeli aircraft and artillery began to bomb Gaza City. Fourteen Indian UNEF soldiers died in the collapse of the hotel where they were waiting to be evacuated from the Middle East. Eytan's parachutists launched an attack on the town in the morning before turning their attention to Khan Yunis in the afternoon. In the evening, the Egyptian governor of Gaza, General Abdelmoneim Husseini, laid down his arms and signed a formal document of surrender on the morning of 7 June. However, the fighting went on at Khan Yunis, just as it had in November 1956, where Tsahal's mopping up continued for several days before all the snipers were finally rooted out.[5] The extremely violent Israeli offensive, with shelling and house-to-house fighting, caused substantial damage. UNRWA estimated that ninety out of its 100 schools were damaged in the fighting, hit by shellfire or both.[6]

The Israeli military governor, General Moshe Goren, once again established Israel's headquarters in the Serai, which had been abandoned by the Egyptians. Although the mayor of Gaza, Ragheb al-Alami, who had been appointed two years earlier, was confirmed in his position, the Egyptian officials working for UNRWA or the former administration, together with their families, numbering around 1,000 people, were expelled.[7] At the end of this so-called 'Six Day War' (which lasted from 5 to 10 June 1967), Israel abolished the former armistice line between Gaza and its own territory. Dayan's expectation was that this 'open door' policy would result in the rapid pacification of the territories occupied by Israel, whose labour market would open up to this new supply of cheap workers.[8] Prime Minister Eshkol went further, likening the Gaza Strip to East Jerusalem, which had been annexed as part of Israel's policy of reunifying the city.[9] Other reports had been submitted to Eshkol suggesting that the Gaza Strip could be annexed after it had been 'emptied' of its refugee population.[10] Gaza was, therefore, viewed from the outset in a different way from the other occupied territories in the West Bank, Golan and the Egyptian Sinai. David Ben Gurion, no longer the incumbent of any governmental post, advocated the annexation of the Gaza Strip, whose population, in his view, could be transferred to the West Bank or to 'some other [unspecified] Arab area'. On 3 September Tsahal published its ordinance Number 78 relating to 'Jewish assets in the Gaza strip and the north of Sinai', which prepared the way for settlement to being with the expropriation of local people. Yet despite these measures, it was in Gaza that Israel was in fact to have the most difficulty establishing its new order.

Guerrilla Warfare

The experience of the first Israeli occupation had profoundly affected the population of Gaza as well as the activists. The spectre of the massacres of November 1956 was part of the reason for the mass exodus of a section of the population. UNRWA estimated that between 40,000 and 45,000 civilians fled the Gaza Strip because of the fighting: equivalent to one person in ten.[11] This figure breaks down into 38,500 refugees from Gaza who found their way to Jordan, where they mainly went to the camp at Jerash, and about 3,000 refugees who registered in Egypt, out of a total of 13,000 civilians who arrived in Egypt from Gaza, according to the Egyptian authorities. This flight of refugees was aggravated by the murder of civilians perpetrated after the end of the hostilities. Palestinian sources report two particular acts of wanton collective slaughter in Rafah, on 11 June 1967. In one of these incidents, a grenade was used to kill eight people including a small girl. The other was a shooting, with ten deaths, which included the sheikh of the Tarabin tribe, a man of seventy, together with his two sons: the bodies, hastily buried by the murderers, were exhumed three months later.[12]

The precedent of the Israeli retreat ten years earlier, in March 1957, tended to discourage collaboration with an occupier whose permanent presence was far from certain. In order not to be trapped in searches for wanted persons like those carried out in the refugee camps in the autumn of 1956, the most determined of the nationalists began to roam from one orchard to another, sleeping rough and keeping away from urban areas. Activists of various tendencies learned from the failures of civil resistance in 1956–7, with the communists, for example, lifting their ban on armed resistance. The first attack on the Israelis took place on 11 June 1967 when a mine was detonated in the port area of Gaza City.[13]

A wide variety of groups engaged in armed opposition against Israel. The largest group, in terms of numbers, equipment and training, was comprised of the officers and men of the PLA (Palestinian Liberation Army). The major part of the units that had formed brigades 107 and 108 withdrew from Gaza with the Egyptian troops, but hundreds of PLA fighters simply removed their uniforms and mingled with the local people, keeping their personal weapons. Captain Hussein Khatib and Sergeant Abdelkader Abu al-Fahm looked after the caches of ammunition, where there were large reserves of mines and even 55 mm mortars.[14] Misbah Saqr, who held the rank of major in the PLA, evaded Israeli pursuit for several weeks before leaving Gaza to make his way to Jordan. He continued his exile in Syria before going on to Egypt, where he took on the leadership of the PLA units that had retreated to Alexandria.

The ANM saw its membership decline after Nasser's apparent invulnerability had been exposed as a myth in June 1967. Although it had more than 1,200 active members before the occupation, only 213 confirmed their membership over the course of the summer.[15] This seepage of activists, however, left the hard core of the organisation untouched, and in particular its secret military wing, 'Sarim', of which even the Egyptians were unaware. Documents found at the Mukhabarat headquarters, on which the Israeli army largely relied in directing its searches in the territory, were not in the event of any great help. The Palestinian Communist Party of Gaza (PCPG) had less than twenty members in 1967 but the removal of the obstacle of Nasserism allowed it to grow in a few weeks to a membership of fifty.[16] Due to its small size and recent recruitment the PCPG was able to escape the Israeli crackdown, at least for the time being.

Fatah remained relatively weak in Gaza, partly as a result of the efficiency of the years of Egyptian counter-measures to which it had been subjected. But it was also due to the fact that its organisation was more focused on the West Bank, to which Yasser Arafat had removed himself shortly after the Israeli invasion. Moreover, the Fatah leader for Gaza, Abdelaziz Shahin, known as Abu Ali, had been arrested and sentenced to fifteen years in prison on 25 September 1967. The Palestine Liberation Front-Pathway of Return (PLF-PR), founded in 1961 in Beirut by Shafiq al-Hout, was also poorly represented in Gaza owing to its overly intellectual image. The Baath Party similarly enjoyed little popular support but was still determined to keep its place in the spectrum of resistance. Finally, the notables of Gaza themselves, such as Haydar Abdel Shafi, Farouk al-Husseini and Mounir Rayess, should not be forgotten. They had never faltered in their defence of Palestinian identity in the territory, whether within the PLO or in their sometimes strained relations with the former Egyptian administration.

The Muslim Brotherhood was the only group that dissociated itself from the patriotic consensus in Gaza. Although they had been in the forefront of the armed struggle between 1948 and 1954, the Brotherhood continued to pursue the policy of resistance within the law on which they had embarked with their refusal to respond to Abu Jihad's call to join the armed struggle in 1957 and then when Fatah was set up in 1959. By this time, Sheikh Ahmed Yassin, to whom Fatah had already made overtures in vain in 1965,[17] had become the leading Islamist personality in Gaza. He categorically refused to join the alliance of anti-Israeli forces despite being asked to do so, though he took the opportunity to gloat over the humiliation that had been inflicted on Nasser, who was loathed by the Islamists for his persecution of the Muslim Brotherhood.[18] Islamist pamphlets described the Arab defeat of June 1967 as a punishment inflicted on the:

false prophets of liberation and revolution: mendacious heroes who have falsely claimed to represent their people, who have imprisoned those who preach Islam, who have thrown into prison the purest of Muslim youth, who have fought against all sincere Islamic preaching, while encouraging moral corruption, intellectual deviation and imported ways of life.[19]

In the closing days of 1967, it was without the Muslim Brothers that Mounir Rayess, (mayor of Gaza from 1955 to 1965), brought together the first secret coordination meeting of the resistance at his residence. Those present were Haydar Abdel Shafi, together with the representatives of the PLA, the ANM and the Communist Party. Some days later, in a second meeting, Haydar Abdel Shafi met delegates from the PCPG, the Baath and the PFL-PR. Also present was Sami Abu Shaaban, the president-elect of the 'League of Arab Civil Servants',[20] who had decided to have no contact with the Israeli authorities and to destroy the archives to prevent the occupying power from using them.[21] The composition of the first of these meetings reflected the influence of the Arab nationalists, whereas the communists put their stamp on the second.

Simultaneously, in Egypt, the PLA units, most of whose men were from the Gaza Strip, were bursting with enthusiasm, and their commanders were putting pressure on Ahmed Shuqayri to authorise them to go into action. Their advocate within the PLO leadership was Bahjat Abu Gharbiyya, a veteran of the nationalist struggle, born at Khan Yunis in 1916, who had taken part in the Palestinian 'Great Rebellion' of 1936 and had been a Baath Party member since 1949.[22] At a meeting in a Cairo hotel the idea emerged of creating the Popular Liberation Forces (PLF), referred to in Arabic as *quwwat al-tahrir al-sha'biyya*, with the intention of equipping the PLA to take guerrilla action against Israel. Shuqayri saw the PLF as a vehicle through which he could reassert himself on the Palestinian scene, in competition with the fedayin organisations among which the leading position was taken by Fatah. In retrospect, the suspicion of such machinations no doubt accounts for the extremely cautious attitude of Arafat, Abu Jihad and Abu Iyad towards the PLF.[23]

The Arab nationalists of the ANM also lagged behind Fatah and its fedayin in operational terms. The young activist Ghazi Sourani, who had been roughly treated while he was detained at the Serai in Gaza, was appointed military commander for the resistance in Shujahiyya, in the south of Gaza City, in August 1967. The ANM's first operations, under the name of the 'Vanguard for Popular Resistance', were in Khan Yunis and Gaza City, where they launched an attack on the Hotel Nasser. The early days were an uphill struggle in which the rhetoric of revolution seemed ill-suited to Palestinian realities. To mark the fiftieth anniversary of the Balfour Declaration, for example, the nationalists demanded that the merchants of the *souq* in Gaza strike for a day. The Israeli army had threatened any protestors with severe reprisals, but when an ANM commando threw blank grenades in the city centre this was enough to justify a general closure of the shops and to allow the resistance to publish a communiqué claiming victory.[24]

In November 1967 the PLO officially recognised the Popular Liberation Forces. Misbah Saqr was infiltrated into the Gaza Strip as their leader in the entire territory, with three regional leaders: Fayez Jarrad for the southern sector (Khan Yunis and Rafah); Yahya Murtaja for the centre (Deir al-Balah and Nuseirat); and Hussein Khatib for the north (Gaza City and Beit Hanoun). Captain Hussein Khatib, still flanked by Sergeant Abu al-Fahm, was reinforced by a young lieutenant from Gaza, Ziad al-Husseini, who had fought at Rafah against the Israel invaders before being forced to retreat into Egypt with the PLA. A month later, the Palestinian branch of the ANM finally renounced its Nasserist origins to become the PFLP (Popular Front for the Liberation of Palestine), led by George Habash. The conjunction of the classic resistance of the Popular Liberation Forces, strongly influenced by their training in Egypt, and the 'revolutionary' ambitions of the PFLP, who liked to hark back to the victorious guerrilla campaigns of China and Cuba, would give the anti-Israeli resistance in Gaza its special character.

Hard Knocks and Bouncing Back

Actions against the invaders were intermittent and largely symbolic: grenades were occasionally thrown, there were ambushes of Israeli patrols, mines were sometimes laid. The PFLP and the communists, however, had some success on the propaganda front: they each produced and distributed their own newspapers, with *Al-Jamahir* (The Masses) for the PFLP and *Al-Muqawama* (Resistance) for the communists. In October 1967, when the execution of Che Guevara in Bolivia was reported, *Al-Muqawama* paid homage to the iconic guerrilla fighter who had been a popular figure in Gaza ever since his visit in 1959.[25] Communist Party membership subsequently increased tenfold, rising to 500 members in the space of six months.[26] Even Fatah, headed locally by Neeman Dib, was taking steps to make itself more visible in Gaza.

However, between 10 and 25 January 1968 the Israeli forces struck a dramatic blow to the Palestinian resistance. The fedayin's carelessness with secret codes enabled the Israeli army to undertake a series of raids where they rounded up resistance fighters.[27] Neeman Dib and the Fatah fighters were the first to be targeted, with the PFLP following shortly afterwards: only four of seventy-one of their fedayin escaped arrest.[28] Those who had eluded arrest stayed on for another three weeks in Gaza before abandoning the struggle and retreating to Jordan. The communists of the PCPG were at least able to safeguard their leading figures, but this was no more than a respite of a few weeks. In April 1968, when the occupation authorities issued an Israeli identity card to take the place of the previous Egyptian document, the PCPG leaders also decided to decamp to Amman, fearing that they would be picked up in the new checks.

Although the Israelis had hoped that their crackdown would destroy the resistance movements, they had failed to reckon with the toughest members of the PLF, who had extensive experience of clandestine activity. The PLF settled down for the long haul, with the active support of the leading Gaza figures who bridged the gap between the notables and the refugee camps: Haydar Abdel Shafi, who embodied the nationalist consensus more than anyone else, was able to transcend factions and regional origins;[29] Farouk al-Husseini sold part of his land to finance the resistance;[30] and Musa Saba pressed into service his contacts in the Christian community and among the merchants in the *souq*.[31] Nahed Rayess, the elder son of Mounir Rayess, fought with the PLF in Gaza until the summer of 1968, when he went to join the Palestinian guerrillas in Jordan, where he took responsibility for liaison between the two groups and propaganda for the internal resistance.[32]

Jordan was at this stage becoming the focal point of the fedayin movement, whose pugnacity contrasted with the rout of the Arab states on the battlefield. The symbolic turning point came on 21 March 1968 with the clash that has become known as the Battle of Karama, from the name of one of the resistance bases in the Jordan Valley, in which 250 Fatah fighters and eighty members of the PLF took on the Israeli army. Only a handful of the fedayin survived the attack, and Israel also conceded that it had lost twenty men, four tanks and five troop carriers. 'Karama', which means 'dignity' or 'honour' in Arabic, sparked off a wave of enthusiasm throughout the region, boosting recruitment among the Palestinian factions. Fatah benefited the most, but the PLF also saw its numbers grow. To provide military training for these new recruits the PLF moved Fayez Jarrad from the Gaza Strip to its Jordanian base at Jerash (where he would be killed in an Israeli bombing raid on 16 March 1969). The PFLP also stepped up its revolutionary rhetoric, particularly in relation to King Hussein. Contrary to its intentions, Israel's 'open door' policy in Gaza, which was intended to conciliate the population, had the incidental effect of facilitating the transit of fedayin and the smuggling of weapons between the Gaza Strip and Jordan.

King Hussein, who was well aware that a majority of his subjects were Palestinians, maintained a bellicose public stance in order not to lay himself open to fedayin subversion within his territory. But this did not prevent him from regularly engaging in secret meetings with Israeli contacts. The fifteenth in this series of meetings since the June 1967 war took place on an Israeli ship in the Gulf of Aqaba. Hussein, whose objective was to regain control of the West Bank, declared that he was prepared to make territorial concessions and allow the frontiers to be redrawn on the condition that he recovered the Gaza Strip. He repeated the argument put to Moshe Dayan by his grandfather King Abdullah twenty years earlier: that in Gaza, Jordan would find its much-needed opening to the Mediterranean, while the unification of all the occupied territories under his rule would serve as a bulwark against Palestinian nationalism, thereby providing a quid pro quo for Israel. Yet the Israelis, who were toying with the annexation of Gaza, and who were in any case determined to 'encourage' emigration from the territory, were unwilling to take up the king's proposal.[33]

In the closing days of 1968 Abdulkader Abu al-Fahm led a PLF attack on the oil pipeline from Ashdod to Eilat, an operation inside Israel's territory that ended badly for the fedayin, many of whom were killed. Abu al-Fahm himself was wounded and detained in Ashkelon before being sentenced to life imprisonment by an Israeli court.[34] Shortly afterwards, aware of how exposed his position was, Hussein Khatib left the Gaza Strip. Ziad al-Husseini, still aged just twenty-five, stepped up as local commander of the 'professional' PLF, and at the same time the 'revolutionary' PFLP was increasingly thrust to the forefront in Gaza.[35]

On 1 February 1969 President Nasser opened a session of the Palestinian National Council in Cairo that saw the fedayin organisations, with Fatah at their head, step up to take the leading role in the PLO. Yasser Arafat became the chairman of the executive committee of the PLO (the PLO-EC), thus relegating Ahmed Shuqayri to history. These machinations were followed with passionate interest in Gaza, in contrast to the lack of concern shown over the various readjustments that took place in 1969 within the fedayin movements. These included the splitting off of the Marxist wing within the PFLP, led by Nayef Hawatmeh, to form the DFLP (Democratic Front for the Liberation of Palestine), and the disappearance of the Palestine Liberation Front-Pathway of Return, which ceased to exist after merging with Fatah. The developments within the PLO in February 1969 were also viewed with interest in Israel, where Prime Minister Levi Eshkol had to admit that 'the Palestinian refugees in Gaza have resisted Egypt almost as forcefully as they have fought against us'.[36] This was little consolation for a head of government who had just eighteen months before declared that the Israeli occupation of Gaza was to be as irreversible as that of East Jerusalem.

Exile in Sinai

The civilian population of Gaza were obliged to endure the petty tyrannies of the occupation in all aspects of their daily lives. Out of the tens of thousands of people who had fled from the fighting, no more than a minute number were permitted to return to Gaza. Only after the intervention of the director general of UNRWA, for example, were 134 of the 180 UNRWA teachers who had been forced into Egypt allowed to return to Gaza, and this was at a date too late to enable the normal start to the school year.[37] The population of Gaza, which was estimated at 385,000 inhabitants in June 1967, numbered only 356,200 after a further two months had elapsed and had fallen to 325,900 by the end of 1968.[38] Israel's office of statistics put the official figure at 352,000 for 1967, 334,000 in 1968 and 340,500 in 1969. Because the 'open door' policy that Moshe Dayan had put in place was not limited to those destined to be absorbed by the Israeli labour market, it also amounted to an incitement to civilians to depart for Jordan. Special coaches were hired for this purpose, and those who expressed the wish to travel to Jordan were seldom informed that their journey could be irreversible.[39] In addition, men pressed into forced labour in Sinai would sometimes have their identity papers confiscated before their journey into the hinterland of the Suez Canal.[40]

Israel's Prime Minister Levi Eshkol was at that time obsessed by the demographics of the Gaza Strip and its implications for Israel's security. This was not a recent obsession. In June 1965 he had questioned the chief of staff on the likelihood of a wave of refugees marching on Israel from Gaza, to which Rabin responded that any such movement would be crushed if Tsahal were to kill 100 civilians.[41] In private, the Israeli prime minister often considered the possibility of transferring 100,000 refugees from the Gaza Strip to Iraq or conceivably to Libya. Eshkol, on the other hand, was much less enthusiastic about either the possibility of transferring a substantial number of refugees to the north of Sinai, the option favoured by Yigal Allon, his deputy, and by the head of Herut, Menachem Begin, or about sending them to the West Bank.[42]

In February 1968 these considerations led Eshkol to set up a unit under his direct authority to cooperate with Mossad and Shin Bet to encourage the emigration of refugees from Gaza.[43] Feelers were put out to Latin America, until the notion of a transfer by air was seen to be impracticable. Financial incentives were offered, however, which was a key factor in the departure of some 15,000 Palestinians from Gaza during the first three months of this secret operation.[44] Yet the majority of those who chose to emigrate were young men who were either single or who were willing to leave their families behind. The process therefore only partly assuaged the demographic obsession of the Israeli leadership, while causing a permanent deficit in the territory's male population.

Despite their vulnerability in the face of the Israeli occupiers, the people of the Gaza Strip gradually became bolder, to the extent of carrying out protests, such as demonstrations and strikes, which, though on a limited scale, grew more audacious over time. To crush the growing tendency to resistance, the occupation forces severely punished all its manifestations. A favourite measure involved detention without trial for renewable periods of six months. Out of fifty-eight UNRWA operatives detained between 1 July 1969 and 30 June 1970, for example, only three were formally convicted by an Israeli military court. The main prisons used to hold detainees were at Ketziot, in the Negev, and at Ashkelon. This procedure was, as before, in breach of the Geneva Convention, which forbids the transfer of any inhabitant of an occupied territory to the territory of the occupying power. When seven residents of Gaza were expelled to Jordan in 1968, and another thirty-six in 1969, Israel justified this by reference to a law enacted in 1945 by the British Mandate authorities during a period of emergency rule.[45] Most of those expelled were men, but on 20 August 1969 a woman named Fatma Mahmud of Khan Yunis was also exiled to Jordan with her five children.

Although Haydar Abdel Shafi was frequently put under house arrest at his home in Gaza, this did nothing to curb his determination. He had qualified as a doctor at the American University in Beirut and had been director of health services in Gaza from 1957 to 1960. In 1969, he set up a branch of the Red Crescent in Gaza, whose existence the Israeli authorities refused to authorise. The occupation authorities considered expelling him to Jordan, but they ultimately found a compromise by exiling him temporarily to Sinai in a measure that had not been used before. In September 1969 he was interned in Sinai at a Bedouin settlement together with Ibrahim Abu Sitta, another founding member of the PLO, as well as the lawyer Faysal al-Husseini. Tsahal was also keen to disrupt the family links that protected the fedayin. In line with this policy, Imad al-Husseini, the brother of the young PLF commander Ziad al-Husseini, was given a four-year prison sentence on 9 October 1969 for having sheltered and assisted his brother. This collective punishment was completed by the banishment to Sinai of the rest of Ziad al-Husseini's family: his father, his mother and his young sister, who was still a minor.

The Israeli intelligence agency, Shin Bet/Shabak, made wide use of Arabic-speaking Jewish agents in disguise as Arabs (known as *mistaravim*),[46] as well as other informers of every kind, with the aim of reinforcing popular belief in their omniscience and to spread alarm. However, the Israeli counterinsurgency apparatus was unable to hold back the wave of agitation that swept over Gaza in October 1969 which had been sparked by the crisis in Lebanon when the fedayin of the PLO engaged the Lebanese government's forces in Beirut and southern Lebanon in order to impose the PLO's military authority over the refugee camps. This was the origin of what became known as 'Fatahland', an area of Lebanese territory that effectively became an autonomous Palestinian base for operations against Israel.

On 26 October 1969 there was a violent demonstration in the Gaza Strip at the refugee camp at Deir al-Balah in Gaza, and another broke out at the Maghazi camp on 28 October. The demonstrators were school and college students, prompting the closure of the establishments concerned by the Israelis. Student unrest continued undiminished over the succeeding weeks, however, until Tsahal decided to strike a decisive blow. On 17 December 1969, Israeli troops entered the UNRWA headquarters in Gaza to arrest the director of education, Shadid Abu Warda, who was sent to Sinai together with five other leading figures, including two school head teachers, two mukhtars and the head of a local chamber of commerce. UN protests about this new violation of international law went unheeded.[47] These measures formed part of the occupation authorities' more general policy of interference in the running of the UNRWA schools, with threats being made against teachers and the censorship of educational materials.[48]

The level of resistance activities in Gaza markedly increased in 1970. Palestinian sources record that in that year more than a quarter of the PLO's operations took place in Gaza, even though the Jordanian and Lebanese fronts were also active in mounting incursions into Israel.[49] An overview of the principal incidents in January 1970 provides a notion of the intensity of the confrontation: on 1 January, there was an attack on an Israeli patrol in Beit Hanoun; on 7 January grenades were thrown at the administrative bloc of the central prison in Gaza; on 16 and 20 January there were grenade attacks in Umar al-Mukhtar Street against Israeli vehicles; on 21 and 22 January Israeli vehicles were destroyed by mines in the south of the Gaza Strip; on 23 January there was a further grenade attack on an Israeli vehicle on the road between Deir al-Balah and Maghazi; and finally, on 24 January a bridge and part of a road were blown up.

The PLF, whose propaganda in Jordan and Syria was organised by Nahed Rayess, reported all these actions in official communiqués that celebrated what it called 'freedom fighters' and their exalted achievements. From 1969 onwards, the PLF produced a monthly magazine entitled *Arab Palestinian Resistance*, published in English in Damascus, which provided a digest of the main military communiqués. The PFLP and Fatah were not to be out-done in reporting the operations of their own fedayin. No less than 352 armed operations were claimed by various groups in the Gaza Strip in the first six months of 1970, of which 139 were by the PLF, fifty-nine by Fatah and fifty-four by the PFLP.[50] The sharp competition between the PFLP and Fatah, especially in Jordan, was no doubt what impelled Arafat's partisans to move into the field, at least in terms of propaganda. The rhythm of insurgency and counterinsurgency led inexorably to further violence and martyrs began to be idealised. The death of Abdelkader Abu al-Fahm, who passed away in prison on 11 July 1970 following a hunger strike, prompted the serious disturbances that followed his funeral at Jabalya. Muin Bseisso, who had become literary editor of the Cairo newspaper *al-Ahram*, wrote a poem in praise of the deceased hero,[51] whose martyrdom and example encouraged new recruits to rally to the cause. Entire sections of the refugee camps became no-go areas for the Israeli patrols. Jabalya was nicknamed 'Vietnam Camp',[52] and the fedayin claimed to have 'liberated' the neigh-bouring zone of Beit Lahya, north of Gaza City.[53]

Between 6 November and 9 November 1970, PFLP commandos hijacked three commercial airliners (one American, one Swiss and one British) before forcing the planes to fly to the Jordanian air strip at Zarqa. Yasser Arafat and Fatah had no longer been able to hold in check the extremism of George Habash's supporters and the resulting mass hostage-taking precipitated a clash between the fedayin and the Jordanian forces. On 12 September, the three aircraft were destroyed on the ground by the PFLP, which freed the majority of the hostages but retained fifty-four who were either Israeli nationals or dual nationals, which resulted in accusations against the PFLP of anti-Semitism.[54]

The following day, Israel deported four leading nationalist figures from the West Bank and two from Gaza to Lebanon. The latter were Haydar Abdel Shafi and the former mayor, Mounir Rayess, the father of the spokesman for the PLF. The six who were expelled were apparently given a message that the PFLP would bear the consequences if any of the hostages were killed.[55] In the end, the remaining hostages were freed by the Jordanian army, which emerged victorious from 'Black September', as the conflict in Jordan came to be known, driving the fedayin out of Amman into the north-west of the country, where they were contained. When the crisis was over, Haydar Abdel Shafi and Mounir Rayess were allowed to return from Jordan to Gaza, via Lebanon and Israel, following two months of exile.

Inside the Gaza Strip, the stand-off had now spread to the local administration, where the staff were unable to boycott the occupying authority but made every effort to frustrate its policies. Some 700 rebellious civil servants were sacked, and the president of their union, Sami Abu Shaaban, was exiled to Sinai for seven months.[56] The fedayin stepped in, physically threatening those they accused of 'collaboration' with Israel. They also saw it as legitimate to take action against those who worked in Israel, whom they accused of siding with the enemy. Within the space of a year, violent intimidation led to a fall in the number of workers from Gaza with jobs in Israel from around 10,000[57] to less than 6,000.[58] In addition, presumed informers allegedly working for Israel were murdered. The PFLP claimed responsibility for twenty-nine such 'executions' in the Gaza Strip over a period of four years.[59] George Habash said at the time that there was 'no conflict against enemy spies in Gaza that was separate from the conflict against the enemy, since the two could not be distinguished'. He added that 'No agent was ever liquidated without being warned beforehand. Any such agents would be properly tried and their confessions were sometimes recorded.' PFLP policy, he insisted, was that no spy was killed 'unless we were 100 per cent sure he was a spy'.

A vicious circle of killing and revenge thus began against a background of the Bedouin custom of vendetta and the blood price. Internecine Palestinian killings became more prevalent after the PLO in Amman was crushed by the Jordanian army in the course of 'Black September'.[60] Rivalry between Fatah and the PFLP was largely responsible for the dangerous escalation, with each faction accusing the other fedayin groups of 'treachery' to the cause, or of accommodating the enemy. Ziad al-Husseini's PLF was largely able to stay out of this fratricide because of their dedication to the armed struggle rather than partisan rivalry. All the same, the struggle between the militias seemed in practice to have caused a split in the patriotic consensus that had prevailed since the summer of 1967.

By the end of 1970, a severe toll had been inflicted upon Gaza. According to the Israeli newspaper, the *Jerusalem Post*, there had been seventeen Israeli deaths, including eight soldiers, and 109 wounded, of whom sixty-one were soldiers, as against 110 Palestinian deaths, of whom seventy-one were fedayin, and 667 Palestinians wounded.[61] French diplomats commented that incidents were by now 'almost a daily occurrence' in the Gaza Strip.[62] Out of the 10,000 or so Gaza Palestinians detained without trial since June 1967, 3,000 were still incarcerated at the end of 1970, amounting to one percent of the population. Meanwhile, 146 residents of Gaza were exiled to Jordan in 1970: four times more than in 1969.[63] Expellees were now sent across Wadi Araba, south of the Dead Sea, since the Jordanian government would no longer permit deportation across the bridges of the River Jordan.

Ariel Sharon, who had succeeded Yehoshua Gavish as military commander of the southern region, nevertheless continued to believe that the Palestinian resistance could not be overcome other than by even tougher measures. This fiery believer in iron-fist tactics, the man who, as long ago as August 1953, had sparked Unit 101 into existence in the course of a bloody raid on Gaza, would once more imprint his characteristic mark on the military approach to the territory and its population.

The Sharon Method

Yehoshua Gavish believed that the counterinsurgency techniques Israel was using in the West Bank were not suitable for Gaza in view of the deep-rooted resistance of the population,[64] but he was unable to persuade Dayan to change his strategy. On 2 January 1971, when two Israeli civilians were killed in a grenade incident, Sharon got his way and was given carte blanche by the Minister of Defence.[65] He dissolved the municipal administration of Gaza, and the mayor, Ragheb al-Alami, though he had been retained in this post after June 1967, was placed under house arrest for refusing to allow Gaza to be linked up to the Israeli electricity grid. Eighty traders were also imprisoned after being convicted for observing strike orders. In other measures, 209 Egyptian passport holders resident in Gaza were deported to Egypt through the intermediary of the Red Cross,[66] and a strict curfew was imposed on the Gaza Strip, extending to twenty-four hours in the case of some of the refugee camps.

140

Israel's frontier police were mainly recruited from among the Druzes and Bedouin who held Israeli nationality: once deployed in Gaza, they spared no brutality in rounding up suspects.[67] The following month, Moshe Dayan was obliged to concede that some thirty Palestinian civilians had been wounded due to the 'excessive use of force'.[68] Despite this, he continued to give his unreserved support to Ariel Sharon, even though the excesses that had been identified were occurrences too regular not to be seen as the result of a deliberate policy. In the case of known fedayin, families were not only punished by having their houses demolished—the family members themselves were also often expelled to Sinai on the pretext of forestalling any assistance they might provide for their rebellious family member. Such collective punishment reached hitherto unheard of heights when 600 women and children were sent to Abu Zeneima Camp in Sinai (Abu Rudeis Camp was reserved for political prisoners).[69] In addition, in 1971, 144 Palestinian prisoners were deported to Jordan.[70]

In the meantime Ziad al-Husseini's PLF continued to attack Israel, and the PFLP appointed a new and charismatic leader: 25-year-old Muhammad al-Aswad, who was nicknamed 'Guevara of Gaza'. As the two fedayin factions were operationally fully independent of each other, they carried out only one joint attack in 1971: a skirmish at Beit Lahya on 31 August. The PLF made up the largest part of the armed resistance, followed by the PFLP and to a lesser extent Fatah. The guerrillas were active across the entire territory, though the refugee camps were especially active. Out of 260 operations in the Gaza Strip in 1971, 127 were claimed by the PLF, fifty by the PFLP and thirty by Fatah.[71] During the day the Gaza Strip gave the appearance of being calm, but nocturnal incidents were frequent and the central hospital was used to being brought the bodies of fedayin who had perished in combat. The wounded were generally taken by ambulance for interrogation in Israel.[72]

Sharon decided that raids on the refugee camps, however intensive, were no longer sufficient, and that the moment had come for the camps to be completely restructured on the ground in order to regain permanent control of what had become the bastions of the guerrilla struggle. More than 2,500 houses were demolished in Jabalya, Rafah and Shati camps from July 1971 onwards, and army bulldozers also widened the principal roads so that military patrols could be more effective.[73] Some 320 kilometres of road were cleared to make them suitable for patrols, and a security fence 85 kilometres long was erected around the Gaza Strip, thereby ending the policy of 'open doors'.[74]

Only three points of access into the Gaza Strip were authorised: Erez, in the north, Rafah to the south, and Nahal Oz, east of Gaza City. Dozens of arms caches and militant hideouts were destroyed in the operation. Many in Gaza also allege that the fedayin who were trapped in their underground redoubts were buried alive by the Israeli bulldozers, although this is impossible to verify. The crackdown on the resistance became so extreme that the PLO decided to fake the death of Misbah Saqr in order to keep him safe. Only Yasser Arafat, Misbah Saqr's wife and three PLF officials were aware of the subterfuge.[75]

Almost 38,000 refugees were uprooted for a second time,[76] with some resettled in other parts of the Gaza Strip and others transferred to Dheishe Camp in Jordan, while 12,000 ended up in Sinai in encampments that were more like detention centres than places of refuge.[77] In Rafah Camp alone, some 4,000 refugees were rehoused in the former quarters of the Brazilian and Canadian UN troops, disused since 1967. 'Brazil', as this new residential area became known, was on the southern edge of Rafah, while the 'Canada' area was actually on the other side of the international frontier with Egypt. On 14 August 1971 a general strike launched in protest at these changes was unceremoniously crushed by Israel, which imposed heavy fines and a variety of sanctions on those involved.[78]

These radical measures, unlike anything Israel had previously used in such a systematic fashion, coincided with the Jordanian army's liquidation of the PLO's last strongholds in the north-west of Jordan. This brought rapid results in the Gaza strip, where the number of guerrilla attacks fell from sixty-nine in July 1971 to just twenty-six in October. Though Ziad al-Husseini was able to pull off a few more spectacular operations, in Jabalya in particular, the three years he had spent in hiding as a hunted man finally took their toll. The net tightened on the rebel chief and the trap that Gaza had now become closed around him. PLF cells fell, one after another, and with Misbah Saqr officially 'dead', Ziad al-Husseini turned in desperation to Rashad Shawa in the hope that this Gaza notable would be able to help him escape to Jordan.

On 21 November 1971 the body of Ziad al-Husseini was discovered in Rashad Shawa's house. The Israeli authorities announced that he had shot himself. Ziad al-Husseini's widow said otherwise: he was left-handed, but the bullet had pierced his right temple.[79] Nationalist circles immediately accused Israel of having arranged the death of the 'martyr' to appear to have been suicide in order to tarnish his memory. The disappearance of the PLF's young commander was a serious blow to the guerrillas, whose activities continued to diminish in December. During 1971, 1,000 fedayin had been arrested. By January 1972, Ariel Sharon was able to organise tours of the Gaza Strip for journalists in order to boast of his achievements, namely the deaths of 104 'terrorists' in 1970, of whom seventy had been killed between July and December, and a fall in the number of fugitives from 160 in April 1971 to fifty-five at the end of the year, of whom many were supposed to have left Gaza entirely.[80] The resistance had by no means disappeared, yet it had evidently been thoroughly trounced.

But Sharon wanted to do more than win on the battlefield. He called on Prime Minister Golda Meir and her cabinet to establish Israeli settlements in the Gaza Strip at the earliest possible opportunity in the five sectors where it was easiest to maintain security.[81] He also wanted to eliminate the refugee camps entirely, with an ambitious plan to resettle their inhabitants over a ten-year period in the towns of the Gaza Strip and the West Bank. He even suggested that 20,000 or 30,000 of the refugees could be allowed to return to Israel and that a compensation fund could be set up to bring closure to the issue by 'meeting the legitimate claims of the Arab refugee families'.[82]

Dayan strongly opposed what he said were unilateral concessions and he also had other disagreements with Sharon. In February 1972, Dayan removed Sharon from his command in Gaza, which was placed under the command of the central military region, falling under the authority of General Rehavam Zeevi who was already in charge of the West Bank. This enabled Dayan to return to the implementation of his 'open door' policy. In February 1974, Sharon, by now a Likud member of the Knesset, expressed his unorthodox views in an interview in the *National Observer* in which he reiterated his original proposal that 20,000 to 30,000 refugees could be resettled in Israel, suggesting also that 100,000 refugees should be transferred from Gaza to the West Bank.

Despite the military triumph of 1967, it took Israel more than four years to take full control of the Gaza Strip. As had been the case in 1956–7, at the time of the first occupation, the inhabitants of the territory paid dearly for the conquest. As well as the liquidation and the arrest of individuals, collective and individual deportations to Sinai, or to Jordan on a permanent basis, were also used as a punishment. Thus systematically depleted, the number of those living in Gaza did not rise to the level of the spring of 1967 until the middle of the succeeding decade,[83] at a time when the occupation had taken on a more permanent character and brutal treatment was less unrestrained.

Yet the intensity of the anti-Israeli resistance in Gaza from 1968 to 1971 aroused only a relatively limited response outside the territory, with little interest in the Arab press or in the Western media. At the time, all eyes were fixed on Jordan, where the PLO had been steadily building a 'state within a state' until its defeat in September 1970 obliged it to retreat into Lebanon. In the meantime serious reservations had emerged regarding the military ethos of the PLF, which Fatah, in common with the other fedayin factions, viewed as insufficiently revolutionary. George Habash, the secretary-general of the PFLP, was at the time insisting that 'the road to Jerusalem goes by way of Amman', and not, therefore, via Gaza. The PFLP eventually began to accord operational priority to Gaza only after the collapse of their Jordanian stronghold, entrusting the Gaza Strip to their iconic leader, Muhammad 'Guevara' al-Aswad.

The fact that a territory of only 360 square kilometres was able to keep up such a prolonged resistance was even more remarkable given the absence of a rearward base from which to draw support and supplies or the backing of a state. Egypt's attention was absorbed by the 'war of attrition' against Israel in which it was engaged on the Suez Canal, and the Baath Party, of which separate branches held power in both Syria and Iraq, had little sympathy or concern for Gaza. The Muslim Brotherhood, which faithfully followed the lead of Saudi Arabia, had opted to boycott the fedayin. The only external support enjoyed by the guerrillas was from the various Palestinian organisations, based first in Jordan and then after 1970–1 in Lebanon. There were increasing difficulties of communication, however, and mounting mistrust. In any case the competition between these external politico-military factions had never played a determining role in the conduct of the internal resistance in the occupied territories. What existed in Gaza was in fact a movement rooted in its own environment, from which it drew the basis of its strength.

A paradoxical outcome of Israel's oppressive policies was the inception of fellow feeling between the towns and villages of the Gaza Strip and the refugee camps. As early as 1956–7, the collective punishments inflicted by the Israelis in both of Gaza's divergent social environments had brought into existence a commonality of suffering and resentment. Finally, the restructuring of Gaza's refugee camps by the Israeli military during the summer of 1971 forcibly integrated the refugee camps into the Gaza Strip's existing urban fabric.

The resistance, highly active in the refugee camps but with nationalist figures from the local elite among its leadership, was driven by social and geographical solidarity between these two elements. For a long period, the fedayin's preferred hideouts were the extensive orchards developed before 1967 by local businessmen for the export of citrus fruit. To achieve military supremacy over the resistance, Ariel Sharon, always inclined to radical options, pondered the complete elimination of the refugee camps. Israel's policy in the end, however, was different: an attempt was made to recruit those local figures who were least compromised by contact with the resistance to Israel's side, on the basis of an Israeli understanding with a Jordan that had now purged itself of the PLO.

9

THE ERA OF THE NOTABLES

In 1972 Moshe Dayan consolidated his position as minister of defence, a post to which he had first been appointed in June 1967 by Levi Eshkol and which he retained, after the latter's death, under Prime Minister Golda Meir.[1] Dayan was a convinced adherent of the 'open door' policy, as he saw an opportunity in the economic integration of Gaza and the West Bank to consolidate Israel's occupation over the long term without making any political concessions. He had permitted Sharon to roll back Gaza's 'opening' in the summer of 1971 in order to crush the fedayin, but once military success had been achieved Dayan removed control over Gaza from the ever-ambitious Sharon, the head of Israel's southern command. In February 1972, Dayan transferred the Gaza Strip from Tsahal's southern command, headed by Ariel Sharon, to its central command, which integrated military oversight of the occupied territories under one command. Henceforth, Gaza was to be seen as 'normalised' in the same way as the West Bank. Ariel Sharon continued at the head of southern command until his retirement from the army in August 1973, although he fought in the October War of that year as a reservist.

The reorganisation also restored power to Gaza's military governor, a post held at the time by General Yitzhak Pundak, a veteran of the Givati brigade and the fighting of 1948 in the Negev who would subsequently serve as Israel's ambassador in Guatemala and San Salvador. General Pundak was later highly critical of Ariel Sharon on the grounds that his brutal methods had created a generation of Israeli enemies.[2] Dayan often went personally to the Gaza Strip, to which he was drawn by his passion for archaeology[3] and where he struck up a relationship with a wealthy and influential Bedouin family in the Deir al-Balah region and a friendship with an Arab watchman who led him to the Canaanite sarcophagi which are today exhibited in the Israel Museum.[4]

Dayan wanted to re-install a mayor with full powers in Gaza City, where the military governor had taken responsibility for municipal affairs since the deposition of Ragheb al-Alami in January 1971. He considered appointing Zuheir al-Rayess, a lawyer with Egyptian links who had been involved in the foundation of the PLO, in order to drive a wedge between elements of the nationalist movement.[5] Yet he eventually chose Rashad Shawa, a member of the notable family that had been frozen out by Egypt in 1957. As Dayan saw it, the three mayors of Gaza, Hebron and Nablus should form an effective counterbalance against the influence of the PLO in the occupied territories.[6]

The Mayor's Dilemma

The Shawa family had historic ties with the Hashemite dynasty that was on the throne in Jordan and had officially honoured them as descendants of the Prophet (*sherif*, plural *shurafa*). Rashad was the youngest of the five sons of Said Shawa, who had been mayor of Gaza from 1907 to 1917, and, like his father before him, he bore the title of 'Hajj', less in recognition of the pilgrimage he had made to Mecca than as a simple mark of respect. 'Hajj Rashad' had served as an administrator for the British Mandate in Haifa in 1935, and while there he had known well the almost legendary Syrian activist Ezzedin al-Qassam, who had utilised his position as a religious judge (*qadi*) to organise the anti-British uprising until his death in 1935 in a pitched battle with the British police.[7] In 1936, Rashad Shawa and his brother Ezzedin Shawa, who was a government official in Jenin, had used their administrative positions to assist the Palestinian uprising, and were obliged to flee the country once their actions became publicly known. Ezzedin Shawa embarked on a lengthy journey that took him to Egypt, Lebanon, Syria and Iraq, before he finally settled in Saudi Arabia as an adviser to Ibn Saud. In 1940, Rashad was allowed to return to Gaza.

Rashad Shawa had promised the British authorities in Palestine that he would refrain from all political activity, though he had agreed to this mainly in order to avoid undermining the position of his elder brother Rushdi, who had become mayor of Gaza. In 1941, Hajj Rashad, acting as a businessman, opened the first cinema in the town, the 'Samer Cinema', which became a popular attraction,[8] and it was this venue that the Muslim Brotherhood used to launch its Gaza section in 1946. In 1951, having become highly critical of the corruption of the Egyptian administration, Rashad backed his elder brother's campaign to transfer the British base to Gaza from Suez. Despite this, Hajj Rashad never abandoned his commitment to the Palestinian nationalist cause and in January 1957 he was imprisoned, first by the Israeli army, and then just a few months later in an Egyptian military prison in Cairo. The public trial of his brother Saadi on a charge of treason was a blow to the whole Shawa clan, who afterwards withdrew from public life to manage their family affairs and held aloof from the entire process that led to the creation of the PLO.

After the renewed Israeli occupation, Hajj Rashad left it to representatives of the other major families of Gaza, such as Farouk al-Husseini or Mounir Rayess, to join up with the resistance. But he was also assiduous in refraining from collaboration with the invaders. However, he eventually indicated which side he was on when he set up the 'Benevolent society' in 1969, which promoted social assistance throughout the Gaza Strip. Rashad Shawa was also the leading light in a group of Gaza landowners who had increased their wealth under the Egyptian administration through the export of citrus fruit and were uneasy about the violence that had become endemic in the territory. With Sharon's successful campaign against the PLO in the summer of 1971, Hajj Rashad felt that his moment had come,[9] but in order not to appear as if he was capitalising on the crushing of the guerrillas he organised a petition to endorse his elevation to the mayoralty. Some 6,000 people responded to his public appeal, on the basis of which Shawa accepted the post in September 1971.[10] Fifty-four years after his father, therefore, and fourteen years after his elder brother, Hajj Rashad became the mayor of Gaza. To prove his independence from Israel, he refused all remuneration for his duties.

Rashad Shawa put his undoubted managerial abilities at the service of those whom he administered. His family links with the Hashemite monarchy enabled him to be generous in issuing transit permits to Jordan for individuals and goods. These permits, which soon became known as 'Shawa passports' and were very much in the spirit of Moshe Dayan's 'open door' policy, were crucial for the resumption of the export of citrus fruit to Iran and the Arab countries. Hajj Rashad also cultivated his patriotic image by making an appeal to the United Nations to take a closer interest in the defence and the integrity of Gaza in view of Israeli ambitions in the direction of annexation. As long ago as 1968, Golda Meir's deputy prime minister, Yigal Allon, had put forward a proposal with government authority that sovereignty in the West Bank could be shared between Israel and Jordan, which would also include the annexation of the Gaza Strip after the transfer of the refugees living in the territory to either the West Bank or Sinai.[11] It may be recalled that Allon, commander of the southern front in 1948–9, attempted a military conquest of Gaza against Ben Gurion's wishes.

To outflank these Israeli projects, Rashad Shawa turned to the plans put forward by Jordan and to international opinion. On 15 March 1972, when King Hussein proposed the establishment of a 'unified Arab Kingdom' on the two banks of the River Jordan, Rashad Shawa endorsed the idea and attempted to ensure that the Gaza Strip would be explicitly mentioned in the Jordanian plan. Hussein's plan was a union within his own Arab kingdom of the territory on both banks of the River Jordan: Transjordan to the east and Palestine to the west, where the latter was to include the West Bank and 'any other Palestinian territories which are liberated and whose inhabitants desire to join it'.[12] Some days later, the mayor of Gaza City welcomed François Mitterrand, the leader of the French socialist party, to the Gaza Strip during his visit to Israel and the occupied territories at the invitation of the 'fraternal' Israeli Labour Party. The future French president's experience of Gaza, though brief, together with Rashad Shawa's forceful expression of his beliefs, left a lasting impression on Mitterrand, confronted as he had been by the reality of the refugee camps and the Israeli occupation.[13]

In his enthusiasm for the United Arab Kingdom the mayor of Gaza was of course unaware that King Hussein was continuing his conversations with Israel, this time at a venue to the south of the Dead Sea. On 21 March 1972, Hussein met Golda Meir, accompanied by Moshe Dayan, whose

150

'open door' policy to the West Bank was precisely intended to preclude any territorial restitution. Hussein had difficulty persuading Meir, who was more hawkish than ever, that his plan was of any interest. Nonetheless, he committed himself to the demilitarisation of the West Bank in the event of an Israeli retreat and restated the claim to the Gaza Strip[14] he had already made in confidence during his meeting with the Israeli prime minister in November 1968. Golda Meir gave him no hope of any significant concession, which did not discourage Hussein from continuing with his programme of parallel diplomacy, if for no other reason than to be prepared for future eventualities.

Rashad Shawa was never to be made privy to such confidences, which was a privilege restricted to a handful of King Hussein's closest circle. He was therefore wholly unaware of just how rigid the intransigence of the Israelis was. On the other hand, he did know how much the king had underestimated the depth of the Palestinians' resentment at the suppression of the fedayin in Jordan at the time of Black September in 1970 and the summer of 1971. His 'Shawa passports' were still acceptable to those who wanted to travel to Jordan for business or other reasons, but he realised he could not continue to ignore Palestinian nationalism in favour of the Jordanian option at a time when the PLO had violently and unanimously rejected what it saw as King Hussein's 'conspiracy'.[15] Subjected to such vehement antagonism, Rashad Shawa made a direct appeal to Yasser Arafat for help and in July 1972 he went to meet the Palestinian leadership which was now based in the Lebanese capital, Beirut.[16] Moshe Dayan was furious that Shawa, as he saw it, should have been seeking the 'blessing' of the PLO,[17] but the mayor returned to Gaza having reassured himself that the fedayin movements, except the PFLP, accepted his position.[18]

For all Rashad Shawa's ability and charisma, however, he could not continue to maintain such a delicate balance indefinitely. His trip to Amman in August 1972, just a month after his journey to Beirut, prompted a vicious campaign against him in the Gaza Strip, led by the imam of the Mosque of Umar, Sheikh Hashem Khazandar. The names of those who would accompany Rashad Shawa to Amman were kept secret until the last moment in a precaution that was more than a mere formality: the mayor would be the object of three assassination attempts, two by the PFLP and one on the part of Fatah.[19] In the event his interview with King Hussein was less than satisfactory, not least because a delegation of nationalist personalities from Gaza had gone to Cairo at the same time.

Rashad Shawa returned to Gaza after being granted permission to issue Jordanian passports. He hoped to be able to consolidate his legitimacy by asking Israel to hold genuine municipal elections. Yet rather than offering him such an opportunity, Governor Pundak instead set him the task of integrating the Shati refugee camp (Beach Camp) into the scope of Gaza City's municipal services. Though the camp was adjacent to Rimal, in the north of Gaza City, it had been under the management of UNRWA since its establishment in 1950, and UNRWA provided its basic services. Its integration into Gaza's municipality, though it might have been justifiable for technical reasons, would be an unambiguous signal of the permanence of the refugees' presence in the Gaza Strip. The mayor was aware that, in 1955, demonstrations against any kind of permanent settlement of the Palestinian refugees had been enough to rattle Nasser himself. He consequently refused to comply with the instructions given to him by General Pundak, who dismissed him from his post on 22 October 1972. Hajj Rashad had been mayor of Gaza for scarcely more than a year.

The Israeli governor henceforth assumed the same kind of direct powers in the Gaza Strip as had been exercised by his Egyptian predecessor, albeit with the absence of anything that could be described as a municipal administration. In Gaza, Israeli officers directed the Palestinian civil servants in the departments of education, health and social services, and the mayors the Israelis had appointed in Khan Yunis, Rafah and Deir al-Balah remained in office, with mukhtars occupying the same role in the refugee camps and the villages. General Pundak attempted to carry out the experiment of integrating Shati Camp into Gaza City himself, promoting the formation there of a local committee which was intended to be one of the eight management committees for the town. However, on 11 February 1972 the head of the Shati committee was murdered, which led to the resignation of his counterparts in the other areas of Gaza City.[20] In Gaza City, bereft of Shawa's intermediary role, Israel found itself directly in the front line.

Last Ditch Efforts

Sheikh Khazandar, who had led the propaganda campaign against Rashad Shawa's visit to Amman, was actually one of Fatah's leaders in the Gaza Strip. He had previously been a leading member of the Muslim Brotherhood, but had left the organisation because of their reticence regarding the armed struggle. He was subsequently able to turn his position as imam of Gaza's largest mosque to advantage in the development of Fatah's structures. Yasser Arafat's movement, long marginal in the Gaza Strip, was looking for local support in Gaza to re-establish itself there following the suppression of the fedayin in Jordan in 1970–1. The task was undertaken by Kamal Adwan, a member of the Fatah leadership who had been trained by Abu Jihad for clandestine operations in Gaza when he was a teenager.[21] Adwan's principal henchman in Gaza was Assad Saftawi, whose commitment had begun early, under the wing of Abu Iyad, and who had taken over from Neeman Dib as Fatah's head in Gaza after the Israeli round-up of suspects in 1968. In Khan Yunis, Fatah was also able to rely on the connections of Zakarya al-Agha, a member of one of the town's leading families.

However, the PLF were unable to recover from the demise of Zia al-Husseini, and the number of their operations consequently declined during this time. In a period of two months in October and November 1972, the PLF claimed responsibility for only three grenade attacks, two exchanges of fire and three bomb attacks. Many activists left the PLF in order to join Fatah,[22] a switch of allegiance also made by Nahed Rayess, who was subsequently based in Beirut. The PFLP now placed its faith in its elusive leader, Muhammad al-Aswad, the 'Guevara of Gaza', whose cunning in evading the occupying forces was increasingly legendary. When the Israeli army decided to punish him and his family by destroying their house, in Shati Camp, Aswad distributed sweets to his neighbours, inviting them to celebrate rather than mourn, in a symbolic act of defiance of Tsahal that was widely celebrated. However, on 9 March 1973 the career of the Guevara of Gaza came to an end when he died in an ambush in the coastal region of Gaza City along with two other PFLP fighters.

The significance of his loss for all the fedayin factions was such that Fatah offered its radio station in Cairo to George Habash to launch a passionate appeal for the continuation of the struggle in Gaza in the name of the PLO on 12 March 1973.[23] A month later Israeli commandos killed three leading Fatah figures in the heart of Beirut, including Yusuf al-Najjar and Kamal Adwan, two of the pioneers of the armed struggle in Gaza. What made this an even worse blow to Fatah was that the Tsahal assassins seized the documentation in Adwan's possession relating to Fatah's networks in the occupied territories.[24] Assad Saftawi, who had previously been able to maintain his cover as a teacher, was now thrown into prison where he was to stay for five years until Israel relaxed its pressure on Fatah. By 1973, Israel was no longer deporting Palestinians to Jordan, though in 1972 it had expelled forty-seven Gaza residents across the Wadi Araba.[25] After the dismantling of the fedayin structures, the leadership of the Palestinian nationalist movement fell to various figures within civil society, or to militant communists within the trades unions and other associations.[26]

All factions were united on one issue: the rejection of the Jordanian option as envisaged by Rashad Shawa. But they were divided on the idea favoured by the communists, according to which a Palestinian state would be created in the territories occupied since 1967. Fatah's official position was to oppose anything less than the total liberation of Palestine, though there was at the same time an internal debate as to whether such an all-or-nothing approach might be counterproductive. The PFLP remained determined not to lay down its arms, even if that meant turning its hand against what it saw as the 'Arab reactionaries'. George Habash was uncompromising. In his opinion: 'Even if a political settlement were to be reached, the resistance should continue the struggle in Gaza, whether against the Israeli occupiers, or against any reactionary regime that may re-impose itself on Gaza, or against any reactionary "Palestinian state" that may emerge from a political settlement.'[27] In diametric opposition to such rhetoric, Gaza's nationalist leaders continued to promote action in a variety of fields in the face of the pressure placed upon them by the Israeli administration and of the patronage exercised by pro-Jordanian personalities.

Notables in the Resistance

In 1967, Dr Haydar Abdel Shafi, who had been the chairman of Gaza's Legislative Council in 1962 and became a founding member of the PLO in 1964, emerged as the creator of a lasting consensus between the different factions of the armed and civilian resistance. In 1969, after being harassed by the occupation authorities and exiled to Sinai, he made a move to contest the dominance of Rashad Shawa's charitable structure by setting up a Red Crescent Association in Gaza. His nationalist credentials were enhanced further when he was exiled to Jordan during the Black September episode in 1970. The Israeli governor, General Pundak, officially authorised the activities of the Red Crescent in the summer of 1972, which enabled Dr Abdel Shafi to set up a free dispensary and medical services, as well as running a public library and sponsoring debates.

Dr Abdel Shafi was assisted in his activities by another veteran of the nationalist struggle, Musa Saba, who had also been in Israeli prisons both during the occupation of 1956–7 and after 1967. A further common factor between the two men was their consistent defiance of the Egyptian administration in Gaza in the name of Palestinian nationalism. The cooperation between the two in the leadership of the Red Crescent was significant at the symbolic level, given that one was the heir of one of Gaza's most prestigious Islamic dignitaries and the other was the son of one of its leading Christian merchants. They were joined by Fayez Abu Rahmeh, a lawyer and former member of the Municipal Council in Gaza, who had distinguished himself by defending nationalist detainees and became known as 'the lawyer of the Palestinian Revolution'.[28]

Yusra Barbari, the president of the Union of Women in Gaza since 1964, was also involved in launching the Red Crescent. In many respects she was one of the leading female figures of Palestinian nationalism. In 1965 she led the Gaza delegation to the PLO working party that resulted in the institution of the General Union of Palestinian Women (GUPW), in which she worked with Intissar al-Wazir, the wife of the fedayin leader Abu Jihad. Intissar al-Wazir was originally from Gaza but had gone into exile with her husband. Yusra's brother, Kamal Barbari, a lawyer who was highly active in the Palestinian cause, disappeared during the invasion of Gaza in 1967, and though his remains have never been discovered he was regarded as a martyr for the resistance.[29] Yusra Barbari endured constant harassment and punishments from the Israeli authorities, and in 1974 she was prohibited from leaving the Gaza Strip. The mobilisation of women was a key issue, particularly since expatriations and repressive action had reduced the male proportion of the population aged between twenty-five and forty-nine to just 41 per cent.[30]

Haydar Abdel Shafi, who was well aware of the setbacks the armed resistance had experienced, was anxious to attract the widest possible spectrum of political actors in support of Palestinian self-determination. In July 1973 he wrote an open letter demanding autonomy to the secretary-general of the United Nations, a move which was endorsed by a range of leading figures in both Gaza and the West Bank and for which Abdel Shafi had gained the support of the mayors designate of Rafah (Fathi Saleh) and Khan Yunis (Suleiman al-Astal).[31] The Astal family, of which Suleiman al-Astal was a member, was one of the three leading families of Khan Yunis, together with the Agha and the Fara families. In August 1973, the communist militants, who were aware of Arafat's reservations regarding any kind of internal leadership, set up the Palestinian National Front (PNF) in both the West Bank and Gaza and insisted on its inclusion in the PLO.[32] Here again, the emphasis was on Palestinian self-determination.

Despite the initial successes of the Egyptian and Syrian armies, the Israeli–Arab war of October 1973, known by the Israelis as the Kippur War and as the Ramadan War by the Arabs, ultimately resulted in another victory for Israel, which prevailed with the help of an air bridge that brought in supplies provided by the United States. In the period that followed the military option seemed to the Palestinians of the occupied territories to be less realistic than ever, and they instead sought to play a larger influence in the evolution of the PLO, which abandoned its previous 'all-or-nothing' ideology in June 1974. The new objective of Yasser Arafat's leadership was to 'establish the independent combatant national authority for the people over every part of Palestinian territory that is liberated'.[33]

The PFLP leader George Habash opposed this goal, which he regarded as a capitulation, and set up a 'rejection front' with the PFLP as its nucleus, against the new direction taken by the PLO. Arafat, however, gained a degree of approval on the international political scene that compensated for what he had lost from the Palestinian radicals. In October 1974, the Arab Summit at Rabat enshrined the PLO as the 'sole legitimate representative of the Palestinian people'.[34] In the following month the PLO was admitted to observer status at the United Nations, and Yasser Arafat issued an appeal to UN members at the General Assembly in New York to allow the Palestinian people to 'live in our national homeland, free and sovereign, enjoying all the privileges of nationhood'.[35]

This diplomatic breakthrough on the part of the PLO came as a boost for Haydar Abdel Shafi's civil resistance in Gaza, to the detriment both of those who went on placing their faith in Amman and of the radicals of the Habash's 'rejection front'. Abdel Shafi had been the leading figure in the nationalist movement ever since the death of Mounir al-Rayess in March 1974 and Farouk al-Husseini's departure for Cairo. His rival Rashad Shawa understood that though his 'Shawa passports' were still vital documents for crossing the River Jordan, his ability to issue them did little to offset the decline in Jordan's standing in the Gaza Strip. He therefore turned back to the process of reinserting himself in municipal affairs, in a way that stressed his patriotic commitment: an approach that differed from his former enthusiasm for the 'United Arab Kingdom'.

On 22 October 1975, when Rashad Shawa agreed to be reinstated by Israel as mayor, three years after he had been deposed, he undertook to 'maintain the Arab character of Gaza and not allow the management of affairs to be left to some ignorant Jewish officer'.[36] The nationalist faction gave Hajj Rashad the benefit of the doubt, acting as if they believed his appointment by the occupying power could be taken in the same spirit as the election of openly pro-PLO mayors in the West Bank six months later came to be viewed. In any case, Sheikh Khazandar's accession to the municipal council served as a tacit endorsement of Shawa on Fatah's part.

By 1976 Haydar Abdel Shafi's Red Crescent was fully operational as a sounding board for the nationalist movement in Gaza, and Yusra Barbari's General Union of Palestinian Women was also increasingly active, especially in the field of labour relations, though women made up only 10 per cent of the work force. Fayez Abu Rahmeh set up the Gaza Bar Association to improve legal assistance for political detainees; and Musa Saba set up a branch of the YMCA (Young Men's Christian Association), whose summer camps and current affairs seminars brought together Palestinians of all faiths. The events of the Lebanese conflict, including the siege and massacre of the Palestinian refugees at the Tall al-Zaatar Camp in August 1976, aroused intense feeling in the Gaza Strip. The violent confrontation at that time between Syria and the PLO brought about a belated reconciliation between Arafat and King Hussein. This new situation finally enabled Rashad Shawa to take a decisive step to reintegrate himself into the nationalist movement. In September 1977, along with Haydar Abdel Shafi, Fayez Abu Rahmeh and Yusra Barbari, he put his signature to a public appeal calling for the establishment of an independent Palestinian state in the occupied territories, under PLO leadership. The Jordanian option in Gaza had survived just five years.

Meanwhile …

Yet there was one political force in Gaza which had discreetly chosen to resume its links with Jordan in contrast to what was happening elsewhere in Palestine. This was the Muslim Brotherhood, which, decimated by Nasser's crackdown in 1966, had adopted a passive stance in face of the Israeli occupation. Sheikh Ahmed Yassin, paralysed since his youth as the result of a sporting accident in 1952, had emerged as the Brotherhood's leader and had imposed its low profile on its members. Yassin, born in 1936 in the village of Al-Jura, near the modern Israeli city of Ashkelon, had been brought up by his mother following his father's death when he was three years old, along with his six brothers. He had attracted a following of young disciples who had been brought up in the Gaza Strip's refugee camps. These included Abdelaziz Rantissi and Musa Abu Marzouk—both of whose families were originally from Yibna, but who had grown up in the camps at Khan Yunis and Rafah respectively—and they were soon joined by Ibrahim Maqadma and Ismail Abu Shanab. In a wheelchair since his youthful accident, Yassin, brought up in Shati Camp, had not enjoyed a prestigious education, having studied English and Arabic for only one year at Egypt's Ain Shams University. He was generally addressed as 'sheikh' in recognition of his austere way of life.

Yassin was the apostle in Gaza of the Egyptian sage Sayyed Qutb, the Muslim Brotherhood's 'martyr' who had been hanged in Egypt in 1966.[37] The paralysed sheikh, who was both a professor and an imam, expressed strong convictions regarding the situation of the Palestinians. In his view, the Palestinians had lost Palestine because they were not sufficiently Muslim—it was only by returning to the sources of their faith and to their daily duties as Muslims that they would ultimately be able to recover their land and their rights, a moral stance that was thus at odds with the nationalist position. Sheikh Yassin was of a similar age to Abu Iyad and Abu Jihad, both of whom were Palestinian refugees who had abandoned the Muslim Brotherhood in order to found Fatah, but was from a younger generation than Rashad Shawa and Haydar Abdel Shafi, Gaza's rival patriarchs. Now, he too was awaiting his hour, which he believed had come with the defeat of the fedayin.

On 7 September 1973, Sheikh Yassin opened the mosque of Jura al-Shams, not far from his home. In a significant gesture, the Israeli governor of Gaza, who had inherited the position of administrator for Islamic affairs from his Egyptian predecessor,[38] participated in the ceremony.[39] This was an important political act. The occupation authorities sought to promote a pietist tendency in Islam that would divert the Palestinian refugees from involvement with the PLO. Sheikh Yassin, for his part, did not deviate from the strict legalistic approach that he had already displayed with regard to the representatives of Egypt's President Nasser (the 'Pharaoh'). As he saw it, the new mosque should become the display case for the 'Mujamma Islamiyya' (the Islamic Collective), a new organisation that was meant to spread throughout the Gaza Strip, organising meetings and distributing literature, running playschools for infants, as well as providing educational support.[40]

Together with Sheikh Yassin and Abdelaziz Rantissi, the Mujamma was run by committed activists, including Mahmud Zahar, Ibrahim Yazouri and Abdelfattah Dukhan.[41] The intention of the Muslim Brotherhood was to take a long-term view, placing the emphasis on family and education in sympathy with the aspirations of ordinary people. The accent was put on the development of what was described as the 'thinking Muslim individual', with the rejection of 'politics: the language of lies and treason'.[42] Emphasis on the superiority of Islam enabled its ultimate victory over the Jews and other evil-doers to be envisaged, allowing the indignities of the military occupation to be forgotten. Gaza's expatriates in the Gulf, who had been inclined to back the nationalist position in the previous decade, now swung round to express their support, with conspicuous generosity, for the Islamic 'awakening' (*sahwa*).

In 1976 the Mujamma set up a Qur'anic school whose social and sporting activities went well beyond what was implied in its title. In the same year, the Muslim Brotherhood completed its provision of services by setting up a charitable organisation, The Islamic Association (*Al-Jam'iyya al-Islamiyya*), which was established by Ismail Abu Shanab, an engineer and one of Sheikh Yassin's earliest associates, with the help of an imam from Gaza, Ahmed Bahar.[43] This organisation also ran a dispensary in Shati Camp, organised by Khalil al-Qawqa, the imam of the camp's mosque.[44] In 1978, a similar organisation, the Association for Islamic Prayer (*Jam'iyyat al-Sala al-Islamiyya*), was set up in Deir al-Balah under the leadership of Ahmed al-Kurd, a UNRWA teacher. The political motivation behind this Islamist mobilisation was demonstrated by the fact that the only religious figures involved were the imams, Ahmed Bahar and Khalil al-Qawqa, as well as Sheikh Yassin himself. Of the others, Rantissi and Zahaar were doctors, Abu Shanab and Abu Marzouk were engineers, Yazouri was a pharmacist, Maqadma was a dentist and Al-Kurd was a teacher.

In 1969 the Muslim Brotherhood in Gaza numbered no more than fifty members,[45] but over time its numbers had grown. According to the Brotherhood's regulations, it was run by an Executive Council or 'bureau' of seven members, with a Consultative Council (*majlis al-shura*) representing the five areas of the territory, namely Gaza, Khan Yunis, Rafah, the Northern Region (including Beit Hanoun, Jabalya and Beit Lahya) and the Centre (comprising Deir al-Balah, Nuseirat and Maghazi).[46] Abu Marzouk took advantage of his studies in Egypt to maintain contact with the Muslim Brotherhood in Cairo, as did Rantissi, Abu Shanab and Maqadma, albeit to a lesser extent. The occupation of Sinai, however, made communications with Egypt difficult and obliged the Brotherhood to turn instead towards Jordan, which had become considerably easier to access since 1967. Sheikh Yassin's followers made connections with the Muslim Brotherhood in the West Bank, which was run as a subsidiary of the Brotherhood in Amman.

Jordan was the only Arab country at the time where the Muslim Brotherhood had complete freedom to operate, in return for which it offered its unreserved support to King Hussein against Nasser and the PLO. The Muslim Brotherhood had also given its blessing to Jordan's annexation of the West Bank in 1950. The Muslim Brothers in Jordan were largely Palestinian by origin, which acted to encourage ever closer collaboration with Sheikh Yassin's followers, while also making available to the Brothers in Gaza new contacts in Amman and further afield in the Gulf. Between 1969 and 1974, Fathi Shikaki, a student activist member of the Muslim Brotherhood at the University of Bir Zeit, who had been born in 1951 and brought up in the refugee camp at Rafah, helped to maintain links between the Brothers in Gaza and the West Bank.[47] The Muslim Brotherhood still had no official existence in Gaza and they refrained from grandiose statements that might have hampered them in building up their networks. Time was on their side, or at least that was what they believed.

The PFLP, in its murderous pursuit of Israeli 'agents' in Gaza, never confronted the Brotherhood. One reason for this was the fact that the Brotherhood did not collaborate directly with the occupiers. More specifically, however, the PFLP's strict focus on politics had the result that they failed to perceive the challenge that the Brotherhood's social activism represented. The relationship between the PFLP and the Brotherhood was not based on mutual tolerance or understanding but sprang from indifference and ignorance. This had the consequence that though the Brotherhood remained aloof from the resistance movements, no incident occurred to cast a cloud over the relationship between the nationalists and the Islamists during the first decade of the Israeli occupation. It was left to the far-sighted Haydar Abdel Shafi to perceive the rise in power of Sheikh Yassin's followers, on the basis of the reports he received from his Red Crescent contacts spread throughout the territory.

The struggle against the process of settlement was not a declared priority of the nationalists, since it seemed to be only a secondary manifestation of the occupation itself, and one which was limited in scale. By 1977 there were only four Jewish settlements in the Gaza Strip, all of which were Nahal settlements, whose numbers were limited and which were initially military in nature (Nahal is a Hebrew acronym from 'Fighting Pioneer Youth', and young Israeli volunteers could perform their military service in these settlements, which were attached to Tsahal). In contrast, in the West Bank, Golan and Sinai there were already forty-eight, twenty-five and twelve settlements respectively, of which only fifteen, or less than one in five, were

Nahal settlements. A Nahal was frequently the initial phase of a settlement that would in due course be transformed into a kibbutz or a moshav.[48]

The first settlement to be established in the Gaza strip, in August 1970, was in Kfar Darom, to the south of the Maghazi Camp, on the site of the former settlement that had been placed there in the 1946–8 period. The settlement, which regarded itself as having inherited the religious nature of the previous settlement, had no agricultural land. The next settlement, Netzarim, founded in February 1972 and situated to the south of Gaza on land confiscated from the Abu Middain tribe, was affiliated to the Herut movement and was only partly agricultural. The same was true of the following settlement, at Morag, set up three months later between Khan Yunis and Rafah. In May 1973 a new settlement appeared at Katif, between Deir al-Balah and Khan Yunis, with the long-term project of introducing agriculture under glass-houses. These scattered settlements had little impact on the population and the land of the territory, in contrast to the ambitious plans harboured by Ariel Sharon, whose goal was to divide the Gaza Strip into five sectors isolated from each other by Jewish settlements.

Although Moshe Dayan ceased to be Israel's minister of defence after the October War of 1973, his 'open door' policy continued well after he left office. The number of Gaza residents who worked in Israel, which at the height of fedayin activity in 1971 had fallen to less than 6,000, increased to 25,000 in 1973 and continued to rise to 42,000 in 1974 and 53,000 in 1977.[49] By this stage over half the salaried population of Gaza, where unemployment remained widespread, worked in Israel. Though the average wage of the Gaza workers was less than half that of their Israeli counterparts,[50] and workers from Gaza were unable to join or benefit from the Israeli Histadrut union, the relative prosperity produced by this massive transfer of workers into Israel nevertheless transformed the mentality in Gaza and the way of life.[51]

In contrast to the situation prior to 1967, where it had been a 'free zone' that was open to the Egyptian market, Gaza now became a captive market, where, for example, the proportion of Gaza's imports that originated in Israel rose from 72 per cent to 91 per cent between 1968 and 1978, while Gaza also provided a pool of unskilled labour for the benefit of the Israeli economy. The inhabitants of Gaza who were employed in Israel could be separated into three different categories. Only a third of them were hired through the nine official Israeli agencies that had been set up in the Gaza Strip, though a further third were in a working situation that was more or less legal as they paid social security contributions on their declared salaries. The final third, on the other hand, were illegally employed, paid in cash and hired through open air 'markets' that sprang into existence in the big Israeli towns.[52]

The fluctuations in relations with Jordan affected the export of citrus fruit from Gaza, as well as travel to the Arab world, which was no longer possible through Sinai, and it also had an impact on cash remittances from expatriates in the Gulf. The varying ways in which Gaza was dependent on circumstances intensified the vulnerability of the population and its sensitivity to regional developments, from which flowed a heightened awareness of political events that spread from the highest to the lowest social class. At the same time, the intensification of the indiscriminate maltreatment that had begun under the Israel occupation of 1956 prompted a common nationalist front to come into existence that included both the towns of the Gaza Strip and the refugee camps. While it was true that the leading figures of the civil resistance were drawn from among the notable citizens of Gaza, the residents of the camps also became involved with the only movements that remained active after the elimination of the last of the fedayin cells in 1973.

The first decade of Israel's occupation of Gaza can be divided into twin segments of comparable length. In the first, the period leading up to 1972, the PLO guerrillas grew in power and influence before they were eventually eliminated. The Jordanian option then emerged, which was resisted tooth and nail by the civil resistance and was finally eliminated in 1977.

The brutality of Israel's behaviour, which peaked in the summer of 1971, though it also continued after that date, had lasting consequences for the Gaza Strip. The nationalist movement was never fully to recover from such a bloodbath and it lost its leadership role to the West Bank, where the mayors elected in April 1976 mobilised the population in support of the PLO. The Muslim Brotherhood, meanwhile, took the opportunity afforded by the damage inflicted on the anti-Israeli resistance to build up its own structure and establish roots in Gaza. It would be Egypt, rather than Jordan, that was destined shortly to overturn the status quo in the Middle East.

10

THE ALIEN PEACE

Jimmy Carter, the Democratic president who took office in the United States in January 1977, was committed to a comprehensive solution of the Israeli–Arab question from the outset. He distinguished himself from his successive Republican predecessors, who, in the spirit of Dr Kissinger's 'shuttle' diplomacy, prioritised bilateral arrangements between Israel and its neighbours without ever taking the Palestinian dimension of the conflict seriously. In contrast to the previous Republican administrations, Carter spoke of the prospect of a 'homeland' for the Palestinians, thus using an expression redolent of the Balfour Declaration of sixty years before which endorsed the principle of a 'national home for the Jewish people'.

However, in May 1977 this new American vision was frustrated by the electoral defeat of the Israeli Labour Party, which lost control of the government for the first time since the country's independence. The new government was formed by the Likud bloc, the right-wing coalition led by Menachem Begin. The defence portfolio was taken by Ezer Weizman, Rabin's deputy, at the general staff during the war of 1967, while Moshe Dayan had quit the Labour Party to become Israel's new foreign minister in Begin's government. Ariel Sharon became minister for agriculture, where his intention was to promote Israeli settlement in the occupied territories. In particular, he intended to develop the implantations already planned south of the Gaza Strip close to the settlement of Yamit (set up in 1967), and the settlement complex known as the Rafah Heights (Pithat Rafiah) at the extreme north-east of the Sinai Peninsula.

165

Menachem Begin, as the new prime minister, abnegated all previous limits on Jewish colonisation within what he called the 'Land of Israel' (*Eretz Israel*); in other words, the full extent of Mandatory Palestine. Likud no longer spoke of the 'West Bank' but instead referred to this area as 'Judaea and Samaria', making it clear that what remained of Jordan (in other words, historical Transjordan) was henceforth to be the only conceivable Palestinian state. The so-called 'Jordanian option', favoured by the Israeli Labour Party since the enunciation of the 'Allon Plan', was therefore no longer available. On the other hand, Egypt's President Anwar Sadat, who had succeeded Nasser in 1970, still hoped to recover by negotiation Egypt's territory in Sinai that he had been unable to liberate by force of arms in October 1973. King Hassan II of Morocco was a confidential intermediary in the first contacts that were made between Israel and Egypt in the summer of 1977.

In the meantime President Carter continued to pursue his search for a comprehensive solution. On 1 October 1977, in a communiqué issued jointly with his Soviet opposite number Leonid Brezhnev, he said Israel should withdraw from the territories it had occupied in 1967 and that the 'legitimate rights of the Palestinian people' should be guaranteed.[1] This statement received a hostile reception in Israel. On 19 November 1977 Sadat, convinced that Egypt would obtain more in a bilateral process than from any kind of international conference, attempted to take matters into his own hands by making his celebrated visit to Jerusalem. In his speech before the Knesset he made a plea for the right of the Palestinian people to have a state of their own but did not refer to the PLO and made no mention of Gaza, though he did speak about the West Bank. In his response, Begin made no reference to any territorial concession within Eretz Israel. On 21 November, in Jerusalem, Sadat received a delegation of four Gaza notables, at the head of which was the mayor, Rashad Shawa. The meeting, however, was nothing more than a formality.

The Rejection of Camp David

Syria, Iraq, Libya and the Palestinian 'rejection front' immediately condemned Sadat's 'treason'. Yasser Arafat, however, waited for some weeks before making a similar statement. Before flying to Jerusalem, Sadat had suggested to Arafat that Egypt might be able to negotiate an Israeli withdrawal from Gaza, a proposal the PLO leader viewed as utterly unrealistic.[2] Arafat pondered the omissions in Sadat's Knesset speech, fearing he had been left on the sidelines by a historic development. A similar uncertainty was evident in December 1977 when Sheikh Khazandar, the imam of the mosque of Umar, assembled a group of Gaza personalities to go to Cairo as a delegation, a move which was undermined by the defection of many nationalist figures.[3] Arafat finally led the PLO into a stance of outright opposition to Egypt, which retaliated with the suspension of all the concessions that had been offered to Palestinian nationals. This was particularly damaging for students from the Gaza Strip as they were forbidden access to Egypt's universities, where 1,500 new Palestinian students had previously been enrolled each academic year.[4]

President Carter concluded that the PLO had excluded itself from the peace negotiations, in the course of which he spent much of 1978 attempting to assemble an Israeli–Egyptian agreement. In February, he received Sadat at Camp David, his country residence, followed by Begin in March. However, he was faced with an Israeli refusal to dismantle its settlements, including those in Sinai, as well as by Egypt's demand for concessions to the Palestinians, at least of a symbolic nature. In July Sadat put to Washington a plan for an Israeli withdrawal from the occupied territories, where security would then be provided by Jordan in the case of the West Bank, and by Egypt in Gaza, 'in cooperation with freely elected representatives of the Palestinian people'.[5] Begin rejected withdrawal from any part of Eretz Israel but agreed to the possibility of an autonomous Palestinian administration being created in the West Bank and Gaza. To break the deadlock the United States proposed that such an autonomous administration could be a temporary stage which would continue for five years, after which the definitive status of the Palestinian territories would be decided upon. This was the formula at the heart of the bitterly contested negotiations that took place between Carter, Begin and Sadat at Camp David from 5 to 17 September, which culminated in an agreement in two parts, one relating to peace in the Middle East and the other to a future Egyptian–Israeli treaty.

While the talks at Camp David were taking place, the magazine *New Outlook* organised an unprecedentedly frank Israeli–Palestinian conversation on 5 and 6 September 1978. In the presence of the 'doves' of the Zionist left and extreme left, and together with other personalities from the occupied territories, Haydar Abdel Shafi again pledged his allegiance to the PLO. 'We don't claim the PLO is the best leadership possible; nobody can claim anything of that sort. But the PLO is the Palestinian leadership. And I think it is a leadership that came about in a democratic way, under the circumstances.'[6]

Abdel Shafi asserted that he wanted to see the coexistence of an Israeli and a Palestinian state, noting however that there must be negotiation on the frontiers of Palestine. Such a future state, to be able to absorb the Palestinian population as a whole, should benefit from a right of return, and must not be limited to the West Bank and Gaza. But he immediately drew another consideration to the attention of his Jewish interlocutors. 'You claim that we seek a Palestinian State in the West Bank and Jordan as a step towards the violent destruction of the State of Israel. I think you are right to harbour such thoughts. You do not trust the Arab people.'[7] He nevertheless concluded that it was up to Israel to make historic concessions to placate the 'Palestinian sentiment of injustice.'[8] These arguments were far from convincing for the Israeli pacifists who attended the meeting, and such exchanges were the antithesis of what the Egyptians, Israelis and Americans were in the process of deciding upon at Camp David.

Sadat gained an agreement from Israel to withdraw from the whole of Sinai, though Israel insisted that the future of the Jewish settlements on Egyptian territory should be subject to a Knesset vote. Yet Begin made no concessions on the Palestinian issue, where the proposal at Camp David had been that there should be a 'self-governing authority' for a transitional period, to be installed by Israeli, Egyptian and Jordanian delegations, which might include 'representatives of the Palestinian people'.[9] King Hussein, who had not been represented at Camp David, refused to participate in any such process, and, speaking to the Knesset, Begin repeated his triple veto: 'There will be no referendum in Judaea, Samaria and Gaza, and on no condition will there be a Palestinian state. Thirdly ... the murderous organisation known as the PLO is not and will not be a factor in the negotiations.'[10] In these circumstances, the Palestinian section of the Camp David accords appeared to be severely compromised from the outset. Meanwhile, as a result of the Israeli–Egyptian process, the Gaza Strip, which had been part of the central command since 1972, again fell under the southern command of Tsahal.

In Gaza, the consensus on backing the PLO, which Haydar Abdel Shafi had persuaded even Rashad Shawa to support in September 1977, was more critical than ever after Camp David. From 16 to 18 October 1978, the chairmen of the Municipal Council in Gaza, and of the local Red Crescent, as well as the mayors designate, the mukhtars, presidents of the chambers of commerce and trade union leaders, and heads of various associations—in short everyone in the Gaza Strip with any pretension to a representative role—attended a meeting at the invitation of Musa Saba. The gathering, which was held at the YMCA, concluded with severe criticism of the Israeli–Egyptian text:

Autonomy, in the sense in which the word is used in the Camp David Accords, is devoid of meaning and content, as it does not measure up to even the minimal demands of the Palestinian Arab people, nor to their rights. Nor will it facilitate the proper exercise by this people of their right to liberty and self-determination. This is the result of the obscurity, ambiguity and complexity of the text.[11]

The impact of this 'national congress' was such that the Israeli governor, General Yossef Kastel, subsequently forbade all political gatherings in the Gaza Strip to prevent a similar event from taking place in the future. He also placed restrictions on the activities of the Red Crescent as well as those of other nationalist organisations. Tension in the territory grew, at the same time as Sadat was attempting to persuade Begin that he should install some semblance of devolved power in Gaza as soon as possible. This formula, officially known as 'Gaza first', took note of King Hussein's refusal to give his blessing to any kind of self-government in the West Bank. However, despite Egypt's insistence, it aroused no interest in Israel.[12]

Rashad Shawa exhorted President Sadat to accept nothing less than 'the realisation of our aspiration to establish an independent and sovereign state'.[13] Haydar Abdel Shafi, together with the mayors of Nablus, Hebron and Ramallah, participated in a 'National Orientation Committee' that opposed the Camp David process. On 26 March 1979 Begin and Sadat signed a peace treaty between Israel and Egypt in Washington. This in turn caused Egypt to be excluded from the Arab League, which moved its headquarters from Cairo to Tunis. The signature of the treaty was also the signal for a general strike and serious disturbances in the West Bank and Gaza. The PFLP accused Sheikh Khazandar of involvement with what they called the Egyptian 'conspiracy', and he was ultimately assassinated in Gaza on 1 June. The murder of such a prominent figure as the imam of the Mosque of Umar, who had failed to find protection either in his links with the Muslim Brotherhood or his commitment to Fatah, inaugurated a wave of violence towards admitted or supposed 'collaborators' with Israel.[14]

Though the resulting wave of intimidation and assassination did not reach the same intensity as that of 1970–1, it was enough to rule out all inclination to accept any kind of 'autonomy' offered by Israel. Rashad Shawa was open in his condemnation of what he called a 'trompe l'oeil' proposal under which the occupying authority would leave Gaza City simply to continue to control the formally self-governing administration from the neighbouring colony of Netzarim.[15] The Israeli plan failed in fact to materialise when negotiations with Egypt on the Palestinian segment of the Camp David Accords collapsed. But the backlash would be a lesson for the nationalist camp.

The Battle of the Crescent

In March 1979, President Carter's anxiety to see Begin and Sadat sign a treaty was especially keen because, a month earlier, the United States had suffered a major strategic defeat in the Middle East when Ayatollah Khomeini's Islamic Revolution in Iran had overthrown the regime of the Shah, an important US and Israeli ally. Many of the Islamist officials now in power in Teheran had been trained in the PLO camps in Lebanon, and Israel's embassy in Teheran, evacuated by its staff, had swiftly become the 'Embassy of Palestine'. Arafat was the first foreign dignitary to visit the victorious Khomeini, and the slogan 'Two Revolutions in One', following the public embrace between the two leaders, was taken up by the Palestinian activists.[16] Abu Iyad stressed this newly proclaimed fraternal relationship in order to improve the PLO's relations with the Shi'ite movements in Lebanon, while Abu Jihad, working from his Beirut base to boost Fatah's presence in the occupied territories, saw Islamic revolution as another opportunity to gain the upper hand in relation to the PFLP and the Palestinian communists.[17]

The Muslim Brothers of Gaza also regarded the fall of the shah as a welcome development, one which they viewed as a demonstration that Islam was able to achieve what the nationalists and the Marxists had failed to do since 1948.[18] The Brotherhood, structured as a single entity on both sides of the River Jordan, leaned on the support of its joint leadership in Amman[19] and was unconcerned by the break with Egypt. Sheikh Yassin, cautious as was his wont, refrained from overt criticism of President Sadat despite hoping to profit from the break with Cairo. The ban on students from Gaza attending Egyptian universities had already led to the opening of the first institution of higher education in the Gaza Strip, the Islamic University of Gaza, in which the Muslim Brothers intended to be fully involved. The founders of the Islamic University used the existing legally recognised framework of the local branch of Al-Azhar University, which had provided a basic education in Gaza up to the row over the Camp David Agreement. The funding for the new institution came from the Organisation of the Islamic Conference, based in Jeddah, from which Egypt had also been suspended, which provided an initial grant of 150,000 dollars.

Another unexpected consequence of the Begin-Sadat peace treaty was the official Israeli recognition of the Mujamma in September 1979, a movement which had until now been tolerated by the Israeli authorities. The Israeli governor, General Yossef Kastel, made this decision with the aim of countering the nationalist campaign against Camp David.[20] As a result, Sheikh Yassin's followers were able to fund their networks, to seek donations for their charitable activities and to distribute financial assistance within a legal framework. Abdel Shafi's Red Crescent, which the Muslim Brotherhood intended to take over, was now the only competitor to the Mujamma. However, the Brotherhood was aware that their resources were still insufficient to carry through such an ambitious plan, and they consequently sought help from former Brothers who had now become members of Fatah.

Assad Saftawi was one of the pioneer Gaza fedayin who had quit the Muslim Brotherhood in order to set up Fatah's local branch. He had been trained in clandestine activity by Abu Iyad and had managed Fatah in the Gaza Strip from 1968 to 1973 under the supervision of Beirut-based Kamal Adwan. One of the effects of Adwan's assassination by Israeli commandos was that Saftawi was apprehended and given a five-year prison sentence. After his release, Saftawi once again took up the role of Fatah's representative in Gaza, this time under the command of Abu Jihad, who, incidentally, had always refused to cut his links with the Muslim Brotherhood. At the same time as running Fatah, Abu Jihad was therefore providing discreet but substantial help to the 'jihad' launched by the Muslim Brotherhood in Syria against the regime of Hafez al-Assad. Fatah viewed this as revenge for the attacks carried out by Damascus against the PLO in Lebanon in 1976. The support base of the Syrian Brotherhood was in Jordan, and Abu Jihad's circles worked closely with the Jordanian Muslim Brotherhood, which opened up the possibility of similar joint action in the Palestinian territories. This process of cooperation would eventually come to an end with the crushing of the Syrian insurrection in Hama by Hafez al-Assad in March 1982. In Gaza, the murder of Sheikh Khazandar, which Fatah blamed on the PFLP, led to closer cooperation between Abu Jihad's followers and those of Ahmed Yassin. Muhammad Awad, the seventy-year-old imam who had become president of the new Islamic University, presided over this anti-progressive alliance in the name of the struggle against the 'atheists'.[21]

Saftawi, who was already a member of the executive committee of the Red Crescent, put himself forward for chairman of the association, though Haydar Abdel Shafi had hitherto been re-elected unopposed since 1972. In December 1979, the 4,000 members of the Red Crescent were asked to choose between two lists, one headed by Abdel Shafi, with the lawyer Fayez Abu Rahmeh as his number two, and the other headed by Saftawi, seconded by Ibrahim al-Yazouri of the Mujamma. The coalition of the Muslim Brotherhood and Fatah swung into action behind Saftawi, and after a vigorous campaign they believed success was within their reach. Yet when the votes were counted the outcome was a major victory for Abdel Shafi's list, which took seventeen of the twenty-one seats on the executive committee. Saftawi, backed by Yassin, lodged an allegation of electoral fraud, which, oddly enough, had to be brought before the Israeli Interior

Ministry, the body with formal responsibility for the management of associations in the occupied territories. This sparked off a crisis in the leadership of the Red Crescent, from which Saftawi resigned after accusing the 'communists' of diverting it from its proper course.[22]

On 7 January 1980 the activists of the Mujamma rallied their sympathisers and mounted a demonstration several hundred strong at the Islamic University, where Sheikh Awad exhorted them to avenge the insult. They set off in procession to the offices of the Red Crescent, which they looted, sacked and burned. Most of the books in the Red Crescent's library, including many Islamic texts, went into the flames. The demonstrators then spread out across the town, attacking cafés, video shops and retailers who sold alcoholic drinks. The Israeli army made no attempt to intervene except to protect Haydar Abdel Shafi's own house and to disperse groups of demonstrators who were trying to attack it.

The Red Crescent accused Israel of 'complicity' in the orgy of violence,[23] while the Islamists complained about the protection that the occupation authorities had afforded to Haydar Abdel Shafi. General Yitzhak Segev, who had just succeeded Yossef Kastel as governor, despite his reservations over whether his predecessor had encouraged Sheikh Yassin, was obliged to conclude that the latitude given to the Mujamma had sown the seeds of unprecedented trouble among the Palestinian militants.[24] Meanwhile, calm was far from having been restored. On 9 January 1980, the Muslim Brotherhood set fire to the local office of the nationalist daily newspaper, *Al-Quds*, before forcing the closure of a cinema, a bar and a billiard hall.

Sheikh Yassin's supporters, though they had failed to infiltrate the Red Crescent, no longer felt inhibited from the display of force in the interests of imposing their own ideas of social order. Even football matches were used as a stage for their battle between Islam and 'unbelief'.[25] They were also adamant that no rival opinion should be heard within the Islamic University, where Abdelaziz Rantissi and Mahmoud Zahar had taken senior positions. The growth in numbers of the university's staff, however, also reinforced the presence of the nationalists, who were therefore able to take seven of the thirteen seats on the Consultative Committee, the only university body not appointed by the administration. In February 1981, the leadership of the Islamic University arranged for the seven nationalists elected as members of the committee to be arraigned by the occupation authorities, which obliged them to resign.[26]

The campus staff, from the fifty college porters upwards, were recruited from among the affiliates of the Mujamma, which ensured the compliance of students with disciplinary standards that were more moralistic than academic. Gaza's only university became the rallying point for the Muslim Brotherhood's most active members. After ten years of patient networking in the refugee camps and the poorer areas, Sheikh Yassin's supporters now enjoyed the benefits of a prestigious location in the heart of Gaza City. The Mujamma was then able to diversify its activities into seven sections: proselytisation, social assistance, education, charity, health, sport and the arbitration of disputes. In 1981, the Muslim Brotherhood set up a highly active female youth branch, the Young Women's Muslim Association (*jami'yyat al-shabbat al-muslima*).[27] The more perceptive of the progressive activists understood that they had never been able to carry out social mobilisation on such a scale.[28] However, a major contribution to the success of the Islamists seems to have come from Israel's forbearance. As one activist put it, 'in Gaza, anyone who does anything the occupation disapproves of, even cleaning the streets for free, knows he will sooner or later be punished for it'.[29]

A Hard Right Turn

Over time, Menachem Begin's intransigence regarding the Palestinian issue led to the defection of those of his political partners who were most committed to the Camp David peace process. Moshe Dayan was the first to give up. In October 1979 he left the government and Yitzhak Shamir became the new minister of foreign affairs. On behalf of the Labour opposition, the Knesset member Avraham Katz-On, formerly administrator at the kibbutz of Nahal Oz, close to the Gaza Strip, proposed a complete change of direction in Gaza. His proposal, published in the newspaper *Yediot Aharonot*,[30] was that the settlements sited among Arab populations should be withdrawn and that the border be redrawn before sealing the land frontier, after which sovereignty should be handed to Egypt. Cairo would then be held responsible for any frontier incidents. This suggestion, being more or less similar to the prevailing regime before 1967, was immediately rejected by Likud, whose policy was the diametrical opposite: to encourage Israeli settlement.

On 7 January 1980 Menachem Begin met Anwar Sadat at Aswan in Upper Egypt, where Sadat made a vain attempt to revitalise the idea of 'Gaza first'.[31] Ezer Weizman resigned as Israel's minister of defence four months later, with the post then taken by Menachem Begin in a return to the practice of David Ben Gurion under which the prime minister also held the defence portfolio. This gave a greater role to the chief of staff, Rafael Eytan, who, as a parachutist commander, had led one of the bloodiest raids on Gaza in 1955 and had taken part in the conquest of the territory in 1967. Far from favouring emollient discussion on self-government for the territories, Eytan was a partisan of the hard-line approach. His philosophy was not so much to strike a targeted blow at the activists as to cow the population in general.[32]

Tension rose between General Eytan and the governor, General Segev, who believed in the need for dialogue and economic development in Gaza.[33] The commander of the southern region, which included the Gaza Strip, was General Dan Shomron, who carried some political weight as the commander of the successful Entebbe raid in 1976 when more than 100 hostages held by Palestinians were freed at Entebbe airport in Uganda in a commando operation. He refused to sack General Segev, and the affair went up as high as Begin himself, who met Segev five times. The prime minister made no secret of his agreement with Eytan and of his view that there needed to be change in Gaza. As he put it, 'We will annex Gaza, but it will not be in my lifetime.'[34] However, following Likud's victory in the August 1981 parliamentary elections, Ariel Sharon became minister of defence and his support for Eytan's tough approach finally resulted in Segev's removal from Gaza.

The position of governor was not subsequently filled, since on 1 December 1981, a month after a similar move in the West Bank, Israel put in place what it called a 'civil' administration in Gaza. In fact, Colonel Yossef Lunz was installed as governor: he had previously been the military governor in the West Bank where he had been a staunch supporter of the Israeli settlers. Rashad Shawa boycotted the new administration and on

2 December he called a strike of the municipal services. The strike came on top of another strike that had been called the previous week by Gaza's professionals (lawyers, doctors and others) in protest against a new Israeli tax. The occupation troops struck back by closing the pharmacies and other businesses belonging to anyone on strike, together with the imposition of heavy fines. The shooting to death of an eleven-year-old boy in a demonstration in Rafah on 7 December caused disturbances to spread throughout the Gaza Strip and led to the imposition of a curfew that lasted almost a week. The professionals' strike was called off on 16 December in return for the withdrawal of the new tax, although the municipal boycott of the new 'civil' administration continued.

Trouble broke out again in the spring of 1982 in coordination with the West Bank. A strike that began in Rafah on 24 March in protest against a military aggression was brutally suppressed. Then, on 11 April, when an off-duty Israeli soldier attacked worshippers at al-Aqsa mosque in Jerusalem, resulting in a large number of deaths, Palestinians responded with a general strike in solidarity with the victims. These events took a serious turn at the Islamic University in Gaza and in Jabalya refugee camp, where the activists began to use the Arabic expression 'intifada' to describe their uprising. On 4 May, Rashad Shawa suspended some parts of Gaza's municipal services. After two months of high-level confrontation, the mayor was deposed by the Israeli minister of the interior, who took direct charge of Gaza City's administration. Neither the 'civil' administration nor the idea of Palestinian 'self-government' had ever taken any concrete form. On the contrary, the transfer of Gaza's administration from the Ministry of Defence to the Ministry of the Interior had only served to further entrench the long-term nature of the occupation.

On 25 April 1982 Israel completed its withdrawal from Sinai, which was carried out in three successive stages after the signature of the Camp David Accords. Anwar Sadat, who had been assassinated six months earlier by an Islamist commando, was not there to appreciate the restoration of Egypt's territorial integrity, which was overseen by his successor, Husni Mubarak. It had not been easy for Begin and Sharon to compel their most extreme supporters to accept the withdrawal of the Israeli settlements in the northern part of Sinai. The evacuation of Yamit, the largest of these settlements, was a psychological battleground for Israel's annexationist right wing. In the end, the Israeli government physically dismantled the settlements before handing the region back, in an action that was received badly in Egypt.

Peace between Israel and Egypt entailed new problems for the residents of the Gaza Strip. The Israeli withdrawal once again rendered visible the line of the international frontier drawn in 1906, a frontier which had been largely theoretical under the British Mandate, the Egyptian administration and the Israeli occupation. The Rafah conurbation was henceforth divided between an Egyptian sector and a Palestinian sector, with barbed wire and fences. The Israeli army set up a monitoring operation along the so-called 'Philadelphia corridor', as the boundary strip along the Egyptian frontier was called.

More than 300 houses in Rafah camp were destroyed in the course of this process, with the transfer of the refugees to Tall al-Sultan, north of Rafah proper.[35] In the meantime some of the refugees who had been displaced during the summer of 1971 to the disused barracks left by the Canadian UN troops in Egyptian territory were moved once more, this time to Tall al-Sultan, while others remained in Canada Camp, and were therefore still in Egypt. The families that this process divided were now only able to communicate with each other by shouting across the barbed wire that marked the frontier. Israel only occasionally allowed repatriations from Canada Camp, and by April 1995, 293 of the original 496 families in the camp were still in Egypt.[36] Gaza's fishermen were meanwhile deprived of their traditional access to Egyptian territorial waters and were only allowed to work by day off Gaza's own short coastline.[37]

The destruction of the settlements in Sinai was accompanied by an upsurge in Israeli settlement activity in Gaza in April 1982. The ultra-nationalist yeshiva at Yamit, where there had been 120 students, withdrew to Gush Katif (the Katif bloc) since the Nahal (military) settlement established there ten years earlier, close to Khan Yunis, had developed into a complex of housing and a centre for economic activity involving 1,000 settlers and extending as far as Rafah and the Egyptian frontier. The military outpost at Nissanit, at the northern edge of the Gaza Strip, had also become a Nahal shortly after Sinai was returned, and was situated at the extremity of an Israeli settlement that had been created to receive settlers returning from Egypt.[38] Lastly, a Nahal was set up at Jabal Muntar, which strategically dominated Gaza City, on lands that had in part been expropriated from the Shawa family.

Though the Palestinian press harked back to the popular uprisings of 1955 and 1957 in their descriptions of the 'intifada' of the spring of 1982, the fifteenth anniversary of the Israeli occupation saw Gaza cast into a general atmosphere of gloom. The unanimous opposition to Camp David had been derailed by the ambitions of the Muslim Brotherhood, unwisely backed by Fatah. As Haydar Abdel Shafi was trying to recover from the destruction of the Red Crescent headquarters, it was his opposite number Rashad Shawa who took the lead in opposing the 'civil' administration, which in the event was effectively stillborn. Israel's Prime Minister Menachem Begin, and his minister of defence, Ariel Sharon, however, were unconcerned by this setback, as they believed they had discovered the formula that would enable them to bury Palestinian nationalism and to pacify the occupied territories. As Begin and Sharon saw it, the crushing of the PLO in Lebanon was the key to the entrenchment of Israeli domination in the West Bank and Gaza. After attempting to impose an alien peace in the occupied territories, a new vision for 'peace in Galilee' stemmed from the resolve to wipe out the Palestinian national movement in Lebanon.

11

THE NEW WAVE

On 6 June 1982 five Israeli divisions invaded Lebanon. As Menachem Begin explained in a letter he sent on the same day to US President Ronald Reagan, Israel's goal was 'to drive the terrorists 40 kilometres north'.[1] This, at least, was the excuse Begin offered both to Reagan and to France's president, François Mitterrand, who happened to be together at Versailles in the context of a G7 meeting. However, the true objectives of operation 'Peace in Galilee', as it had been designated, soon became apparent. The goal of Ariel Sharon, the minister of defence, was nothing less than the destruction of the PLO and the humiliation of Syria. On 8 June, the brigade led by General Yitzhak Mordechai attacked the town of Saida and the Palestinian refugee camp at Ain Hilweh, the largest in Lebanon. On 9 June, there was a major air battle between the air forces of Israel and Syria over the Beqaa, which compelled Damascus to accept a ceasefire forty-eight hours later. On 11 June, Israeli forces began to surround Beirut, where Yasser Arafat and thousands of PLO fighters were dug in.

This siege of an Arab capital by Israeli forces continued for two months, sending shockwaves throughout the entire region. The images and reports of the savage fighting in Beirut came to Gaza in the midst of the Israeli authorities' confrontation with the municipal administration of Rashad Shawa, who was ultimately compelled to resign. The people of Gaza were anxious to donate blood for the wounded in Beirut, which the International Committee of the Red Cross transported to Saida. On the other hand, the

Bank of Palestine, which had been authorised to resume its operations in Gaza in the previous year, was prohibited from sending financial donations to Lebanon. On 25 August, a grenade was thrown at an Israel vehicle in Gaza, without causing any injury.

On 30 August 1982 Yasser Arafat was evacuated from Beirut under French protection. Around 10,000 fedayin left Lebanon by sea, but only 1,000 of them accompanied Arafat, Abu Jihad and Abu Iyad to Tunis, where the Palestinian leadership now installed itself not far from the head-quarters of the Arab League.[2] The Gaza-born communist poet Muin Bseisso, with others from Gaza who faced death if they remained in Lebanon, also embarked on this journey into exile. On 1 September, President Reagan put forward a new plan for the settlement of the Palestinian question that would be based on a negotiated Israeli withdrawal from the West Bank and Gaza under which there would be an autonomous Palestinian entity linked to Jordan. This so-called 'Reagan Plan', which would have halted Israeli settlement in the occupied territories, was immediately rejected by Begin.

The massacres that Lebanese militiamen perpetrated in the Palestinian camps at Sabra and Shatila on 16 and 17 September sowed fear and revulsion. The Gaza hospital, in the Sabra Camp, which had already been in an exposed position during the siege of Beirut, now found itself at the heart of the carnage. In the Gaza Strip, the reaction was one of impotent rage though none dared accuse the PLO of having abandoned civilians to their worst enemies. The Israeli opposition blamed Begin and Sharon, and on 25 September 400,000 protestors marched through the streets of Tel Aviv. An official commission of inquiry set up soon afterwards concluded that Israel's responsibility for the bloodbath in Sabra and Shatila was indirect but that Ariel Sharon should bear personal responsibility.[3] Though he rallied the settlers in his support, Sharon was obliged to resign as minister of defence but remained in the government as minister without portfolio. The chief of staff, Rafael Eytan, was also found responsible. He, however, had in any case come to the end of his military career and went on to establish a new extreme right-wing party, Tzomet.[4]

THE NEW WAVE

The Rise of Extremism

The PLO had strived to salvage its own honour through the evacuation of its fighters in good order from Beirut, but the massacres in Sabra and Shatila disturbed even its most faithful supporters. In Gaza, the Muslim Brotherhood drew what advantage it could from the situation, and in January 1983 it took 51 per cent of the votes in student elections at the Islamic University.[5] Since the Islamists already controlled the administration, the support staff and a large section of the teaching staff, they now held almost complete control over the university—those students who did not concur with their idea of moral order were subject to intimidation, and were occasionally also subject to violent assaults.[6] Fatah, which belatedly realised that its activists were no more exempt than the communists in this Islamist cleansing process, attempted to regain the upper hand. This was the cause of the collective brawls that took place on the campus in June 1983 in which dozens were wounded.[7] The Muslim Brotherhood were nevertheless able to maintain supremacy within the Islamic University in Gaza and went on to send busloads of their 'Islamic Bloc' supporters to the West Bank campuses, and in particular to Bir Zeit, to challenge the militant nationalists there.[8]

This deleterious atmosphere was aggravated further by the internal 'dissidence' (*inshiqaq*) that tore Fatah apart in the refugee camps in eastern and northern Lebanon. The dissidents, led by one of Fatah's military leaders, Abu Musa (Said Musa al-Mughara), were openly supported by President Assad's Syria, whose prime goal was to reassert his power inside the territory of Lebanon and also in the Palestinian political sphere. Arafat and Abu Jihad, who had secretly returned to Lebanon to put down this internal revolt, were gradually driven back from Beqaa before being finally surrounded in Tripoli in the autumn of 1983. This time, thousands of loyal fedayin were besieged by the Syrian army, assisted by Fatah dissidents fighting alongside pro-Iranian militiamen.

Although George Habash's PFLP maintained a position of neutrality in this conflict, the PFLP-General Command (PFLP-GC) led by Ahmed Jibril took up arms against Arafat's supporters. Ahmed Jibril was a Palestinian serving as an officer in the Syrian army who had been a founder member of the PFLP in 1967 but subsequently split off to set up his

'General Command', which remained outside the PLO. Fighting raged across Tripoli in November and December 1983, under bombardment both by Syria's artillery and by the Israeli navy offshore. In the end, Arafat and his supporters were evacuated for a second time, once again under French protection. Upon being extracted from the net that was tightening around him in Lebanon, he went to Egypt to see President Mubarak in order to settle the feud that was sparked by the Camp David treaty. Arafat also announced that he had decided to move forward together with Jordan in a peace initiative.

Though well received in Gaza and the West Bank, these approaches were condemned by Damascus and its Palestinian supporters. Yitzhak Shamir, who had become Israel's prime minister in October 1983 after Begin's retirement from political life, was as strenuous as his predecessor in refusing to have any dealings with Palestinian nationalism. Likud and the Labour Party were similarly at one in refusing all dialogue with the 'terrorists' of the PLO. The occupation authorities made a particular scapegoat of one of the early adherents of the PLO in Gaza, Abdelaziz Shahin, known as Abu Ali. He had already spent fifteen years in prison from 1967 and 1982, but was put under house arrest in a Bedouin village and threatened with expulsion.[9] In February 1985, he was finally deported to Lebanon.

The wait-and-see policy of the Muslim Brotherhood and the crisis inside Fatah led to the emergence of a small nucleus of activists in Gaza who combined Islamist commitment with anti-Israeli principles. This was the 'Islamic Jihad', led by Fathi Shikaki, who, as a medical student from Rafah, had served as a link between the Muslim Brothers in Gaza and the West Bank ten years earlier. After moving to Egypt he took up jihadist extremism, modelling his ideas both on the Islamic Revolution in Iran and on the group who had murdered President Sadat. Now a renegade from the Brotherhood, he returned to Gaza to work as a doctor, but also secretly set up the movement for Islamic Jihad in Palestine (*harakat al-jihad al-islami fi filastin*), known as Palestinian Islamic Jihad (PIJ).[10] This movement is to be distinguished from a separate Islamic Jihad founded in 1980 in Amman (*harakat al-jihad al-islami: beit al-maqdis*) by Sheikh Assad Bayud al-Tamimi, who was celebrated for an apocalyptic pamphlet prophesying the inevitable disappearance of Israel. ('*Beit al-Maqdis*', 'the house of sanctity', refers to the city of Jerusalem.)[11]

One of Shikaki's leading supporters was Sheikh Abdelaziz al-Awda, who had been expelled from the Muslim Brotherhood in 1974 after an internal inquiry headed by Ibrahim Maqadma, an associate of Sheikh Yassin. Another of Shikaki's followers was Ramadan Shallah. Both were teachers at Gaza university, and both had been educated in Egypt, Awda in Islamic sciences and Shallah in economics. Shikaki argued that the Muslim Brotherhood's order of priorities should be reversed, since, as he put it, 'the Palestinian cause is the central cause of the Islamic movement',[12] and the latter should therefore be at the service of the former. For the PIJ national liberation consequently took priority over social re-Islamisation.

The murder of an Israeli civilian in the market at Gaza on 10 March 1983 was followed by reprisals against Arab workers in the Negev town of Netivot. It also brought about a change of emphasis for the Israeli intelligence services. Hitherto focused on the PLO, they now began to pay more attention to Islamist fringe movements and homed in particular on the inflammatory sermons that Awda and Shallah tended to deliver to students along with their courses. Awda also preached in Gaza City, in the Anan mosque close to Shati camp, and at Beit Lahya in the Ezzeddin al-Qassam mosque, named after the celebrated Syrian jihadist who lost his life in 1935. In the same spirit of homage, for a long time the favoured pseudonym of Fathi Shikaki was Ezzedin al-Faris (Ezzeddin the Knight). The Israelis estimated that there were several dozen activists and a larger number of sympathisers for what they called a 'Khomeinist' movement.[13] In August and September 1983, there was a wave of arrests of those linked to the PIJ. Shikaki was imprisoned for a year, while Awda and Shallah were banned from teaching and put under house arrest for 'incitement to violence'.[14] The PIJ's own propaganda claimed the movement was the only true heir of a tradition of anti-Israeli resistance that went back to Ezzedin al-Qassam and the origins of Fatah.[15]

In April 1984 a major incident took place for which the PFLP was responsible. On 12 April 1984, four PFLP fighters from Gaza seized an Israeli bus carrying forty passengers to Tel Aviv. The hostage-takers, armed with knives and threatening to detonate a bomb, drove the captured bus to Deir al-Balah where they demanded the release of hundreds of Palestinian prisoners in exchange for the freedom of the hostages. Moshe

Arens, Israel's minister of defence at the time, Moshe Levi, the chief of staff, and Avraham Shalom, the director of Shin Bet, all went to the scene of the incident. At dawn on 13 April, an elite unit of Tsahal, led by General Yitzhak Mordechai, stormed the bus. One Israeli soldier and two of the hostage-takers died in the operation.[16] The two other Palestinian activists, it later emerged, were beaten to death by Shin Bet, with Mordechai and Shalom each blaming the other for the summary execution. Israel's President Chaim Herzog would later put an end to the affair by granting an amnesty in 1986 to all the Shin Bet agents involved. At the time, following the customary procedure of collective reprisal, the houses of the four PFLP militants were destroyed by Tsahal.

Although the PFLP headquarters in Damascus claimed responsibility for this incident, Israel blamed Fatah with the aim of compromising the talks between Yasser Arafat and King Hussein of Jordan. The PFLP, unable to take further action against Israel, resumed its policy of eliminating those it accused of being 'agents' of Israel, an activity George Habash had always insisted was legitimate. On 25 October 1984, the PFLP took responsibility for bullet wounds inflicted on Abderrahman Darabaya, a Gaza resident accused of collaboration with the Israelis. The previous month, Abdelhamid Kishta, who had been appointed mayor of Rafah by Israel, had been murdered by masked assassins. On this occasion the PFLP maintained its silence, no doubt hoping to evade the outbreak of a blood feud in this southern area of the Gaza Strip where tribal custom and the practice of the 'blood price' continued to be more observed than elsewhere in the territory. Southern Gaza was also a hotbed of smuggling across the Egyptian border: the new mayor of Rafah installed by Israel, Suleiman Zurub, was sacked after only a couple of months when he was accused of drug smuggling.

The Sheikh in Prison

Ahmed Yassin had drawn substantial benefits from his strategy of remaining within the law. The official authorisation Mujamma had received in 1979 had enabled it to develop its social and financial network. For example, in 1981 and 1983 it took five of the eleven seats on the board of the doctors' association.[17] Its supporters controlled the Islamic University in

Gaza, and they had no hesitation in physically assaulting Sheikh Awda.[18] In addition, many of the private mosques in the Gaza Strip were under their control (under the Egyptian administration, only ten of the seventy-seven mosques active in Gaza were privately run while seventy out of the seventy-eight mosques constructed under the Israeli occupation were in private hands).[19] Israel's attitude to the construction of mosques was illuminated by a remark made by Abdelaziz Rantissi's brother. As he put it, 'at the time, the Israelis believed that the faith could make us forget our rights to our land'.[20] The Mujamma also strengthened its links with the Jordanian branch of the Muslim Brotherhood, which ran the Islamist organisations of the West Bank and controlled access to Islamist sympathisers in the Gulf and the sources of funds they represented.

Such external support was crucial if the Mujamma was to occupy the ground left vacant by the PLO, which had been weakened by the loss of its base in Beirut and the funds to which this gave it access. Sheikh Yassin enjoyed active support from the executive leadership (Political Bureau) of the Jordanian branch of the Muslim Brotherhood in Amman, one of whose officials, Yusuf al-Azm, went to Gaza in April 1983 to help with the expansion of the Mujamma.[21] At the same time, another leading Jordanian Islamist, Muhammad Saqr, became president of the Islamic University in Gaza, defeating the Fatah candidate for the post, Riyad al-Agha, despite the fact that the latter was a member of one of the most influential families in Khan Yunis.[22] As a Muslim Brotherhood activist said at the time, 'the problem was having devoted too much time to the armed struggle to the detriment of the ideological struggle. The people were suffering from a spiritual vacuum and had to rediscover their awareness of Islam in order to fill the void created by the occupiers', adding that, 'the left wing activists were sick people [whom we] needed to care for'.[23]

Sheikh Yassin's supporters kept up the tension in Gaza City. On 18 March 1984, dozens of masked Islamists broke up a party at the Samer Cinema where licentiousness was alleged to have been taking place. This was an irony since the same cinema had been the venue where the founding conference of the local Muslim Brotherhood had been held in 1946, a fact of which Sheikh Yassin's men were doubtless unaware. Despite many people being injured, no complaint was made to the security services. On

21 April 1984, aggressive intolerance reached a new level when the mausoleum of the Prophet Muhammad's great-grandfather in the Daraj area of the city came under attack. Islamist activists alleged that the customary pilgrimage to the tomb of Hashim was reprehensible idolatry of a pagan figure. The sacrilege involved was all the more irksome because of the habit of Islamic chroniclers over the centuries of referring to the city as 'Hashim's Gaza'. Sheikh Yassin's faithful, however, adhered rigidly to their 'Salafist' convictions: respect was to be accorded solely to the two first generations of Muslims, *al-salaf al-salih*, literally, 'the pious ancestors'.[24] But such violence also increased the numbers of the Mujamma's enemies, which in turn led the organisation to accumulate an armoury of guns against the possibility of confrontation with other Palestinian factions.[25] The official history of Hamas's security, published in Gaza in 2009, records that, by 1983, 'the major concern arose from the competition from other Palestinian forces'.[26]

The reaction of the occupation authorities to the activities of the Muslim Brotherhood was ambiguous. Some viewed the Brotherhood as a highly useful counterweight both to the PLO and to the jihadist tendency, whereas others condemned the growing prevalence of the Islamists and their brutal methods.[27] On 13 June 1984 the latter view prevailed when Shin Bet raided Sheikh Yassin's residence and some sixty pistols and submachine guns were discovered in a nearby mosque. Two months later, the sheikh was sentenced to thirteen years imprisonment, a heavier sentence than those of his supporters who were arrested alongside him (Ibrahim Maqadma, for instance, only received an eight-year sentence). The sheikh appointed Abdelaziz Rantissi and Ibrahim al-Yazouri to stand in for him at the head of the Mujamma. Recruitment to the Islamist cause was boosted by anger at the treatment of the sheikh, whose prestige and charisma were enhanced. The sheikh's sentence also enabled the Mujamma finally to give the lie to the accusations of collusion with Israel that other Palestinian factions had levelled at it.

In the event Sheikh Yassin was only to remain in detention for less than a year. His name was at the head of a list of detainees to be freed that was conveyed to Israel by Ahmed Jibril's PFLP-General Command, the implacable adversary of Yasser Arafat's PLO, in exchange for the liberation of three Tsahal soldiers captured in Lebanon in 1982. The exchange of prisoners took place under the aegis of the International Committee of the Red Cross on 20 May 1985. Israel freed 1,150 prisoners, of whom 605 were released in Israel and in the occupied territories. Sheikh Yassin received a triumphal welcome when he returned to Gaza. Though he had been obliged to agree not to resume his role in the Mujamma, he retained his position at the heart of the Islamist movement, whose rise in Gaza appeared to be unstoppable. He also ran an extensive support network outside Gaza, whose key activists were Musa Abu Marzouk (one of his earliest disciples who was now based in Egypt), as well as Ibrahim Ghosheh and Khaled Meshal, both of whom travelled between Jordan and Kuwait.

The Jordan–Palestine Interlude

Rashad Shawa did not abandon the idea of pursuing a new political initiative even after he had been deposed as mayor of Gaza in July 1982. What alarmed him was the potentially catastrophic result both for Gaza's economy and for its population if nothing was done. In January 1984 he went to Tel Aviv to meet the leadership of Mapam, an opposition group to the left of the Israeli Labour Party. Two months later, Rashad Shawa addressed the Labour Party conference in Jerusalem, which was, however, more concerned about the outcome of the impending parliamentary elections than about the fate of Gaza.[28] In practice, the elections of July 1984 inaugurated the laborious process of constructing a coalition between Likud and Labour, which in a novel arrangement was to be led for the first two years by Shimon Peres for Labour and then by Yitzhak Shamir for Likud. Mapam rejected this arrangement and broke its electoral alliance with Labour.

Yasser Arafat, meanwhile, continued to pursue his rapprochement with King Hussein, and, significantly, it was in Amman that the next Palestinian Political Council (PNC) was held from 22 to 29 November 1984. The session was boycotted by the PFLP and scorn was poured on it by the pro-Syrian 'dissidents'. However, it gave the PLO chairman a mandate to reach an agreement with Jordan. On 11 February 1985 Arafat and King Hussein agreed on a programme of 'common action' during a meeting in Amman. In future peace talks, a joint Jordanian–Palestinian delegation would participate in anticipation of the formation of a confederation between Jordan and a future Palestinian state. Rashad Shawa's name was inevitably mentioned as a participant in such a delegation, and it was in light of this that he was received by France's President Mitterrand the following month.[29]

Yet the two elements of the governing coalition in Israel were resolute in their refusal to deal with the PLO. The Labour minister of defence, Yitzhak Rabin, went further when, on 21 March 1985, as he visited Jewish settlers in the Gaza Strip, he asserted that the territory should remain 'an inseparable part' of the State of Israel.[30] Two months later, when Sheikh Yassin was freed, many Gaza-based militants who were equally opposed to the PLO's compromise were also liberated. Opposition to Yasser Arafat, and calls for the resumption of the armed struggle against the occupiers, were soon to begin again in earnest,[31] though such grenade attacks or attempted ambushes as in fact took place were almost all without effect.

In this context, informal discussions on the Palestinian element in the putative future joint Palestinian–Jordanian delegation seemed to be increasingly divorced from the realities on the ground. In early June 1985, an initial list of nine Palestinian personalities including Rashad Shawa was circulated. In mid-July, a different list of only seven names was approved, in which Rashad Shawa no longer featured with Fayez Abu Rahmeh representing Gaza in his place. The choice of the 'Lawyer for the Palestinian Revolution', the founder of the Gaza Bar Association and a long-term colleague of Haydar Abdel Shafi in the Red Crescent, met with approval in nationalist circles, especially as Abu Rahmeh was careful to declare both his allegiance to the PLO and his commitment to non-violence.[32]

Inside the Israeli government, the Jordanian option, dear to Shimon Peres, was passionately opposed by Shamir, and a fortiori by Sharon. Though the former minister of defence now held the industry portfolio, he nevertheless insisted that the PLO must be fought relentlessly on every front. From August 1985 onwards, Rabin instituted what he called his 'iron hand' policy in the occupied territories, endorsed by the Israeli government on 4 August, and resumed Israel's deportation of Palestinians to Jordan and Lebanon.[33] On 25 September 1985, the murder in Cyprus by a Palestinian guerrilla group of three Israelis on board a leisure craft prompted the Labour leader to strike a blow of unprecedented severity against the PLO. On 1 October, two squadrons of F-16 fighters bombed the offices of the Palestinian leadership in the southern suburbs of Tunis, killing seventy-three people including twelve Tunisians. The raid encouraged extremist reprisals and undermined efforts to construct a joint Palestinian–Jordanian initiative, whose failure was acknowledged by King Hussein some months later, putting an end to Jordan's efforts at 'common action' with the PLO.

Glory and Guns

In Gaza, the resultant political blind alley led to an increase in anti-Israeli activism and to tensions between the Palestinian factions. On 1 January 1986, Fatah mustered its supporters to celebrate the twenty-first anniversary of its first guerrilla actions. The occupation authorities responded by imposing a curfew on the entire Gaza Strip. On 18 February, five soldiers of an Israeli patrol were wounded in a grenade attack, and two weeks later a remote-controlled bomb was detonated, though without causing any casualties. On 27 September, Fatah claimed responsibility for the killing of an Israeli settler who had been stabbed in the marketplace in Gaza. A second settler was murdered in similar circumstances on 7 October, resulting in anti-Arab reprisals by the settlers. The following day, the minister of housing, David Levy, visited to Gaza to announce the establishment of further settlements. On 19 October, an Arab labourer from Gaza was stabbed in Ashdod. In general terms, all 40,000 Gaza inhabitants working in Israel paid a heavy price for the upsurge in violence.

Fatah's return to militancy led to growing tension with the supporters of Sheikh Yassin. The Muslim Brotherhood had already accused Fatah of having murdered Ismail Khatib, a professor at the Islamic University of Gaza, on 17 November 1984.[34] On 18 May 1986 there was an exchange of fire between Fatah and the Brotherhood, with the Islamists accusing the nationalists of not strictly observing the fast of Ramadan. The Muslim Brotherhood, rather than accusing Fatah directly, turned against its favourite scapegoat, the 'communists'. On 26 June, the deputy head of the doctors' union, Rabah Mohanna, who was well known as an official of the PFLP, was beaten up in the street. Both his legs and one of his hands were broken. On this occasion, Fatah took the side of the Palestinian left wing and incidents spread like wildfire across the entire Gaza Strip. On 1 July, the Israeli 'civil' administrator, General Yehoshua Erez, summoned 100 of Gaza's religious dignitaries to make an appeal for calm.[35] The nationalists and Islamists refused to call off their mutual settling of scores until a meeting was held at the headquarters of the Gaza Bar Association the following day.

Sheikh Yassin, who took the view that this was only a truce, immediately decided to furnish the Mujamma with a clandestine security apparatus, the Organisation for Jihad and Preaching (*munazzamat al-jihad wa al-da'wa*), which was known by its Arab acronym 'Majd' (literally, 'Glory'). The stated objective of this apparatus, which was the first armed organisation to be set up by the Muslim Brotherhood, was to counter Israeli attacks and to deter Shin Bet.[36] The suppression of collaborators, however, would soon provide Majd with a plausible excuse for violence towards other Palestinian factions and also for the forcible suppression of 'vice', including alcohol, drugs, prostitution and pornography. Salah Shehada, the official responsible for student affairs at the Islamic University, became the head of Majd.[37] Despite its rhetorical designation of Shin Bet as its adversary, the Palestinian enemy within remained the clear priority of the Muslim Brotherhood.

Fatah and Palestinian Islamic Jihad, on the other hand, remained in the front line against Israel. Their activism brought them numerous recruits but also made them the target of the occupying power's 'iron fist'. In March 1986, Fathi Shikaki, the political head of PIJ, was arrested and sentenced to four years in prison, leaving only Sheikh Awda as the public face of Islamic Jihad (Ramadan Shallah had left the Islamic University in Gaza to continue his studies in economics in the United Kingdom). In December, a series of grenade attacks against Israeli patrols led to the arrest of some fifty members of Palestinian Islamic Jihad.

This group in fact exercised an increasing attraction for young radicals, as the trajectory of three of them demonstrates. Misbah Suri and Abdurrahman al-Qiq came over to the PIJ from the PFLP, while Imad Saftawi was the son of a staunch Fatah man, Assad Saftawi, who had organised Fatah's rapprochement with the Muslim Brotherhood before being attacked by Sheikh Yassin's supporters. Yet on the Fatah side others remained loyal. Muhammad Dahlan, a refugee from Khan Yunis, where he had set up Fatah networks, had already been jailed a number of times and was deported to Jordan in

January 1987. His expulsion sparked off troubles across the Gaza Strip in which one demonstrator was killed in front of the Khan Yunis mosque. Dahlan became a member of the PLO delegation in Baghdad and was then ordered by Abu Jihad to come to Tunis to take charge of liaison between the PLO and the activists in the 'interior' of Palestine.

From February 1987, agitation became endemic in the Gaza Strip. The Islamic University was regularly closed and on occasion even the secondary schools joined in the disturbances, with demonstrations that involved stone throwing and setting tyres ablaze. Frequent arrests of students and school pupils led to solidarity strikes to demand their release, while collective punishments, such as the demolition of houses, bans on the exercise of professions and arbitrary fines, simply fed the protests rather than putting a stop to them. The punishments inflicted were certainly very heavy: ten to fourteen years in prison, for example, for four teenagers accused of having thrown stones and Molotov cocktails in a sentence handed down by the military tribunal of Gaza[38] (in comparison with just thirteen years in prison for Sheikh Yassin himself when he was arrested in 1984). But punishments such as these had begun to lose their deterrent effect. Arrests were so numerous that the central prison in Gaza was full, leading to the opening of a new detention camp called Ansar-2 to take the overflow. (Ansar had been the name of the principal internment centre opened by the Israelis in southern Lebanon, though there had been room for 5,000 prisoners in the original Ansar detention camp in 1983 as against only 250 in Ansar-2 in 1987.)[39]

At the same time, Yasser Arafat, in his headquarters in Tunis, was still trying to bring all the nationalist factions together under Fatah's umbrella. This process was formalised at the next PNC session in Algiers on 20 April 1987. This session of the Palestinian parliament in exile was boycotted only by the unaffiliated factions based in Syria, foremost among which was the PFLP-GC headed by Ahmed Jibril. In contrast, George Habash's PFLP and the DFLP run by Nayef Hawatmeh joined the PLO executive committee, its supreme governing body. Arafat even went as far as to co-opt the three PNC members from the administration of the Islamic University of Gaza, thus bringing Islamic figures into the fold who had previously subscribed to Sheikh Yassin's rejection of the PLO. These three were Abdallah

Abu Azza, Abdurrahman al-Hourani and Salim Amin al-Agha, of whom the latter was the only one who had previously been a member of the PNC. All three denied their previous membership of the Muslim Brotherhood, even though this was what Fatah had emphasised in order to stress the importance of their recruitment.[40]

On 18 May 1987, six Islamic Jihad activists, including Imad Saftawi, Misbah Suri and Abdurrahman al-Qiq, escaped from Gaza prison. Over the following days, only one was recaptured. On 25 May, Fatah claimed responsibility for the death of an Israeli businessman who had been killed in Gaza for hiring female workers. On 31 May, Jewish settlers roamed the streets of Gaza City, firing into the air and throwing stones at houses. The Israeli army tried to avert direct confrontations between the settlers and the population. Yitzhak Shamir, who had replaced Shimon Peres as prime minister under the terms of the agreement on national unity made after the election, paid a surprise visit to Gaza on 25 June. He was accompanied by General Yitzhak Mordechai, the commander of Israel's southern military region, whom the Palestinians regarded as having been responsible for the devastation of the camps in South Lebanon five years earlier.

On 2 August 1987 Islamic Jihad ambushed and killed an Israeli officer, Ron Tal, who was in charge of security at Ansar-2. Yitzhak Rabin, as minister of defence, immediately went to the scene with Dan Shomron, now the chief of staff. Rabbi Meir Kahane, an extreme right-wing agitator, exhorted his supporters to go to Gaza to call for the expulsion of all the Palestinian inhabitants. Tsahal imposed a three-day ban on entry to Gaza, which was placed under a curfew. Jabalya Camp, the largest in the Gaza Strip, was subsequently enclosed by a barbed wire fence. Israeli employees of the 'civil administration', moving in groups and shunning the most frequented roads, were anxious to leave Gaza before nightfall.[41]

The nationalist organisations secretly coordinated their efforts, with Zakarya al-Agha representing Fatah, Rabah Mohanna the PFLP, Jamal Zakout the FDLP and Fadel Burnou the Communist Party.[42] This reflected the new make-up of the PLO leadership, where left-wing groups were included together with Fatah. All the factions were intensely concerned about the possibility of infiltration by Israel and of confrontations that could lead to bloodshed. Tsahal, for its part, tightened the rules of engagement for its units. On 1 October 1987, three Palestinians were killed at a roadblock, allegedly because they had not stopped soon enough. Two of the victims were notables who were known to be politically inactive. The identity of the third was not disclosed until later: this was Misbah Suri, the former PFLP militant, now a member of Islamic Jihad, who had been on the run for four months.[43]

On 6 October 1987 there was a vicious clash between an Israeli patrol and an Islamic Jihad guerrilla group in the heart of Gaza City in which a Shin Bet officer and four Palestinians were killed. The Palestinians included two of those who had escaped from prison in the spring. Two days later a general strike had spread throughout the Gaza Strip and a bus full of Israeli tourists was attacked. The imposition of a curfew brought new protests, this time led by women from the Shujahiyya area. On 19 October, three buses sent to bring workers from Gaza to Israel were burned. On 9 November, a Jewish settler, at whom schoolchildren had thrown stones at Deir al-Balah, chased some young girls and killed one of them, Intissar al-Attar, aged seventeen, in the courtyard of her school. An Israeli court released the murderer on bail.[44] A week later Sheikh Awda was arrested and threatened with deportation. This was enough to arouse a reaction from a much wider section of the public than the supporters of Islamic Jihad. The sheikh was defended in court by Fayez Abu Rahmeh.

The Muslim Brotherhood stayed out of this activity, going as far as to clash with the supporters of Islamic Jihad on the campus in Gaza. Sheikh Yassin declared that, for a Muslim, membership of Fatah was as sinful as the consumption of alcohol or pork.[45] His supporters expended a vast amount of effort in entrenching themselves in whatever positions of power they were able to hold. The student elections at the Islamic University in Gaza were conducted in separate polls in the men's and women's colleges. In early December 1987, the Mujamma took the majority of the seats in the two colleges, with 75 per cent of the women's votes and 60 per cent of the men's.[46] The Islamist activists, preoccupied with their procedural manoeuvres, were taken by surprise when violence erupted in Gaza. On 6 December, a Jewish shopkeeper was stabbed in the open street in Gaza. Two days later, on 8 December, four Palestinians were killed when they were hit by an Israeli truck, in an accident that was taken as an act of reprisal for the previous murder.[47]

On 9 December 1987, the funerals of three of the victims, from Jabalya refugee camp, attracted thousands of demonstrators. The three men were Shaaban Nabhan, Ali Muhammad Ismail and Issam Hamouda. The fourth victim, Taleb Abu Zeid, was a refugee resident in Maghazi Camp. The protestors defied the Israeli soldiers, pelting them with stones, to which the Israelis responded by firing directly at the crowd. A fifteen-year-old boy, Hatem Sissi, fell with a bullet through the heart. The rioting spread from Jabalya Camp to the whole of the Gaza Strip. The occupying forces went into the principal hospital to seize wounded suspects, while incidents also broke out in Rafah, Khan Yunis and the other camps and a curfew was imposed and frequently renewed, without effect. The troubles spread to the West Bank and began to be described as an intifada, the Arabic word for uprising.

Sheikh Yassin convened the leadership of the Mujamma at his residence. The attendees included Abdelaziz Rantissi, Ibrahim al-Yazouri and Salah Shehada, as well as Abdelfattah Dukhan from Nuseirat and Issa Nashar from Rafah.[48] This was a bad period for the Muslim Brotherhood. They had been spat at during the funeral of Hatem Sissi, who was declared to be the first martyr of the intifada: their lack of action against Israel had become insupportable. But the majority of the Mujamma officials still believed that it was too early to confront Israel while the balance of power was tilted in Tsahal's favour. Ahmed Yassin, however, ordered his Islamist supporters to adopt a nationalist position. Within a week, Israel's reprisals in Gaza had led to half a dozen deaths and a large number of wounded.

On 14 December 1987 the Muslim Brotherhood in Gaza finally called for a struggle against the occupation. Though the text in which this call was made would later be cited as Hamas's founding document, the name 'Hamas'(which means zeal, enthusiasm, fervour or even exaltation) was not used. 'Hamas' is an acronym for the Arabic title, *harakat al-muqawama al-islamiyya*, (Movement of the Islamic Resistance), in whose name the 'intifada of our people' would be waged.[49] The option of resistance had already been chosen by those dissident Muslim Brothers who had departed to join Fatah in 1959. In 1987 Sheikh Yassin's authority was sufficient to transform the Mujamma into Hamas, with the change in ideology this entailed, without dividing the organisation itself.

In the five years from Israel's resumption of direct administration of the Gaza Strip to the outbreak of the intifada, three complex and tragic developments occurred which had important implications for the territory's population. The first of these was the internal Israeli political debate. After the 1984 elections, a national unity government was formed in which Rabin's 'iron fist' policy was consistent with the hard-line demands of the right wing. Second, there were the disagreements inside Gaza between the Palestinian factions, with polarisation between the nationalists and the Muslim Brotherhood against the background of Islamic Jihad's increasing influence. Finally, there was the issue of the PLO's tribulations outside Palestine, in Lebanon and Tunisia, with an inter-Palestinian reconciliation in 1987 that excluded the pro-Syrian dissidents.

However, while these political and ideological developments preoccupied the attention of observers, major changes were also taking place within the Gaza Strip itself. The first of these pertains to Gaza's demographic situation: the population of the Strip had increased to more than half a million inhabitants, and a majority of Gaza's residents were now young men and women with no knowledge of any situation other than the Israeli occupation. By 1987, the UN estimated Gaza's population at 650,000 inhabitants, of whom 59 per cent were under nineteen years of age (Israeli sources give lower figures). The Strip, which had seen its geography transformed by the *nakba* (the Catastrophe) of 1948–9, and the establishment of the refugee camps on a permanent basis, had seen its population more than double since that period. Urban areas expanded into the remaining green spaces, beginning with the loss of the date palm oases. The continual construction work even swept away the orchards that had been carefully developed under the Egyptian administration. The density of the population, meanwhile, placed an increasing amount of strain on Gaza's available public resources.

The relative prosperity that had been inaugurated in the 1970s by the opening up of the Israeli labour market subsequently gave way to a widespread and onerous culture of dependency. Half of Gaza's population continued to work in Israel, in construction rather than in agriculture or industry, and these workers were the object of discrimination in terms of salaries and working conditions. Citrus exports continued to decline, exacerbated by the closure of the Iranian market after Iran's Islamic Revolution and by the restrictions put in place both by Israel and by the Arab countries (ironically, this was in pursuit of the boycott of Israel).[50] Such small-scale local industry as had previously existed remained underdeveloped, not least because of regulations that protected Israeli businesses and their markets.[51]

Finally, the stress resulting from Israeli settlement activities was increasingly apparent. The fourteen settlements that existed by 1987 still comprised only 2,500 settlers, most of them in Gush Katif in the area of Khan Yunis.[52] Each settler, however, had 400 times as much land at his disposal as a Palestinian refugee and twenty times more water than a peasant farmer in the Gaza Strip.[53] This predatory intrusion in a region already overexploited strengthened yet further the solidarity between the towns and the refugee camps, both of which were faced by the same rapacity. The intifada was ultimately sparked by the shooting of the teenager Hatem Sissi by an Israeli soldier, only a month after the killing of the schoolgirl Intissar al-Attar at Deir al-Balah on 9 November 1987, who was shot by a settler. Both these adolescents were born under the occupation, after the fedayin movement had been suppressed, and had grown up under the shadow of Israeli settlement and the 'iron fist'. These two were thus typical of the young people who would give the intifada in Gaza its unique character.

1987–2007

THE GENERATION OF THE INTIFADAS

12

THE REVOLT OF THE STONES

On 9 December 1987, the intifada began. It spread like wildfire from its origins at Jabalya Camp to the rest of the Gaza Strip before igniting the West Bank. This nationalist uprising in the occupied territories aroused the passions of the frustrated youth, who challenged the troops of the occupying forces with nothing more than stones. The Israeli government intensified its 'iron hand' policy, taking a heavy toll among the stone throwers. Strict curfews and collective punishments were imposed in a futile bid to stop the nascent movement. The PLO called for the intervention of an international force to protect the Palestinian population, and though the UN Security Council stopped short of endorsing this suggestion it nevertheless passed Resolution 605 on 22 December (with the abstention of the United States), which 'strongly deplores those policies and practices of Israel, the occupying Power, which violate the human rights of the Palestinian people in the occupied territories'.

Israel's Foreign Minister Shimon Peres publicly declared his preference for the demilitarisation of the Gaza Strip, with a freeze on Israeli settlement, adding somewhat unexpectedly that security should be provided by the Jordanian police force. This formula was rejected by Prime Minister Yitzhak Shamir as well as by the minister of defence, Yitzhak Rabin. Although Rabin was also a member of the Labour Party, he was much more of a hawk than Peres. In the Gaza Strip, the four Palestinian parties which had placed their cooperation on a formal basis in August 1987

(Fatah, the PFLP, the DFLP and the Communists) set up the Unified National Command for the Uprising (UNCU). UNCU's members were in the first instance Ihab al-Ashkar (aged twenty-five) for Fatah, Marwan Kafarna (thirty-two) for the PFLP, Jamal Zakout (thirty-one) for the DFLP and Tawfiq al-Mabhouh (forty-one) for the Communists. Israeli action had the consequence that there needed to be repeated changes in the composition of the committee. UNCU declared its allegiance to the PLO and called for 'international protection for the Palestinian people'.[1]

UNCU, which was represented at the local level by 'popular committees', organised civil resistance in the form of demonstrations and strikes in the Gaza Strip and the West Bank. Funerals for victims of Israeli counter-action were often the occasion for new clashes, setting off a cycle of violence that tended to increase popular involvement rather than reducing it. UNCU called for boycotts of the occupation authorities: the public was asked to refuse to pay taxes, officials were told to resign from their posts and workers were called on to refuse any work in Israel. Its communiqués began with the slogan: 'No voice takes precedence above the voice of the intifada.'[2] The PLO's leadership in exile added its weight to the demands made by UNCU and created a system of formal cooperation between Tunis, the West Bank and Gaza, under the authority of Abu Jihad.

National Disobedience

On 3 January 1988 Yasser Arafat declared that the PLO would 'not resort to armed action during the intifada'.[3] There was a broad consensus between the various elements of the Palestinian leadership that the intifada must not become an armed movement, echoing the position already taken by a wide range of nationalist associations and groups. Islamic Jihad, whose spectacular attacks had punctuated 1987, also suspended their armed operations.[4] Sheikh Yassin was unable to call for armed jihad even if he had wished to as the Muslim Brotherhood had only recently adopted 'Islamic resistance', while its armed wing, Majd, remained small.

The objective of the Palestinian leadership and the various nationalist groups was to create a balance of power that was more political than military in order to compel the occupiers to withdraw. This was a dramatic change for a national movement that had previously celebrated the symbol of the fedayin's gun. In an 'unarmed' variant of the Molotov cocktail, the activists of Nuseirat Camp began to use a bottle filled with excrement rather than petrol, which became known as the Kharatov cocktail (*khara'* means 'shit' in Palestinian Arabic).

Yet despite the consensus on preventing the intifada from becoming an armed movement, the Israeli forces continued to use live ammunition against protestors, as well as rubber bullets which, although purported to be more suitable for crowd control, have a metal core that can be deadly in the case of direct fire. The occupiers' violence attracted increasingly severe criticism from the international community, including the Western countries. On 4 January 1988, David Mellor, the deputy British foreign minister, speaking in Gaza, said that the treatment being inflicted upon the population was 'an affront to the values of civilisation'.[5] A correspondent for the French newspaper *Le Monde* spoke of 'vistas of desolation' across Gaza City.[6]

On 13 January 1988 the eight refugee camps across the Gaza Strip were placed under a week-long curfew, which included a ban on the movement of the UNRWA trucks that brought in food aid. At Jabalya Camp, which had been declared to be a closed military zone, this collective punishment was maintained for a week. Between December 1987 and January 1988, twenty-six of the forty-one Palestinians killed by Israel were in Gaza. On 8 February, the European Economic Community (the EEC) condemned what it referred to as 'violations' of human rights and international conventions in the occupied territories. On 24 February, President François Mitterrand declared that the 'daily slaughter', as he called it, 'had become truly unacceptable'.[7]

But this did little to dissuade Shamir and Rabin from taking even tougher action. Israel had dismantled the Gaza branch of UNCU by mid-February with the arrest of Jamal Zakout among others. Even the Muslim Brotherhood was not exempt, as was illustrated by the imprisonment of Abdelaziz Rantissi, the deputy head of the Mujamma, and of Khalil al-Qawqa the head of the Islamic Association. Despite international disapproval Israel increasingly used deportation as a weapon. The leaders of Islamic Jihad were expelled to Lebanon: Sheikh Awda was deported on

201

11 April, together with Qawqa, and then four months later Fathi Shikaki himself was compelled to depart. With a nod to the dismal celebrity of the Gaza City detention centre known as 'Ansar 2', Israel's Ketziot prison in the Negev came to be known as 'Ansar 3'. Before the spring of 1988 had come to an end, more than 2,000 Palestinian detainees were held in Ketziot, usually without trial.[8] There was still insufficient room for all the prisoners, however, and an 'Ansar 4' was consequently set up in Rafah to absorb the victims of the round-ups and the house-to-house searches.

Despite the grass-roots character of this uprising, Tsahal continued to believe it could halt the intifada by eliminating the PLO official responsible for the affairs of the occupied territories. On 16 April 1988, an Israeli commando group was infiltrated into the northern suburbs of Tunis to assassinate Abu Jihad, who died after being hit by sixty bullets in front of his wife and his children. But far from calming the uprising, this only provoked an upsurge of violence both in Gaza and in the West Bank. Seven Palestinians aged between fourteen and twenty-two were subsequently killed in a single day in the Gaza Strip,[9] the population of which responded by raising black flags and displaying PLO emblems throughout the territory.[10] Once the forty days of mourning (the *arba'in*) for Abu Jihad had been completed, the troubles broke out again in a militant display of respect in which even the Islamists became involved. Respect for the memory of the 'martyr Abu Jihad' and his sacrifice became a dominant theme of nationalist propaganda.

The occupation authorities then attempted to dismantle the system that the leadership of the resistance used to disseminate its instructions. These efforts began with a prohibition on the ownership of fax machines. The authorities then closed all of the printing works in the Gaza Strip, giving them permission to re-open only on a case-by-case basis, with the result that UNCU, and later Hamas, were obliged to commission its printed material from the West Bank. But this also presented difficulties because transit between the two Palestinian territories was strictly controlled. The 'green line' of 1967, between Israel and the occupied territories, which twenty years of the 'open door' policy had sought to erase, returned between Israel and the Gaza Strip, where the only point of entry was now the closely supervised Erez crossing. In the absence of printed material, nationalist instructions were henceforth painted on the walls despite severe Israeli reprisals against individuals whose houses were marked with such graffiti. The Israelis also put out fake communiqués themselves, with the aim of spreading confusion or causing dissension between the Palestinian factions.

'National disobedience', to use the expression of UNCU's leaflets, continued to be the order of the day in the Gaza Strip. Officials resigned by the dozens, including many policemen. It was hard to boycott Israeli products, given Gaza's economic dependence on Israel. Yet the practice of refusing to pay tax to the occupying authority was widespread. In May 1988, the Shamir government responded with the imposition of new identity cards for the Gaza Strip that were only issued once evidence had been provided that taxes had been paid. Two months later, the obligatory renewal of licence plates on cars was similarly used to check the payment of tax and to extract what was overdue. UNCU in turn responded by increasing the number of days of action and with calls for 'total' or 'general' strikes, though the Communist activists expressed certain reservations due to their fear of exhausting the population of Gaza, which was facing relentless pressure from activists and the military alike.[11]

On 31 July the intifada achieved its first victory when King Hussein formally severed the ties between the two banks of the River Jordan under which he had continued to assert Jordanian sovereignty over the West Bank. The king declared that the future of Palestine was henceforth for the Palestinians to decide. Although Amman's disengagement largely concerned the West Bank, it also consigned to history the 'Jordanian option' which Shimon Peres continued to believe was still a possible route towards a resolution of the status of Gaza. The leading protagonists of this option in Gaza itself had in any case already changed their views: Rashad Shawa, who had been one of its leading supporters for many years, had abandoned his previous position on the issue in order to become part of the nationalist consensus, and by this stage he had lost much of his standing in the eyes of the new intifada generation—after Israel had removed him from the position of mayor in Gaza in 1982 he had devoted himself to charitable works and the cultivation of his personal circles. On 28 September 1988 Rashad Shawa suffered a heart attack and passed away. With his death, a chapter of Gaza's history came to a close. Despite the limited public profile he had maintained in the years prior to his death, his funeral became the occasion for a nationalist demonstration that was violently broken up by the occupying troops. His daughter, Rawya Shawa, pointedly refused to acknowledge Shimon Peres and Yitzhak Rabin when they came to offer their condolences.[12]

Hamas Against the State

The formal severance of the two banks of the River Jordan had the unanticipated consequence of accelerating Hamas's progress in installing a formal institutional structure. Sheikh Yassin's movement, which had been established on 14 December 1987 as the result of a schism in the Palestinian branch of the Jordanian Muslim Brotherhood, declared its affiliation to Hassan al-Banna and to the mainstream Muslim Brotherhood in February 1988.[13] However, on 18 August 1988 it went a stage further with the promulgation of a 'Charter' which was intended to be viewed as an alternative to the Charter of the PLO.[14] In contrast to the position of classical Islamic jurisprudence, which had regarded Palestine as an integral part of the 'land of Islam' since the time of the crusades, Hamas asserted that the entire territory of Palestine was a *waqf* (an Islamic bequest), and was therefore inalienable.[15]

In contrast to the PLO Charter, which was first endorsed by the Palestinian National Council (PNC) in 1964 and then amended in 1969, Hamas's Charter was simply imposed on the movement by Hamas's founder and chief, which, in the authoritarian tradition of the Muslim Brotherhood, accepted it without any opposition. The document is representative of the eschatological vision of the Islamist militants, for whom confrontation with the 'Jews' is inevitable and divine victory is guaranteed. The text is steeped in conspiratorial language according to which international Zionism's historic links with freemasonry enabled it to manipulate 'the French revolution, the communist revolution and most other revolutionary upheavals'.[16] This polymorphous enemy was now accused of causing the First and Second World Wars and subjecting the League of Nations and then the United Nations to its control in order to realise its plan to seize the territory of Palestine.[17]

This kind of rhetoric was intended to emphasise the 'purity' of Hamas's stance in comparison with the compromises that the PLO had made. Sheikh Yassin's movement, which had complied with the strike calls issued by UNCU until this point, subsequently established its own calendar of action and threatened punishment for any 'collaborators' who failed to respect it. Numerous clashes ensued in the Gaza Strip. On 30 August 1988 the nationalists retaliated by denouncing what they regarded as 'Hamas's attempt to impose its supposed predominance'.[18] Tension rose throughout the occupied territories until Arafat held talks in Cairo with the supreme guide of the Egyptian Muslim Brotherhood, Sheikh Muhammad Abu Nasr, on 2 September. The summit issued a call for reconciliation with which Sheikh Yassin complied, as a result of which Hamas abandoned its own calendar of action and again began to call for strikes on the same dates as those declared by UNCU. Yet relations between the nationalists and the Islamists still remained tense: on 10 September 1988, the Arabic service of Israeli TV broadcast an interview with Sheikh Yassin which was strongly critical of the PLO.

But this divergence of views within the resistance did not impede the momentum that the intifada had generated in the direction of the proclamation of a Palestinian state. The nationalists of Gaza and the West Bank pressed the PLO leadership to launch a diplomatic process that would culminate in Israel's withdrawal from the occupied territories. The PNC session scheduled for 12–15 November in Algiers was expected to be the occasion for the first move towards such a historic breakthrough. The Israeli authorities ordered Gaza's schools to close for the week in which the session took place. UNCU openly demanded that the PLO should commit itself to the proclamation in advance by declaring 15 November to be Palestine's 'independence day'.[19] The entire Gaza Strip was placed under curfew two days before this date. When the day came, the PNC voted by 253 against forty-six in favour of an Israeli withdrawal from the occupied territories in the West Bank and Gaza and called upon the United Nations to establish an interim mandate. The 'State of Palestine' was thus proclaimed, and it was soon to receive recognition from some forty nations. In Gaza, UNCU celebrated the realisation of the 'dream of every free Palestinian'.[20]

On 13 December 1988 Yasser Arafat addressed the UN General Assembly, which had convened in Geneva due to the US refusal to grant a visa to the chairman of the PLO. Arafat's recognition of Israel on this occasion finally persuaded the United States to open an official dialogue with the Palestinian leadership. However, the concessions Arafat had made were condemned by George Habash's PFLP, which had already voted against the resolutions passed by the PNC in Algiers. The PFLP, thus finding itself in opposition, made overtures to Hamas in a historic change of direction that made a lasting impression in Gaza. In a remarkable turn of events, Sheikh Yassin's faithful followers, who had previously demanded the 'liberation of all Palestine',[21] found themselves joining with a group of long-standing left-wing Palestinian nationalists to condemn a plan to achieve an independent state in the West Bank and the Gaza Strip.

The first year of the intifada ended with an especially high toll of dead and wounded in the Gaza Strip. Whereas 142 Palestinians had died, not a single Israeli had been killed in the territory. Seventy-seven Palestinians fell to gunfire and thirty-seven died after inhaling teargas (most of whom were older people and very young children or infants who are especially vulnerable to this kind of attack). Seventeen lost their lives after being beaten by Israeli soldiers or police, nine were killed in traffic accidents that may have been deliberate and two died in detention, their bodies bearing the marks of torture.[22] The Gaza Strip emerged from this period of twelve months scarred and impoverished. Never, on the other hand, had the ambition for a sovereign Palestine appeared to be nearer to fulfilment.

A Futile Eighteen Months

Despite the PFLP's evident bid for control, Yasser Arafat was determined to maintain the intifada's commitment to a non-armed strategy, in which the prospect of an early diplomatic breakthrough by the PLO could even lead to an agreement with Israel. Hamas's leaders had also made contacts with Israeli Labour ministers during the early months of 1988. Mahmoud Zahar, for instance, has acknowledged that he met Shimon Peres on 23 March 1988 to propose a tacit recognition of Israel in exchange for its withdrawal from the territories occupied in 1967. Similar exchanges with Yitzhak Rabin have never been confirmed. However, in the period that followed Hamas chose to abandon these contacts and instead emphasised the clear distinction between its stance and that of the nationalists, thereby keeping to the position adopted by the Mujamma in 1973. As the PLO was making preparations for a permanent agreement with Israel, Sheikh Yassin was consequently banking on the failure of the peace initiative. Though he maintained his commitment to Hamas's political and social functions, he also decided to initiate a programme of armed action against Israel. Due to the fact that Salah Shehada and Yahya Sinwar, the two chiefs of Majd, Hamas's internal security service, were both in prison, Hamas secretly set up a new apparatus known as Unit 101, headed by Mahmoud al-Mabhouh, whose modus operandi was the abduction of Israeli soldiers.

On 16 February 1989, led by Mabhouh, Unit 101 crossed into Israel and kidnapped an army sergeant, Avi Sasportas, who was hitch-hiking back to his home in Ashdod. Sasportas was killed shortly afterwards and his body was buried. In Israel his disappearance was initially regarded as a mystery. On 3 May, Ilan Saadoun, another Israeli sergeant, was kidnapped and executed by the same group.[23] While searching for Saadoun, Tsahal units found the body of Sasportas, which in turn prompted an extremely violent Israeli response against Hamas. Hundreds of Hamas leaders and activists were arrested, including Sheikh Yassin himself and Mahmoud Zahar. Sheikh Yassin admitted that he had authorised the execution of collaborators with Israel but denied all responsibility for the abduction of Sasportas and Saadoun.[24] His desire to protect Hamas's political wing from suspicion of involvement in the kidnappings led him to refuse any prisoner exchange, and in fact this seems likely to have contributed to the tragic outcome of the incidents.[25] Mabhouh evaded arrest by fleeing to Egypt. He would meet his end in Dubai on 20 January 2010 when he was killed by Mossad agents (he had earlier been subject to three failed assassination attempts in Lebanon and Syria).

Much of Hamas's structure had been dismantled as a result of the Israeli response, including Unit 101. Musa Abu Marzouk travelled back to Gaza from Louisiana, where he was studying for a doctorate, in order to rebuild the Islamist organisation.[26] Abu Marzouk, who had been one of Sheikh Yassin's earliest supporters, had been involved in channelling the support the Mujamma received from Egypt over a long period. With the assistance of Sayyid Abu Musamih he divided the Gaza Strip into five administrative sectors, each with three heads of department responsible for security, activities and propaganda respectively.[27] Internal procedures were tightened up, with senior officials no longer being able to evade the chain of command by making direct contact with individual activists. The basic organisational unit on the ground continued to be the 'section' (*usra*, literally 'family').

Abu Marzouk returned to the United States once his mission had been accomplished. This was the first time in the history of the Islamist movement in Gaza that the 'exterior', which had hitherto always been subordinate to the 'interior', had intervened at the heart of the organisation. It was a turning point for Abu Marzouk, as well as for his associate Khaled Meshal, who had been travelling between Jordan and Kuwait to promote Hamas's interests.[28] The external support structure, dating from the days of the Mujamma, grew in size and importance after the incarceration of Sheikh Yassin and his principal collaborators, a process which ultimately culminated in the creation of a Hamas 'Political Bureau' abroad. This 'Bureau' inherited the powers of the 'Executive Council', which previously constituted the collective management of the Muslim Brotherhood in Gaza. Hamas also began to expand the scope of its operations with the creation of four separate 'shura' councils for Gaza, the West Bank, the Palestinian diaspora and for prisoners held by Israel respectively (the Mujamma had previously operated within the Gaza Strip alone, with five consultative councils (*majlis al-shura*, plural: *majalis al-shura*)). These four councils were in due course placed under the authority of the Political Bureau.[29]

The intifada continued in Gaza while these changes were taking place inside Hamas, with a rhythm of strike days and popular demonstrations, each met by Israeli counter-measures and collective punishments. In the course of the initial 500 days of the uprising, Shati Camp was placed under curfew for 190 days, Jabalya was closed for 164 days and Rafah was closed for between 122 and 137 days, depending on the zone involved. Deir al-Balah was placed under curfew for 116 days, and Khan Yunis for 105 days. Gaza City also suffered, with forty days of curfew in the Shujahiyya area.[30] General Matan Vilnai, who took over as Tsahal's southern commander in June 1989, persevered with Israel's 'iron fist' policy: the houses of those regarded as terrorists were demolished, schools from which stones had been thrown were shut and the families of activists were targeted. After two years of the intifada, sixty-eight children under sixteen years of age had been killed in the Gaza Strip. Children were 40 per cent more likely to die a violent death in the territory than in the West Bank.[31]

The violence Israel inflicted on Gaza was accompanied by an increase in the murders of so-called collaborators, which was reminiscent of the settling of accounts that took place in 1970–1. Out of every ten Palestinians killed during the intifada, it has been estimated that eight lost their lives as the result of Israel's actions while the remainder were murdered by their compatriots. The brutal circumstances of these murders, some of which were perpetrated by the PFLP and Hamas, as well as Fatah, often led to protest strikes.[32] The major losers from these internecine struggles were the nationalists of civil society who had hoped to find an escape from factional conflict through the intifada, but whose professional associations now became subject to inter-party rivalries.

Inside the Gaza Strip, the savagery of Israel's reaction alongside the mounting internal discord became ever harder to bear, especially as the goal of an independent Palestine increasingly appeared to be vanishing from sight. There was now a striking lack of substance in the dialogue conducted in Tunis between the United States and the PLO leadership. Israel's Prime Minister Yitzhak Shamir did not retract his plan for elections to be held in the West Bank and Gaza under the framework of autonomy envisaged at Camp David, but he specifically excluded the PLO from participation. In October 1989, James Baker, the US secretary of state, made a bid to break out of the stalemate with the proposal of an Israeli–Palestinian dialogue in Cairo that would not be limited to issues related to the elections.

Yasser Arafat, who had been agitating for Egypt's re-inclusion in the Arab League, as well as the return of the League's headquarters to Cairo after its ten-year absence, made it known that he endorsed the choice of Egypt's President Mubarak as a mediator. Shimon Peres, with the support of Yitzhak Rabin, also supported an active role for Egypt and proposed that Palestinians exiled from the occupied territories could be included in future discussions in Cairo. Shamir accused him of wanting to bring the PLO into the negotiations, which contributed to the collapse of the national unity government of Likud and Labour in March 1990. Shamir, who remained prime minister, was subsequently able to construct a new right-wing government in which Ariel Sharon regained the housing portfolio and hence responsibility for settlement policy.

On 20 May 1990 the murder of seven day-labourers from Gaza on the outskirts of Tel Aviv led to violent disturbances across the occupied territories. A month later, Washington declared that the PLO had failed to fulfil its commitments in the struggle against terrorism and suspended the dialogue between the United States and the PLO leadership.

The Road to Madrid

On 2 August 1990 the news of Iraq's invasion of Kuwait reached the Palestinian population. To a large section of Arab public opinion, Saddam Hussein appeared to be a new Salah ad-Din, passionate to restore Arab national rights, or even a modern-day Robin Hood, set to distribute the wealth of the Gulf to the Arab world's poorest. This fateful blindness to the cynical reality of the Iraqi dictator's objectives brought cheering crowds into the streets across the Middle East, from Amman to Sanaa. In the Gaza Strip the effect was if anything even more pronounced owing to the distress of the people. Arafat decided that a trade-off between Kuwait and the occupied territories was the only way to unblock the Palestinian stalemate. He declared his support for Baghdad, despite warnings from his faithful lieutenant, Abu Iyad, the second-in-command in both the PLO and Fatah, who had limited confidence in Saddam Hussein.

In Gaza, UNCU took an unreservedly pro-Iraqi line, matching the popular feeling in the territory. Hamas adopted a more balanced view, condemning both the invasion of Kuwait and Saudi Arabia's appeal for American forces to come to its aid. On 8 October 1990, the Israeli police ruthlessly put down a demonstration on the Haram al-Sharif in Jerusalem (the Temple Mount), causing the deaths of twenty-two Muslims, which was followed by bloody clashes throughout the occupied territories. While the PLO continued to call for its supporters to refrain from the use of arms, Hamas made no secret of its determination to exact vengeance for Palestinian victims. On 14 December two Hamas militants from Gaza stabbed three Israeli workmen to death in Jaffa. The two assassins went underground, where they joined hundreds of other *mutaradun* (fugitives), a term denoting respect for the most resolute activists.[33]

On 14 January 1991, Abu Iyad was murdered in Tunis by a mole who had been infiltrated into the Palestinian security services, possibly at the instigation of Iraq. Arafat subsequently lost his ability to control the consequences for the PLO of his support for Saddam Hussein. Abu Iyad's death left Arafat as the sole survivor of the original group who had founded the PLO, all of them fedayin originally from Gaza. Kamal Adwan and Yusuf al-Najjar had been killed by Israeli agents in Beirut in April 1973, and in 1988 an equally brazen operation had resulted in Abu Jihad's death in Tunis. Arafat had never been so isolated, and this was at a juncture when the PLO was suffering one disaster after another.

Arafat's financial supporters in the Gulf, with Saudi Arabia at their head, were the first to punish him for his support of Saddam Hussein by suspending their payments to the PLO. Hamas, which had never supported Saddam Hussein, also saw its budget curtailed, albeit to a lesser extent. In September 1990, Khaled Meshal returned permanently from Kuwait to Jordan, while Musa Abu Marzouk was allowed by the Jordanians to remain in Amman, which had now become the seat of Hamas's Political Bureau.[34] From 17 January 1991 onwards the Iraqi positions in southern Iraq and Kuwait were bombed and shelled by a US-led coalition as part of operation 'Desert Storm'. On 24 February, the land operation to liberate Kuwait was launched from Saudi Arabia, freeing the country in less than five days.

With the Iraqi occupation over, reprisals against Palestinians in Kuwait who were accused of having collaborated with Iraq soon took on alarming proportions. More than 400,000 Palestinians, half of whom were originally from Gaza, were expelled from Kuwait and the rest of the Gulf.[35] Although most of them went to Jordan, which received a third influx of Palestinian refugees (after the arrivals of 1948 and 1967), it is estimated that some 20,000 to 30,000 Palestinians returned from the Gulf to the Gaza Strip. This was a disaster for the economy of the Gaza Strip. The intifada had already ruined the export of citrus fruit and it had also reduced the number of employment opportunities in Israel. With the cessation of the remittances of the Palestinian emigrants in the Gulf, at the same time as the disappearance of the transfers made by the PLO, the population of Gaza now descended into poverty. The territory's GNP, which had already fallen by a third since the beginning of the intifada, dropped by another 10 per cent, with unemployment at 40 per cent.[36]

The economic situation was further compounded by Israel's decision to revoke the 'general exit order' on 15 January 1991, which extended freedom of movement across the frontiers to all but a few Palestinians from the occupied territories. It was cancelled as a precaution against troubles arising out of the offensive against Iraq. But it was never to be restored—the residents of Gaza, who were already obliged to carry electronic identity cards renewable on a yearly basis in order to enter Israel, were now obliged to seek personal exit permits unique to themselves. Workers employed in Israel were immediately affected, as well as students from Gaza attending West Bank universities, who made up, for example, a third of the students at Bir Zeit. It also became increasingly difficult for families split between the West Bank and Gaza to arrange family meetings.[37]

The population of the Gaza Strip now had little choice but to place its faith in US diplomacy, with the hope that this would lead to a diplomatic solution. President George H. Bush, who sought to lay the foundations of a 'New World Order' in the Middle East, and his secretary of state, James Baker, took steps to convene an international peace conference. Washington nevertheless refrained from compelling Israel to negotiate with the PLO, and the following months were marked by intense negotiation over the construction of a Palestinian–Jordanian delegation to attend the impending conference. Three technically independent delegates, who were in fact closely linked to Fatah, acted as intermediaries between the United States and the PLO, which had engaged in no further direct dialogue since June 1990. These were Faisal al-Husseini, for East Jerusalem; Hanan Ashrawi, for the West Bank; and Zakarya al-Agha for the Gaza Strip.

The United States sent letters of invitation to each of the parties involved in the conference, which was scheduled to take place in Madrid on 30 and 31 October 1991. The Soviet Union, which would soon split into its constituent parts, in theory held the joint presidency of the conference, in an arrangement dictated by President Bush's desire to conciliate Mikhail Gorbachev and nationalist sentiment in the emerging Russian state. Haydar Abdel Shafi, now seventy-two years old and an active lifelong nationalist, was ultimately appointed to head the Palestinian element of the joint Palestinian–Jordanian delegation, rather than Faisal al-Husseini, who was too closely identified with the PLO. Of the fourteen members of the Palestinian delegation in Madrid four were originally from the Gaza Strip. In addition to Abdel Shafi, the members included Zakarya al-Agha, who was president of the Doctors' Association, Freih Abu Middain, the head of the Bar Association, and Abderrahman Hamad, the dean of the Faculty of Engineering at Bir Zeit University in the West Bank, who was born in Gaza. Yet none of the seven members of the steering committee, headed by Faisal al-Husseini, had any connection with Gaza.

Despite this, Abdel Shafi was accorded the same amount of time to give his opening address as Jordan's foreign minister, and his speech, an impassioned plea for lasting peace between the peoples of Israel and Palestine, contrasted sharply with the acrimonious exchanges between Israeli Prime Minister Yitzhak Shamir and the foreign minister of Syria. In his opening address Haydar Abdel Shafi celebrated the uprising in the occupied territories:

Our intifada is a testimony to our perseverance and resilience, waged in a just struggle to regain our rights. It is time for us to narrate our own story, to stand witness as advocates of a truth which has long lain buried in the consciousness and conscience of the world. We do not stand before you as supplicants, but rather as the torch bearers who know that in our world of today ignorance can never be an excuse. We seek neither an admission of guilt after the fact, nor vengeance for past iniquities, but rather an act of will that would make a just peace a reality.[38]

Fatah activists came out in force to silence all opposition to the negotiations. On the eve of the peace conference, members of Fatah demonstrated in Gaza with olive branches which they pointedly offered to the Israeli soldiers. On 30 October 1991, thousands turned out on the streets of Gaza and Khan Yunis in support, defying Hamas's call for a strike in protest against Madrid. Although the occupation authorities allowed these displays of strength to proceed, they waited until 3 November to lift the curfew they had imposed on the Gaza Strip for the duration of the peace conference. The next day, in elections for the Gaza Chamber of Commerce, the first held since 1964, the PLO took thirteen of the sixteen seats contested, as against a mere two for Hamas, thus demonstrating the level of popular approval for the principle of negotiation.

The Qassam Effect

On 16 October 1991, shortly before the talks at Madrid, Sheikh Yassin, who had been imprisoned by Israel since May 1989, was sentenced to life imprisonment by Gaza's military tribunal with an additional sentence of fifteen years. He had been found guilty of all seventeen charges brought against him, including responsibility for the deaths of the soldiers Sasportas and Saadoun, though he continued to deny this latter accusation. The two and a half years that Sheikh Yassin had already spent in prison had done nothing to quell his pugnacity, and his supporters continued to condemn what they saw as the PLO's surrender to the United States and Israel. In practice, nothing changed in terms of day-to-day life in Gaza after the Madrid conference. The occupation was as hard to bear as ever and the peace talks themselves, now transferred to Washington, soon became bogged down.

In the context of this fermentation and polarisation, Hamas took the momentous decision to set up a fully fledged armed wing, whose existence would, of course, remain secret. This new armed wing would not simply be an extension of its internal security service, Majd, whose leaders, Salah Shehada and Yahya Sinwa, were in any case still serving prison sentences. It was instead constructed from 'cells' constituted by the *mutaradun*: fugitives from the Israeli authorities who had already been living in hiding for months, or even years in some cases. These Islamist 'brigades', in Arabic *kata'ib* (singular, *katiba*), took the name of Ezzedin al-Qassam, the Syrian sheikh who had fought in Palestine against the British and was killed in action by British troops in 1935. The reference to Ezzedin al-Qassam represented an attempt to outbid the PLO's claim to historical legitimacy by harking back to an even more distant past, paying respect to the pioneer sacrifices of the 'Great Arab Revolt' of 1936–9 as well as to the Muslim Brotherhood in 1948. This kind of manipulation of the pre-*nakba* legacy was intended to rule out any deal with Israel on the basis of the armistice lines that were operative from 1948 to 1967.

The Ezzedin al-Qassam brigades were led by Imad Aqel, who had been born in Jabalya Camp in 1971. It was in this camp that the 'brigades' first appeared in public, in a procession to commemorate the fourth anniversary of Hamas on 14 December 1991,[39] in which a masked fighter brandished a submachine gun[40] in a display of overt defiance of Israel and the intifada's doctrine of abstaining from the use of arms. As Israeli targets remained beyond Hamas's reach, its 'brigades' targeted other Palestinians whom it accused of being 'collaborators' or drug dealers. In the course of 1992,[41] the brigades assassinated at least thirteen Palestinians (though some sources estimate that the figure was ten times higher and assert that the number of killings perpetrated by Hamas in Gaza soon overtook those inflicted by the occupying troops).[42] Repeated pleas by UNCU to halt the execution of 'collaborators', which was often accompanied by torture, remained unanswered: 114 so-called 'collaborators' were killed in the Gaza Strip in 1991, a figure that rose to 199 in 1992.[43]

On 23 May 1992, Haydar Abdel Shafi made a plea for a halt to inter-Palestinian violence while addressing a meeting attended by thousands in Shati Camp, the stronghold of Sheikh Yassin and his supporters. But this was to no effect. On 7 June, Fatah announced it had agreed a 'Charter of Honour' with Hamas to put an end to the mutual violence. Yet Hamas denied the existence of any such document and on the very same day the 'mukhtar' of the camp at Deir al-Balah was assassinated in the market by masked assailants, in full view of shoppers and traders. On 7 July, clashes between the supporters of Fatah and Hamas left dozens wounded across the entire Gaza Strip. On the following day, Haydar Abdel Shafi made a bid to reconcile the two factions, asking delegates from Hamas to his residence and those from Fatah to the Red Crescent headquarters. On at least two occasions, Israeli agents disguised as Arabs (*mistaravim*) succeeded in passing themselves off as Hamas members (on 19 May in Rafah) or as Fatah activists (on 13 July in Gaza City), which increased the tension. From the start of the intifada, Tsahal had put in place a unit of *mistaravim* to operate in the Gaza Strip known as 'Samson' (Shimson).

The nationalist activists found themselves in an extremely difficult position—whereas the armed Islamist fighters condemned their alleged collusion with the occupiers, Israel continued to ban contact with the PLO, to whom even the peace negotiators were forbidden to speak. This had bizarre results. On 13 May 1992, two of the Palestinian negotiators at Madrid, Zakarya al-Agha and Abdurrahman Hamad, were refused entry to Gaza at the Rafah crossing, before eventually being admitted. On 16 June, Walid

Zakout, one of the Palestinian delegation's advisers, was placed under administrative detention in Gaza for six months. Even Haydar Abdel Shafi was not exempt: on 17 July he was interrogated by the police in Jerusalem about a meeting he had held in Amman the previous month with Yasser Arafat. In the meantime the intifada continued with as much vigour as Israel's attempts to suppress it. On 1 April 1992, four Palestinians were killed in disturbances in Rafah. During the first two weeks of October there were serious troubles throughout the territory in sympathy with a hunger strike by Palestinian prisoners, while the Erez crossing was the scene of violent protests on the part of day-labourers held in the 'no-man's land' between the Gaza Strip and Israel.

Likud had been defeated in the Israeli parliamentary elections of June 1992. In July a majority Labour government was formed, headed by Yitzhak Rabin with Shimon Peres as foreign minister. However, this change in government did not lead to an improvement in the situation in the Gaza Strip. Those in the Palestinian 'peace camp' were naturally encouraged by the change of government in Israel, but it also had the incidental effect of intensifying the clashes between Hamas and Fatah over the summer of 1992. Hamas was determined to carry off a major coup, in order both to unsettle Israel and to see off its nationalist rivals. A year after the formation of the Ezzedin al-Qassam brigades, they were ready for action, both in the Gaza Strip and the West Bank, where Imad Aqel had secretly remained from May to November 1992.[44]

On 7 December 1992 the Qassam brigades claimed responsibility for the deaths of three Israeli soldiers at Beit Lahya, the bloodiest loss for Tsahal in the five years of the intifada. The Gaza Strip was sealed off and searched from end to end, as was the West Bank, where Hamas struck the next blow. On 12 December, an Israeli soldier was killed in Hebron and the following day a frontier guard, Nissim Toledano, was kidnapped on the road to Ramallah. The kidnappers demanded the immediate release of Sheikh Yassin, who was interviewed at length about the situation on Israeli television. The hostage was executed within a few hours, and when his body was discovered on 15 December there was a major round-up with some 1,200 Islamist militants being arrested in the occupied territories, half of them in the Gaza Strip. Israel's Prime Minister Yitzhak Rabin deported 415 of the detainees to Lebanon, including 164 of those from Gaza.

216

The UN Security Council, with the endorsement of the United States, issued a severe condemnation of this collective banishment in Resolution 799, which was adopted on 18 December 1992.[45] With the support of the international community, Lebanon refused to allow the deportees access to its territory. For its part, Tsahal fired on anyone who attempted to return to the Israeli frontier. The 415 who had been expelled set up a makeshift camp at Marj al-Zuhur (literally, 'Meadow of Flowers'), just inside the Lebanese border, which they soon began to call the 'Camp of Return'. The charismatic Abdelaziz Rantissi, with the backing of Mahmoud Zahar, became the informal leader of this militant community and in this straitened situation these two Hamas leaders contrived to attract an extraordinary degree of international publicity. Their influence over their fellow exiles was increasing, especially with regard to the supporters of Islamic Jihad, who had previously been more inclined towards Fatah, and lasting ties were made with Lebanese Hezbollah.

The deportees of the 'Camp of Return' were feted as heroes in the Gaza Strip. UNCU and Hamas published their first ever joint communiqué to call for their unconditional repatriation, and anti-Israeli rioting once again resumed with unprecedented intensity. On 19 December 1992, in Khan Yunis, the place of origin of twenty-three of the deportees, six Palestinians, including two children, were killed on a single day. The Israeli army imposed seventeen days of curfew in Khan Yunis during the month of December, including a consecutive period of ten days, and eleven people were shot dead, including four children. The momentum of the crisis prompted the PLO to inaugurate a new high-level dialogue with Hamas, which took place outside the country, first in Tunis and then in Khartoum. These exchanges ultimately foundered on the number of seats to be reserved for Hamas in the Palestinian National Council, with Hamas seeking 40 per cent while the PLO was only prepared to concede eighteen seats out of 452. But, thanks to the Qassam brigades, Hamas had returned to the centre of the Palestinian stage, a year after the Madrid conference had seemed to edge the Islamists out.

Hamas's new standing was reflected in the fact that the US diplomats in Amman held two working sessions with the Hamas representative in Amman, Muhammad Nazzal, after the dialogue between the United States and the PLO had been suspended. However, as a result of the controversy that subsequently ensued following these meetings, Hamas was placed on the US State Department's list of terrorist organisations. On 1 March 1993 a member of Islamic Jihad stabbed two Israelis in Jerusalem. Tsahal's reprisals included a complete ban on all entry to the Gaza Strip, and such total closures, which had previously been unusual, subsequently became increasingly common. Although Haydar Abdel Shafi, the Palestinian negotiator in Madrid, condemned Islamic Jihad's attack, his influence over events on the ground now seemed to be in decline. On 8 March, he called for calm in the Gaza Strip between Hamas and Islamic Jihad, who had begun to compete for control of the mosques. On 2 March an Israeli was shot dead in Rafah, but no group claimed responsibility. Other armed groups were also active. On 18 April, the armed group affiliated to the PFLP, the Red Eagles, joined forces with the Islamist groups to murder another Israeli in Gaza.

In March 1993, in an Israeli opinion poll published in the newspaper *Maariv*, less than a quarter of the Israeli respondents wanted the occupation of the Gaza Strip to continue indefinitely. An immediate retreat was the option favoured by 33 per cent, with 34 per cent opting for a negotiated retreat, while only 23 per cent wanted the occupation to continue.[46] Two Israeli ministers even went as far as to call for immediate withdrawal: these were Aryeh Deri, minister of the interior (Shas Party) and Haim Ramon of the Labour Party who was minister of health.[47] By this stage it was the increasing level of violence, rather than the peace process, which animated the Israeli debate on Gaza's future. On 23 May 1993, Prime Minister Yitzhak Rabin put forward the 'Gaza first' option: a negotiated withdrawal from Gaza as an initial stage of a settlement that would in due course also take in the West Bank. (The settlement, as envisaged by Rabin, would not affect East Jerusalem as it had been formally annexed by Israel in June 1967.) Haydar Abdel Shafi had come to the conclusion that nothing could come from any talks he held with Israel under the auspices of the United States. He therefore published an 'open letter' addressed to the Palestinian people in which he called on the PLO to practise 'collective leadership'.[48] He was of course unaware that representatives for Arafat and Rabin had been conducting secret negotiations for some months in Norway, which eventually led to mutual recognition between the PLO and Israel.

News of the diplomatic breakthrough at Oslo only began to emerge at the end of August 1993. Concerns grew among the Palestinian factions with the revelation of the secret deal. The PFLP and the DFLP dissociated themselves from Arafat's leadership, while Hamas, Islamic Jihad and the pro-Syrian groups went further, crying treason. The people of Gaza, however, seemed to support the agreement: according to poll results broadcast on Israeli TV on 30 August 1993, 76.4 per cent of the inhabitants of Gaza backed the agreement between the PLO and Israel. The PLO leadership swiftly endorsed the 'Gaza and Jericho first' formula, which gave notice, albeit symbolically, that it intended in due course to establish itself in the West Bank.

In September 1993 events quickly began to move forward. On 3 September the final touches were put to the 'Oslo Accords' in Paris, and in Tel Aviv tens of thousands of Israelis demonstrated in support on 4 September. On 7 September, a similar number of Israelis gathered in Jerusalem to show their opposition to the peace process. In the same month, Yitzhak Rabin gave an interview to an Israeli newspaper in which he elaborated on his position with regard to the Palestinians:

I would prefer to see the Palestinians take upon themselves the problem of keeping order in Gaza. They will be more effective than we have been, since they will not allow appeals to the Supreme Court. They will prevent the Association for Civil Rights in Israel from entering the territory to criticise them. They will govern in their own way, and, what is more important, they will take over responsibility for the task from the Israeli military.[49]

The process continued on 9 September when Arafat signed a document recognising Israel, with Rabin declaring Israel's recognition of the PLO ten hours later. On 10 September, thousands of Fatah supporters marched in Gaza in support of the Oslo Accords, with scuffles breaking out between them and a Hamas counter-demonstration. On 12 September, Islamic Jihad carried out a lethal ambush in Gaza. On 13 September, President Clinton welcomed Yitzhak Rabin and Yasser Arafat to Washington, while Shimon Peres and Mahmoud Abbas officially put their signatures to the peace agreement between Israel and the Palestinians.

On 14 September 1993 Hamas carried out its first suicide bombing in Gaza. A young militant named Baha ed-Din al-Najr attempted to enter the police station in Gaza with an explosive charge attached to his body, but his bomb blew up prematurely causing no casualties.[50] A week later, a local Fatah figure, Mohammad Abu Shaaban, the treasurer of the Gaza Bar Association, was murdered as he returned from a meeting held in support of the Oslo Accords. More than 2,000 people attended his funeral, on the occasion of which Yasser Arafat, speaking from his headquarters in Tunis, made an appeal for the Palestinians to reject all forms of 'violence and terrorism'.[51] On 21 October, another Fatah veteran, Assad Saftawi, the principal of an UNRWA school in Bureij Camp, was assassinated by masked killers. Assad Saftawi was a former Muslim Brother and the father of a notorious Islamic Jihad activist. Forty years before, he had been inducted as a militant alongside Abu Iyad and had lived through every kind of trial and danger, until at last, peace or its prospects, had cut him down. On 24 November, Imad Aqel, the founding leader of the Ezzedin al-Qassam brigades, was killed by Israeli soldiers. At just twenty-two years of age, having taken the lives of so many 'collaborators', it was ironic that Aqel himself fell victim to an informer.[52]

Throughout the intifada, Fatah and Hamas, sworn enemies despite having sprung from the same roots, competed for the allegiance of the Palestinian population in Gaza, each to the detriment of the other. Fatah gradually abandoned the reflexes it had developed as a rootless bureaucracy whose guerrilla war was fought outside Palestine, turning instead to identify itself with a Palestinian people in rebellion in their own land against the occupying power. Hamas, on the other hand, developed out of its initial territorial base in Gaza: it extended itself into the West Bank, it set up its Political Bureau abroad and it learned lessons from the anti-Israeli struggle of Hezbollah in south Lebanon. Fatah broke with its historic fedayin legacy to endorse the unarmed struggle of the intifada and to accept the possibility of a peace agreement with Israel. Hamas, in contrast, moved away from the strategy of pietism and obedience to the law that had originally been espoused by the Mujamma, its parent organisation, and, with the Ezzedin al-Qassam brigades, explored the possibilities of an armed option. For both Hamas and Fatah, however, the Gaza Strip was the chosen sphere in which these developments took place.

The six years of the uprising bled the territory dry. From December 1987 to May 1994, the Israeli forces killed 523 inhabitants of Gaza, 462 houses were demolished by Tshahal, and close to 78,338 hospitalisations had been registered as the result of wounds inflicted by the occupying troops.[53] The entire social fabric was also disrupted, and street violence and the disruption of the educational framework took a heavy toll on the lives of the young throughout the occupied territories, especially in the Gaza Strip. In the course of the apparently interminable intifada, 85 per cent of Gaza's children saw their homes attacked, 42 per cent were beaten by the occupying forces while 55 per cent had seen their parents beaten.[54] The 'armed wings' of the various Palestinian factions, with their self-important titles, 'Hawks', 'Eagles' and 'Brigades', frequently drew their recruits from the more desperate margins of Palestinian youth: young people deprived of an education who saw no other future for themselves. The frontier between militancy and delinquency became blurred, and the prevalence of attacks on so-called 'collaborators' enabled it to be crossed without compunction.

The intifada was not a golden age of patriotic consensus, but a period of collective violence against the Palestinian people, some of which was inflicted by part of that people against itself. Civil society, which entered unarmed into the intifada, responded with the creation of associations and NGOs intended to stem this dramatic decline. Of the 114 NGOs operating in the Gaza Strip in 1994, half had been established during the last two years of the intifada, which were in many respects the worst. Yet the wounds were deep, and no provision of the Oslo Accords was calculated to heal them. Even an ideal peace would not have healed such profound and deep trauma. This is why the very vista of such an awaited breakthrough was to open upon a series of profound misunderstandings.

13

A SHARPLY LIMITED AUTHORITY

The 'Declaration of Principles' agreed between the PLO and Israel in Oslo envisaged an interim five-year period during which a 'Palestinian Interim Self-Government Authority' would come into existence in the territories from which Israel had withdrawn, and that 'in order to guarantee public order and internal security', this Authority 'will establish a strong police force, while Israel will continue to carry the responsibility for defending against external threats'.[1] The two parties committed themselves not to take any step during the transition period that would be prejudicial to the final status of the West Bank and the Gaza Strip. The Oslo process was based on Israeli–Palestinian cooperation, from which enhanced autonomy was intended to result. However, the agreement did not provide any mechanism to resolve tension or crisis other than open-ended negotiations since any Israeli withdrawal was conditioned by guarantees from the Palestinian Authority.

Haydar Abdel Shafi had noticed this apparent weakness, especially as Yasser Arafat had conceded a number of points in Oslo on which the Palestinian negotiators had stood firm since Madrid. Abdel Shafi saw the settlements as the most urgent issue, though under the Oslo Accords these were left in suspense until the end of the interim period, in the same chapter as the issues of frontiers, refugees and Jerusalem. Rabin, however, had insisted on not tying his hands on this subject, limiting himself to drawing a distinction between 'political' settlements, whose removal could be accepted, and settlements to be retained for reasons connected with Israel's security. This latter category applied particularly to settlements in the Jordan Valley. Security grounds as a justification for the retention of settlements were for the time being, however, applied by Israel to the protection of settlers already in situ, which led Tsahal to demand the continuance of its control over at least a quarter of the Gaza Strip. In the months after the signature of the Oslo Accords, some 850 additional settlers came to Gaza. This became a cause for concern, even though the total number of settlers in Gaza was still less than 5,000.

A further issue that affected the implementation of the Oslo Accords was the fact that the Israeli–Palestinian peace agreement had begun with a major misunderstanding between the people of Gaza and those to whom the Gazans referred, with no particular affection, as the Tunisians.[2] The exiled PLO fighters felt that their combat and sacrifice over a period of many years had obliged Israel to agree to withdraw from some of the occupied territories, and if they were not greeted as saviours they at least expected to be welcomed as liberators. By contrast, the population of Gaza, including the most politicised groups, believed the intifada had been the determining factor in the retreat of the Israelis. They consequently felt that the Tunisians should acknowledge that the indigenous Palestinians had struggled ceaselessly on behalf of the exiles and that it was this struggle that had enabled them to return. Each group therefore believed that the other was in its debt, a source of incomprehension that was exacerbated by the divergence in the experience of the two groups: occupation for one and exile for the other, with a complex relationship between the two.[3]

The Return of the 'Old Man'

Yasser Arafat had always sought to retain personal control over the affairs of the PLO, down to the smallest practical details. After the deaths of his two companions, Abu Iyad and Abu Jihad, the decision-making process within the PLO became even more centralised. Though Mahmoud Abbas, known as Abu Mazen, had been part of the first generation of Fatah, having taken responsibility for liaison between Gaza and the Gulf in the 1960s, his lack of legitimacy as a fedayin fighter and his public image as a manager had deprived him of reliable support within Fatah. Within the organisation, he was often nicknamed the 'administrator' (*al-Muwazzaf*). On 28 November 1993, Israeli troops killed a 23-year-old activist, Ahmed Abu Rish, who was the head of Fatah's armed organisation, the 'Hawks' in Khan Yunis. A new group, the Abu Rish brigades, was formed in response. This independence on the part of the most radical element of Fatah in Gaza encouraged Arafat's authoritarian tendencies. He subsequently appointed Zakarya al-Agha, a man from a notable family in Khan Yunis, as the head of Fatah in the Gaza strip in preference to Sami Abu Samhadana, the head of the Fatah Hawks in Gaza who had spent most of his adult life in Israeli prisons. In his management of the Palestinian territories Arafat evidently preferred to rely only on those who had always supported him unconditionally, thereby keeping all important decisions in his own hands.

Thus when Haydar Abdel Shafi met Arafat in Tunis on 2 January 1994 there was little likelihood that the veteran Gaza personality's plea for an inclusive and collective approach to the administration of Gaza would be enough to persuade the PLO leader. Arafat had already put his own men into key positions, juggling with their allegiances and networks. The 'Old Man' (*al-Khityar*), as his supporters called him in a spirit of affectionate respect, selected Mansour al-Shawa, Rashad Shawa's son, to be the future mayor of Gaza. But Arafat's plans were derailed by a new spiral of violence. On 25 February, an American-Israeli settler massacred twenty-nine Muslim worshippers at the Ibrahimi mosque in Hebron, known to the Jews as the Tomb of the Patriarchs; on 28 March, six Fatah activists were killed at Jabalya Camp by a Tsahal hit squad, which later admitted they had mistaken the six for a group of 'fugitives' for whom they were searching; and on 6 and 13 April, Hamas carried out its first suicide bombings inside Israel, with eight and six victims respectively, including the bombers themselves.

It was in this particularly delicate context that Arafat and Rabin finally succeeded in signing an interim agreement establishing Palestinian autonomy in Gaza and Jericho on 4 May 1994. Part of the agreement was that the 'territorial jurisdiction' of the Palestinian Authority would exclude Israeli settlements and military zones, which amounted to a quarter of the Gaza Strip.[4] Israeli security posts in the urban zone were evacuated, however, in order to be handed over to the Palestinian police, while the 600 detainees in Ansar 2 in Gaza were transferred to Ketziot, in the Negev, with the former prison becoming a Palestinian police training centre. Israel and the PLO agreed that the Palestinian police force should be 9,000 strong, with 7,000 members drawn from Palestinians repatriated from abroad. Palestinian detainees were also to be released, with some 5,000 to be freed in two stages. On 10 May, the first 157 new Palestinian police recruits came in through the Rafah crossing, led by General Nasser Youssef and cheered on by the population. Four days later, the Israeli army transferred control of Jabalya Camp to the Palestinians. On 16 May, 250 members of the Ain Jalout brigade of the PLA, who had already been deployed under Nasser before 1967, took up various Tsahal positions around the Gaza Strip, though they were still banned from having heavy weapons, just as they had been a quarter of a century earlier.

The new strong man of Gaza was Muhammad Dahlan, to whom Arafat assigned responsibility for security in the Strip. The police force, which Ghazi Jabali was appointed to lead, was only one department of the security apparatus in Gaza. Dahlan took direct responsibility for 'preventive security' (*al-amn al-waqa'i*) but he also had oversight of the criminal police (*al-bahth al-jina'i*) and the coastguard (*al-hirasa al-bahriyya*), the latter of which was feared by Arafat's political opponents despite its apparently innocuous title. On the other hand, the chairman of the PLO himself kept direct control of Force 17, which was the equivalent of a presidential guard and also functioned as a Special Forces unit. He gave his cousin, Musa Arafat, command of military intelligence (*al-istikhbarat*) for the Gaza Strip, and put Amin al-Hindi in charge of civil intelligence (*al-mukhabarat*).

The popularity Dahlan had gained as a former Fatah leader in Khan Yunis prior to January 1987—when his expulsion led to disturbances throughout the whole territory—worked in his favour. While in Tunis, Dahlan had served as a link between the PLO chairman and the Palestinians of the 'interior' throughout the six years of the intifada. He was now the PLO's nominated interlocutor with General Amnon Shahak, Tsahal's deputy chief of staff who had previously served as head of Aman, the Israeli military intelligence arm. On 20 May, two Israeli soldiers were killed at the Erez crossing point in an attack for which both Hamas and Islamic Jihad claimed responsibility. On 23 May, Tshahal and the Palestinian police set up joint roadblocks in an attempt to track down the culprits, which led to a major protest by Hamas on the campus of the Islamic University. The newly appointed Palestinian minister of justice, Freih Abu Middain, who had defended many militant Islamists in Israeli courts as head of the Gaza Bar, attempted to calm the popular mood. When he detained twenty-six alleged collaborators, however, the Israeli government condemned what it said was a violation of the accords made with the PLO, and this argument was advanced to excuse delay in releasing Palestinian detainees.

On 1 July 1994 Yasser Arafat returned for his first visit to the Gaza Strip after some four decades. Arafat entered the Gaza strip at Rafah, beneath a sea of Palestinian flags, then went on to Gaza City for a ceremony at the Square of the Unknown Soldier, Gaza City's largest open space. Before tens of thousands of people, he paid his respects to the martyrs of the intifada and made a solemn promise to strive for the liberation of Sheikh Yassin. This gesture of reconciliation towards Hamas was repeated the following day, during visits to Shati Camp and Jabalya. Arafat was then flown in an Egyptian army helicopter to Jericho, which had now become an autono-mous Palestinian enclave in the occupied West Bank. In Jericho, he chaired the first meeting of his government, in which Freih Abu Middain and another four of the twelve ministers present were from the Gaza Strip.

On 12 July 1994, Arafat took up permanent residence in Gaza. Yet Israel was soon to remind him of the limits of the autonomy to which he was entitled. In his official car, when he crossed into the Gaza Strip at Rafah, the PLO chairman had brought with him one of his old associates. This was Mamdouh Noufal, the military leader of the DFLP, whom Tsahal accused of involvement in an attack at Maalot on 15 May 1974 in which twenty-five people had died when a school was held hostage.[5] In response, Israel closed the crossing point into Gaza and suspended all permission to enter for members of the Palestinian Authority until Arafat relented and accepted the de facto deportation of one of his entourage. This humiliation for the Palestinian leader was related to two broader issues. First, Israel retained exclusive control over access to the 'autonomous' territories. More broadly, it also retained the right to forbid entry to anyone who in its view continued to be a 'terrorist'. These arrangements emphasised the extent to which Israel continued to be the 'occupying power', even after Oslo. Around the Gaza Strip, Tsahal constructed a fence some 60 kilometres in length, a measure undertaken on the orders of Tsahal's commander in Gaza, General Doron Almog, who, ironically, had been the Israeli commander who had formally welcomed Yasser Arafat on his return to the territory on 1 July 1994.[6] Arafat exacted compensation by appointing Aoun Shawa as mayor of Gaza rather than Mansour Shawa, his cousin and brother-in-law, the candidate which the Israelis had expected to be appointed. With this apparently arbitrary act, Arafat intended to demonstrate to the population and to the notable families that it was he who, in spite of all, was master in the territory.

The Palestinian security services were also quick to make their mark in Gaza. On 7 July 1994, Farid Hashem Jabou, a 28-year-old taxi driver detained by the police, died following interrogation in Gaza's central prison. The Palestinian minister of justice spoke of an 'excessive use of force' and held three police officers for questioning. Human rights advocates quickly claimed that this was a case of 'torture'.[7] This incident hastened the signature of an agreement between the PLO and the International Committee of the Red Cross (ICRC) which allowed the latter to inspect locations where prisoners were held by the Authority. On 17 July, disturbances that broke out at the Erez crossing point involving day-labourers from Gaza who set fire to dozens of Israeli buses degenerated into an exchange of fire between Israeli and Palestinian police. Two Palestinian civilians lost their lives and two days later Hamas claimed responsibility for the killing of an Israeli soldier in Rafah, apparently in reprisal. On 14 August, a further anti-Israeli incident in which Hamas was involved led to the arrest of thirty-five militant Islamists by the Palestinian police. Meanwhile, Hamas, in this instance with the backing of the PFLP, demanded elections in Gaza City, where the municipality was exclusively in the hands of Yasser Arafat's favourites.

The Palestinian Authority had set in train a '100-day plan' to kick-start the Gaza Strip's ruined economy, with the World Bank opening a Gaza office and international donors promising to contribute sums up to a total of 2.6 billion dollars for the development of the autonomous Palestinian territories. The urgent need of the Palestinian police for equipment and training was deemed to be a priority, though it was not until January 1996 that the Palestinian security forces finally acquired a functional communications system in Gaza.[8] The American State Department insisted on the importance of transparency: the antithesis of the practices of the chairman of the PLO. For a quarter of a century, Arafat had personally signed all cheques, both large and small, relating to the PLO's expenditure. Ahmed Qureia, better known by his PLO name of Abu Ala, a former banker and one of the leading negotiators in Oslo, was given responsibility in his new capacity as minister for the economy for the management of the new structure put in place by the Authority: the Palestinian Economic Council for Development and Reconstruction (PECDAR). Nabil Shaath, the minister for planning and cooperation, had no direct access to the budgetary mechanism.

The Islamist Challenge

Arafat was well aware of Hamas's strength in Gaza and was keen to neutralise it by encouraging splits within Hamas on the one hand and selectively co-opting its members on the other, as had long been his practice with the radical factions within the PLO. He talked to those Hamas leaders most likely to be attracted by a role in politics, such as Mahmoud Zahar, still cloaked in the prestige that had accrued from his expulsion to Marj al-Zuhur, and Ismail Haniya, the rising star of Sheikh Yassin's movement, encouraging them to form a new political party to contest future elections. He also gave permission to Imad Falluji, a Hamas member from Jabalya Camp, to launch a new periodical that embodied Islamist ideas.[9] These machinations were condemned by the Hamas leadership imprisoned in Israel, particularly Abdelaziz Rantissi (who was not released until 20 April 1997) who had been jailed in Israel when he was allowed back from Lebanon, and Salah Shehada, the historic leader of Hamas's military wing. It was against this background that the Ezzedin al-Qassam brigades repeated their coup of December 1992 by abducting another Israeli soldier, Nachshon Wachsman, in October 1994.

The Israeli Prime Minister Yitzhak Rabin demanded urgent action by Arafat and accused the kidnappers of hiding their prisoner in the Gaza

Strip. In return for the soldier's release the Qassam brigades not only demanded the liberation of Sheikh Yassin and the Hamas leaders, but also the leading figures of Hezbollah that were imprisoned in Israel. This was the first occasion on which the 'militant fraternity' avowed by the Palestinian and Lebanese Islamists at Marj al-Zuhur emerged clearly into view. Rabin told Arafat he was prepared to release Sheikh Yassin. However, Wachsman's whereabouts became known when the Palestinian intelligence services, pursuing their own investigations, picked up hundreds of Hamas members in Gaza and ultimately tracked him down in a part of the West Bank under the control of the Israeli army. On 14 October, an assault mounted by Tsahal to retrieve the hostage ended with his death together with that of another Israeli soldier and three Qassam brigade militiamen. The cooperation between Israel and the Palestinian Authority to bring this operation to a conclusion resulted in three consecutive days of violent demonstrations by Hamas's supporters in Gaza. On 19 October twenty-three people died in Tel-Aviv in a suicide bombing by the Qassam brigades. The Gaza Strip was immediately sealed off.

Israeli counter-terrorist operations, about which serious questions were being asked in Israel, started to be launched without any consultations taking place with the Palestinian security organisations. On 2 November 1994, Hani Abed, a leader of Islamic Jihad, was killed by a car bomb in Gaza. Arafat went to the funeral but was pushed away by the dead man's family and friends.[10] Thousands of demonstrators marched in protest against the collaboration between the Authority and Tsahal on the following day. On 11 November, an Islamic Jihad suicide bomber on a bicycle blew himself up at the Netzarim roadblock, killing three Israeli army reservists. The Palestinian police picked up 180 members of Islamic Jihad in Gaza, which Yitzhak Rabin regarded as insufficient. The Islamist demonstrators, for their part, grew bolder despite appeals for calm from Mahmoud Zahar. On 18 November, after the Friday prayers in Gaza City, the Palestinian police were swamped by thousands of protestors and fired on the crowd, killing fourteen people and wounding hundreds.

This bloodbath, coming only a few months after Arafat's return to Gaza, was a shock to the population regardless of individual political sympathies. Arafat placed the blame on external manipulation, but his standing was seriously affected. The 'Old Man' turned back to the discredited Fatah Hawks, under the leadership of Sami Samhadana (who would shortly be promoted to the rank of colonel in Force 17, Arafat's presidential guard), placing them on a fully operational footing to counter the 'danger' from Hamas.[11] He gave Dahlan carte blanche to recruit those he trusted to his 'Preventive Security', whose numbers doubled over the space of a few weeks.[12] Tension rose to such a point in the Gaza Strip that it had to be defused by bringing in Palestinians of Israeli nationality to mediate between Fatah and Hamas in negotiations. On 23 November, Ahmed Tibi, a member of the Knesset and an Arafat sympathiser, signed an agreement with Nimr Darwish, the leading Israeli Islamist. Three days later, Hamas and Islamic Jihad put 20,000 people into the streets of Gaza on the anniversary of the murder by Israel of Imad Aqel, the first leader of the Qassam brigades. The Palestinian police, faced with such an impressive show of force, maintained a low profile.

Criticism of Arafat began to emerge within the PLO, and even within Fatah itself. Arafat appointed Mahmoud Abbas to the position of chief negotiator with Israel, in the hope of achieving a substantial and non-phased Israeli withdrawal from the West Bank. Abdel Shafi pointed out with some annoyance that what actually held back all development in the autonomous territories was the continued presence of Israeli settlements. Arafat suppressed dissidence in Gaza, whether from preachers, journalists or human rights activists, with increasing severity. His principal concern continued to be the looming Islamist threat: on 9 April 1995, there were two suicide bombings against Israeli settlements in Gaza, killing eight people, for one of which Hamas claimed responsibility while Islamic Jihad took responsibility for the other. Round-ups and arrests by the Palestinian security services were on this occasion immediately followed by closed nocturnal sittings by the Authority's military tribunals, which imposed heavy sentences on members of the Islamist leadership. The crackdown was not restricted to military officials: on 14 May, for example, Sayyid Abu Musamih, who had helped to reorganise Hamas after Sheikh Yassin's arrest in 1989, was sentenced to two years in prison for having fomented 'sedition' against the Palestinian Authority.[13]

The 'Old Man' was well aware that it was impossible to destroy Hamas through repression alone. He therefore resumed his conciliatory approaches to the less intransigent of the Islamist leaders. Hamas's internal debate, meanwhile, soon began to focus on the modalities of setting up a political party, which, given that the accords between Israel and the PLO explicitly provided for future elections, would justify passive acceptance of the peace process. The majority rejected any such change, opting instead for abstention from the political process. However, some of Hamas's members, such as Ismail Haniya, argued that the organisation could be marginalised by the emergence of a new Palestinian entity. In Israel, the Rabin government, probably swayed by Arafat's arguments, gave Haniya and three other leading Hamas figures permission to travel to Jordan and thence to Sudan to win the support of the Hamas Political Bureau for their position. Khaled Meshal, however, insisted on sticking to Hamas's traditionally rejectionist standpoint, thus confirming the newly emergent dominance within Hamas of the 'exterior' over the 'interior'.

In the Gaza Strip the process of integrating the Tunisians into the local population was not proceeding smoothly. The issue of housing for the thousands of functionaries of the Authority and their families caused a high degree of tension. They were accused of being responsible for an unreasonable increase in rents, and of unauthorised building in the already overcrowded camps.[14] Other than a minority of higher-ranking officers, who had been assisted when they arrived by Gaza's notable families, the majority of the PLO staff detailed to work for the Palestinian Authority lived on modest salaries and were resentful of the restrictions imposed on them. Mutual lack of understanding exacerbated a cultural divide between those who had seldom if ever been outside the Strip and the former fedayin who, even if they had originally come from Gaza, had also known the more open societies of Beirut and Tunis. Their degree of tolerance, itself entirely relative, was frequently denounced as 'alien' by the Islamist militants, who were proud of never having left the territory.[15]

Arafat Without Rabin

Yitzhak Rabin had signed a peace treaty with King Hussein of Jordan on October 1994 and he held at least some hope that a similar agreement could be reached with Syria's President Hafez al-Assad. His relationship with Arafat had always been difficult. However, his principle, as he often put it, was to negotiate as if there were no terrorism and to fight terrorism as if there were no negotiations. On 28 September 1995, in Washington, DC, Rabin and Arafat signed an interim agreement on the West Bank, which became known as Oslo II (despite being negotiated in the Egyptian border town of Taba). Oslo II divided the territory of the West Bank into three separate zones. In areas classified as Zone A, the Palestinian Authority was in charge; in Zone B, control was shared, with Palestinian administration and Israeli security; and finally, in Zone C, Israel remained in control. Though this put 90 per cent of the Palestinian population under the control of the Authority, the proportion of the territory assigned to each category was highly significant. In the absence of subsequent withdrawals, it left only 3 per cent in Zone A, with 25 per cent in Zone B and 72 per cent in Zone C.

The 'Old Man' experienced great difficulty in getting the text endorsed by the PLO, mustering only nine out of twenty members of the PLO's executive committee to vote it through. But he disregarded this setback in the hope of quickly moving on to an agreement on the final status of the autonomous territories and therefore to the formal installation of a Palestinian state. His reluctance to allow any obstacle to intervene was also the reason Arafat refrained from reaction when Fathi Shikaki was assassinated in Malta by Mossad agents on 26 October. The murder of Islamic Jihad's founder gave rise to violent demonstrations in Gaza, however, especially as his successor, Ramadan Shallah, who was also from Gaza, had made an explicit appeal for anti-Israeli reprisals during a speech in Damascus. Two suicide bombings were carried out on 2 November against settlement buses, one at Kfar Darom and the other at Gush Katif, but in each case only the Islamic Jihad bomber was killed.

Yitzhak Rabin also encountered major problems in gaining acceptance for Oslo II on the Israeli side, with protests against him becoming increasingly vituperative. On 3 November, at a meeting in Tel Aviv, he was shot dead by a right-wing Jewish extremist. When Arafat heard the news of the attack, as he was working in his office in Gaza, he dropped everything to follow the news on Israeli television which, however, restricted itself to reporting that the prime minister had been taken to hospital in a grave condition. The PLO chairman finally learned that Rabin was dead from one of his staff who had a direct link to sources in Israel. When he heard the news he was overcome with grief. An eye witness describes Arafat, with tears flowing, holding his head in his hands as he repeated: 'It's over, it's over.'[16]

President Clinton, Egypt's President Mubarak and King Hussein of Jordan all came to Jerusalem for Rabin's funeral. As Arafat realised that he would not be welcome, the PLO leader secretly visited Rabin's widow during the night of 8 November 1995 to express his condolences, making the return trip from Gaza to Tel Aviv on board an Israeli helicopter.[17] In Jerusalem, Shimon Peres took over as prime minister. On 15 November, Arafat had been scheduled to make a speech to mark the seventh anniversary of the proclamation of the 'State of Palestine' in Algiers, but after the interception of a death squad coming from Libya sent to assassinate him, he cancelled the event. He would never cease to be haunted by the ghost of Rabin.

The first elections to the presidency and the Palestinian Legislative Council (PLC) were due to be held in the West Bank and Gaza on 20 January 1996. The outcome of the presidential election was scarcely in doubt, as Arafat had only one rival: a woman candidate from El-Bireh, Samiha al-Khalil, who was herself a militant nationalist. Questions remained, on the other hand, in relation to the election of the members of the PLC, despite years of estimating the strengths of the various parties on the basis of union and student elections. The Gaza Strip had been assigned thirty-seven seats out of the eighty-eight that would make up the future parliament, and was comparatively better represented than the West Bank. The Strip was divided into five constituencies: Gaza North, Gaza City, Gaza Centre, Khan Yunis and Rafah. These accounted for 42 per cent of the seats in parliament, whereas the population only comprised 35 per cent of the electorate as a whole (in numerical terms, 350,000 of the million voters who had been registered).

The PFLP and the DFLP declared their intention to boycott the elections, though a number of their officials and activists intended to stand as independents. There was also a lively debate inside Hamas, where the option was being considered of running under the name of the 'National Salvation Party', an entity which had been created specifically for the occasion. In the end, Sheikh Yassin decided not to pursue the idea. Ismail Haniya, who was personally inclined to run as an independent in Gaza, was persuaded not to put himself forward,[18] which gave rise to a certain amount of internal discussion within Hamas.[19] On the other hand, Hamas no longer called upon its supporters to boycott the vote, even after the murder of Yahya Ayyash, the operational leader of the Qassam brigades, killed in Beit Lahya by means of a booby-trapped telephone on 5 January 1996. Around 100,000 people turned out for Ayyash's funeral, where calls for revenge were heard. Once again, this was an instance where Israel had opted to take direct action in Gaza rather than turn to Palestinian security, though the Palestinian security services had effectively kept Ayyash and his supporters under control over a period of seven months.[20]

On 21 January 1996 Yasser Arafat gained 87 per cent of the vote for the presidency and, in the absence of serious competition, Fatah won a comfortable majority of fifty seats out of the eighty-eight seats in the PLC. The turn-out was almost 80 per cent in the Gaza Strip, 12 per cent higher than in the West Bank.[21] Haydar Abdel Shafi received more votes than any candidate in the territory, easily beating those elected for Fatah in Gaza City, though these included two local veterans of the armed struggle who had long been in exile. These were Nahed Rayess, one of the pioneers of the PLF in 1967, and Intissar al-Wazir, the widow of Abu Jihad (who was also known as Umm Jihad) who had been a Fatah activist in her own right from the very beginning. Rawya Shawa, who was the daughter and granddaughter of mayors of Gaza, was elected as an independent, as were two Gaza sheikhs who were identified with Hamas, Wajih Yaghi and Musa Zaabout. In the constituency of Gaza North, dominated by Jabalya Camp, Imad Falluji, a Hamas renegade who had joined Arafat, received the lowest number of votes of those who were elected.[22]

Under the leadership of Freih Abu Middain, one of Arafat's ministers, Fatah took all five seats that were contested in Gaza Centre, both in its own right and through the intermediary of 'independent' candidates. In Khan Yunis, the Fatah list, headed by another Palestinian Authority minister, Nabil Shaath, took six of the eight seats that were in contention. (Zakarya al-Agha was beaten on his own turf, despite attempts at electoral fraud so blatant that even Fatah attempted to put a stop to them.)[23] In

Rafah, two of the candidates elected were former Fatah exiles, Abdelaziz Shahin and Rawhi Fattouh. In the eyes of Arafat's supporters, the electoral success of Fatah's candidates was a ringing endorsement. Tsahal's disengagement from Ramallah and Jenin, with Nablus and Hebron (Al-Khalil) soon to follow, further consolidated the basis of the Authority. However, such optimism failed to take into account the consequences of the undeclared war that was emerging between Hamas and Israel.

Two Hamas suicide bombers, claiming to be disciples of Yahya Ayyash, went into action in Jerusalem and Ashkelon on 25 February 1996, killing twenty-five people. Shimon Peres, who lacked the authority that had accrued to his predecessor Yitzhak Rabin from his status as a former general, suspended all negotiations with the PLO. With diplomacy suspended, it fell to Peres's military chief of staff, Amnon Shahak, to meet Arafat at the Erez crossing point to demand that he wage war without mercy against the Islamist movement. The Palestinian president, whose intelligence services had already laid hands on 200 Hamas supporters, set a date for the surrender of illegal arms in the Gaza Strip, after which there were to be systematic searches of the residences of activists. Tsahal sealed off the Palestinian territory, though it was in fact from the Israeli-controlled zone in the West Bank that the next two suicide bombers came, who struck at Jerusalem on 3 March, with ten dead, and in Tel Aviv the next day, with fifteen people killed. On this occasion, incidentally, the Tsahal closure caused a diplomatic incident between Israel and Germany on 9 March 1996 when Klaus Kinkel, the German foreign minister, refused to allow Tsahal to inspect his official car following a meeting with Yasser Arafat in Gaza.

In Gaza, Fatah's supporters demonstrated in their thousands to condemn these attacks, going as far as to carry placards in Hebrew (for the benefit of the Israeli media) proclaiming: 'Yes to peace, no to violence.' The Palestinian security forces, whose numbers had been boosted as part of the struggle against Hamas, were now 40,000 strong, all the separate services taken together.[24] They took control of the Islamic University and of the most radical mosques, arresting thirty-five of the thirty-seven activists most wanted by Shin Bet over the course of a few days. They also demolished a monument in Khan Yunis erected to the memory of Yahya Ayyash. On 13 March 1996, the Sharm el-Sheikh summit was held on the initiative of

President Clinton, under the auspices of President Mubarak. This was attended by the leaders of thirty-one states including Presidents Yeltsin, Chirac and Demirel, the British prime minister, John Major, and Germany's Chancellor Kohl, as well as the leaders of fourteen Arab states, with the exception of Syria, Lebanon and Libya. Arafat laid great stress on the extent of the measures he had taken against the Islamists. Clinton was extremely concerned about the consequences of the outbreak of suicide bombings on the upcoming Israeli elections, particularly as Shimon Peres's poll ratings had begun to fall in relation to the Likud leader Binyamin Netanyahu, who was a vocal opponent of Labour's peace strategy. The deadly offensive waged by Tsahal against Hezbollah in Lebanon in April 1996, under the title 'Grapes of Wrath', did nothing to reverse Labour's slide in the polls.

Arafat, who was also banking on a Labour victory, convened the Palestinian National Council in Gaza on 24 April 1996. He was anxious to abrogate, prior to the Israeli elections, the articles of the PLO Charter that called for the destruction of the State of Israel. Because of various restrictions imposed by Tsahal, only 536 of the 669 members of the PLO's 'Parliament' were able to reach the autonomous territory by the date of the meeting. The historic PNC session was presided over by Selim Zaanoun, Abu Iyad's former companion during his time underground in Gaza. What was at issue was a symbolic transfer of power towards the Palestinian Authority, whose remit related to the West Bank and Gaza, and which cooperated in conjunction with the Palestinian Legislative Council, elected just three months earlier, and away from the PNC, hitherto the most representative institution of the Palestinian people in all its diversity, including the Palestinian diaspora. Arafat, who continued to be active as the leader of Fatah, the dominant faction within the PLO, and also as the head of the Palestinian Authority, thus inaugurated a major step forward in Palestinian history. Further, the amendment of the Charter, by means of which the PLO put into action one of the provisions of its peace agreement with Israel, the transition from the PNC to the PLC, was also part of the 'territorialisation' of Palestinian aspirations: necessarily a restrictive process.

Seven of the twenty-three members of the new Palestinian cabinet were from Gaza. Those who kept their previous posts were Intissar al-Wazir at the

Ministry of Social Affairs, Nabil Shaath as planning minister, Freih Abu Middain as justice minister and Riyad Zaanoun at the Ministry of Health. Three other Fatah personalities from Gaza also entered the government. Abdurrahman Hamad, a former member of the Palestinian delegation at Madrid, became minister for housing, a largely nominal post of minister of supply was created for Abdel Aziz Shahin (Abu Ali), and Imad Falluji, who had recently joined Fatah after leaving Hamas, was rewarded with the post of minister without portfolio. All seven ministers were also by convention drawn from the elected membership of the PLC, which was why Zakarya al-Agha lost his position as minister for housing and left the government when he was defeated in the polls at Khan Yunis in January 1996.

Arafat now moved his focus from Gaza to the West Bank, spending more time at the Muqatta in Ramallah, the administrative and military complex built under the British Mandate which had successively been used by the Jordanians and then by Israel. Most of the Authority's leading figures who were able to do so had already chosen the relative ease of life in the West Bank in preference to the overbearing constraints of Gaza. The new Palestinian team had scarcely had time to install itself, however, before there was a further upheaval in Israeli political life, comparable to the end of the Labour domination in Israel that had taken place in 1977. On the evening of 29 May 1996, Shimon Peres, who had been forecast to win the election on the basis of the early counting of the votes, was overtaken during the night by Binyamin Netanyahu, who was declared the victor. For Arafat, this blow was even harder to bear than the assassination of Yitzhak Rabin.

As the Palestinian Authority leaned progressively towards the adoption of a permanent base in the West Bank rather than Gaza, UNRWA moved its headquarters to Gaza City. Until 1978, the UN agency set up for the Palestinian refugees had been based in Beirut, but due to the Lebanese civil war it withdrew to Vienna. The return of the UNRWA structure to the Middle East was favoured by major donors, such as the United States, Norway and Japan. But it also fulfilled an operational need. The Gaza Strip was in practice the only possible choice, since a quarter of the refugees registered with UNRWA lived there, with a unique concentration of refugees in the camps set up for the purpose by the United Nations. On 15 July 1996, UNRWA's commissioner-general, Peter Hansen, a Danish national, together with his administrative team, officially transferred the organisation's headquarters from Vienna to Gaza City.

Peace on Hold

In accordance with his election campaign, which had been characterised by hostility to the PLO and the Oslo Accords, the new Israeli prime minister allowed it to remain in doubt as to whether he was even willing to meet Yasser Arafat. Indeed, it was not until 22 August, after a conversation between Mahmoud Abbas and Dore Gold, the adviser Netanyahu had designated to make such contacts, that Tsahal grudgingly agreed to resume the routine permission granted to 150 of the Palestinian Authority's officials to move freely between the West Bank and Gaza. This reluctance even extended to the movements of the Palestinian president. Arafat was accustomed to travel between Ramallah and Gaza by helicopter, but on 22 August Shimon Peres was obliged to go to Gaza for a planned meeting with the Palestinian leader because Arafat's helicopter had not been given permission to make the flight to Ramallah. Six days later, upon returning to Ramallah, Arafat's helicopter was left circling for more than an hour until it was permitted to land in Gaza. It should be mentioned that Mahmoud Abbas was subsequently able to develop a wider range of official contacts in Israel, both with Ariel Sharon, the infrastructure minister, and with Aryeh Deri, the leader of the religious Shas Party, who had been an early advocate of Israel's unilateral withdrawal from Gaza when he had been minister of the interior in the Rabin government of 1993.

Arafat pleaded with Ezer Weizman, the president of Israel, to intervene to end Tsahal's obstruction, while Netanyahu accused the Palestinian president of heightening the tension. Arafat and Netanyahu finally met at the Erez crossing on 4 September 1996, though their conversation was limited to the technicalities of the impending Israeli disengagement in Hebron. Three weeks later, Netanyahu, without consulting Tsahal, initiated archaeological excavations under the Temple Mount in Jerusalem, in other words, under the mosques of the Haram al-Sharif (The Noble Sanctuary). This led to violent confrontations throughout the occupied territories, with exchanges of fire between Israeli troops and Palestinian police, in Nablus in particular. Tsahal later gave the Palestinian Authority the names of seventy police officers accused of firing on Israeli troops, whom they asserted they had the right to arrest.

Israeli helicopters went into action in Gaza and Rafah against protestors who attacked Tsahal positions or settlements. After three days of riots, a fragile calm returned. President Clinton invited both Arafat and Netanyahu to Washington, together with King Hussein of Jordan, for an Israeli–Palestinian summit which ultimately failed to result in an agreement. On 23 October 1996, in this tense atmosphere, Gaza gave an exceptional welcome to the French President Jacques Chirac. To commemorate the occasion, Arafat renamed one of Gaza City's avenues after Charles de Gaulle (incidentally, Gaza already had a Victor Hugo Street, which had been the site of the French Cultural Centre since 1994). During the visit Arafat took the French president to the port of Gaza, where building works had been suspended due to the political blockade.[25]

The Likud government increased the pace of settlement as the talks between Israel and Palestine began to falter, which in turn led to angry debates in the Palestinian parliament that was meeting in Ramallah; in Gaza, meanwhile, Hamas dedicated the ceremonies marking its ninth anniversary to the struggle against Israeli settlement. This was a very popular theme, and the Palestinian Authority gave its blessing to a rally in Gaza where Mahmoud Zahar made a passionate address to 15,000 activists and sympathisers. The agreement on Hebron was finally signed by the Palestinians on 15 January 1997, with the Israeli cabinet adding its signature a day later. To achieve this, however, much more diplomacy had been required. There had been three meetings between Arafat and Netanyahu, and a shuttle by US envoy Dennis Ross between meetings with Arafat in Bethlehem and discussions with Netanyahu in Jerusalem, together with a mission by King Hussein of Jordan.

Three years after his return to Gaza, the 'Old Man' even found himself challenged within the fledgling Palestinian institutions. In April 1997, the PLC held a number of highly emotional debates on the mismanagement of international aid, with accusations raised of nepotism and corruption, based in part on a report by the General Control Office, the Palestinian body set up to scrutinise government expenditure. Questions were raised in particular about the role of Nabil Shaath, the planning minister and Fatah member of parliament for Khan Yunis. Fathi Subuh, a professor at Al-Azhar University in Gaza, was arrested on 2 July 1997 after daring to include a question about corruption inside the Authority in one of his exam papers. He was held for five months without charge before being released under caution with an order to report to his neighbourhood police station.

On 30 June 1997 the death of an inhabitant of Gaza after questioning by Force 17, effectively the presidential guard, sparked off violent demonstrations against arbitrary behaviour by the Palestinian police. A dozen people had already died in the Authority's detention centres, and in this case the presidential guard was found guilty of torture. Arafat decided to make an example of the culprits, and on 3 July a military tribunal condemned three of the police officers involved to death, while two others were sentenced to five years in prison.

Last but not least the arrangements for Israeli settlements in the Gaza Strip, which involved expropriations and demolitions,[26] were a frequent cause of disturbances in which the Palestinian security forces were obliged to contain the demonstrators, in effect protecting the settlers in order to prevent the situation from escalating.

The Sheikh's Glory

On 30 July 1997, a Hamas suicide attack which left fifteen dead, including the two suicide bombers, led to Israeli reprisals against the Gaza Strip on an unprecedented scale. Not only was the territory closed off, but fishing boats were also prevented from going to sea. Israel additionally suspended the transfer of tax revenue to the Palestinian Authority as specified in the peace agreement. This related to the transfer of revenue from VAT in Israel to the Authority, which represented as much as half of the latter's operating budget. Arafat was furious and prepared to take action, but at the same time he invited to Gaza the head of Shin Bet, Ami Ayalon, to discuss improved anti-terrorist cooperation. On 4 September, however, the effect of such gestures of good will was swept away when a triple suicide attack was carried out by the Qassam brigades in Jerusalem in which four Israelis died. Though none of the suicide bombers was identified as coming from Gaza, the territory was once again isolated from the world by Israel. Arafat arrested dozens of Hamas members, closed down its various publications and shut its social centres. Netanyahu insisted that these measures were insufficient, and his strictures were largely supported by the Clinton administration.

However, Israel's prime minister was well aware that the Hamas leadership inside Gaza, Abdelaziz Rantissi, only recently released from prison, and Mahmoud Zahar, both veterans of Marj al-Zuhur, had no control over the Qassam brigades. He gave instructions to Mossad to strike instead at the Hamas Political Bureau, which he identified as the highest tier of Hamas's management. Musa Abu Marzouk had just been tried and acquitted in the United States on a charge of financing terrorism, obliging the Israeli authorities to drop a demand for his extradition, which made it difficult for Israel to justify targeting him. For this reason, Israel's choice of target fell on Khaled Meshal, who was living in Jordan. On 25 September 1997, in a bizarre sequence of events, two Israeli agents carrying Canadian passports contrived to jostle Meshal while he was walking in the street in Amman, injecting him with a slow-acting poison.[27] The Jordanian intelligence services uncovered the plot and arrested the would-be assassins. King Hussein, enraged at the affront, threatened Clinton with the possible abrogation of his peace treaty with Israel. Under American pressure, Netanyahu agreed to supply the antidote to the poison, thus saving Meshal's life. But in exchange for the discreet release of his two assassins he also agreed to a move with momentous consequences—the release of Sheikh Yassin.

Arafat, who had spent weeks attempting to root out Hamas in the Gaza Strip, was taken aback by the fall-out from Netanyahu's blunder. On 2 October 1997, the Palestinian president made a bid to mitigate the impact of this spectacular turn of events by going to Amman to congratulate Sheikh Yassin in person on his release, and to invite him to return to Gaza. On 6 October, Sheikh Yassin's return brought tens of thousands of people out into the streets of Gaza City. Not all who celebrated his return were Islamist militants, by any means, but for the Islamists in particular this white-haired sexagenarian, imprisoned since 1989, had the advantage of being neither associated with the darkest hours of the intifada, nor tainted with the lies and scandals of the Palestinian Authority. Sheikh Yassin declared that a halt to attacks against Israel would be contingent on a total Israeli withdrawal from the West Bank and Gaza, together with the dismantling of all settlements.

Though Sheikh Yassin did not contest the representative character of the Authority, Arafat was henceforth obliged to take account of a personality whose charisma in the Gaza Strip was as powerful as his own. Arafat's paternalistic image as the 'Old Man' of Palestine had lost its leverage. Among Sheikh Yassin's right-hand men were not only Abdelaziz Rantissi and Mahmoud Zahar, who had been his faithful companions since the launching of the Mujamma a quarter of a century before, but also Ismail Haniya, who was his preferred henchman from the new generation. On the other bank of the Jordan, Khalid Meshal, the miraculous survivor, had acquired unprecedented status proportional to the humiliation that had been inflicted on Mossad. Arafat, by contrast, was alone, increasingly isolated in his 'trompe l'oeil' presidency, which had in fact cut him off more from his people than had any of the tribulations he had suffered in the past. He had been elected by the popular vote in January 1996, and held in his own hands the leadership of the Palestinian Authority, the PLO and Fatah, but his titles paled by comparison with the aura of the frail survivor of Israel's prisons. Still haunted by the shadow of Rabin, Arafat would be obliged to eke out his existence steering a course between Netanyahu and Yassin. In February 1998, Sheikh Yassin was authorised by Israel to travel to Egypt for medical reasons and went on afterwards to visit Saudi Arabia, Iran, the United Arab Emirates and Kuwait. Wherever he went, his reception was as warm, if not warmer, than that accorded to Yasser Arafat.

The inhabitants of the Gaza Strip continued to be subjected to periodic closures of the territory, and were sometimes banned from using the main roads when Israel decided to reserve them for the use of the settlers. In fact, between 1993 and 1996, Tsahal closed off the Gaza Strip for a total of 342 days, and the situation grew worse after Netanyahu came to power. From 1994, the loss of revenue due to closures was larger than the inflow from international aid. In these circumstances, the population was increasingly sceptical about a peace process that appeared to have become indefinitely protracted. On 14 May 1998, Palestinians participated en masse in two minutes of silence, observed across all the occupied territories, to mark the fiftieth anniversary of the 'nakba'. Marches took place and clashes with the Israeli soldiers broke out. A nurse was killed while evacuating the wounded. Arafat, who was becoming more impotent each day, held discussions in Gaza with senior Israeli defence and intelligence officials and stepped up cooperation against terrorism, with the help of the United States and Britain, in the hope of resuming the negotiations with Netanyahu that had been suspended since January 1997 and the partial Israeli withdrawal from Hebron.

The Clinton administration's preference was for parallel conversations with the antagonists rather than direct mediation, but as a method this failed to lead to better results. For this reason, on 7 October 1998, the US secretary of state, Madeleine Albright, agreed to meet Arafat and Netanyahu at the Erez crossing for tripartite talks. The atmosphere gradually became more relaxed and Arafat issued an invitation to the Israeli prime minister to lunch in Gaza. This was a first for Netanyahu, who had never been into the autonomous territories. Yet the improvement was only temporary as on the very next day the Israeli leader announced new settlement plans. In the aftermath of this he appointed Ariel Sharon as his foreign affairs minister and designated him as Israel's interlocutor with the Palestinian Authority, which caused considerable consternation in Gaza.

On 15 October 1998, President Clinton invited Netanyahu and Arafat for talks at the White House before leaving them to negotiate face to face at Wye Plantation, a historic house in extensive grounds on Wye River in Maryland, under the supervision of Madeleine Albright. The talks stalled, and King Hussein and President Clinton himself were both obliged to become involved at length. On 23 October an agreement was reached that would result in the Authority's control of 40 per cent of the land area of the West Bank and the establishment of an industrial zone in Gaza, together with an airport and a commercial port. Five years after the original festivities at the White House, Clinton and Arafat were both painfully aware of the grave consequences of Rabin's demise.

The 'Wye River' Agreement, as the Israeli–Palestinian accord was designated (on the principle of 'Camp David' and 'Oslo', as earlier agreements were known), was strongly criticised in Gaza, not only by Hamas and Islamic Jihad but also by the PFLP and the DFLP. The Qassam brigades, which had been observing a de facto truce that had lasted for more than a year, went back into action. On 29 October 1998, a suicide bomber crashed his booby-trapped car into a school bus from a settlement close to Khan Yunis, but was headed off by an Israeli military jeep whose driver died with him in the explosion. There was a quick reaction from the Palestinian security services, with Sheikh Yassin placed under house arrest and hundreds of Hamas activists arrested, including Mahmoud Zahar. Abdelaziz Rantissi had already been arrested some months earlier because of his criticisms of the Authority.

The threat of reprisals against Arafat's administration by the Qassam brigades was repudiated by the Hamas leadership, both in Gaza and Amman, but this did not prevent Hamas from being subjected to even tougher action. The Authority found it more difficult, however, to halt the popular movement of solidarity with the hunger strike of Palestinian prisoners in Israel whose release Yasser Arafat had failed to achieve, not even obtaining the freedom of a proportion of those held. On 23 November, more than 1,000 protestors targeted Mahmoud Abbas's residence while Sheikh Yassin symbolically joined the hunger strike of his former fellow prisoners.

But Yasser Arafat had other priorities. He was anxiously making preparations for a visit to Gaza by President Clinton, which he hoped would give a boost to Palestinian hopes for a state of their own. On 14 December 1998, Yasser Arafat and his wife Souha, welcomed Bill and Hillary Clinton to Gaza's newly opened airport. (The passengers of Air Palestine, created under the aegis of the Palestinian Authority, were otherwise obliged to travel to El-Arish by coach in order to start their flights from there.) The details of protocol for the day had been scrutinised and re-scrutinised so that each element of the ceremony was appropriate to a future sovereign state, with the proper deployment of flags, anthems and guards of honour. On that day, Gaza sought to present itself as the capital of the State of Palestine, proclaimed in Algiers ten years before, which Arafat had believed himself to be inaugurating when he had signed the Oslo Accords. The interim period of five years would be completed in May 1999, with nothing yet agreed on the permanent status of either the West Bank, where the majority of the territory continued to be occupied, or of Gaza, where a quarter of the land area was still in the hands of the settlements.

On the occasion of Clinton's visit, Arafat played his last card. In Gaza, not only did he convene the Palestinian National Council (PNC), the 'parliament' of the PLO, but also his Palestinian Central Council, whose role was to make decisions when the full PNC could not be summoned, as well as the PLO Executive Committee. He also called for a session of the Palestinian Legislative Council to meet in Gaza rather than at its principal seat in Ramallah, supplementing it with a gathering of dozens of Palestinian notables and personalities. The intention of this muster of 1,000 Palestinian representatives was to renew his commitment to live in peace with Israel, in the presence of the US president. The amendment of the PLO Charter, already approved in 1996, was voted through for a second time by a show of hands. Meanwhile, Hillary Clinton was visiting a refugee camp, and the US commerce secretary, William Daley, was taking part in the inauguration of the Gaza industrial zone at Qarni. For a period of a few hours, Gaza again began to hope. However, at the summit at Erez which met after these events, attended by Clinton, Arafat and Netanyahu, the latter produced a new list of twelve conditions that had to be fulfilled by the Palestinians before the Wye River Agreement could come into effect.

On 17–19 December 1998, US air strikes against Iraq led to violent protests in Gaza which the Palestinian police uncompromisingly suppressed. The American operation 'Desert Fox', carried out in coordination with Britain, was initiated after the Americans forced UN observers out of Iraq, thus terminating their mission to supervise the destruction of Iraq's weapons of mass destruction in accordance with UN resolutions. The air strikes coincided with a debate in the US Congress on the impeachment of President Clinton, who was at the time politically exposed at home, having been accused of dishonesty with regard to his extra-marital relations with Monica Lewinsky. Operation Desert Fox undoubtedly helped to counteract the fallout from the Monica Lewinsky scandal.

Long gone were the days when Arafat's judgement was obscured by his support for Saddam Hussein—eight years after the latter's invasion of Kuwait, Arafat had provided hospitality for an American president who was to launch a bombing campaign against Saddam's Iraq upon returning from Gaza to the United States. Netanyahu continued to refuse to apply the Wye River Agreement. Arafat named the 'Yasser Arafat International

Airport' for himself in Gaza, and called the new port installations the Abu Ammar Naval Base (the industrial zone, however, soberly retained its technical appellation). On 10 March 1999, Arafat went to Amman to visit the new Jordanian monarch King Abdullah II, who had succeeded his father, King Hussein. While he was there, the Palestinian police crushed a protest in Gaza against a death sentence passed on two individuals that was seen as unjust. Arafat delayed his return to Gaza. Once he had arrived home, he took steps to make it clear that he was in charge and then set off for a month-long tour abroad, consulting all and sundry on the idea of a unilateral declaration of the independence of Palestine on the date of expiry of the interim period.

On 24 April 1999, Yasser Arafat convened a meeting in Gaza of the Central Council of the PLO to address this subject, attended, most unusually, by Sheikh Yassin in the capacity of an observer. In the presence of the Islamist patriarch, the Palestinian president declared that his preference was to delay any unilateral declaration, a position which received the support of a majority of the delegates present. Khalid Meshal and his Hamas Political Bureau colleagues in Jordan disapproved of Sheikh Yassin's attendance at this meeting, even in an observational role.[28] This was the first occasion on which the founder of Hamas had been so brusquely disowned by his own supporters. Any such challenge on the part of Fatah would have been unimaginable, though Fatah had in any case been somewhat sidelined by the existence of the Palestinian Authority. As a Fatah activist in Gaza put it, 'Arafat is like a fire: if you come too near you get burned, but if you stay too far away from him, it gets cold.'[29] On 4 May 1999, the day the interim period expired, the Palestinian president was visiting Ireland. On 17 May, parliamentary elections in Israel brought a key development when Netanyahu, who was still refusing to implement the Wye River Agreement signed the previous autumn, won only 44 per cent of the vote in the direct poll for prime minister, while the new Labour leader, Ehud Barak, won by a landslide, with 56 per cent of the vote. Arafat's hopes were aroused: he must have asked himself whether he had found a new Rabin. Sheikh Yassin maintained his silence, while the Gaza Strip as a whole gave the appearance of total indifference.

Camp David in Reverse

Despite the scale of Barak's personal victory in the prime ministerial poll, the Knesset elected in May 1999 was the most divided in Israel's history. It took Barak more than six weeks to construct a coalition government out of seven separate parties. Yossi Beilin, one of the architects of the Oslo Accords, became minister of justice, while the foreign affairs portfolio went to David Levy, a Likud dissident. On 11 July, Arafat met Barak at Erez for the first Israeli–Palestinian summit since the fruitless tripartite meeting with Clinton and Netanyahu. The Israeli prime minister agreed to take the Wye River Agreement forward, but refused to enter into any discussion of settlements. A few days later in Washington, Barak announced that the 'majority' of Israeli settlements would be maintained, both in the West Bank and the Gaza Strip.[30] In any case, Tsahal units were currently helping settlers to build new greenhouses and prefabricated residences near Khan Yunis. Israeli–Palestinian negotiations, now conducted by Saeb Earakat, minister for local government, for the Palestinians and Gilead Sher, Barak's cabinet director, quickly came up against the issue of the calendar for the application of Wye River.

On 25 July 1999 Arafat was able to speak to Clinton and Barak during the funeral ceremony in Rabat for King Hassan II of Morocco. In contrast, the emir of Kuwait, who had never forgiven the PLO chief for his support of Saddam Hussein in 1990, refused to even shake his hand. Arafat was more fortunate with the ruler of Qatar, Sheikh Hamad Ben Khalifa al-Thani, who accepted his invitation to visit Gaza. When the Qatari sovereign arrived in Gaza on 8 August 1999, he became the second head of state to visit the Palestinian autonomous territory: the first had been the late King Hussein of Jordan. Meanwhile, President Mubarak of neighbouring Egypt continued to hold back from any such gesture in Arafat's direction. Sheikh Hamad was accompanied by a reporting team from Al Jazeera, the 24-hours news satellite TV station based in Qatar, many of whose staff had previously worked for the BBC Arabic Service, which had revolutionised television news coverage in the region. Qatar took the opportunity to open a diplomatic mission in Gaza.

After weeks of sometimes acrimonious negotiations, Erakat and Sher reached an agreement on the modalities of the application of the Wye River

Agreement, which became known as Wye II. On 4 September, at the Egyptian resort of Sharm el-Sheikh, under the auspices of Egypt's President Husni Mubarak, the text was signed by Yasser Arafat and Ehud Barak, as well as by the US Secretary of State Madeleine Albright and King Abdullah II of Jordan. (Jordan, incidentally, had just closed the Hamas office in Amman after which Khaled Meshal and his staff, after spending two months in detention, left Jordan for the Qatari capital, Doha. The Hamas Bureau would ultimately find its new permanent home in Damascus.) The Palestinian president also achieved the release of 350 prisoners, only a small proportion of those held by Israel, but whose release was a gesture the Palestinian population, especially in Gaza, had eagerly awaited. On 15 September 1999, during a televised debate in Gaza, mothers of Palestinian prisoners accused the Authority of not putting enough pressure on Israel to obtain their freedom. The producer of the TV programme in which these views were aired was arrested soon after by the 'Preventive Police' and held without charge until 4 October. When he was freed, he revealed the names of police officers who had allegedly tortured him and challenged them to re-arrest him. The day after the signature of Wye II, three suicide attackers detonated their bombs in northern Israel, one in Haifa and two in Tiberias, in which only the bombers were killed. The Palestinian security services, which had detained 300 Hamas members as a precaution during the preceding weeks, confirmed that the attacks had not been prepared in the areas under their control. As it transpired, the bombers were Arabs of Israeli nationality, the first time this had been the case.

On 16 September, Arafat and Ehud Barak met inside Israel in an encounter that was intended to be secret but was revealed the following day by the Israeli press. Arafat was able to extract some concessions from the Israeli prime minister, which though significant, were nonetheless somewhat limited. (Arafat was to hold a further clandestine meeting with Barak in Tel Aviv on 7 March 2000, which was also soon publicised.) As a result of the Palestinian leader's efforts, the second in command in the PFLP, Abu Ali Mustafa, was given permission to return to the West Bank after thirty-two years in exile, which helped the Authority to make peace with the Palestinian left wing. George Habash continued to refuse formal reconciliation with Arafat, taking the same hostile attitude towards Fatah as that adopted by Syria as well as by Hamas. However, Abu Ali Mustafa soon succeeded Habash as head of the PFLP and reintegrated it into the PLO. In another concession, a 50-kilometre long passage between the Gaza Strip and the West Bank was finally opened, though Israel retained its sovereignty and the right to intervene as it saw fit. Barak also challenged the relevance of UN resolutions relating to Palestine and made no secret of his preference for a unilateral agreement on separation, with terms to be laid down by Israel, or at least for long-term interim arrangements to be similarly reached. This augured badly for the final status negotiations that were soon to follow. During a visit to Gaza on 19 October 1999 Nelson Mandela, the former South African president, called on Israel to withdraw quickly from both the West Bank and the Gaza Strip.

In Gaza there were increasing complaints about the Authority, which, with the territory in such a deprived situation, was blamed for everything that went wrong. Taxi drivers frequently went on strike because of increases in the price of fuel and teachers walked out because their salaries were too low. More or less spontaneous calls were made to refuse to pay electricity and telephone bills, drawing attention to the difference in the rates charged from those that prevailed in Israel. Arafat cajoled some and threatened others, sometimes making concessions and sometimes digging in his heels, all of which enabled the Authority to steer a course between the hazards it faced. Any accusations of corruption were forcefully rebutted, resulting in the detention of journalists, as well as union and human rights activists.

No one was spared, not even within the Palestinian administration itself. On 20 June 2000, for instance, Force 17 occupied the Gaza offices of one of the officials in charge of refugee issues, who had been too critical of Arafat, and the official himself was arrested the following day in Ramallah. The various security services began to behave like out-of-control militias, sometimes settling disputes between each other by force of arms. On 8 June 2000, for example, an outbreak of shooting inside the intelligence headquarters left two officials wounded. Tsahal had its own share in these repeated incidents. For example, a force of 100 Israeli soldiers burst into the Gaza international airport on 1 June 2000 to arrest a Palestinian suspect, wounding some twenty people in the process. On 9 July, a woman was accidentally killed at a roadblock at Kfar Darom, in an event which failed to lead to any revision of the rules of engagement.

The Israeli withdrawal from Lebanon in May 2000 was undertaken unilaterally by Ehud Barak as the result of military pressure from Hezbollah. For Arafat, this was a negative development because it undermined his negotiating strategy towards those who clung to the principle of 'Islamic resistance', to borrow the term used by Hamas itself. It also meant that the Israeli prime minister was even less inclined to make substantial concessions, increasingly subject as he was to constant criticism from Likud. The final status talks eventually got under way in secret in Stockholm between Israeli and Palestinian negotiating teams, but they rapidly ran into the ground. On 3 July 2000, the PLO's governing institutions met in Gaza and mandated Arafat to proclaim a Palestinian state in the Palestinian territories occupied in 1967. In response, Ehud Barak threatened to annex a large part of the West Bank. To avoid an open confrontation, Clinton invited the two leaders to Camp David where talks on the final status began on 11 July 2000, only for it to be accepted two weeks later that they had failed to progress, largely because of irreconcilable differences on the question of Jerusalem.

Seven years after the signature of the Oslo Accords, and six years after the installation of the Palestinian Authority in Gaza, the record of Arafat's achievements was very mixed. The authoritarian style of leadership characteristic of the 'Old Man' had hindered the establishment of an administration appropriate to his ambition to establish a state. It also led to his failure to generate enthusiasm among the Palestinian youth, despite their having been battle-hardened by the experience of the first intifada. The Palestinian president soon decided to shake off the dust of Gaza, preferring to make his headquarters in Ramallah when he was not travelling abroad. The PLO's officials, long in exile in Beirut and then in Tunis, were also not slow to quit Gaza when the possibility of installing themselves in the West Bank was on offer. This early loss of love between the Palestinian Authority and Gaza evidently suited the interests of Hamas, which thrived on the cult of personality that surrounded Sheikh Ahmed Yassin, which stretched far wider than Islamist circles.

By 2000, the Gaza Strip was still waiting for the dividends that should have accrued from the peace process. Its high degree of dependence on the

Israeli economy, which the occupation tended only to intensify, left the population especially vulnerable to the closures of the territory by Tsahal that became more and more frequent. The inflation of the Palestinian bureaucracy only partially made up for this loss of revenue, and brought with it, through the activities of the Authority, a pernicious growth in dependency and nepotism. None of the major infrastructure projects foreseen in the various donor conferences had taken practical shape, whether in the port of Gaza or relating to such projects as commercial tree plantations, and the industrial zones of the frontier regions, such as Erez and Qarni, continued to be closely tied to the Israeli market.

At a time when Palestinian farmers and fishermen were struggling to find a market for their products, the Israeli settlers seized the best irrigated land in Gaza and were able to make profits from the export of the harvests they gathered from their agricultural greenhouses, equipped with the latest technological advances. For Tsahal, the security of the Israeli settlements took priority over all other considerations, and this was an imperative that complicated still further for the Palestinians of Gaza an existence that was already difficult. A quarter of the territory remained under the exclusive control of Tsahal, which had set up fifty strongpoints at sensitive positions.[31] According to General Tzvi Fogel, deputy commander in Gaza, Tsahal had been preparing for a confrontation in the territory since December 1999; the fortification of these positions increased the likelihood of what was becoming a self-fulfilling prophecy.[32] Faced by the realities of the peace, which were so distant from the dreams that had been nourished by the intifada, the population was gripped by blind rage. Hamas bided its time, while the Palestinian Authority imagined itself to be stronger than it was. The Gaza Strip was ready to boil over.

14

DAYS OF FURY

When he returned to Gaza after the fruitless Camp David summit of 11–25 July 2000, Yasser Arafat, who was confident in the outcome of future negotiations, persuaded the PLO leadership to delay the unilateral proclamation of a Palestinian state. On 25 September, Arafat went to the Tel Aviv residence of Israeli Prime Minister Ehud Barak for a three-hour meeting, during which President Clinton spoke to the two leaders by telephone from Washington. The Israelis and Palestinians agreed to send their negotiators back to the United States to take up the talks where they had left off.

On 28 September 2000, Barak authorised Ariel Sharon to visit the Temple Mount (the Haram al-Sharif) in Jerusalem, together with a Likud parliamentary delegation. The party was accompanied by a police escort 1,000 strong. The visit, which the Palestinians saw as an unprecedented provocation, was repeated the following day. This was a Friday, the day for collective prayer in the mosques, and on this occasion there were 2,000 police to protect Sharon and his colleagues. On that day, six Palestinians were killed in East Jerusalem. Over the following three days, disturbances spread across the whole West Bank, into the Gaza Strip, and then into the regions of predominantly Arab population inside Israel. In all, forty-four Palestinians died, including ten of Israeli nationality. The menacing sound of Israeli drone engines became familiar to Gaza's inhabitants.[1] General Yom-Tov Samia, the southern region commander who was responsible for the Gaza Strip, took a hard-line view and was sympathetic to the settlers. To quell the troubles, he ordered the use of cluster bombs whose showers of steel flechettes were deadly in the urban environment.[2]

There was no question that this new uprising was nationalist in its inspiration, but since it was inspired by the urge to defend the holy place of Jerusalem it became known as the 'Al-Aqsa Intifada'. In contrast to 1987, the Gaza Strip was not its point of origin. However, it was on 30 September at the Netzarim crossroads in Gaza that its first emblematic martyr fell: twelve-year-old Muhammad al-Durra. The use of firearms had been banned by the nationalist command during the first intifada: this time, the rioters soon began to carry guns. On 7 October, seven people were wounded when a bus carrying Israeli workers was ambushed. Gaza airport was closed in response. Extremists on both sides quickly took the lead. Ehud Barak explored the formation of a government of national unity with Sharon, while Arafat met the leaders of Hamas and Islamic Jihad in Gaza to coordinate Palestinian action. The closure of Gaza and the West Bank was not enough to halt the escalation. At the international level, a number of attempts were made to mediate.

Last Chance Talks

On 12 October 2000, the Palestinian president was preparing for a visit to Gaza by the head of the CIA, George Tenet, who had been sent by President Clinton to restore calm through the re-establishment of tripartite security arrangements involving the United States, Israel and the Palestinian Authority. This was the moment that Barak chose to order an air raid on Arafat's offices, on the same day as an attack on the port of Gaza. The bombing, from which both Arafat and the CIA chief emerged unscathed, were part of Israel's reprisals for the lynching of two Israeli army reservists at a Ramallah police station, an incident in which fifteen Palestinian policemen had themselves been wounded when trying to protect the two soldiers from summary execution. The following day, disturbances broke out in Gaza City to express popular outrage against the Authority's inability to resist Israel's aggression. The demonstrations continued until 16 October, this time in protest against Arafat's decision to travel to Sharm el-Sheikh, where he conferred with Ehud Barak in an attempt to resolve the crisis, under the auspices of President Mubarak and with the presence of President Clinton, King Abdullah of Jordan and the secretary-general of the United Nations, Kofi Annan. Dissatisfaction with Arafat, which was first expressed by Hamas, quickly gained ground within Fatah. A 'Supreme Committee for the Supervision of the Intifada' was set up, known as the 'National-Islamic Committee', which brought together various PLO and non-PLO factions with the intention of rejecting any commitment made by Arafat at Sharm el-Sheikh. As the situation seemed to be sliding beyond control, Barak continued to play a double game. On the one hand, on 30 October 2000, he blatantly attacked installations belonging to Fatah and Force 17 in Khan Yunis. The following day, on the other hand, he sent Amnon Shahak, his former chief of staff and now his minister of transport, to hold talks with Arafat in Gaza City. The spiral of violence continued to mount throughout the Palestinian territories, but on 11 November the violence reached new heights around the settlement bloc of Gush Katif, with eight Palestinians left dead and one Israeli soldier killed by 'friendly fire'. Two days later, Palestinian gunmen killed two Israeli soldiers and an Israeli lorry driver in the Gaza Strip. On 18 November, a Palestinian policeman fatally wounded an Israeli soldier before being shot dead himself.

On 20 November, a bomb attack against a bus in Kfar Darom, in which two Israeli settlers died, prompted reprisals across the Gaza Strip, with attacks by tanks and helicopter gunships on targets related to the Palestinian Authority, Fatah's preventive security and Force 17. The Palestinian TV and radio buildings were also hit in the raids, in which two died, while at the same time combat helicopters went into action in Rafah. Despite appeals for calm, clashes between the Palestinian police and the Israeli armed forces only increased. Barak then played his political trump cards. First, he proposed a minimal peace agreement on his terms, under which a Palestinian state would be established in 75 per cent of the Gaza Strip and a third of the West Bank. On 10 December, once this offer had unsurprisingly been rejected by the Palestinians, he announced his resignation, opening the way for a new direct election to the position of prime minister within the next two months. In the United States, President

George W. Bush, who was highly critical of the Middle East policy of his predecessor, Bill Clinton, had been declared the victor in the American presidential election that had taken place the month before, after a lengthy legal challenge by his rival, the former vice-president Al Gore. Against this background, Hamas was easily able to bring more than 30,000 demonstrators on to the streets to condemn any resumption of the peace process.

During the closing weeks of Ehud Barak's period in office and of the Clinton administration, Arafat tried to act as positively as possible. On 2 January 2001, the Palestinian president visited the White House where he gave his approval, albeit with some reservations, to the so-called 'Clinton parameters' for a lasting peace that had their origin in a formula for a comprehensive settlement Clinton had proposed on 15 December 2000. The main lines of the proposal embodied in the Clinton parameters were that the State of Palestine would have sovereignty over the entire Gaza Strip and 94–6 per cent of the West Bank. Israel's annexation of the main settlement blocs was to be compensated for by a territorial exchange, while East Jerusalem would be divided and the 'right of return' of the Palestinian refugees would be abrogated in exchange for Israel's formal recognition of the 'suffering' inflicted upon them in 1948. Finally, the Israeli armed forces would retain their presence in the Jordan Valley. On 7 January, Arafat sent Muhammad Dahlan to Cairo to meet the head of Israeli military intelligence under the auspices of George Tenet, the CIA chief. On 11 January, Dahlan was also one of three emissaries designated by Arafat, together with Saeb Erakat and Ahmed Qureia (Abu Ala), to resume high-level Israeli–Palestinian talks at a meeting in Erez. On 14 January, the body of an Israeli settler was discovered in Khan Yunis. But the fragile détente survived this development.

The violence continued, and the escalation of the level of the armed exchanges even took its toll on the inner circles of the Palestinian Authority. On 17 January 2001 in Gaza City, three masked killers murdered the director of Palestinian radio and television, Hisham Makki, who was an associate of Yasser Arafat. Despite this incident, Arafat held talks on the same day in Cairo with the Israeli foreign minister on the possibility of concluding a comprehensive agreement before the direct prime ministerial election in Israel that would decide whether Barak would continue to be prime minister or if he would be succeeded by Ariel Sharon. Lengthy talks in Taba resulted in a draft agreement. On 6 February, however, the prospects for these 'last chance' talks were swept away by the scale of Ariel Sharon's electoral victory, who took 62.4 per cent of the vote as against just 37.6 per cent for Barak.

The New Situation

The people of Gaza were devastated by the news of the election of the Gaza Strip's former military commander who had crushed the armed resistance in 1971. Arafat was also dismayed by Sharon's election: he had been the architect of the siege of Beirut in the summer of 1982, and had done everything in his power to ensure that the PLO chairman would be killed in the fighting.[3] Arafat nevertheless sent the new Israeli prime minister a letter of congratulation, subsequently making a telephone call to urge him to resume the peace process. Sharon's reply was that no discussions could be contemplated without a complete halt to the violence, and that even then only a provisional agreement could be considered. The new Bush administration also did its bit to close this particular door by confirming that the Clinton parameters were no longer operational.

Despite Ariel Sharon's victory in the prime ministerial poll, he did not necessarily command an obvious majority in the Knesset. Ehud Barak therefore entered into talks with Sharon in relation to the possibility of a government of national unity. Meanwhile, on 13 February 2001, while he was still caretaker prime minister, Barak ordered a raid on Jabalya Camp. As a result, one of Force 17's commanders, Massoud Ayyad, who had faced accusations from Israel of maintaining links with Hezbollah and Iran, was killed in his car by air-to-ground missiles. Ten days later, a volley of four homemade mortars was fired into an Israeli settlement in Gaza, without causing any casualties. In reprisal, two Palestinian police posts were destroyed, the Gaza Strip was sealed off and a ban was placed on driving along the territory's main north–south road. Tsahal planned to widen the security perimeters around the Gaza settlements to give them greater security. On 7 March, Sharon's coalition government was approved by the Knesset, with the inclusion of two Labour members: Binyamin Ben Eliezer became minister of defence and Shimon Peres took the foreign affairs port-folio. Ehud Barak, infuriated at being left out of the cabinet, went to the United States to work in the private sector.

In April 2001 there was a dramatic escalation in the number of clashes in the Gaza Strip. Palestinian mortar attacks were now being aimed not just at the settlements but also into the territory of Israel itself, including the frontier kibbutz of Nahal Oz. Tsahal held the Palestinian police and Force 17 responsible for these mortar attacks, which rarely caused casual-ties, and in reprisal launched attacks on Palestinian police installations. On 4 April a convoy of Palestinian security personnel, who were returning from a coordination meeting with their Israeli opposite numbers at the residence of the American ambassador at Herzliya, came under sustained Israeli fire at the Erez crossing point in which two Palestinian agents were wounded. A week later, Israeli tanks and bulldozers went into the camp at Khan Yunis to destroy Palestinian targets, demolishing twenty-eight houses in one day. On 14 April an operation of similar size was conducted at Rafah, and on 16 April at least seven positions belonging to Force 17 were shelled at the police headquarters in Gaza City. Tsahal divided the Gaza Strip into three sections sealed off from each other. In Rafah, on 25 April, four Fatah activists were killed in unexplained explosions, and on 30 April two Hamas militants died in similar circumstances. Whereas Israel claimed that they were 'terrorists' who had blown themselves up as they were pre-paring bombs, the Palestinian factions accused Tsahal of having detonated remote-controlled explosives.

Arafat appealed for an end to the Palestinian mortar attacks on Israel and for all attacks on non-military targets to cease. Hamas, Islamic Jihad and the PFLP rejected his requests and even grass-roots Fatah members were no longer willing to listen to such calls for restraint. They were in any case deemed insufficient by Israel, which demanded an end to all forms of violence and accused Arafat of duplicity, in view of the degree to which the Palestinian security services were themselves implicated in operations against the settlements. Israeli incursions with tanks and bulldozers went deeper into the 'autonomous' territory and were ever more destructive. On 2 May 2001, twenty houses were razed to the ground in Brazil Camp, and on 15 May, in Deir al-Balah, five houses and a police post were demolished. Israeli attacks were not solely directed at the Palestinian Authority. On 2 April Tsahal helicopters were used to target and kill an Islamic Jihad official in Rafah, and on 15 May one of Sheikh Yassin's bodyguards was killed by a tank round in Gaza City.

The United States tried in vain to achieve a ceasefire, or at least to reopen a dialogue between the Israeli and Palestinian security services. The mood of the moment, however, tended towards escalation. On 18 May, when a Hamas suicide attack killed five Israelis in Netanya, Sharon ordered Israeli F-16 aircraft to attack Palestinian Authority targets in both Gaza and the West Bank. This was the first time Israeli fighter aircraft had been used to attack the Palestinian territories since the occupation in June 1967. A week later, Israel responded to an attempted Hamas attack on an Israeli position in Gaza with the destruction of a police post and the bombardment of an area of Rafah. The same pattern was repeated on 29 May, when Israel felt it was appropriate to respond to a failed attack with a sustained assault on residential areas in both Rafah and Khan Yunis. On 4 June, exchanges of fire and grenades in Rafah left twenty-five wounded, including three Israeli soldiers. Meanwhile, Tsahal reported that it had now refined its technical capacities to include advanced technology for detection of movement on the border of the Gaza Strip both by day and by night. New 'rules of engagement' were handed down to the occupying troops which allowed Tsahal to treat any person inside a buffer zone a kilometre deep as a legitimate target.[4] The buffer zone was designated as one of the 'regions of special security', referred to by Tsahal as ABAM (*Ezor Bithoni Meyuhad*). They were first instituted by General Doron Almog, who had succeeded General Samia as southern region commander in December 2000.

George Tenet was again sent to the region to try to halt the violence. But the Bush administration took the view that it was for Arafat rather than Sharon to give guarantees, and in the meantime the civilian population of Gaza was continuing to pay a very heavy price for Israel's attacks. On 9 June 2001, for example, three Bedouins were killed in an attack near the Netzarim settlement; on 17 June, a twelve-year-old demonstrator was killed in Khan Yunis; and on 7 July another boy aged just eleven was killed in Rafah. During a meeting on 4 July, the Israeli 'security cabinet', consisting of those ministers with security responsibilities, approved a list of twenty-six Palestinian individuals to be eliminated. This was followed by a series of more or less targeted assassinations, taking place in the first instance in the West Bank. On 23 July, 3,000 demonstrators gathered in Gaza to protest against the Palestinian Authority's undertaking to put into practice various provisions put forward by George Tenet. The protest soon began to escalate before spreading to Nuseirat camp, where the demonstrators attacked the residence of Musa Arafat, Yasser Arafat's cousin and the head of military intelligence.

The Israeli programme of targeted assassinations began to include Fatah activists as well as Hamas militants. On 26 August 2001 a Fatah official in Rafah was killed when his house was bombed, together with two of his children. Three days later, in Gaza City, Israeli helicopters fired missiles at a car in which the military chief of Hamas, Muhammad Dayef, was travelling. Dayef escaped on this occasion, though one of his bodyguards and the son of his deputy died in the raid. Dayef was a graduate of the Islamic University in Gaza who had succeeded Yahya Ayyash as the head of the Qassam brigades in January 1996: over the coming months, he was to be targeted by helicopter gunships three more times.

On 25 August, two fighters from the DFLP, which had historically been identified with the negotiation process, captured an Israeli army position near Gush Katif and killed three Israeli soldiers before being shot down themselves. Ayman Bihdari, who planned this attack, was later killed alongside four other DFLP activists when an Israeli helicopter fired on their car in Rafah on 4 February 2002. On 26 August, Israeli F-15 and F-16 aircraft bombed Musa Arafat's offices, and Israeli helicopters overflew the Palestinian president's offices, though without opening fire. On 1 September Israel's next target was no mere factional militant: a colonel serving in the Palestinian intelligence in Gaza City died when an explosion destroyed his car. A week later, there was a similarly unexplained explosion at a Fatah office in Rafah.

The Shadow of 11 September

Some 3,000 people lost their lives in the terrorist attacks in New York and Washington perpetrated on 11 September 2001 by al-Qaida, which led the

Bush administration to declare a 'global war on terror'. None of the nineteen suicide attackers was Palestinian, and Osama Bin Laden, the instigator of the attacks, was highly critical of the nationalist emphasis not only of the PLO but also of Hamas.[5] At the same time, Arafat was ostentatious in his determination to give blood for the victims of the terrorist carnage in New York. This did not discourage Ariel Sharon from confounding the Palestinians with those responsible for the incidents in the United States. As he put it, 'Everyone has their Ben Laden: Arafat is our Ben Laden.'[6] This belligerent rhetoric was entirely consonant with the wave of emotion that was sweeping over the United States. Yet at the same time as Ariel Sharon was making a public display of his prejudices, the Israeli Labour Party's Shimon Peres, foreign minister in Sharon's government, was playing a contrary role. He arranged a meeting with Arafat in Gaza airport on 26 September.

Following their meeting, Arafat and Peres issued a joint statement committing themselves to put into effect the provisions proposed by George Tenet for the achievement of a ceasefire. However, when a bomb exploded at the frontier with Egypt soon afterwards, which slightly wounded three Israeli soldiers, Tsahal's reaction was brutal. Fourteen houses were demolished in Rafah during the night and six Palestinians were killed in the course of the following twenty-four hours. On 28 September 2001, the violence that marked the first anniversary of the outbreak of the 'Al-Aqsa Intifada' effectively buried the already tenuous hopes of a ceasefire. On 2 October, two Hamas members infiltrated into the settlement of Aley Sinai, at the northern edge of Gaza Strip, killing three Israelis before being killed themselves. Four policemen and two Palestinian farmers were killed on the following day by Tsahal during an operation to widen the security perimeter of Aley Sinai using bulldozers. None of the commentators saw fit to remark that Ariel Sharon had already 'pacified' the Gaza Strip using the same methods thirty years before.

The Palestinian president appeared to have lost his legendary ability to weather such storms, torn as he was between demands from the United States and Israel on the one hand and the fury of his own population on the other. Hamas fanned the flames by accusing the Palestinian Authority of criminal cooperation with Israel. On 8 October 2001, there were violent demonstrations in the streets of Gaza against the launch of the Western offensive in Afghanistan. Some 2,000 students faced the Palestinian police, whose response, which involved the use of live ammunition, caused the deaths of three people. Police stations and other symbols of the Palestinian Authority were sacked. The troubles continued the next day, at the same time as Tsahal was hitting Palestinian targets in Gaza City. Arafat, increasingly helpless, was buffeted by events over which he had no control. He clung to his dialogue with Shimon Peres, with whom he held a private meeting on 3 November in Spain. At the United Nations General Assembly in New York, where the fifty-sixth session opened on 10 November 2001, after being postponed for two months owing to the events of 11 September, President Bush refused to meet Arafat because of the 'failure' of the Palestinians in the struggle against terrorism.[7]

Deaths were once more widespread in the Gaza Strip. On 22 November 2001, five schoolboys died in Khan Yunis when a bomb that Tsahal said it had placed to trap Palestinian fighters exploded. Hamas, responsible for the proliferating suicide attacks inside Israel, also targeted the settlements in the Gaza Strip. On 24 November, a soldier died in Kfar Darom as the result of mortar fire, and on 2 December a settler was shot dead. On 3 December, ensconced in the Muqatta, his headquarters in Ramallah, Arafat ordered the arrest of Sheikh Yassin, but hundreds of Hamas activists prevented the Palestinian police from entering his residence. After a three-day stand-off, with some exchanges of gunfire, Ahmed Yassin agreed to place himself voluntarily under house arrest. This compromise was immediately rejected by the Israeli government of Ariel Sharon. In reprisal, Israeli bulldozers ploughed up the runways at Gaza's airport, while Arafat's two presidential helicopters were destroyed and F-16s bombed Palestinian installations in Gaza belonging to the Palestinian police and the presidential guard.

On 16 December 2001, Arafat, who had outlawed the military wings of Hamas and Islamic Jihad, now declared them to be 'a danger to the highest interests of the [Palestinian] nation'.[8] However, an attempt by the Palestinian police in Gaza to arrest Abdelaziz Rantissi, the Hamas spokesman, was no more successful than the earlier bid to arrest Sheikh Yassin. On 20 December, an Islamic Jihad militant was killed in a raid by the

Palestinian security forces in Gaza whose objective was to prevent a mortar attack on an Israeli settlement. There were riots against the Palestinian Authority in which six people were killed at the funeral of the victim the following day in Jabalya Camp. The Sharon government confirmed that it had banned Arafat from leaving Ramallah, even to attend the Christmas Eve mass at Bethlehem, and that he was certainly forbidden to return to Gaza. On 20 January 2002, several thousand Palestinians, who were unaware that Arafat would never see the Gaza Strip again, demonstrated in Gaza in support of their president. Sharon continued to make no secret of his regret that he had failed to kill Arafat during the siege of Beirut, twenty years earlier.[9]

The Islamic Resistance

Sheikh Yassin and the founders of Hamas, among whom Abdelaziz Rantissi now played a leading role, remained entrenched in the heart of the Gaza Strip, where they organised ever more daring attacks against Israeli targets. The other factions competed with Hamas to be at the forefront of armed activism. On 14 February 2002, the Saladin brigade of the Popular Resistance Committees (PRC) destroyed an Israeli tank near Netzarim, killing three Israeli soldiers. The Israelis identified the PRC activist they accused of responsibility for this attack as Mustafa Sabah (who was to be killed on 2 December 2002 when five missiles were fired at his house in Gaza). No Israeli tank had previously been destroyed in the occupied territories. The immediate response of the Sharon government was to send F-16s to bomb Palestinian police positions, this time at Jabalya. Israel's attacks on the Palestinian Authority's installations, which they were able to strike at will, did absolutely nothing to halt the rise in the power of the partisan militias.

On 18 February 2002, a suicide bomber from the 'Al-Aqsa Martyrs' brigades', affiliated to Fatah,[10] killed three settlers from Gush Katif. Israeli F-16s bombed police positions in Gaza in response, yet the following day saw further escalation when Israeli naval guns were fired at Force 17 and Arafat's presidential complex was shelled, killing a total of nine Palestinian soldiers. On 21 February, Tsahal launched a major operation in Gaza City, just before dawn, destroying the Palestinian radio and television complex among other targets. It was in Brazil Camp in Rafah that this incursion took its deadliest form, with six Palestinians losing their lives. The cycle of violence continued, while all attempts by the United States to use mediation by the CIA to renew cooperation between the Israeli and Palestinian intelligence services were to fail. Arafat, besieged in his headquarters in Ramallah, began to lose his grip over the Gaza Strip.

At this stage, Hamas was congratulating itself on having begun to produce the locally made rockets known as Qassam-2, which were named after the eponymous founder of the Qassam brigades. The Qassam-1 had been a small mortar shell with a range of only 2 kilometres and a charge of 1 kilogram.[11] Tsahal assessed these new rockets, which carried 5 kilos of explosive, as having a range of between 5 and 8 kilometres, and accused Hamas of having fired them for the first time at a target outside the Gaza Strip on 10 February 2002.[12] This missile launch, a response to Israel's F-16 attack on the Ansar 2 prison, caused no casualties. On 5 March, when Israeli F-16s once again struck the Gaza Strip, two Qassam rockets landed in the Israeli town of Sderot, wounding two children. The following day Tshahal responded with an all-out attack on the Palestinian Authority buildings in Gaza, by air, land and sea. At least four police officers were killed. Hamas, however, fully intended to stay on the front foot. On 7 March, a Hamas fighter penetrated the Atzmona settlement and killed five settlers before being killed himself. This was Muhammad Farhat, who was nineteen years of age: the same age bracket as the Israelis he killed. His five brothers were all equally committed to the fight against Israel: over time two were to be killed and one imprisoned. After Muhammad Farhat's attack, the move towards extremism gathered pace. The next day, forty Palestinians were killed in the West Bank and Gaza; on 9 March, fourteen Israelis were killed in two suicide bombings, one in Netanya carried out by the Al-Aqsa Martyrs' Brigade and one carried out by Hamas in Jerusalem. Then, on 10 March, thirty Israeli missiles demolished Arafat's offices in Gaza. Eighteen Palestinians died in a bloody raid on Jabalya Camp on the following day.

The Israelis partially re-occupied the West Bank in the spring of 2002. Armed confrontations flared up in Ramallah, Bethlehem and Jenin, as well as elsewhere. In contrast, the Gaza Strip, though still racked by disturbances, was spared a similar offensive. Troops were massed around the territory in early May but they did not go into action. The 5,000 inhabitants of the village of Mawassi, an enclave of Palestinian population in the heart of Gush Katif, were isolated from the outside world for fifty days. Hamas nevertheless kept up the pressure from its side, and on 15 June two Israeli soldiers were killed at the settlement of Dugit, at the northernmost tip of the Gaza Strip. On 20 June, some 2,000 unemployed Palestinians, who had been unable to work in Israel since the start of the second intifada, staged a hunger march in Gaza City. The Palestinian Authority's struggle for survival was far from their thoughts. At the same time, the Sharon government made a revealing statement about how it viewed the Gaza Strip when it threatened to deport the families of suicide bombers in the West Bank to Gaza, in order to 'discourage such attacks'.[13] This principle, agreed by Sharon's cabinet, was at least partially endorsed by the Israeli Supreme Court when it acquiesced in the expulsion from the West Bank to Gaza of two relatives of an Al-Aqsa brigades suicide bomber, who were being punished for having helped with the bomber's preparations. Within the overall catastrophe that Palestine had become, Gaza was worse than the West Bank.

The Israeli army began to fret about Hamas's production of a new rocket in Gaza, the Qassam-3, which had a range of 12 kilometres. During the night of 23 July, an F-16 dropped a ton of bombs on a building in the densely populated Daraj area of Gaza. Amid the ruins, rescuers found the body of Salah Shehada, who had overseen Hamas's first steps into the field of armed conflict. Salah Shehada is described in Hamas's official history as the leader (*qa'id*) of the Qassam brigades, whose earliest members were Imad Aqel and the 'group of the martyrs' (*majmu'at al-shuhada*): those who had been killed at one time or another during the previous decade. Fifteen civilians were killed in the Daraj attack, including seven children and two infants, while Muhammad Dayef, the operational head of the brigades, was still on the run. From this point on, Tsahal's policy was to target Hamas militants with murderous incursions into the Gaza Strip by dozens of tanks supported by helicopters. On 24 September eight Palestinians were killed in Gaza City and Beit Lahya, and then on 7 October in Khan Yunis a further fourteen died. Such large-scale operations resulted in many clashes in which Palestinian civilians were the principal victims. As this was happening, there began to be more infighting between Islamist fighters and the Palestinian police. In Gaza City on 7 October, the head of the riot police and five Hamas men died in such an internecine settling of accounts.

No one was spared as the situation deteriorated. On 7 November 2002, in Khan Yunis, four masked militiamen kidnapped the representative of the International Committee of the Red Cross (ICRC), a German national. He was soon released, but a new red line had been crossed in the Gaza Strip with the targeting of a senior foreign aid worker. On 6 December, as the end of Ramadan was being celebrated, an incursion by four Israeli tanks at Bureij led to the deaths of ten Palestinians, including two local employees of UNRWA. Israel swept aside accusations levelled by the United Nations of 'the indiscriminate use of heavy firepower in a densely populated civilian area'.[14]

Westerners also became subject to the violence in Gaza. On 16 March 2003, Rachel Corrie, a 23-year-old American student who was demonstrating against demolitions in Rafah on behalf of the International Solidarity Movement (ISM), was fatally crushed by an Israeli army bulldozer. On the same day, incidentally, two Palestinian civilians were killed, one in Rafah and the other in Khan Yunis. On 11 April, Thomas Hurndall, a British photographer aged twenty-two, also working with ISM in Rafah, was shot in the head: he died the following year, having spent nine months in a coma. On 2 May, James Miller, a British journalist aged twenty-two, was killed by Tsahal in Rafah while making a documentary under the only too appropriate title of *Death in Gaza*.

Not a week passed without Hamas attempting to attack the Israeli settlements in Gaza, often successfully. On 17 January 2003, the Islamist militia even tried to seize an Israeli gunboat offshore, but its own boat sank before the guerrillas aboard could go into action. On 24 January, the firing of eleven Israeli missiles at Gaza City brought a reprisal from Hamas in the shape of three Qassam rockets fired at Sderot. Hamas's ability to respond, which was unprecedented despite two years of repeated and bloody Israeli raids, enhanced Sheikh Yassin's prestige. But the trial of strength was only just beginning. Tsahal destroyed the four bridges linking Gaza City to Beit Hanoun in the north of the territory, before sending its tanks into the heart of Gaza City itself, devastating the market area. Sharon's aggressive image served him well in internal Israeli politics, enabling his Likud bloc to trounce Labour in the Knesset elections on 28 January 2003. Out of the 120 Knesset seats, Likud took twenty-three (having held nineteen before the election), while Labour fell back from twenty-five seats to nineteen.

With Arafat confined within his offices in Ramallah, the impression gained ground that the fate of Gaza was being settled in his absence through direct confrontation between Sharon and Hamas. On 15 February 2003, four Israeli soldiers died in the Gaza Strip when their tank exploded just outside Dugit settlement. The next day, six Hamas fighters perished in Gaza City following the detonation of a car full of explosives in which they were travelling. Their funerals were attended by 100,000 people, while at the same time an Israeli guerrilla unit assassinated an officer of the Qassam brigades on the Netzarim road. On 18 February, forty tanks with helicopter support entered the centre of Gaza City, killing eleven people. The next day, Hamas fired four rockets into Sderot. Tshahal responded by dividing the Gaza Strip once more into three sections sealed off from each other. In the course of the following weeks there were Israeli incursions in Beit Hanoun, Khan Yunis, Bureij, Nuseirat and Jabalya, all of which took a heavy toll.

Mahmoud Abbas, speaking on behalf of the PLO, made appeals for the demilitarisation of the intifada, but these were categorically rejected by Hamas. Arafat, still besieged in his redoubt in Ramallah, finally agreed to share the absolute power he had wielded for so long by creating a position of Palestinian prime minister to which he appointed Mahmoud Abbas, who was recognised by both Israel and the United States as having made a decisive contribution to the conclusion of the Oslo Accords. All of this left Hamas unmoved, particularly in Gaza. On 8 May, Ibrahim Maqadma, one of Sheikh Yassin's earliest supporters, died in a missile strike on his car, along with three of his body guards. Reprisal rockets fired at Sderot by Hamas caused no casualties. In Jabalya Camp, where Ibrahim Maqadma was born and had grown up, a mosque was named in honour of the 'martyr'.

In his inaugural speech to the Palestine Legislative Council on 29 April 2003, Mahmoud Abbas emphasised his determination to combat terrorism. Muhammad Dahlan was appointed to the position of minister of state with responsibility for security. Two days later, an Israeli incursion into Gaza City with thirty tanks left thirteen dead, including a Hamas official and his two brothers. On 15 May, sixty-six Israeli tanks rolled into Beit Hanoun before dawn, killing five people, including a child of twelve whose medical evacuation was prevented for hours. After the Israeli tanks withdrew, hundreds of people demonstrated in protest against the Hamas rockets that had been fired from their locality. This unprecedented demonstration said much about the despair of a population caught in the crossfire.

Ariel Sharon twice met Mahmoud Abbas, both to emphasise the exclusion of Arafat from the new dispositions in the region and also to reach an agreement on putting into practice the 'Road Map' for the resumption of negotiations. This concept, which originated with the Americans, was endorsed on 30 April 2003 by the so-called 'Quartet', made up of the United States, Russia, the United Nations and the European Union. An initial phase, in which there would be a freeze on Israeli settlements accompanied by a cessation of violence on the part of the Palestinians, was supposed to lead to two international conferences, one to get the peace process under way and the second to agree on a definitive solution. The Palestinian militias were unanimous in their opposition to the new approach. Hamas gathered its supporters for an anti-Abbas protest in Gaza at the close of Friday prayers on 6 June 2003. Two days later, three Hamas fighters, disguised in Israeli uniform, killed four Tsahal soldiers at the Erez crossing point. Islamic Jihad and the Al-Aqsa Martyrs' brigades symbolically joined together to claim responsibility for the attack. On 10 June, Israel responded by attempting to eliminate Abdelaziz Rantissi in a missile attack on Shati Camp. Hamas's spokesman, however, escaped with superficial wounds, though one of his bodyguards and a passer-by were killed. A suicide attack by Hamas in Jerusalem on 11 June in which eleven people were killed brought four reprisal raids by Tsahal in the space of forty-eight hours, in which seven Hamas officials, as well as thirteen civilians, were killed in rocket attacks from helicopters.

Truce and Blood

Hamas did not conceal its admiration for Hezbollah, whose stubborn guerrilla warfare had eventually led to Israel's unilateral retreat from southern

Lebanon in May 2000, after more than twenty years of occupation. In the Gaza Strip, this was the sole route that Sheikh Yassin's movement intended to pursue. Tsahal's command, which had been careful not to embark on a major re-occupation of Gaza such as that carried out in the West Bank in 2002, wanted to disengage from a territory that it knew was unmanageable. Ariel Sharon was well aware that the settlements, which he had envisaged in 1972 as a defensive forward perimeter for Israel, had become a costly focus for trouble in Gaza. Rather than putting his cards immediately on the table, however, he appointed his security adviser, Amos Gilad, to negotiate with Muhammad Dahlan on the technicalities of disengagement.

For the ambitious Dahlan, this was too good a chance to miss to establish a fief for himself in the Gaza Strip, in which he had been born and raised and where he had cultivated his own clientele. Arafat was still besieged inside his headquarters in Ramallah, West Bank, and Mahmoud Abbas was stigmatised as one of the Tunisians, incomers whose lifestyle was viewed as being overly extravagant. On 27 June 2003, Dahlan and Gilad signed an agreement on Israeli redeployment out of Beit Hanoun, and shortly afterwards joint Israeli–Palestinian patrols re-opened the north–south road that ran the length of the Gaza Strip. Delegates from Fatah, Hamas and Islamic Jihad agreed to declare a 'truce' (*hudna*) of three months, in which there would be no further attacks on Israel, during a meeting in Cairo. However, in return the militias demanded the release of their prisoners by Tsahal. On 11 July, this was the conclusion reached by a Hamas meeting in Jabalya, against a background of sporadic exchanges of fire under cover of darkness between Palestinian police and Islamist fighters.

The tension continued to mount during the summer of 2003. The murder of an Islamic Jihad official in Hebron on 14 August was followed by a suicide bomb in West Jerusalem five days later in which fifteen Israelis and five Americans were killed. Islamic Jihad claimed responsibility, but the attack had in fact been carried out by Hamas militants from Hebron. President Bush telephoned Ariel Sharon to reassure him that he enjoyed the support of the United States. On 21 August, Ismail Abu Shanab, a member of Hamas's political leadership, was killed in an Israeli helicopter attack, together with two of his bodyguards, while travelling in his car in the middle of Gaza City.

From 1997 to 1999 Abu Shanab had been the head of the engineers' syndicate, where he had been Hamas's nominee, and had been responsible for recent contacts with the PLO. With his death, the 'truce' signed in Cairo, and ratified by Abu Shanab himself, had been broken by Israel after only two months. His funeral on 22 August 2003 was attended by tens of thousands of Palestinians. In the meantime Tsahal had once again taken direct control over the Gaza Strip's north–south road and had re-imposed its security division of the territory into three sectors, as before. Dahlan's police moved in on the sites from which rockets were being fired at Israel, and for the first time closed three of the tunnels that had been dug under the frontier fence at Rafah for smuggling purposes.

Israeli missiles killed four leading Hamas figures in the space of a few days, including Hamdi Kalakh, who died on 28 August in Gaza City, Abdulla Aqel and Farid Mayat, killed on 31 August at Nuseirat, and Khadir al-Husary, who died in Gaza on 1 September. The Palestinian Authority froze the funds of a dozen Islamic associations, prompting violent demonstrations in Gaza. On 6 September, Israeli aircraft bombed the residence of Sheikh Yassin, who escaped unscathed. On 9 September, Hamas responded with two suicide bombs in which five Israeli soldiers and seven Israeli civilians lost their lives. The following day, Mahmoud Zahar escaped when a half-ton bomb fell on his house in Gaza, though one of his sons and two other people were killed. Mahmoud Abbas, whose support was ebbing away as the violence mounted, stepped down as prime minister to be replaced by Ahmed Qureia (Abu Ala), the Oslo negotiator. To be able to take the post of prime minister, Qureia stepped down from his position of Speaker of the Palestinian Legislative Council, where he was succeeded by Rawhi Fattouh, a Fatah member of the PLC for Rafah. In the reshuffle that followed, Muhammad Dahlan lost his ministerial responsibility for security but refused to admit defeat and continued to run his own organisations.

Tsahal carried out two major ground operations in the Gaza Strip in October 2003. Between 10 and 14 October, 100 houses were demolished in Rafah along the line of the Egyptian frontier in order to clear a security corridor. This was followed by another operation on 26 October within Gaza City itself. At the same time as Palestinian police buildings continued to be attacked by Israeli raids, the Palestinian security services themselves became increasingly involved in clashes with Islamist militiamen. A police-man kidnapped in Shati Camp on 17 September was liberated only when an exchange was arranged for seven of Sheikh Yassin's supporters who had been arrested in reprisal. On 15 October, a US embassy convoy was hit at Erez, with three American security personnel killed in the explosion. This was a clear challenge to Dahlan, and the Palestinian police rounded up suspects with increasing vigour.

Israeli incursions continued in Rafah, and to a lesser extent in Khan Yunis, with the objective of putting an end to arms smuggling from Egypt. On 10 and 11 December 2003, Tsahal blew up two tunnels before sending twenty armoured vehicles into Rafah, killing two Hamas members, together with a doctor and three other civilians. Even Fatah's grass-roots membership was disgusted by the Palestinian Authority's inactivity. On 29 December, young Fatah activists kidnapped the governor of Gaza, who was also an adviser to Yasser Arafat, when he was on his way back from Egypt, holding him for some hours in order to compel him to see for himself the scale of the damage inflicted by Israel. The gap between the PLO leadership and activists of varying political inclinations had never been so wide.

It was in this context that Sheikh Yassin adroitly adjusted his stance as part of his efforts to keep Hamas at the forefront of the Palestinian question. On 7 January 2004, he proposed a prolonged 'truce' with Israel, (albeit of indeterminate length), although he insisted that this would be conditional on a retreat to the frontiers of 1967.[15] However, five days later, on 12 January, Hamas took responsibility for the first suicide attack carried out by a woman. When she exploded her bomb at Erez, Rim Rayashi, a 22-year-old student with two young children, killed three Israeli soldiers and a security agent. After this attack, the 3,600 Palestinians who crossed at Erez to work in the industrial zone at the frontier, or in Israel itself, were held there for several days. This did not prevent Abdelaziz Rantissi from putting forward another proposal for a truce on 25 January, this time for ten years, to be effective after an Israeli withdrawal from Gaza and the West Bank.[16] Such a suspension of hostilities was not to be taken as implying any recognition of Israel, nor the end of the conflict. Theologically, it was justified by the precedent of the 'truce' concluded in AD 628 at

Hudaybiyya between the Prophet Muhammad and the polytheists of Mecca. This provided that 'war between us will cease for ten years, during which people will go about in security with no thefts ambushes or aggressions'. Two years later, it should be noted, the Prophet Muhammad took control of Mecca, whose inhabitants had converted to Islam. In any case, Tsahal failed to see in the offer of a truce any reason to halt its campaign to eliminate Islamist officials from the Gaza Strip.

The Era of the Assassins

As 2004 began, three years after he had taken over as prime minister in Israel, Ariel Sharon remained determined not to make a peace agreement with the Palestinians. He had never previously accepted anything but temporary arrangements. However, he now declared that he sought unilateral disengagement. All the political and military prestige he had won as the daring hero of the Israeli right wing were necessary to obtain acceptance for such a breach of the principle of the inviolability of Eretz Israel, with the Knesset backing his plan by fifty-one votes to thirty-nine on 12 January 2004. The Separation Wall that was being constructed in the West Bank followed the same principle. Sharon had evidently decided that the moment had come to make the best of a bad job, dismantling seventeen of the twenty settlements in the Gaza Strip within two years, since, as he put it: 'In future there will be no Jews in Gaza.'[17]

Far from relieving Tsahal's pressure on the Gaza Strip, the prospect of disengagement seemed in the short term to prompt yet more military incursions, apparently with the objective of permanently crippling the Palestinian factions. The militias, meanwhile, were laying the groundwork for their role under the new dispensation by attacking the police and representatives of the Palestinian Authority. On 19 February, the office of a Fatah PLC member in Khan Yunis was attacked, and on 1 March one of Arafat's advisers in Gaza, Khalil Zabin, was riddled with bullets. On 6 March, coordinated suicide attacks hit Tsahal positions at Erez as well as the Palestinian security services. Eight days later, on 14 March, at the Israeli port of Ashdod, Hamas carried out a suicide attack in which eleven Israelis lost their lives. The two bombers were from Jabalya and the Islamist militia had linked up for the occasion with the 'Al-Aqsa Martyrs' brigades' in a new challenge to the Palestinian Authority. Israeli reprisals continued from 15 to 17 March, with incursions, bombings and demolitions, particularly on the campus of the Al-Aqsa University in Gaza. This was an establishment that had tried to maintain a neutral position between the Islamic University, still under Hamas control, and Al-Azhar University, backed by the Palestinian Authority. In general, these universities had developed in response to the impossibility for Palestinian students of taking courses outside the Gaza Strip.

Sheikh Yassin was killed on 22 March 2004. Sharon had never abandoned his policy of striking Hamas at its head. Three Israeli missiles armed with flechettes were fired at the founder of Hamas as he left morning prayers at a mosque in Gaza City. Three of his bodyguards and four passers-by died in the same attack. Tsahal sealed off the Gaza Strip once more, as hundreds of thousands of Palestinians went into the streets across the territory to vent their anger, with bloody clashes with the Israeli troops. These were particularly violent at Khan Yunis, where Palestinian rockets were fired at the neighbouring Israeli settlements. The next day, a crowd of 200,000 turned out for Sheikh Yassin's funeral. The Palestinian police, desperate to squash rumours that they had been complicit in the murder, provided a guard of honour of twenty-one policemen for the cortège. The popularity of Hamas was enhanced by the 'martyrdom' of its founder. On 9 April, a collection organised by the Islamist movement in the mosques and the public squares of Gaza brought in 3 million dollars in funds in a single day, a startling sum in view of the low standard of living to which the territory had been reduced.[18]

Khaled Meshal, at his headquarters in Damascus, was confirmed as the head of the Political Bureau, while Abdelaziz Rantissi became Sheikh Yassin's successor in Gaza. Rantissi was killed with two of his bodyguards on 17 April 2004 when an Israeli missile attack struck his car. Hamas refused to disclose the name of its new leader in Gaza, though Mahmoud Zahar and Ismail Haniya seemed the most likely successors. Four days later, the Palestinian prison in Gaza was stormed by masked fighters who liberated their comrades who were being held on suspicion of involvement in Islamist attacks. On 2 May, an Israeli woman living in Gush Katif was killed together with her four children by Palestinian guerrillas, in an attack jointly claimed by Islamic Jihad and the Al-Aqsa Martyrs. Collaboration between factions was increasingly widespread, both against Tsahal and against the Palestinian security forces.

Israeli incursions were now habitually accompanied by fierce street fighting, with unprecedented losses for Tsahal. On 11 May 2004, six Israeli soldiers were killed in Gaza City, and the next day five lost their lives in Rafah. Following the example of Hezbollah in southern Lebanon, the Islamist militiamen took care to retain the remains of dead Israeli soldiers, which were valuable commodities for exchange in any future transactions. On 17 May in Rafah, Tsahal inaugurated 'Operation Rainbow'. The clashes extended over a week, while Israeli bulldozers demolished sixty houses to widen the security corridor along the Egyptian frontier. Tsahal announced the destruction of three tunnels used for smuggling. Fifty Palestinians were killed in the operation, eight of whom were civilians killed by helicopter fire on a peaceful demonstration on 19 May. On 30 May, a Qassam brigades' commander, Wael Nassar, was killed by Israeli missiles while riding a motorcycle in Gaza City. On 28 June 2004, five Qassam rockets fell in Israel in an attack which caused the first Israeli civilian casualties in such an incident, after so many rockets that had caused only material damage or slight wounds: an adult and a child of three were killed. Sharon replied with the Israeli offensive known as 'Active Shield', a wide-scale search-and-destroy operation that focused for more than a month on Beit Hanoun. This onslaught actually suited the purposes of the militias, who effectively ran whole sections of the territory and inflicted public humiliation on the apparently ineffectual agents of the Palestinian Authority. On 16 July, the Gaza chief of police was kidnapped and paraded by his masked abductors through the streets of Bureij Camp, before being released unharmed. Security officials in Gaza condemned what they called 'anarchy and chaos',[19] before submitting their collective resignation to Yasser Arafat.

Arafat, still confined in Ramallah, believed he could calm the situation. On 17 July 2004, he appointed his distant cousin Musa Arafat to be head of security in Gaza. However, the appointment of a figure already accused locally of corruption triggered an uprising of the Fatah grass-roots against the security services. Muhammad Dahlan was suspected of encouraging the trouble in order to better sabotage his rivals.[20] Hundreds of supporters of the Al-Aqsa Martyrs' brigades attacked and looted the Palestinian military intelligence offices in Rafah and Khan Yunis. The Palestinian president eventually made a compromise by placing Musa Arafat under the authority of a well-respected general, Abderrazak al-Majayda. But this did not prevent the split at the heart of Fatah from growing ever wider—on 28 July, for example, militiamen blocked the entry of two Palestinian ministers at the Erez crossing point, thereby preventing them from entering the Gaza Strip.

There was a spectacular contrast between Fatah's impotence on the one hand, with its energies absorbed by its internal quarrels, and the combativeness of Hamas on the other, despite the constant Israeli attacks that it was being subjected to. Helicopter raids on Hamas officials were still continuing, and on 7 September 2004 fourteen activists were killed in an attack on a disused sports stadium in Gaza that was being used as a training centre. On 24 September 2004, Hamas mortar fire killed a resident in the Israeli settlement of Neve Dekalim and Israeli reprisals intensified over the succeeding days. On 26 September 2004, Hamas accused Mossad of responsibility for the death of Ezzedin al-Sheikh Khalil, a senior military figure in the Islamist movement, who died in an explosion in Damascus. On 1 October, Israel officially launched an operation called 'Days of Penitence' in which some 3,000 soldiers and 200 tanks were thrown into action in a bid to establish security in the far north of the Gaza Strip. For two weeks there were daily clashes in Jabalya, Beit Lahya and Beit Hanoun, which disclosed the relative lack of success of 'Active Shield', the operation that had taken place during the summer.

Hamas, which referred to the Israeli offensive in the north of Gaza as 'Days of Rage' rather than 'Days of Penitence', intensified its propaganda against the Israelis. The head of Hamas's military wing gave press conferences, in which he wore a hood for security, and detailed communiqués were published about its operations with graphics of actions carried out against Tsahal.[21] Hamas also produced detailed casualty lists with names of the forty-three Qassam brigades' martyrs killed in two weeks of combat and of the 135 Palestinian civilians killed, enumerating the twenty-eight Qassam rockets fired as well as the twenty-six Yassin missiles, eponymously named for Sheikh Yassin. Their accusations against Fatah were indirect but nonetheless damning. Hamas said its own leaders, as distinct from those of Fatah, were 'in the trenches and not in the hotels' (*min al-khanadiq, la min al-fanadiq*). At the same time, mutual recriminations continued to torment the Palestinian Authority, with an attempted assassination of Musa Arafat and internecine exchanges of fire between the agents of the Authority's own security agencies.

As the Palestinian Authority's security apparatus in Gaza began to fall apart, and with it the Authority's ability to govern, a clandestine drama was unfolding within the presidential complex in Ramallah. Arafat, paralysed by more than two years of siege and deprivation, collapsed on 27 October 2004. Doctors were urgently summoned from Egypt and Jordan, but the health of the 'Old Man' deteriorated rapidly. Sharon was concerned that Arafat's death could lead to widespread turbulence in the West Bank, which had previously been more stable than the Gaza Strip. It was for this reason that Israel discreetly asked France to intervene before it was too late.

On 29 October Arafat's powers were provisionally transferred to Mahmoud Abbas as the Palestinian president flew to Paris. He was admitted to intensive care at the Percy military hospital at Clamart, where he fell into a coma a few days later. On 6 November, the prime minister, Ahmed Qureia, was delegated by the PLO leadership to go to Gaza, where he sought to pacify the various services and factions. As Arafat's health worsened, Israel announced that it would not permit the 'Old Man' to be buried in Jerusalem. Clashes with Tsahal continued undiminished in the Gaza Strip, where five Palestinians were killed on 9 November and another five on 10 November. On each of those days there was also a militia rocket strike on an Israeli settlement, though these attacks did not result in any casualties.

Yasser Arafat died in Paris on 11 November. His coffin, covered with the Palestinian flag, was accorded full republican honours by the French state at the airport at Villacoublay, from which it was flown to a military airfield in the outskirts of Cairo. On the same day six Palestinians were killed by Tsahal in the Gaza Strip. The next day, Arafat's remains were transferred by helicopter to Ramallah to be provisionally interred there until the late president's wish to be laid to rest in Jerusalem could be met. Tens of thousands of Palestinians gathered in Ramallah for the funeral ceremony. In Gaza, there was just as large a gathering for a symbolic ceremony, with which Hamas associated itself. The open split that had prevailed during the second intifada was forgotten in the process of mourning. However, the conflicting visions for Palestine held by Yasser Arafat and Ahmed Yassin had not yet finished their work of dividing the Gaza Strip, now the orphan child of both its iconic leaders.

15

ONE PALESTINE AGAINST ANOTHER

The succession to Yasser Arafat was officially decided on 12 November 2004, before the remains of the 'Old Man' had even been consigned to the ground. Mahmoud Abbas was to become head of the PLO and of Fatah; Ahmed Qureia (Abu Ala) would remain prime minister, with oversight of day-to-day events; and Rawhi Fattouh, the Speaker of the PLC, according to the provisions of the constitution, would become interim president for the two months it would take to arrange a presidential election. The speed with which the arrangements were made was indicative of the prevalent fear of a vacuum in the upper echelons of the Fatah and the PLO following the disappearance of the historic leader who had been so intimately identified with these movements.

In April 2004, the identities of the leaders of Hamas in the Gaza Strip had not been publicly acknowledged for fear that any successor to Abdelaziz Rantissi might be eliminated as quickly as Rantissi himself had been. However, the death of Sheikh Yassin had diminished neither Hamas's dynamism nor its popularity. Ariel Sharon's stratagem of unilateral disengagement from the Gaza Strip had undermined the Palestinian Authority to the benefit of the armed militias, since the latter credited themselves with responsibility for the Israeli decision to withdraw from the Strip without any concession in return. Hamas counted on deriving as durable an advantage from this as that which had accrued to Hezbollah in southern Lebanon after the Israeli retreat of May 2000. On 6 December 2004, when Mahmoud

Abbas and Ahmed Qureia visited Damascus, the shift in the balance of power between Hamas and the PLO meant that the two Palestinian statesmen felt obliged to call on Khaled Meshal, not least to ask him to declare a truce during the impending presidential election campaign.

States of Tension

In Israel, the prime minister's own right-wing supporters were accusing him not only of betraying the settlers in Gaza but also of repeating the error made in Lebanon by his Labour predecessor, who had not been able to prevent Hezbollah from strengthening its positions along Israel's northern frontier after Tsahal's withdrawal. In order to outflank these criticisms, Sharon ordered the Israeli forces to take even tougher action in the Gaza Strip. On 18 November 2004, nervousness on the part of the Israeli troops resulted in a serious incident in Rafah that involved Egypt, when three Egyptian frontier guards were killed after being mistaken for a Palestinian guerrilla group. Clashes between Tsahal and the Palestinian factions were an everyday occurrence in the Gaza Strip, though the frequent strikes by locally made rockets only occasionally caused damage and rarely inflicted casualties.

Hamas claimed responsibility for a booby trap that killed an Israeli soldier in Qarni on 7 December 2004 and for a remote-controlled device that left six more soldiers dead at the Rafah crossing on 12 December. After a series of reprisal attacks, Tsahal began to comb out the Khan Yunis region for suspects in order to counter the threat to neighbouring Israeli settlements. On 4 January 2005, a shell from an Israeli tank killed seven Palestinian children aged between ten and seventeen who were gathering strawberries in a field at Beit Lahya. Yet this had little effect on the level of violence involved in the continuing Israeli operations, creating a sombre atmosphere for the Palestinian presidential election, which was in any case officially boycotted by Hamas and Islamic Jihad.

Mahmoud Abbas was elected president of the Palestinian Authority on 9 January 2005 with 62 per cent of the votes. Mustafa Barghouti, a doctor from Ramallah, whose supporters in the Gaza Strip included Haydar Abdel Shafi and Rawya Shawa, received 19 per cent of the vote. On the following day, Sharon's new coalition cabinet, which included Labour, narrowly won a vote of confidence in the Knesset, with fifty-eight votes in favour and fifty-six against. A revolt within Likud had induced three of its Knesset members, who remained opposed to the retreat from Gaza, either to abstain or vote against. The ongoing Palestinian attacks further undermined Sharon's position. On 12 January a settler was killed at Morag, six more Israeli civilians were killed at Karni the following day and a Shin Bet officer was killed at Gush Katif on 18 January. Sharon later blamed Mahmoud Abbas for the attacks, accusing him of inaction against what Israel regarded as terrorists. On 19 January, the newly appointed Palestinian president left his headquarters in Ramallah to rally the Palestinian security services in Gaza and initiate a thorough search of the territory by the Palestinian police.

Muhammad Dahlan, Mahmoud Abbas's security adviser, was finally able to return to his command after more than a year of plotting in the wings, particularly against Musa Arafat and the police command structure in Gaza. Dahlan played a key role in the negotiations relating to Israel's physical withdrawal from the territory, with Dov Weisglass, Sharon's closest adviser, as his interlocutor. Weisglass openly admitted that the intention of the Israeli initiative was to 'pre-empt the peace process', as he put it, and thus to prevent the establishment of a Palestinian state. The Israeli withdrawal from Gaza would be presented as having fulfilled all of Israel's obligations, and there would be no further discussion of 'the refugees, frontiers, and Jerusalem'.[1] It was on this basis that Israel refused to regard the Gaza disengagement as part of a broader process, and restricted its dealings with Dahlan to putting practical arrangements into effect without touching on their political context. Ever ambitious, however, Dahlan intended to use his role in implementing the technical details of the withdrawal to entrench his own position within the Gaza Strip once it was free from Israeli occupation.

On 8 February 2005, Mahmoud Abbas and Ariel Sharon held their first summit meeting at Sharm el-Sheikh, under the auspices of Egypt's President Mubarak, who received each of them separately afterwards. Palestinian demands for coordination with Israel over the withdrawal from Gaza were blocked by Likud's refusal to become involved in formal negotiations of any kind. As Prime Minister Ahmed Qureia wryly commented, 'the Sharon plan is in fact the opposite of the restoration of Palestinian sovereignty over a part of our territory'.[2] The de facto truce that still held in Gaza was broken by occasional incidents, for which both sides refused to acknowledge responsibility. Yet this was a period of relative calm and one that was much appreciated by the population. Even Islamic Jihad respected the cessation of hostilities, and when a suicide bombing took place in a night club in Tel Aviv its leadership in Gaza denied all responsibility. Four Israelis died in this incident, for which responsibility was eventually accepted by Islamic Jihad's branch in Damascus: this was the reason why Israel directed its anger on this occasion at Syria rather than at the Palestinian movement.

On 19 March 2005, the Palestinian factions met in Cairo to formulate an official offer of truce (*tahdi'a*: literally 'calming') that was intended to last until the end of the year, on condition that Israel exercised the same restraint. The resilience of the truce, implemented by both sides in parallel without direct negotiation, was put to the test on 9 April when the Israeli army killed three adolescents in Rafah. The three, all aged fourteen, were playing football close to the security corridor next to the Egyptian frontier and were targeted because of their alleged 'suspicious' behaviour: one of them had apparently tried to retrieve a ball from the no-go area. Hamas and its allies fired five mortar rounds at the neighbouring settlements in response, without causing major damage, while issuing a statement that this was an isolated attack and not a breach of the truce. Tsahal accepted this limited action and the incident was deemed closed by both sides. In the meantime Muhammad Dahlan continued to advance his own interests, entering the Palestinian government as minister for 'civil affairs'. His rival Musa Arafat, meanwhile, lost his post as chief of the Palestinian police in Gaza, which was assigned to Dahlan's former deputy Rashid Abu Shibak.

Twists and Turns

Sheikh Yassin, consistent with his rejection of the Oslo Accords, had excluded Hamas from standing in the elections that followed from the agreement. The Islamist movement restricted itself, as it had done in the past, to participation in the professional and student elections, the sole means they had of judging their popularity on the ground. The substantial level of popular participation in the presidential and parliamentary elections of 1996, however, which was even higher in Gaza than in the West Bank, indicated that a large proportion of the Islamist movement's grassroots supporters had in fact cast votes. After the death of Sheikh Yassin, the Islamist movement seriously considered the candidature of an 'independent' Islamist in the presidential election of January 2005. Participation in the elections for the Palestinian municipalities no longer appeared as an end in itself but rather as a preliminary step in the revision of the erstwhile policy of abstention.

The municipal elections of 27 January 2005—the second of five waves of municipal elections were held, the first of which had been those in the West Bank in 2004—proved a success for the Islamist movement's new strategy in the Gaza Strip, where seven of the nine municipalities involved came under Hamas control. The victory was somewhat discredited by the low turnout, which was around 20 per cent, for example, in Deir al-Balah, where the mayor elected was Ahmed al-Kurd, who had been the head of the Association for Islamic Prayer since 1978. However, the turnout was enough to confirm Hamas's decision to participate in parliamentary politics. The Islamic movement took the decision to organise itself in preparation for the parliamentary election scheduled for July, and in order to blunt the impact on the public of apparent disrespect for a policy to which Sheikh Yassin had been committed, the Hamas election campaign was launched on the anniversary of the Sheikh's death. Hamas reaped ongoing benefits from this political switch. In the municipal elections of 7 May in Rafah, Bureij and Beit Lahya, its percentage of the vote was sufficiently high for Fatah to accuse it of electoral fraud, an allegation which had legal consequences. Sharon issued dire warnings of the implications of a parliamentary victory for the Islamist movement, which he said could even compromise the principle of the disengagement from Gaza.

Mahmoud Abbas was concerned about the possible implications stemming from any delay in the disengagement and deferred the parliamentary elections. He also hoped to encourage the Americans to play a larger part in the Gaza disengagement. On 26 May 2005, during a meeting with

President Bush at the White House, it was agreed that General William Ward, who had been appointed three months earlier to supervise the restructuring of the Palestinian security forces, should also mediate with the Israelis over the withdrawal from Gaza. Ward quickly came to believe that the Palestinian police force, even without the limits Israel imposed on the weapons it was permitted to deploy, was not sufficiently large to be able to control the militias operating in the Strip.[3] At the same time, an ambitious plan for the economic re-launch of the Gaza Strip was being proposed to the G8 group of nations by James Wolfensohn, the former director of the World Bank, who had become the Middle East representative for the Quartet: the international negotiating body that had been given responsibility for overseeing the Road Map in 2003, whose members were the United States, Russia, the UN and the EU. Wolfensohn's plan would require an investment of 3 billion dollars over three years and involved the re-opening of the road system and the airport and the construction of new installations at the Port of Gaza. In order to allow Ward and Wolfensohn to work in Gaza, the US State Department also lifted its ban on US citizens visiting the Gaza Strip, which had been in place since the attack on the American diplomats at Erez in October 2003.

Early in the summer of 2005, Karen Abu-Zayd, another American national, became director of UNRWA, whose offices had been in Gaza City since 1996, succeeding Peter Hansen at the end of his ten-year term. The UN hoped that her appointment would ease relations with Israel, which had been much exercised by Peter Hansen's supposedly too close cooperation with Hamas. The accusations against Hansen could not be substantiated but were nevertheless echoed in the United States.[4] In addition to the aid dispensed to a large proportion of the population of the Gaza Strip, UNRWA had 8,200 salaried employees, mainly in the educational and health sectors. Because of the repeated closures of the territory, UNRWA's offices in Amman and Jerusalem had also expanded over the years.

The Palestinian Authority also took steps to extract the maximum benefit from the impending Israeli disengagement. On 4 August 2005, Mahmoud Abbas, together with Ahmed Qureia and Muhammad Dahlan, assembled thousands of his supporters in Gaza to celebrate what he called 'Victory Week'. Yasser Arafat's birthdate was chosen for the start of the celebrations.

The propaganda outcome was somewhat marred by tensions within Fatah that were still very much alive. On 7 August, Suleiman al-Fara, a Fatah official in Khan Yunis, was arrested. In order to obtain his release, his henchmen kidnapped two foreign volunteer workers on the following day. In general, the Al-Aqsa Martyrs' brigades and the Popular Resistance Committees (PRC), which were themselves splintered according to the allegiances of local group leaders, tended to incline more towards Hamas, or even Islamic Jihad, than to the official Palestinian security services.

Scorched Earth

The Israeli settlements in the Gaza Strip had been declared a military zone, which allowed the Israeli army to deny access to Israeli citizens other than residents. They were thus able to exclude political opponents of the withdrawal from Gaza. Two new security fences, one with razor wire and the other with electronic sensors and surveillance cameras, were being installed that would completely surround the Gaza Strip. The Israeli soldiers also demolished a dozen unoccupied bungalows on the coast where a group of settlers from the West Bank had set up a protest camp. On 18 July 2005, more than 20,000 Israelis came to demonstrate in southern Israel close to the Strip to declare their rejection of Sharon's policy. The movement of solidarity with the Gaza settlers lost some of its impetus, however, when a Tsahal deserter killed four Israeli Arabs in Galilee on 4 August before being lynched by a mob.

On 8 August 2005, the Gaza settlers were told that they had only a week left to depart voluntarily from the territory and thus to qualify for full compensation. After the deadline had expired, at midnight on 16 August, less than half of the 8,500 settlers remained. On the other hand, those who refused to leave had been joined by a similar number of young settlers from the West Bank. When the Israeli forces moved in, however, there were only a few disturbances, despite the provocation offered to the Palestinians by the settlers of Kfar Darom and Neve Dekalim. Among the soldiers, only one case of refusal to obey orders was recorded, when two soldiers refused to clear the synagogue at Kfar Darom with water cannon on 18 August.

The same scenario was repeated from one settlement to the next. The settlers demolished or rendered unusable their residences and the agricultural greenhouses before handing their settlements over to Tsahal. This scorched-earth policy represented the failure of the plan James Wolfensohn had devised for the transfer of the greenhouses to the Palestinian Authority for which he had raised 14 million dollars from philanthropic sources, including half a million dollars of his own money. On 22 August 2005, the disengagement came to a conclusion with the evacuation of Netzarim. Sharon, who had been minister of defence in April 1982 at the time of the dismantling of the colony of Yamit in Sinai in accordance with the Israeli–Egyptian peace treaty, had this time brought to fruition an even more complex operation. The dramatic removal of the settlers in fact enhanced his international stature as a statesman who was ready if necessary to impose painful concessions on his own side. However, the Sharon government reneged on an earlier agreement to destroy the synagogues in the abandoned settlements, thus leaving the Palestinians to take responsibility for an act of sacrilege.

After the disappearance of the settlements, Tsahal continued to occupy its own positions in the Gaza Strip, from which it made occasional sorties. The countdown to the Israeli withdrawal had in the meantime exacerbated the internal feuds within Fatah. On 7 September 2005, 100 militiamen seized Musa Arafat's residence, killing him on the spot and kidnapping his son Manhal, who was released the following day. This was a blow for Mahmoud Abbas, who had to cancel a scheduled visit to the UN General Assembly. The last Israeli units withdrew from the Gaza Strip shortly after dawn on 12 September. It immediately became clear that the Palestinian security forces were unable to halt the looting of what remained of the abandoned settlements. The Egyptian frontier guard was also swamped and simply opened the Rafah crossing point with unrestricted access.

These scenes of anarchy cast a shadow over the Palestinian Authority's celebration of Israel's withdrawal from the Gaza Strip. On 13 September, Hamas organised a demonstration involving tens of thousands of its supporters in Gaza City to claim the withdrawal was a victory for the 'resistance'. While Hamas was careful not to make a show of arms, Islamic Jihad, which attracted less support, went on parade with its full panoply of weapons. The appearance of the Palestinian security forces across the territory, however, particularly on the frontier with Egypt, brought about a rapid change in Hamas's position. On 16 September, thousands of masked Hamas militants paraded with their weapons on the site of the former settlement of Neve Dekalim, and the following day Hamas put on a similarly ostentatious display of force in Gaza City itself.

Sharon's Last Battle

On 23 September 2005, Hamas organised a procession of its militiamen with a Qassam rocket proudly displayed on a launch pad mounted on a truck. The accidental explosion of the rocket's charge killed at least fifteen people. Hamas refused to admit responsibility and accused Israel of having fired a missile at the demonstration. Caught up in its own propaganda, Hamas retaliated against Israel. The following day, Hamas and Islamic Jihad fired thirty rockets at Sderot and into the Negev, causing slight injuries to five Israeli civilians. Israel's reprisal was ferocious. For the first time since 1967, heavy artillery shells were fired into Gaza, and a senior official of Islamic Jihad was killed. Hamas ordered an immediate ceasefire. The Tsahal operation, given the title 'Operation First Rain', continued until 2 October, with F-16 aircraft breaking the sound barrier at regular intervals over the Gaza Strip.

At the end of October, in response to Palestinian mortar fire, Israel unleashed a further operation, 'Eternal Renewal', accompanied by air attacks and the scattering of threatening leaflets over the Gaza Strip. Tsahal banned the international press from the territory. Artillery emplacements were set up in the border zones around the Gaza Strip and work began on a concrete wall several metres high. Palestinian fishing boats, which had been authorised under the Oslo Accords to fish up to a limit of 20 nautical miles from the coast, were henceforth limited to a 9-mile zone. The industrial area at Erez was simply shut down, with no compensation given to the thousands of Palestinians who worked there.

All the economic plans made by Wolfensohn ahead of the withdrawal simply collapsed. Though freedom of movement was now no longer a possibility, Wolfensohn needed at least to ensure that the crossing points would not be arbitrarily shut. He threatened to resign in a bid to persuade the US Secretary of State Condoleezza Rice to become personally involved.

After a night of arduous negotiation, an Agreement on Movement and Access (AMA) was finalised on 15 November 2005. This was the first occasion in which Israel and the Palestinian Authority had engaged with each other over an issue relating to the future of territory evacuated by Israel. The agreement, however, was of a purely technical nature, detailing the arrangements made to check persons and vehicles at the crossing points at Rafah and Qarni, where large-scale scanners were planned for use on trucks en route for the West Bank. A European mission (EUBAM: the European Union Border Assistance Mission), which was in permanent contact with Israel, was given the task of monitoring freedom of passage at the Rafah crossing point, which was jointly administered by the Palestinian Authority and Egypt.

On 24 November, conscious of the reluctance of many within Likud to support disengagement, Sharon established a new centrist political party, Kadima ('Forward'), which was intended to bring together Likud dissidents with like-minded members of the Labour Party. As this major rearrangement of the Israeli political scene was taking place, he put sustained military pressure on the Gaza Strip. During the five years of the second intifada, the ratio of Israeli to Palestinian deaths in and around the Gaza Strip had been one to eleven. In the three months following the disengagement in Gaza, thirty Palestinians had been killed without the death of a single Israeli.

During December 2005 the application of the AMA was frequently suspended by Israel, but rather than being a response to infractions by Fatah in Gaza, this was in reprisal for attacks undertaken in the West Bank (and by Islamic Jihad). Israeli helicopters also targeted the Al-Aqsa Martyrs' brigades and the Popular Resistance Committees. Rockets were fired at Israel in return, though in general without hitting any targets. The Palestinian security services, as the American mediator General Ward had foreseen, showed themselves unable to keep order in the territory. On 21 December, the principal of the American School in Gaza and his deputy, an Australian and a Dutch national respectively, were kidnapped for a period of several hours by PFLP guerrillas. Three days later, Hamas fighters opened fire on a police roadblock where an attempt had been made to disarm them.

The tension was such that Israeli military intelligence began to envisage that a political separation was likely within a year between what they had begun to call 'Hamastan' in Gaza and 'Fatahstan' in the West Bank. This was the conclusion of a report to the Israeli cabinet by General Aharon Zeevi, head of military intelligence.[5] Even before the so-called Separation Wall constructed by Israel had begun to eat into the edges of Palestinian territory in the West Bank, isolating East Jerusalem, the Gaza Strip was already closed off by a continuous barrier that had been reinforced in the months before the withdrawal of the Israeli army from the territory. By this stage nobody dared to dream of the possibility of a land corridor between the two Palestinian territories.

Sharon suffered a minor stroke on 18 December 2005 and had to step down for a week from the day-to-day conduct of his government for health reasons. When he returned on 25 December 2005, his first move was to initiate Operation 'Blue Sky'. This was intended to create a no-go zone in the areas of the northern Gaza Strip previously occupied by Israeli settlements that had recently been evacuated, in order to prevent the area being used to fire rockets into Israel. The prime minister's objective was in part to enhance his strong-man image, as he looked for support from the right for Kadima, his new party. But on 4 January 2006 everything changed. Having recovered from the apparently minor stroke he had suffered in December, Sharon was struck down by a massive second attack. He lapsed into a coma from which he did not emerge. All his powers were transferred to his deputy, Ehud Olmert. The Sharon era was at an end.

A Bitter Victory

It was against the background of this ongoing crisis in Israeli politics that the Palestinian parliamentary elections took place in the West Bank and the Gaza Strip on 25 January 2006. As president, Mahmoud Abbas had approved an electoral law intended to preserve the dominant position of Fatah. Under the new law, half the 132 seats of the future parliament would be allotted from lists on the basis of proportional representation, which was supposedly more favourable to Fatah, while the other half would continue to be decided as before, by voting in electoral constituencies. Mahmoud Abbas had difficulty in finalising his Fatah list: there were serious incidents during the primary elections the presidency had decided to hold for the selection of Fatah candidates in the Gaza Strip which had led to the cancellation of this unprecedented exercise in democracy. Fatah candidates were instead nominated by the party machine, which fuelled many bitter disputes. On polling day, the presence of 100 dissident candidates greatly undermined Fatah in some of the most highly contested constituencies, and in Khan Yunis in particular.

While Fatah suffered the consequences of internal splits, Hamas produced its own list under the banner of 'Change and Reform', led by the pragmatic Ismail Haniya, with the more radical Mahmoud Zahar in ninth position on the list. Two other historic members of the Hamas leadership, Abdelfattah Dukhan and Sayyid Abu Musamih, appeared in tenth and twenty-third place respectively, while Sheikh Marwan Abu Ras, popularly known as the 'mufti of Hamas', was in twenty-fourth position. The turnout was high, at 77 per cent, and the international observers reported that the vote was reasonably trustworthy and honest. In contrast to Fatah's calculations, Hamas took 44 per cent of the votes in the proportional ballot, with twenty-nine seats as against twenty-eight for Fatah. Hamas actually received fewer votes in the constituencies, with 36.5 per cent of the votes. However, the lack of unity among its opponents meant that it took forty-five of the seats allocated this way. Hamas consequently received seventy-four of the Palestinian Legislative Council's 132 seats, achieving an overall majority for which it had been unprepared. There was a strong polarisation between the north and the south of the Gaza Strip. Hamas took the five seats in Jabalya, while Fatah took the three seats in Rafah. In the three other constituencies, Hamas took the lead and no independent candidate was elected except in Gaza City. When the voting was over, Fatah supporters in the Gaza Strip and some elements from the Palestinian security services showed their anger at the Hamas electoral victory by attacking the local parliament building as well as by pulling down Hamas symbols. Muhammad Dahlan, who had himself been elected as a PLC member for Khan Yunis, was accused by his opponents as being the instigator of these disturbances.[6]

The Western powers, which had not envisaged this outcome, immediately responded with a demand that Hamas make three undertakings as a condition for Western cooperation with a future Hamas government. These were a commitment to non-violence; the recognition of Israel; and respect for agreements already made. Within the Quartet, both Russia and the United Nations supported this demand.[7] The United States, meanwhile, made tougher demands than the European Union, both making their continued assistance conditional on these three requisites. Mahmoud Abbas promoted Muhammad Dahlan to his personal staff and attached the Palestinian security services directly to the presidency, while also putting in place a number of key administrative posts whose holders would report solely to himself. Palestine's international paymasters, who had compelled Arafat to give up some of his powers to a Palestinian prime minister in 2003, warned that powers could be withdrawn from a future Islamist government and be returned to the presidency.

George W. Bush's advisers, together with Ehud Olmert's ones, devised a strategy to isolate Hamas in the Gaza Strip by simply forbidding the Islamists who had been elected members of the PLC to travel to the West Bank. As a result the first session of the newly elected PLC, held on 18 February in Ramallah, had to be conducted as a video conference with Ismail Haniya, who had been chosen to form a new government. Israel's next move was to suspend the transfer to the Palestinian Authority of the so-called clearance revenues collected by the Israeli government on the Palestinian authority's behalf, which represented the VAT on trade with the West Bank and Gaza. The United Nations condemned this as a violation of the peace agreements, while Ismail Haniya offered the political compromise of setting up a national unity government. As he declared to the *Washington Post* on 26 February 2005: 'If Israel withdraws to the 1967 borders, then we will establish a peace in stages.' He added that Hamas was ready to recognise Israel, 'if Israel declares that it will give the Palestinian people a state and gives them back all their rights'.[8]

The inter-Palestinian negotiations ran aground on Hamas's refusal to recognise the extent to which the PLO was still representative of the Palestinian people. Hamas's demand was to be allocated 40 per cent of the seats in the longest-standing Palestinian organisation before it would concede that the PLO still enjoyed its pre-eminent position as the representative of the Palestinian people. With this demand frustrated, rather than going ahead with a national unity government, Ismail Haniya set up a predominantly Hamas government with eighteen Hamas ministers out of twenty-four and the other six less important portfolios going to 'independents'. Ten of the twenty-four ministers were originally from the Gaza Strip, including the two pillars of the cabinet: Said Siyam at the Ministry of the Interior and Mahmoud Zahar at the Ministry of Foreign Affairs. Europe's refusal to deal with Hamas resulted in the suspension of the agreement on freedom of movement at Rafah, while the closure of the crossing points between Gaza and Israel became the rule, with the occasions when they were open being the exception and occurring only with the good will of Tsahal. Moreover, as 37 per cent of the wages paid in the Gaza Strip came from the Palestinian Authority, the boycott of Hamas by the Authority's Western paymasters meant the suspension of the payment of the employees' remuneration. The population of Gaza was thus plunged into a humanitarian crisis requiring urgent aid from the European Union and the World Bank. Problems soon arose: for example, from mid-March onwards, it was impossible to buy flour in the territory.

The field of security arrangements became the battleground on which Mahmoud Abbas and Ismail Haniya challenged each other over their respective legitimacy. Abbas appointed Abu Shibak, Muhammad Dahlan's former deputy, as coordinator of security services on his immediate staff. Said Syam, the Hamas minister of the interior, drawing confidence from the size of the majority he achieved in the election in Gaza, responded by setting up a new force he described as 'executive' (*tanfiziyya*), under his direct control, appointing as its director Abu Samhadana, an official of the PRC, thus formalising the alliance between the most militant elements of Fatah and the Islamist movement. Five hundred members of the PRC joined this 'executive' force while Dahlan's supporters blockaded or emptied the arsenals of the Palestinian police force in Gaza. Clashes became widespread, and as a counterbalance to the 'executive force' the United States encouraged the involvement of Force 17, the presidential guard, 1,500 of whose 2,600 members were deployed in Gaza.

In the Israeli parliamentary election held on 28 March 2006, Ehud Olmert and the new Kadima party took twenty-eight seats out of the Knesset's total of 120. This put Kadima in the position of being the largest single party and enabled Olmert to form a government. On 6 April he formed a coalition government including Labour and Shas. Olmert's plan was to continue with the policy of unilateral disengagement initiated by Sharon and to withdraw from 70 per cent of the West Bank, retaining settlements and strategic areas. This was known as '*hitkansut*' in Hebrew, variously translated as 'convergence' and 'consolidation'. For the moment, Olmert left Mahmoud Abbas's requests to resume negotiations unanswered. On 11 May, an eighteen-point programme was issued by a group of Palestinian activists currently held in Israeli prisons, signed on behalf of Fatah by Marwan Barghouti, from Ramallah, and for Hamas by Abdelkhaliq Natche, a former resident of Hebron, in addition to other signatories. This joint statement called for the establishment of a Palestinian state in the West Bank and Gaza, since it was in these territories and not inside Israel that the 'resistance' struggle should be waged. Mahmoud Abbas endorsed this programme, officially entitled the 'National Reconciliation Document'. In Gaza, Ismail Haniya welcomed what became known as the 'Prisoners' Document'.[9] But Khaled Meshal rejected the agreement from his base in Damascus. This was not the first occasion on which the leader of Hamas in exile would complicate the already arduous task of the new Palestinian prime minister. The Hamas ministers had already been obliged to resign their partisan affiliations so that Hamas would not become compromised by involvement in everyday administration. Such contradictions shed light on the covert conflict within the Hamas cabinet in which Haniya and Siyam were in opposition to Zahar and Atallah Abu Siba, the culture minister, a strict Islamist educated in Sudan.

Abbas believed that this was an auspicious moment to take the initiative in his confrontation with Hamas. On 25 May 2006, during a video-link between Gaza and Ramallah that brought together hundreds of nationalists and Islamists, he asked the Hamas leadership to clarify its position on the establishment of a Palestinian state in the territories occupied in 1967 and announced his decision to hold a referendum on this question, as prescribed by the 'Prisoners' Document'. Ismail Haniya disregarded Meshal's veto and opened talks with Abbas. However, he insisted that the inter-Palestinian negotiations should take place in Gaza in order to escape the ambit of the Hamas Political Bureau in Damascus, which was more influential on the West Bank-based officials of Hamas.

The security situation in Gaza continued to deteriorate with daily clashes between Fatah and Hamas supporters. Tension between the government's 'executive force' and the security services that answered to the presidency (which in practice meant to Dahlan), reached a point where the Egyptian advisers serving in Gaza were obliged to mediate between the various police forces. Nothing seemed able to halt the decline: exchanges of fire were followed by mortar bombs and booby-trapped cars. On 12 June 2006, Fatah and Hamas fought a pitched battle in Rafah in which RPGs were used. As the clashes became a vendetta, the death toll grew. At the same time the number of supply trucks that crossed into the Strip at Qarni dwindled due the substantial bribes taken by local officials.[10]

Summer Rains

Ehud Olmert, heartened by the welcome given to him by President Bush in Washington on 23 May 2006, stepped up Tsahal's aggressive posture in Gaza. On 30 May, Israeli armoured vehicles went into Gaza for the first time since the withdrawal of September 2005, killing three Islamic Jihad fighters. On 8 June, Jamal Abu Samhadana was killed in a raid in Rafah, together with three members of the PRC who had recently joined up with the pro-Hamas executive force. Eight Palestinian civilians were killed in an explosion on the beach at Beit Lahya the following day. Hamas retaliated by firing ten rockets into Israel each day for a week before resuming its observance of the year-long ceasefire with Israel on 15 June. Tsahal claimed the right to strike Hamas in response to each rocket fired, even if they had been fired by another faction. Air raids on Gaza grew more frequent.

At first light on 25 June 2006, an eight-member Palestinian group, including militants from Hamas, the PRC and the newly founded 'Army of Islam' carried out a daring raid on Israel's strong point at Kerem Shalom, on the border with the Gaza Strip. Emerging dressed in Israeli uniforms from a secret tunnel that led under the border fence, they were able to capture a nineteen-year-old Tsahal tank-crew member, Gilad Shalit. Two Israeli soldiers and two Palestinians died in the exchange of fire. The attack was described as retaliation for the murder of Abu Samhadana by the Israeli forces and their abduction in Rafah the previous evening of two

Hamas fighters. However, it was evident that there was also an intention to undermine the Abbas–Haniya talks. The Palestinian president demanded the immediate return of Gilad Shalit, while the prime minister restricted himself to asking that the prisoner be treated humanely. On 27 June, despite this difference between their positions regarding the current crisis, Abbas and Haniya finalised a platform for a future national unity government committed to the establishment of a Palestinian state in the West Bank and the Gaza Strip. Some hours after the announcement of this political breakthrough on the Palestinian side, the Israeli forces launched a general offensive against the Gaza Strip. This operation, which Israel called 'Summer Rains', began with the destruction of Gaza City's power station, leaving the city dependent on power imported from Israel. The Hamas ministers and members of parliament who lived in the West Bank were seized at their residences and imprisoned. As a result, the responsibilities of these eight ministers had to be shared out among their colleagues who were in Gaza, with day-to-day authority devolved to the administrative directors of their departments in Ramallah. Tsahal's inability to trace Shalit led it to shift the target of its attacks from the south to the north of the Strip after significant destruction of Gaza's infrastructure. On 1 July 2006, the kidnappers agreed to free Shalit in return for the release of 1,000 Palestinian prisoners, including all of the women and children who were being held in Israel. The Olmert government rejected these demands and intensified its campaign against Gaza, leading the head of the Egyptian military intelligence to suspend his efforts at mediation.

During the night of 3 July 2006, the Givati tank brigade crossed into the north of the Gaza Strip. The settlements abandoned less than a year before were reoccupied and used as bases for raids into Jabalya and Beit Lahya. Hamas responded by firing a new model of Qassam rocket at Ashkelon, where a school was damaged. After several days, Tsahal shifted its target to the centre of the territory, attacking from the industrial zone at Qarni. UNRWA was forced to shelter 1,000 refugees who had fled from the bombings in two schools in Rafah. In one day, on 6 July, Israel carried out 221 raids in the Gaza Strip. On 12 July, Muhammad Dayef, the leader of the Qassam brigades, escaped when two 250 kilogram bombs were dropped on the building in which he lived. A Hamas militant was killed in the bombing together with his wife and seven children. The offices of the members of Ismail Haniya's cabinet and the headquarters of Force 17 were repeatedly targeted. Despite the scale of the destruction, 70 per cent of the 1,197 inhabitants of the West Bank and Gaza polled on 6–7 July approved of the continued detention of Gilad Shalit, as well as the refusal to release him unless a prisoner exchange took place. Support for Hamas's strategy in relation to the use of arms was marginally higher in Gaza than in the West Bank.[11]

On 13 July 2006 Israel launched a major offensive against Hezbollah in Lebanon, which had seized two Israeli soldiers. The Hezbollah action was apparently taken in an attempt to relieve the pressure on the Gaza Strip by creating a diversion. But this had no effect on events on the ground, where Israeli raids continued, directed particularly at Gaza city at the end of July and in early August at Rafah. In August, UN agencies assessed the damage of the six weeks of conflict that had just taken place. Up to 27 August, at least 213 Palestinians had been killed, the majority of whom were civilians, and material damage had been inflicted to the value of at least 15 million dollars. Tsahal had fired between 200 and 250 mortar shells each day, against nine rockets a day from Hamas. In addition, 79 per cent of the inhabitants of Gaza were now assessed as living in poverty, while urban areas were supplied with electricity for only six to eight hours a day and received running water for only two or three hours.[12] For five months, Hamas had been unable to pay the salaries of its employees, which, together with the closure of the territory by Israel for such a long period, had aggravated the crisis to an unprecedented degree.

To avert the humanitarian crisis in Gaza that would result from the bankruptcy of the Palestinian Authority, the European Union had constructed a complicated procedure to bypass the Hamas government. Known as the TIM (Temporary Interim Mechanism), whose purpose was to provide direct assistance for the Palestinian population, the procedure established a parallel channel for the distribution of aid. This untested procedure led to a noticeable increase in the costs of the aid supplied, at the very time when the situation of the civilian population was deteriorating dramatically. The cumbersome nature of the boycott on Hamas explains why the European Union ended up paying more to help less of the Palestinian population. The European Union's position had now grown closer to that of the United States, or even to that of Israel itself, due to France's aggressive attitude towards Hamas. The French President Jacques Chirac was convinced that the assassination of his 'brother' Rafic Hariri, the prime minister of Lebanon from 1992 to 1998 and again from 2000 to 2004, had been carried out on the instructions of Bashar al-Assad, the president of Syria.[13] Hariri had been killed along with twenty other people when a bomb was detonated as his motorcade travelled through central Beirut on 14 February 2005. Chirac's anger against Damascus was also directed against Assad's regional allies, namely Hezbollah in Lebanon, but also Hamas.

The French president shared the belief of the monarchs of Jordan and Saudi Arabia in the existence of a 'Shi'ite crescent' that was acting to destabilise the region, which included Iran and Iraq as well as Syria and the Gaza Strip. Perversely, the militancy of Hamas's Sunni Islam appeared to count less in this blinkered view than the supposed links between the Palestinian Islamists and Teheran. Such an analysis was consonant with Israel's condemnation of what it said was Iran's plan to bring about the destruction of the Israeli state, in which Hamas in Gaza was only one element. The highly personalised antagonism between Chirac and Assad thus served to exacerbate the Western demonisation of Hamas. The French president's hostility was fortunately no hindrance to the activity of the French Cultural Centre in Gaza, which continued to serve as a window on the world for the youth of the territory and those involved in the arts. From 1987 to 1994, the French Cultural Centre had been the only outside institution that continued to operate while the intifada was in full swing.

Though a ceasefire between Israel and Hezbollah was signed on 14 August 2006, Israel's operation 'Summer Rains' continued in the Gaza Strip. A particularly striking episode occurred when Israel sent troops into the eastern suburbs of Gaza City from 27 to 31 August, leaving some twenty Palestinians dead. Mahmoud Abbas and Ismail Haniya nevertheless resumed their talks on the formation of a government of national unity including Fatah and Hamas. The United States reiterated the three conditions it had first imposed on Hamas the day after the Palestinian elections: recognition of Israel, renunciation of violence and adherence to existing agreements. To these, Israel added the supplementary condition that Gilad Shalit must be unconditionally released. The Palestinian president and his prime minister disregarded this, announcing on 11 September an agreement in principle that was immediately rejected by Washington on the grounds of what were described as its omissions and imprecision. For example, Hamas did not extend formal recognition to Israel but merely undertook to 'respect' existing agreements. Two thirds of the Palestinian public questioned in the Gaza Strip took the view that Hamas should not recognise Israel as the result of international pressure.[14]

The Mecca Agreement

The United States openly appealed for new elections to be held at an earlier date than scheduled in the belief that the deteriorating situation had turned the population against Hamas. In this hope, the Americans earmarked 42 million dollars for the reinforcement of Fatah. To Washington, Muhammad Dahlan appeared to be the ideal protagonist for the political re-conquest of the Gaza Strip. On 1 and 2 October 2006, clashes between the competing security services degenerated into a pitched battle in Gaza in which eight died: four pro-Fatah combatants, one pro-Hamas and three passers-by. Small-scale settling of accounts continued throughout the following weeks. On 12 October, a senior official in the Palestinian intelligence was killed together with a senior Hamas official. The vendetta between the militias culminated on 20 October in a failed attack on Ismail Haniya's motorcade. Kidnappings of journalists and foreign aid workers were a frequent occurrence, though Hamas always contrived to free such hostages unharmed after a few days.

The year wore on in the besieged territory without any relaxation of Israel's military pressure. From 1 to 8 November 2006 in the north of the Gaza Strip, Tsahal conducted an operation known as 'Autumn Clouds', in which eighty Palestinians died. Of these, fifty were civilians, including two women and sixteen children. Two of the dead were doctors. A twelfth-century mosque at Beit Hanoun was destroyed, together with dozens of other buildings. A further offensive two weeks later, involving 1,000 Israeli troops, was met by the first Hamas suicide attack for two years when a sixty-year-old woman wounded three Israeli soldiers in an incident at Beit Lahya on 23 November. In the light of the escalation in the violence, Mahmoud Abbas obtained the agreement of all the Palestinian factions to suspend rocket attacks and tunnel digging in exchange for a halt to the Israeli operations.

Khaled Meshal, urged by Ismail Haniya not to risk such an agreement, said he would give Israel six months' grace in which to make progress towards the establishment of a Palestinian state within the 1967 frontiers. This carefully judged declaration resulted in the withdrawal of Tsahal from the Gaza Strip, with a ceasefire that was operative from 26 November 2006. The truce with Israel, however, once again left the field wide open for rivalries between the militias, which reached an unprecedented level of violence in the Gaza Strip. On 10 December, the Hamas interior minister narrowly escaped an attack and the following day the three young children of a Palestinian security colonel were killed in an attack on his car before a Qassam brigades' commander fell victim to a deadly Fatah ambush at Khan Yunis.

Ismail Haniya, who was in Sudan as part of a regional tour, returned to Gaza immediately. Upon his arrival the Israeli army refused him entry at Rafah on the grounds that he had brought back millions of dollars in cash that had been donated abroad. Hamas militiamen challenged the presidential guard for control of the Palestinian representation at the frontier post, which was re-opened thanks to Egyptian intervention on 14 December 2006. This did not prevent the prime ministerial convoy from being attacked and one of his bodyguards was killed. Hamas accused Muhammad Dahlan of responsibility and took its revenge with a wave of attacks to which Fatah in turn responded. Seventeen Palestinians were killed during a week of fratricidal combat, including two Fatah men who were executed in cold blood after being kidnapped. A French journalist from the newspaper *Libération* was seriously wounded on 17 December in an exchange of fire in Gaza City near the Palestinian ministries. On 23 December, the two factions accepted a ceasefire.

This inter-Palestinian truce collapsed eight days later after an armed confrontation at Jabalya. Fatah and Hamas kidnapped hostages from each other and the conflict became increasingly vicious. On 4 January 2007, an imam who had criticised Hamas was murdered at Maghazi Camp. Four days later, Muhammad Dahlan addressed tens of thousands of his sympathisers in Gaza City, the biggest crowd to attend a Fatah meeting in the territory since Yasser Arafat's return in 1994. He told his audience that no Hamas provocation should be left without response and gave his oath that he would emerge triumphant from the escalation of violence. There were shouts of 'death to the murderers', and 'Shiites, Shiites', indicating that the plan was to identify Hamas with its Iranian patron in order to isolate it from the Palestinian community. Incidents became less frequent after 13 January, though there had by that time been seventeen deaths.

On 23 January 2007 the conflict began once more, this time with a Hamas attack against a seaside hotel which had been opened by Muhammad Dahlan on the site of an abandoned settlement. Mahmoud Zahar's residence was attacked by Fatah and Rashid Abu Shibak's house was the target of a Hamas attack. On 26 January, Fatah guerrillas raided a pro-Hamas mosque in Gaza City, killing five worshippers and taking ten hostages. These were later freed in return for Hamas's lifting of the siege of a senior Fatah official in Jabalya. On 1 February, a clash between the presidential guard and Hamas's executive force left five dead when the Islamists ambushed a convoy on its way to Dahlan's headquarters. Fatah attacked the campus of the Islamic University in Gaza and in response Hamas caused serious damage to various institutions linked to Fatah. The death toll from what had increasingly begun to look like a civil war was seventy-four dead in two weeks.

These episodes of extreme violence, all of which were broadcast on satellite TV news programmes, aroused passions in Jordan and elsewhere in the Arab world. King Abdullah of Saudi Arabia had given his name to the Arab peace plan adopted in March 2002 by the Arab Summit in Beirut, which had offered Israel peace with the whole Arab world in exchange for a withdrawal from the territories occupied in 1967. Now he invited Mahmoud Abbas, Khaled Meshal and Ismail Haniya to come to Mecca for a meeting on 6 February 2007 to put an end to what he saw as their increasingly shameful confrontation. He promised to donate a billion dollars in aid to the Palestinian territories on condition that an agreement was reached to stop the violence at the earliest possible date. In less than forty-eight hours, the negotiators agreed on the formation of a national unity government, to be led by Ismail Haniya, with nine Hamas ministers, six from Fatah, five independents (three to be nominated by Hamas and two by Fatah), and finally four ministers representing the smaller parties. Mahmoud Abbas's right of veto over appointments was recognised, but though it was agreed that the future Haniya government would commit itself to 'respect' for international legality and the agreements already made, no reference was made to recognition of Israel.[15] In a survey taken in the Gaza Strip and the West Bank, half of those questioned believed the agreement would put an end to the clash between Fatah and Hamas, but an equal number thought it would only result in a temporary truce.[16]

The Descent to Hell

After a month of negotiations the Palestinian national unity government was inaugurated on 13 March 2007. At Ismail Haniya's side was his Fatah deputy prime minister, Azzam al-Ahmad. Two independents, who were endorsed both by Hamas and Fatah, took key portfolios: the minister of the interior was Hani Qawasmeh and the minister of foreign affairs was Ziad Abu Amr, a professor at Bir Zeit University specialising in Palestinian Islamism who had been elected as a deputy in Gaza in 1996 and was re-elected ten years later. The leaders of two small parties, Salam Fayyad (Third Way) and Mustafa Barghouti (National Initiative) also joined the government, with the former becoming the minister of finance and the latter the minister of information. In his policy statement, Ismail Haniya acknowledged Mahmoud Abbas's right to negotiate with Israel on behalf of the PLO. On 17 March, the PLC gave a vote of confidence to the new government by a majority of eighty-three votes to three (forty-one Hamas members of the PLC were currently imprisoned by Israel and four others were in hiding).

Mahmoud Abbas called for the siege of Gaza to be lifted and for negotiations on the final status of the occupied territories to begin. He also appointed Muhammad Dahlan to be his coordinator for security, answering directly to the presidency. This move was intended to placate the United States and Israel, but it greatly irritated Hani Qawasmeh at the

Interior Ministry as well as Hamas. The only foreign country that immediately issued a positive response to the formation of the Haniya government was Norway, which sent its minister of foreign affairs to Gaza (his Israeli opposite number retaliated by refusing to meet him in Jerusalem). Member states of the European Union said they were ready to cooperate with Palestinian ministers who were not Hamas members. The United States refused to alter its previous position, insisting that it would collaborate only with Mahmoud Abbas, or, if the issue arose, with Salam Fayyad. The US determination to impose early elections, a position supported by Egypt, clearly emerges from confidential documents published by the Jordanian and Israeli press. The Jordanian weekly *Al-Majd* was banned and confiscated on 30 April 2007, the day it had announced it would publish the first 'leak' relating to American policy. A revealing document was in fact published by *Haaretz* on 4 May.

Hani Qawasmeh, the new interior minister, proposed that Hamas's executive force should be merged into the Palestinian security forces. In Gaza, this formula met with stark rebuttal from Rashid Abu Shibak, supported by President Abbas. Dahlan had the help of the United States to set up a 1,400-strong special force recruited to contain Hamas. On 10 May, Mahmoud Abbas announced the deployment of 3,000 of his own supporters to restore 'law and order' to the Gaza Strip. Clashes with Hamas grew more severe, leaving twenty-four dead over the space of a few days. Qawasmeh abandoned his efforts and left the government, after which Ismail Haniya took on the interior portfolio in addition to his existing responsibilities. The crisis was all the more alarming because the truce with Israel that had been in force since 26 November 2006 was regularly being broken by bombing and rocket strikes.

The impression began to gain ground among the Islamists that Fatah's manoeuvres were being coordinated with an increase of aggression on the part of Israel. On 16 May 2007 Ehud Olmert launched a series of attacks on Hamas positions in Gaza, even though Hamas, as distinct from Islamic Jihad, was continuing to observe the truce. Thirty-two Palestinians were killed in three days, and up to thirty rockets a day were launched in reprisal. Half of the 24,000 inhabitants of Sderot left the town, which was the political base of the Labour defence minister, Amir Peretz. The escalation once again sparked off the vendetta between the Palestinian militias: fifty-five died in a new round of clashes between Fatah and Hamas. Joint appeals for a ceasefire made by Mahmoud Abbas and Ismail Haniya had no effect. Calm was restored on 20 May, but only through the mediation of the delegation of Egyptian officers which was in Gaza to promote security cooperation. The Egyptian themselves were exposed to physical danger, and on 16 May in Rafah an Egyptian officer was wounded by Fatah militiamen while he was holding a reconciliation meeting between Fatah and Hamas representatives.

In early June 2007, rumours were rife in the Gaza Strip that a major arms delivery was about to be made to Dahlan and his men.[17] A Fatah 'Special Forces' unit some 500 strong had just arrived in the territory. On 6 June, a clash in Rafah set off a series of further incidents throughout the Strip. Hostages taken by both sides were now routinely being tortured, and kneecapping was common. The settling of accounts by militias had become so routine on the ground that it was beyond the political control of the leadership of either Fatah or Hamas. On 10 June, a member of Mahmoud Abbas's presidential guard was thrown from a tall building in Gaza City in an attack that was avenged some hours later when an Islamist militiaman was thrown from a neighbouring building.[18]

On the morning of 11 June 2007, Mahmoud Abbas and Ismail Haniya proclaimed the seventh ceasefire between their forces in a month. However, the Qassam brigades could not resist taking advantage of the absence of Muhammad Dahlan, who was undergoing surgery in Egypt. Despite the overwhelming numerical superiority of Fatah and its security services, the military wing of Hamas now launched a determined offensive that seemed impossible to resist. Police and militiamen loyal to Fatah and the president, disregarding Mahmoud Abbas's order to resist, often surrendered or deserted in the face of the determination of the Islamists.[19] Yet in such savage fighting surrender was often no guarantee of survival. On 14 June 2007, at the headquarters of the Fatah-linked 'preventive security', Islamist militiamen murdered at least seven police officers who had already laid down their arms. UNRWA suspended its activities in the Gaza Strip after two of its employees were killed in crossfire. Hundreds of Fatah's senior officials and activists fled by sea to Egypt or queued up at Erez to leave the territory. In four days, the rout of Mahmoud Abbas's supporters in the Gaza Strip was complete and the victory of Hamas, now sole master of the territory, was total. The houses of the Palestinian Authority's hierarchy were ransacked, Muhammad Dahlan's own villa in Gaza City was demolished with sledge hammers and hooded militiamen paraded and disported themselves in the office of the Palestinian president.

Mahmoud Abbas could have attempted to take matters into his own hands by returning to the Gaza Strip, which had after all elected him in January 2005. However, in private, he often expressed his relief at being able to concentrate his attention on the West Bank alone.[20] The Palestinian president declared a state of emergency from his headquarters in Ramallah, dissolved the government of national unity and installed Salam Fayyad as prime minister with a cabinet of technocrats. On 15 June 2007, the United States gave him its full support, soon to be followed by the Quartet and the European Union. Aid money that had up to now been frozen was unblocked with a degree of alacrity that contrasted with previous bureaucratic slowness. Thanks to this international generosity, it was possible for the Authority to resume paying the salaries of its employees in the Gaza Strip, which were paid on condition that they refused to work for the Hamas administration. Throughout the West Bank, Islamist militants were tracked down and their networks were dismantled.

The Quartet's special envoy, James Wolfensohn, who had invested so much of his effort and good will in Gaza, stepped down to be replaced by Tony Blair, very much an exponent of the principle of 'West Bank First'. After a year-long siege by the Israel forces, the Gaza Strip was ill-equipped to heal the wounds of the inter-Palestinian civil war. Electricity and water supplies, already stringently rationed, were no longer available at all except on a very erratic basis. Light industry, cut off from raw materials and markets, was running at only 20 per cent capacity,[21] creating a situation of hidden unemployment that was still insufficient to disguise the disastrous lack of work. The United Nations, due to the Israeli ban on the import of building materials, was compelled to suspend construction projects on which tens of thousands of Palestinians were employed.[22]

The only government officials in the Gaza Strip who were regularly paid were those who absented themselves from their places of work, because of the edict on the part of Palestine's international paymasters that there should be no cooperation with Hamas, while Hamas was already having great difficulty in settling its wages bill at the end of each month. The chaos grew worse with the institution by the presidency in Ramallah of a Friday and Saturday weekend, as against the Thursday and Friday weekend that had prevailed in the Strip since 2006. (Initially Friday had been the only free day recognised by the Palestinian Authority but Thursday had been added as it was already a day on which few government officials actually worked.) In another intrusive action, the Palestinian president issued a decree invalidating all travel documents issued in Gaza. The Israeli scenario of a division between 'Hamastan' in the Gaza Strip and 'Fatahstan' in the West Bank had effectively come to pass. On 13 June 2007, even before Hamas had definitively gained control, the head of Israeli military intelligence, Amos Yadlin, told American diplomats in Tel Aviv that 'Israel is pleased to see Hamas take control of Gaza, which will permit us to treat it as hostile territory.'[23] One Palestine had turned against the other, with both the losers in a fratricidal battle. The trap was closing on the Gaza Strip.

Forty years after the beginning of the Israeli occupation of Gaza, and two years after the unilateral disengagement ordered by Sharon, the noose had finally tightened, with tragic effect. The dismantling of the settlements had allowed the inhabitants of an overcrowded territory access to more space, but the locations that had been evacuated were often reoccupied by Tsahal as forward posts and bases for the implementation of aggressive incursions into the Strip. Only the land surface of the Gaza Strip was independent, since its frontier posts, its airspace and its territorial waters all remained under the intrusive control of Israel. After the limited autonomy with which Arafat had been obliged to be contented, the occupying power had constructed a new form of domination at a distance, dividing and ruling to the benefit of Fatah and the detriment of Hamas.[24]

The Gaza Strip had already paid a high price during the first intifada but the armed conflict involved in the second substantially increased the human cost. Some 3,000 Palestinians had been killed by Israel in Gaza since the beginning of the second intifada,[25] in other words a proportion three times greater than in the West Bank. Tsahal's 'targeted' assassinations were especially deadly in the Strip, with 363 dead between 2000 and 2007, of whom 148 were accounted for by collateral civilian damage.[26] The military option, once the Israeli retreat was under way, had fed into an unprecedented spiral of inter-Palestinian violence. Between 2005 and the summer of 2007, 668 Palestinians were killed by Israel in the Strip, including 359 civilians; but during the same period 357 Palestinians were killed by other Palestinians, of whom half were civilians caught up in incidents. During this same period, just four Israeli soldiers were killed in incidents connected with Gaza. Some 2,800 rockets or mortars were fired from the Gaza Strip into Israel, where they killed a total of four people.

Gaza had been the cradle of the fedayin and the cauldron of the intifada: it now became the focus of the bloodiest of inter-Palestinian quarrels. Sheikh Yassin's supporters had refused to join the armed resistance when the occupation began in 1967—two generations later they became its fiercest exponents, accusing the PLO of doing deals with Israel. The liberation struggle waged by Hezbollah in southern Lebanon, which was ignominiously evacuated by the Israeli army in 2000, was a major influence in bringing about this change of mind. The situation in the Gaza Strip, however, was very different from that on Israel's northern frontier: Gaza was no more than scrap of territory squeezed between south-west Israel and the Egyptian border in Sinai. The destruction of thousands of houses during Tsahal's offensives freed up a buffer zone that ran the length of the carefully constructed fence around the territory. The disengagement of 2005, far from being a liberation, proved only to be the start of a new episode in the dispossession of Palestine.

Hamas's success in the Palestinian elections of January 2006 could have staved off the territory's fate if the Islamist movement had chosen to engage fully in political life, but only if the active interference of the United States and the passivity of the European Union had not sabotaged this experiment in government. The anger generated by the frustration of Hamas's electoral victory reignited popular fury against what were seen as the double standards of the West and the international community. It was the cause of an open wound that was then aggravated by the armed escalation between the militias. Haydar Abdel Shafi, a founder member of the PLO and head of the Palestinian delegation at the Madrid peace conference, looked on with mute despair as the descent into hell took place. On 25 September 2007, when this nationalist hero passed away in Gaza City, a particular conception of a united Palestine, sovereign and democratic, also died.

CONCLUSION

THE GENERATION OF IMPASSES?

16

FIVE YEARS IN THE RUINS

The Gaza Strip came into existence only at the behest of Israel, which herded the mass of those expelled in 1948 into it, defining its narrow confines in the heat of war. Ben Gurion, far-sighted as ever, soon saw the risks inherent in this concentration of refugees in the north-west of the Negev: the natural obstacle presented by the Sinai desert to the south would prevent the refugees from dispersing. By contrast, in the other three neighbouring countries, the refugees had moved away from Israel's frontiers and refugee camps had grown up around the capital cities: respectively, Amman, Beirut and Damascus. For the two thirds of its population who were refugees, Gaza became one huge refugee camp. Ben Gurion's offer to annex the Gaza Strip, which he believed could resolve the problem, was rejected by Egypt at the Lausanne conference of 1949. The territory therefore became the focal point of Israel's problems on its southern front. Israel launched military incursions to intimidate the Palestinians in Gaza; carried out indiscriminate bombing raids against them; and then occupied the territory in 1956 in order to crush any kind of local resistance. In 1957, however, under international pressure, Israel was compelled to retreat from Gaza. When Israel's withdrawal from Gaza was inevitable, Ben Gurion, with no other option, had to place his trust in Nasser's authoritarianism to keep the peace in Gaza. In practice, this ensured that calm reigned until 1967.

Israel's re-occupation of the Gaza Strip at the outset of the Arab–Israel war of 1967 immediately brought with it the threat of a renewed insurgency given the uniquely determined attitude of the Palestinian guerrilla movements. Moshe Dayan made an attempt to dissolve the problem presented by Gaza through his 'open door' policy with Israel and the West Bank, an unequal partnership which, over the space of two decades, brought some benefits. In 1993, Yitzhak Rabin opted for the principle of closure of the territory while at the same time initiating a dialogue with the PLO. Getting rid of Gaza became an obsession for the Israeli military, which envisaged the devolution of responsibility for keeping order to a Palestinian force while it would retain the right to intervene in the event of any threat. There was no change in Israel's strategy on this issue between the partial withdrawal of 1994 and the unilateral disengagement of 2005. The difference was that while Rabin saw himself as initiating a peace process, Sharon simply imposed a unilateral fait accompli.

For Israel, however, there were problems in an approach framed exclusively in terms of security, whose brutal nature elicited sporadic outbreaks of international interest in response to the various crises. The humanitarian emergency threw into stark relief the lack of prospects for the people of Gaza, caught up in the trial of strength between Hamas and Fatah. Thus Israel's fruitless strategy exposed the insolubility of the humanitarian crisis, itself exacerbated by the intractability of the inter-Palestinian conflict. The 1.5 million inhabitants of the territory, already subject to exceptionally rigid physical isolation, also found themselves the prisoner of this triple impasse.

The Israeli Impasse

The Olmert government was backed to the hilt by the Bush administration in its policy of inflicting collective punishment on the Gaza Strip, which was more isolated from the outside world than the relatively better off territories in the West Bank that were under the control of the Palestinian Authority. On 16 July 2007, President Bush made a speech in favour of the 'West Bank First' option ahead of a peace conference planned for the autumn of that year. In the meantime Israel continued its air attacks and ground incursions into the Gaza Strip, where forty-three people were killed in the month of August alone. Despite Hamas's observation of a de facto ceasefire, the frequent salvos of rockets by Islamic Jihad were sufficient to prompt sustained aggression on the part of the Israeli army. Ismail Haniya could no longer find sympathy for his suggestion that the entry points to Gaza could be put under the control of Mahmoud Abbas's presidential guard in exchange for an alleviation of the Israeli blockade.

On 19 September, Olmert and his security cabinet took a further step when they classified the Gaza Strip as 'hostile territory', against which 'military and anti-terrorist operations' would be intensified. Sanctions against Gaza were strengthened, with a ban, for example, on the import of paper into Gaza to discourage Hamas's propaganda activities, while the Israeli government continued to proclaim its wish to avoid a 'humanitarian catastrophe'.[1] Israeli incursions continued throughout September, with some twenty people dead and the demolition of fifteen houses. Five activists were also killed in 'targeted' raids. Hamas urged Islamic Jihad to halt the rockets, but to no avail. From his base in Damascus, the head of Hamas's Political Bureau, Khaled Meshal, made a similar plea, also without result. The tension between Hamas and Islamic Jihad came to a head on 21 October, when Hamas's executive force and Islamic Jihad militiamen clashed directly in Rafah in an engagement that left at least two dead.

On 26 November 2007 President Bush convened his anticipated peace conference in the American city of Annapolis in the state of Maryland. On the eve of the meeting, Ehud Olmert, in what was supposed to be a gesture of good will to Mahmoud Abbas, announced a temporary suspension of the ban on the export of flowers from Gaza and permission for the import into Gaza of a hitherto proscribed cargo of sheep. The conference itself did not lead to any significant breakthroughs, since Israel made it a condition of any advance in relation to the establishment of a Palestinian state that Mahmoud Abbas's Palestinian Authority must regain effective control of the Gaza Strip. Two thousand inhabitants of Gaza were permitted to go on the pilgrimage to Mecca that year solely because their names had been conveyed to the Israeli military authorities by the Palestinian Authority in Ramallah (rather than the Haniya government in Gaza). After six months of stringent blockade, Ismail Haniya conveyed the offer of a ceasefire in Gaza to Israel through various channels, conditional on the lifting of the Israeli siege. On 18 December 2007, he made the proposal to the Israeli Knesset member Yossi Beilin; he then repeated it in an interview with

Israeli television the following day; and finally he put it in a letter forwarded to Ehud Olmert by the Egyptian president, Husni Mubarak.

Olmert disregarded Hamas's proposal, keeping up the military pressure. As a result, at least thirty-five Palestinians were killed in Gaza in the first two weeks of January 2008. Ismail Haniya had nothing to show for his diplomatic efforts and was therefore obliged to bow to the wishes of the Qassam brigades. Between 15 and 17 January, the seven months of undeclared truce came to an end with the firing of 150 rockets at Israel. Eight Israelis were wounded and one Ecuadorian immigrant worker was killed. This time, Israel's reprisals were economic as well as military. On 20 January, the Israeli authorities forced the closure of the power station in Gaza. The rockets ceased after a few days, but on 4 February there was a suicide attack at Dimona in which one Israeli was killed. A new cycle of attack and counter-attack began in which twenty-seven Palestinians and seven Israelis were killed. On 28 February, Tsahal launched a new offensive known as 'Hot Winter' against the Gaza Strip, in the course of which 111 Palestinians were killed, half of whom were civilians, together with three Israelis. It was in response to 'Hot Winter' that Hamas had fired its first Grads at Israel, between 28 February and 3 March 2008. The use of Grad rockets, which the Palestinians also called Katyushas, was a definite escalation. They had a calibre of 122 millimetres and a range of 20 kilometres, well in excess of the range of Qassam-2 or Qassam-3 rockets. They had in fact previously been used on a smaller scale by the Islamic Jihad, which had fired its first Grad on 20 March 2006, without causing any injury, and launched three other Grads at Israel before the end of 2007.

Egypt and the European Union offered to mediate to obtain a ceasefire, but this was blocked by the United States which wanted to ensure that Hamas was not able to extract any political advantage. On 12 March 2008, Ismail Haniya called for a ceasefire, but to no avail. In early April, Israeli incursions into the Strip were so prolific that the different Palestinian factions began to cooperate in response. They mounted joint raids, striking two frontier posts at Nahal Oz on 9 April and at Kerem Shalom on 19 April, provoking a murderous Israeli reprisal on 23 April. Egypt was alarmed by the escalation and on 30 April it obtained an agreement from all the Palestinian factions to implement an immediate ceasefire in Gaza.

This was rejected by Ehud Olmert, who was beginning to have his own difficulties in domestic politics: multiple and serious allegations of fraud and corruption were being made against him.

It required all of President Mubarak's determination to change Olmert's mind on the ceasefire proposal, with the Egyptian head of military intelligence General Omar Suleiman conducting a shuttle mission between Israel and Gaza. A letter from the kidnapped soldier Gilad Shalit, who had by now been Hamas's prisoner for two years, was conveyed to Israel by way of former US president Jimmy Carter: this also carried some weight. At last, Israel and Hamas reached an agreement to observe a truce for six months, to begin at dawn on 19 June 2008. Ismail Haniya undertook steps to punish any violation of the truce from the Palestinian side, by whatever faction. There remained little trust between the two sides, however, and Hamas reiterated its original demand for the liberation of 1,000 Palestinian prisoners in exchange for Shalit's release. Yet the violence diminished markedly. October 2008 was the quietest month since the outbreak of the second intifada eight years before, with only one attack on an Israeli target and seven on the Palestinians, of which four took the form of shells fired by the Israeli navy at Gaza's fishing fleet. There were no deaths on either side.

Uncertainty prevailed in Israel's domestic politics. Ehud Olmert had stepped down and had been succeeded as leader of Kadima by his foreign affairs minister, Tzipi Livni. But she was unable to form a government. This left Olmert as caretaker prime minister despite the fact that he had resigned. On 28 October 2008, new elections were announced in Israel, but were not to be held until February 2009. On 4 November 2008, the day of the American presidential election, the Israeli army launched an attack on Deir al-Balah in which five Hamas militants died. Tsahal's pretext was the continued construction of tunnels from the Gaza Strip into Israel like the one used in the operation to capture Gilad Shalit. The subsequent escalation was swift, despite Ismail Haniya's appeal to Egypt to return to the ceasefire. On 14 November, Hamas fired eleven Grad rockets, damaging a house in Sderot in which one Israeli was injured. Once more, Israel sealed off the Gaza Strip completely, maintaining the closure even when rockets began to be fired less frequently. Within Hamas, internal tensions emerged. On 14 December 2008, in Damascus, Khaled Meshal declared that the ceasefire was officially due to expire in five days at the end of its six-month period. At the same time, Hamas officials in Gaza were saying that they wanted the truce renewed. On 22 December, Mahmoud Zahar took this line when speaking on Israeli TV.

Ehud Olmert, who was still continuing as caretaker prime minister, together with his minister of defence, Ehud Barak, who had returned to Israeli politics as a leader within the Labour Party in 2005, set in train the necessary arrangements for an unprecedented offensive against the Gaza Strip. On 24 December 2008, when Hamas fired eighty rockets and mortar shells into Israel, the rest of the Israeli cabinet unanimously backed the plan. The following day, Olmert spoke on the television channel Al-Arabiyya, which broadcasts from Dubai, threatening the population of Gaza with dire consequences if the rockets continued. On 25–6 December, some thirty Palestinian missiles landed in Israel, though no injury or damage resulted. On 27 December, at the end of the morning, a wave of aerial bombing raids on Gaza got under way that led to the deaths of 228 Palestinians. Dozens lost their lives at a ceremony to award diplomas to newly qualified police personnel. This was the beginning of the major Israeli operation, 'Cast Lead'.

This 'War on Gaza', as the Arab media soon began to call it, began with a week of intensive shelling and bombing, from the air, and from artillery and naval guns, which was directed at Hamas's offices and security installations as well as at the tunnels that had been dug for smuggling goods into the territory. On the night of 3 January 2009, four Tsahal brigades (three made up of infantry and parachutists and one armoured brigade) moved into the Gaza Strip: a total of some 10,000 troops. Instead of advancing into heavily populated areas, the tanks pushed forward to bisect the territory, from Nahal Oz to the former colony of Netzarim, destroying all obstacles they found in their way. Drones were now being used not just for surveillance and cover, but also in attack operations. On 12 January, a third phase began, with repeated shelling of targets that had already been hit, with the intention of delivering a supposed 'coup de grâce' to Hamas.[2] On 18 January, Israel declared a unilateral ceasefire, apparently at the behest of Barack Obama, whose presidential investiture was to take place two days later.

In the course of the twenty-three days of conflict that constituted 'Cast Lead', nine Israeli soldiers were killed in the Gaza Strip, of whom four were the victims of a friendly fire incident, and three civilians and one soldier were killed on Israeli territory.[3] There is controversy, however, over the scale of Palestinian losses. According to an organisation linked to the International Federation for Human Rights, 1,417 Palestinians were killed, including 236 combatants.[4] In contrast, the Israeli government claimed that 1,166 Palestinians were killed, a figure which included 709 'Hamas terrorists'.[5] The disparity was in part related to the status of the Gaza police, who were regarded as civilians by the human rights organisations but assimilated to Hamas in the eyes of Tsahal. However, one of the main problems facing the Olmert government involved persuading Israeli public opinion that the operation had been justified—despite all the attacks, rockets were still being fired into Israel even while the offensive was in progress, and there had been no positive news with regard to the fate of Gilad Shalit.

Only one Hamas leader lost his life in the course of 'Cast Lead'. This was Said Siyam, the minister of the interior, who was killed in a bombing attack on 15 January. Siyam, however, came from the political side of Hamas, as did Ismail Haniya himself. Hamas's military wing, on the other hand, consisting in effect of the Qassam brigades, was undamaged by the Israeli assault and its leadership was left intact. Internal Hamas sources admitted the loss of 150 fighters from the Qassam brigades, whose total strength was 10,000 men on active duty with a similar number of 'reservists'.[6] The Israeli media played up the death of the radical preacher Sheikh Nizar Rayyan, killed on 1 January when his house in Jabalya was bombed, also causing the deaths of his four wives and eleven of their children, but the sheikh had no organisational role in the structure of the Qassam brigades. It was in fact the other factions, Islamic Jihad and the Popular Resistance Committees, which paid the highest price for the Israeli onslaught. On the Israeli side, the originators of operation 'Cast Lead', Tzipi Livni's Kadima and Ehud Barak's Labour Party, drew little political benefit from it, performing disappointingly in the Israeli parliamentary elections that were held on 10 February, with twenty-eight seats for Kadima and thirteen for Labour. In contrast, Likud, now headed by Binyamin Netanyahu, held twenty-seven seats and fifteen went to the secular extreme right-wing party Yisrael Beytenu, headed by Avigdor Liebermann. Interestingly, in the town of Sderot, the Israeli population centre most exposed to the rockets fired from Gaza, 33 per cent of the vote went to Likud, 23 per cent to Yisrael Beytenu, 12 per cent to Kadima and only 5 per cent to Labour. On 31 March Binyamin Netanyahu formed a Likud–Labour coalition government in which Ehud Barak kept the defence portfolio, bringing a moderating Labour presence to a cabinet that also contained the extreme right-wing Avigdor Liebermann as minister of foreign affairs.

In the Gaza Strip, the civilian population had been deeply traumatised by the three weeks of hostilities, during which none had escaped the sensation of vulnerability and impotence. Some began to refer to what had happened as the 'Nakba of 2009', in a reference to the original 'Catastrophe' (*nakba*) of 1948.[7] Hamas's rhetoric was badly received by the civilian population, who accused the Islamist militias of having failed to protect them, while ensuring the safety of their own fighters. When the initial wave of anger died down, it was followed by a general mood of depression at the scale of the consequences. The number of public buildings that had been destroyed or very seriously damaged was 6,400, including thirty-four hospitals and clinics, 214 schools and fifty-two places of worship. In addition, 46,000 private residences had been hit, leaving 100,000 people homeless and there was 600,000 tons of rubble and mess to remove; 80 per cent of the harvest and of the agricultural infrastructure had also been destroyed. The overall estimate of the damage was between 1.6 and 1.9 billion dollars.[8]

The Western press, whose reporters had been banned by Israel from entering the Gaza Strip during 'Cast Lead', were soon able to report the scale of the destruction and the widespread despair. As international criticism grew, the Netanyahu government spared no effort to justify the actions of the previous cabinet, refusing to cooperate with the UN Commission of Inquiry led by the South African judge Richard Goldstone and virulently criticising the conclusions of his report. The Goldstone report, which was issued on 15 September, accused both Israel and Hamas of committing war crimes. It was adopted by the UN Human Rights Council on 16 October by twenty-five votes to six with eleven abstentions.

Among those voting against it was the United States. On 1 April 2011, Goldstone told the *Washington Post* he was prepared to reconsider his conclusions, which Israel took as a pretext to call for the retrospective rejection of the report, though the other three members of the Commission of Inquiry stood by it. Despite eye-witness accounts published in Israel as well as elsewhere by dissident soldiers,[9] 'Cast Lead' continued to enjoy the underlying support of the vast majority of Israeli public opinion. If criticism was levelled at the operation, the question raised was not so much whether it should have been carried out, but whether it had been sufficiently effective. In the two months that followed 'Cast Lead', the Palestinian rockets continued, with no less than 180 falling in Israeli territory.[10] As regards Gilad Shalit, the offensive against Gaza had not induced Hamas in any way to modify the demands they made for his release.[11]

From now on, Tsahal instituted a military routine that kept the Gaza Strip under constant pressure. In early May 2009, Israeli F-16s carried out a series of bombing raids on the tunnels used for smuggling goods and people from Egypt, though without much impact. It soon emerged that while the Israeli raids complicated the task of those who ran the tunnels, they did not stop the underground traffic.[12] The tunnels were dangerous, however: the UN had estimated that between June 2007 and July 2008 at least eighty-five Palestinians had died in the tunnels to Egypt either in cave-ins or by being electrocuted. Israel's determination to install a buffer zone some hundreds of metres deep on the Palestinian side of the border was the cause of repeated incidents in which the local people involved in the tunnel trade were more often the victims rather than armed militiamen. On 4 September 2009, a Palestinian adolescent of fourteen was killed when shots were fired by Tsahal without warning. During the nine months that followed 'Cast Lead', Tsahal killed forty-four Palestinians in Gaza, including five children. In contrast, only one Israeli soldier was killed by Palestinian fire in the same period.[13]

On 25 September 2009, Tsahal resumed its 'targeted' raids with the bombing of three militants in their car in the eastern part of Gaza City. A further sequence of violent incidents, between 6 and 10 January 2010, involving mortar fire by the Palestinians on one side and Israeli air raids on the other, cost the lives of seven Palestinians including three civilians. A further deadly outburst took place at the end of March. During the first six months of 2010, the Israeli forces killed a total of thirty-four Palestinians in the Gaza Strip, eighteen of whom died in air raids. Eleven of these Palestinian victims were civilians, while the three Israelis killed during the same period were all soldiers.[14] On 12 September 2010, three Palestinian farmers including a ninety-year-old and two teenagers were killed on their land by an Israeli tank round. On 3 and 17 November, targeted raids by Tsahal killed a number of 'Army of Islam' militants in a vehicle in which they were travelling in Gaza City. The second half of 2010 saw a toll of thirty-seven Palestinians dead, including twelve civilians, with no Israeli victims during the same period.[15]

Tsahal believed it had found the formula for the management of Israel's southern frontier, at a cost that was exorbitant for the population of Gaza but acceptable to Israeli public opinion. The Egyptian Revolution, which broke out on 25 January 2011, obliging President Mubarak to step down eighteen days later, soon put an end to this strategic delusion. In a reversal of the usual relationship, the Gaza Strip found itself feeding the Egyptian half of the town of Rafah, which had been cut off from the world due to rioting in Suez. Israel had made it a condition of its peace treaty with Egypt in 1979 that there should be no Egyptian military build-up in Sinai. Now, Israel found itself compelled to agree to an unprecedented deployment of Egypt's armed forces to the east of the Suez Canal in order to contain the revolutionary disturbances.

The second half of March 2011 was particularly bloody in the Gaza Strip, with the deaths of fourteen Palestinians, of whom six were civilians. On 20 March, two boys of just fourteen years of age were killed by an Israeli tank outside the camp at Bureij, and on 22 March two adults and two children died in an Israeli mortar bombardment east of Gaza City. The eight Palestinian militiamen killed during this period were for the most part targeted in air attacks. Six Grad rockets and 100 locally made mortar shells were fired into Israel during this period, wounding three people. On three occasions, the Palestinian projectiles actually fell short, in Palestinian territory, causing some material damage. On 7 April, an Israeli teenager was seriously wounded in an ambush on an Israeli school bus on a road close to the border of the Gaza Strip, leading to three days of violence in which seventeen Palestinians lost their lives.

On 18 August 2011, eight Israelis including six civilians were killed in a major attack between the Israeli town of Eilat and the Egyptian frontier in the far south of the Negev. The Israeli army reacted with extreme violence, killing the seven attackers but also causing the deaths of five Egyptian policemen who were mistaken for members of the guerrilla group that had infiltrated into Israel. On 21 August these deaths, though inadvertent, led to riots outside the Israeli embassy in Cairo. Confusion over the incident deepened when Israel accused the Gaza Popular Resistance Committees of having crossed through Egyptian territory, an accusation denied by the PRC, an organisation that was never shy to make claims of responsibility. Soon, air strikes were once more hitting Gaza, with thirteen dead including two very young children, to which the Palestinian response took Israel by surprise. On 20 August, an Israeli was killed by a Grad rocket at Beersheba, relatively far from the Strip. The following day, another Grad was fired but it was faulty and caused the death of a Palestinian teenager at Beit Lahya. Hamas broke the truce it had unilaterally observed since 'Cast Lead' by firing a rocket that hit the Israeli town of Ofakim, where a small child and a baby were wounded. The violence continued for another week, and in one incident four workers were killed in the bombing of a tunnel at Rafah on 24 August. From 28 August, Hamas returned to its self-declared 'calming' (*tahdi'a*), imposing it also on the other factions including Islamic Jihad. This was similar to the first *tahdi'a*, which had been declared by Hamas and its partners in March 2005, and was conditional on a parallel restraint on the part of Israel.

On 11 October 2011, Hamas and Israel reached agreement on a prisoner exchange, with Egyptian mediation and the involvement of the German intelligence services, the BND (*Bundes Nachrichten Dienst*). The head of the BND's Middle East office, Gerhard Konrad, had negotiated a previous prisoner exchange with Israel. A week later, Gilad Shalit was released in exchange for 1,027 Palestinian detainees, of whom 477 were freed at once according to a list agreed by Hamas and Israel, and a further 550 to be chosen solely by Israel were to be freed two months later. Of the 477 who were freed, 292 were from the West Bank, 130 were from Gaza and six were of Israeli nationality. Out of the total number, twenty-seven were women. This was the first time Israel had agreed to release its own nationals who had been sentenced under the Israeli justice system. The second tranche of releases, which took place on 18 December 2011, included only forty-one prisoners from the Gaza Strip. Of the 550 Palestinians released on that day, 300 had been due in any case to be freed in 2012.

Hamas failed on this occasion to obtain the release of any of the key Fatah figures who were being held by Israel, such as Marwan Barghouti, or the PFLP leader Ahmed Saadat. It did, however, arrange the liberation of numerous militants from Fatah, the PRC and Islamic Jihad. Most importantly, it succeeded in freeing dozens of its own senior officials and long-standing members, some of whom had been given several life sentences for their involvement in anti-Israel operations. For example, it obtained the freedom of Yahya Sinwar, one of the founding members of Hamas's military wing, and the release of militants involved in the abduction and murder of the two Israeli soldiers in Gaza in 1989.

Hamas was able to present itself as having scored a major victory with this agreement, despite Fatah's complaints that forty of the freed prisoners were subsequently deported, and that 145 of those released who were originally from the West Bank were forcibly released in Gaza. On 18 October 2011, a holiday was declared in the Gaza Strip, with tens of thousands of Palestinians gathering to celebrate the prisoner releases. To mark the occasion, Hamas banned celebratory fusillades of shots in the air and erected tents to receive visitors outside the houses of each of the released detainees, irrespective of their party affiliations. Ismail Haniya held a reception at Rafah for the returned heroes, before going on to give a public speech in one of Gaza's main squares, with Yahya Sinwar at his side. In Jerusalem, Yoram Cohen, the head of Shin Bet, justified the release of some 200 Hamas 'terrorists' by saying that 'with 20,000 members of the Qassam brigades in Gaza, 200 more will make no difference'.[16] (Yoram Cohen was later to write an account of 'Cast Lead' as he saw it.)[17] His reasoning in relation to the releases was all the more revealing as it marked a change in the rhetoric adopted by the security establishment: 'Cast Lead' had previously been presented by Tsahal as a success on the grounds that several hundred 'terrorists' had been removed from Gaza.

It had taken Israel some 2,000 days to accept the basic principle of the demands Hamas had expressed from the first moment of Gilad Shalit's capture. For five and a half years, Tsahal had unleashed attacks intended to break Hamas, or at least to induce it to bend. However, the Netanyahu government failed to draw any conclusions either from the lack of success of the strict military option, or from its failure to loosen the grip of Hamas on the Gaza Strip. Hamas kept the conflict in Gaza going, but at the lowest possible level, while at the same time subverting the blockade by means of its use of the tunnels that it directly managed. Most of the tunnels between Gaza and Egypt, of which the UN has estimated there were around 600, were operated by private businessmen who pay fees to Hamas. However, Hamas also runs a small number of tunnels itself, which are reserved for the passage of military equipment or other sensitive items. Hamas's tough and efficient internal security guarantees the continuation of this system. The failure of the Israelis to discover the whereabouts of Gilad Shalit during his captivity, incidentally, is a testament to the efficacy of Hamas's security procedures. The lack of success of Israel's policy in Gaza perpetuates the impoverishment of Gaza's civilian population, due to the persistence of the split between the two halves of Palestine.

The Humanitarian Impasse

International leaders and foreign analysts have often referred to Gaza as an 'open air prison'.[18] Another frequent metaphor points out that the territory and its population owe their survival to the 'drip feed' of international aid.[19] This tale of perpetual vulnerability is not the result of some fatal structural problem but has rather been the outcome of a history of violence and subjugation. The occupation of 1967 had indeed opened the Israeli labour market to Gaza's active population, but this same possibility of selling Gaza's labour had rendered the territory basically dependent, while it simultaneously became a captive market for Israeli industry, fatally undercutting local alternatives. Agricultural exports, which had been a major source of revenue for Gaza since antiquity, gradually came to be the exclusive prerogative of the Israeli settlements, which specialised in intensive cultivation under glass.

This growing dependence, which undermines the potential basis of home-grown development in the Gaza Strip, has been described as 'de-

development', an expression devised by the Harvard political economist Sara Roy. According to Roy, 'de-development' is the process of 'deliberate, systematic and increasing dismemberment by a dominant economy of an indigenous economy, whose economic and therefore social potential are not merely damaged but actually negated'.[20] Industrial zones that had been launched as part of the peace process were all sited on the border with Israel and were subservient to the needs of Israeli entrepreneurialism. There is a parallel with similar zones on the Mexican–US frontier, whose contribution to the Mexican economy has been, to say the least, of doubtful value. The projected port of Gaza has never seen the light of day, and the Gaza airport functioned for only two years, from 1998 to 2000, when it benefited for the most part only a self-appointed élite. The increasingly stringent and protracted closures of the Gaza Strip have also served to underline its weaknesses and dysfunctional nature. The day-to-day circumstances of the Strip's population, which had been severely tested by the first intifada, did not improve with the establishment of the Palestinian Authority. In many ways, the much-vaunted 'peace process' had been experienced in the Gaza Strip as a 'regressus' (a downward spiral),[21] which could not help but bring succour to those who were sceptical with regard to the 'Oslo spirit'.

One advocate of Oslo, James Wolfensohn, emboldened by his experience as head of the World Bank, had come to believe that Israel's disengagement in the summer of 2005 was an unmissable opportunity to realise Gaza's potential. However, his schemes foundered, one after the other, and the agreement on free movement, the so-called AMA, which he only managed to bring into being, itself collapsed after just a few weeks. The agreement was robbed of its substance after the Palestinian election of January 2006, when the West took the decision to boycott the Hamas government, which had in practice become identified with the Gaza Strip. As one commentator summed up the situation, in a lapidary phrase, 'The US decides; the World Bank leads; the EU pays; the UN feeds.'[22] After the abduction of Gilad Shalit in June 2006, Israel's grip on the Palestinian territory tightened, and a year later the expulsion of Fatah by Hamas removed Egypt's lingering reservation over the consolidation of the blockade.

The methodical siege raised the levels of poverty and long-term unemployment in the Gaza Strip to unprecedented heights—80 per cent of the population now depended on international aid, as against just 10 per cent a decade earlier. In 2008, in reaction to the sharp decline in the refugees' standard of living, UNRWA spent 20 dollars a day per person in Gaza as against only 8 dollars in 2004.[23] Water was rationed; electricity was available for only two hours a day; and the shortage of fuel grew worse. It was in the context of this dire economic situation that thousands of Palestinians crowded through a hole that Hamas militants had blown through the frontier wall at Rafah on 23 January 2008. The Egyptian security forces, rather than trying to block the human tidal wave, settled for trying to keep them within Sinai. The Palestinians who had entered Egypt spent their savings in the shops of El-Arish, which soon ran out of stock, and then were gradually forced back into the Gaza Strip. The episode lasted only a week.

In the occupied Gaza Strip, notables, nationalists and Islamists all constructed their own circles of influence through the medium of charitable societies and financial assistance. The West Bank, by contrast, had tended towards the formation of cooperatives and trade unions.[24] This political paternalism was accentuated by the degradation of the standard of living in Gaza and was paralleled by the increasing clientelism of the Palestinian Authority, as it became the principal employer in the territory. The sudden break with the Palestinian Authority in 2007 aggravated the excessive growth of bureaucracy by creating a second administration, technically under the control of Ramallah, which mirrored the existing civil service that remained loyal to the elected Hamas government. These 70,000 functionaries were instructed by Salam Fayyad not to turn up for work, under threat, if they did offer to do their jobs, of losing their salaries,[25] which were now paid by Ramallah thanks to international donors.

The 'Donor Conference for the Palestinian State', held in Paris on 14 December 2007, ended with an overall promise of 7.4 billion dollars to be provided over three years. This generosity was intended to support Mahmoud Abbas's negotiating option and to make it attractive through material improvements for the Palestinian people. It was the West Bank, however, and Ramallah in particular, that drew the most direct benefit from this munificence. In fact, this further deepened the split with the Gaza Strip, since the international transfers that were supposed to promote development in the West Bank actually led in Gaza to the forced inactivity of all public servants who wished to retain their salary from Ramallah. The limitations of the Israeli blockade, with only 100 products authorised for import as against 4,000 in the period before June 2006, made their own contribution to the ruination of Gaza's productive economy.

In addition, Operation 'Cast Lead' was all the more devastating because the continuation of the blockade stood in the way of substantial reconstruction. A year after the conflict, 20,000 Palestinians remained without homes.[26] Less than 200 workshops and businesses, out of a total of 3,750, were still able to operate, which implies that more than 100,000 jobs had been lost.[27] This semi-extinction of the private sector raised the level of unemployment to two thirds of the active population.[28] Attacks by the Israeli navy[29] had led to a fall in the number of fishermen to 3,500, from a figure of 10,000 before the second intifada.[30] The collapse of the banking sector, on the other hand, was compensated for by the increase in informal transfers, mainly under the control of Hamas.[31] The blockade of the Gaza Strip, though it led to a decrease in the popularity of the Islamist movement, did nothing in practice to diminish its practical control over the territory. This paradoxical strengthening of Hamas's authority could be seen in the flourishing contraband trade through the tunnels dug under the frontier with Egypt.[32] At the beginning of 2010, economists estimated that two thirds of Gaza's economic activity was accounted for by the import of consumer goods and building materials from Egypt through the tunnels.[33]

The level of activity of foreign militants against the blockade of the Gaza Strip increased over the years. The so-called 'Free Gaza' movement was formed with the explicit objective of 'breaking the siege of Gaza', and of 'awakening the conscience of the world'.[34] Two Nobel Peace Prize winners, Mairead Maguire of Northern Ireland and Archbishop Desmond Tutu of South Africa, actively supported it. On 28 October 2008, Mairead Maguire succeeded in entering in Gaza by sea aboard the vessel SS *Dignity* in company with the Palestinian PLC member and former minister, Mustafa Barghouti. A month later, when Maguire and twenty other passengers attempted to force the blockade for a second time, they were intercepted by the Israeli navy, transferred to the Israeli port of Ashdod and detained for a week before being deported. Operation 'Cast Lead' once more prompted gestures of solidarity. A new and younger generation of

Arabs, upset by the broadcast images of the conflict, paid homage to the solidarity of the Turkish government regarding the issue of Gaza.[35]

The so-called Peace Flotilla was put together in the spring of 2010 at the initiative of the Free Gaza movement together with a Turkish NGO known as IHH, which stands for 'Human Rights and Freedom' (the full name of the NGO is 'Foundation for Human Rights, Freedom and Humanitarian Aid'). As a result of its initiative, six ships were prepared to make the journey to Gaza. Three carried passengers, including the MV *Mavi Marmara*, and the other three were carrying more than 6,000 tonnes of humanitarian aid. In the early hours of 31 May 2010, they were attacked by Israeli commandos in international waters. Nine Turkish citizens were killed on the *Mavi Marmara*. Israel claimed seven of its men were injured in the incident. A seventh ship, named the *Rachel Corrie*, in memory of the American pacifist killed in Gaza in 2003, was unable to leave Malta because of mechanical problems. It later sailed with Mairead Maguire on board and was intercepted without violence by Tsahal on 5 June 2010 before it was able to reach the Palestinian coastline. The prime minister of Turkey, Recep Tayyip Erdogan, accused Israel of 'state terrorism'[36] and recalled the Turkish ambassador. International emotions ran high, with the result that Israel agreed that the aid that had been on board the vessels should be sent on to Gaza from Ashdod, after being checked for banned commodities. Ismail Haniya made it a point of honour to refuse to accept it until the flotilla activists were released by Israel (even though they were deported to their countries of origin).

On 20 June 2010, in an attempt to repair its international image, which had been seriously damaged by these events, the Netanyahu government announced an alleviation of the blockade of Gaza.[37] In effect, this was to be a reversal of the burden of proof: what was not specifically forbidden to be brought in would now in principle be allowed, rather than permission having to be specifically sought for all imports. Two weeks later, Israel published a list of forbidden products, some of which were products that supposedly had the potential to be used for military as well as for civilian purposes. The import of building materials was still conditional on prior authorisation by the Palestinian Authority in Ramallah for the building projects for which they were intended and to certification of the final use of the materials by whichever organisation was responsible for the construction. From this point, imports of consumer goods and commodities rose by a quarter, but imports of building materials went up by only 10 per cent.[38] The effective continuation of the blockade on building materials continued to contribute to the fortunes made by those running the smuggling trade with Egypt: for example, the UN estimated that in September 2011, 90,000 tonnes of cement were brought into the Gaza Strip through the tunnels, in other words ten times the authorised amount brought in through the only official crossing point for this trade at Kerem Shalom.[39] Israel continued to ban all exports from the Gaza Strip, and the number of exit permits through the Erez crossing point remained at around 2,000 per month (1 per cent of the number authorised before the second intifada).[40] In contrast to the principle enshrined in the Oslo Accords, which treated the West Bank and Gaza as a single entity, the Israeli authorities stipulated that a Palestinian was obliged to choose one territory or the other as his or her place of residence: this ruling included married couples between partners where one came from each territory. On 13 April 2010, Tsahal promulgated Military Order 1650, officially the 'Order Regarding Prevention of Infiltration', which officially classified any person residing in the West Bank without a valid permit as being an 'infiltrator'. Palestinians from Gaza, whose numbers in the West Bank had in any case fallen over the previous several years, were liable to immediate deportation or to a penalty imposed by a military tribunal that could be as much as seven years in prison.[41]

Despite all these hurdles, Israel claimed, not entirely without justification, that there was no humanitarian crisis in the territory, contradicting the somewhat apocalyptic view expressed by certain campaigning groups. Meanwhile, foreign aid workers, some with long experience on the ground in Gaza, expressed their misgivings that policies formulated quickly and on the basis of indignation could sometimes lead to a regrettable disparity in the policies of different international NGOs.[42] The Hamas government also took consistent care to monitor the activities of foreign humanitarian groups in its territory, in the interests of coordinating their programmes, especially in the health field. Health problems were sometimes serious: the scale of the H1N1 influenza epidemic in Gaza, with nineteen deaths between 5 December 2009 and 14 January 2010, was such that in order to cope with it, the minister of health in Gaza had to obtain 38,000 doses of vaccine from his opposite number in Ramallah. There was also a permanent tension between Hamas's insistence on oversight and the desire of the NGOs to maintain their autonomy and preserve their direct relationship with civil society. This offers some explanation of why the emphasis on humanitarian activities, even in a situation that appeared desperate, sometimes had counter-productive effects in the Gaza Strip.[43] The focus on the basic day-to-day needs of a population that had been subjected to terrible strains could obscure the requirements of longer-term development and reconstruction.

As one of the last Palestinian consultants still operative in the Gaza Strip points out, the flow of aid is in itself insufficient to halt the slide into impoverishment. Between 2006 and 2007, the economy bottomed out, when the trade in commodities began to offset the crisis of liquidity brought about by the international boycott on Hamas. On the other hand, the situation for individual Palestinians grew worse as the black market gained ground. The Gaza consumer pays the additional costs of the smuggling tunnels from Egypt. Gaza, which otherwise is no more than a captive market for Israel, has become an outlet for goods that are beyond their expiry date or have otherwise been rejected elsewhere. Even if the frontiers were re-opened, the recovery of productivity would be delayed by one or two years until trained personnel could be put in place, either as returnees from abroad or newly trained staff. Only inter-Palestinian reconciliation would permit the reversal of the long-term downward spiral, while international remittances only serve to exaggerate yet further the disparity between the governments in Ramallah and Gaza.[44]

The Palestinian Impasse

On 23 June 2007, Ismail Haniya called for an unconditional inter-Palestinian dialogue, conducted on the principle of 'no loser and no winner'.[45] This proposal, unsurprisingly, elicited no response from Ramallah, where Mahmoud Abbas had endorsed Salam Fayyad's 'emergency cabinet' after condemning what he referred to as the Islamist 'coup' in Gaza.[46] On 14 July, in Amman, the Palestinian president said, 'we have no intention of opening a dialogue with Hamas until they repair with their own hands the damage they have done'. Hamas's police, however, the so-called 'executive force', was well aware that the defeat they had inflicted on Fatah in Gaza resolved only part of the security problem that Hamas faced. The more powerful families in the territory had in recent years developed what were in effect private militias of their own, taking advantage of the confrontation between Hamas and Fatah to set up what amounted to an indigenous 'mafia' system. In this situation, the Dughmush family had played a double game to its own profit. Mumtaz Dughmush, a former officer in Muhammad Dahlan's police force, had first assisted Jamal Abu Samhadana to set up the Popular Resistance Committees before going over to Hamas. Now, as leader of the so-called 'Army of Islam', which was recruited from among his kin and those who owed him favours, he once again distanced himself from Hamas in order to re-open a dialogue with Fatah.[47]

There were two issues at stake for the Haniya government and the Qassam brigades. First, it was necessary to halt the clan vendettas, which seemed likely to lead to an unprecedented outburst of violence. In the four days of confrontation between Hamas and Fatah in June 2007, the number of amputees doubled because of the spread of the practice of kneecapping captive opponents.[48] Meanwhile, it was also important for Hamas to be able to restore order on a permanent basis and ensure security for a population that had been traumatised by the anarchy of the militias. The first challenge came with the Bakr family, who controlled a force of 300 men in Gaza City, who were determined to avenge the death of a clan member, a Fatah officer, who had been killed by Hamas. The part of town where the Bakr clan lived was literally besieged by the executive force for three days, and nine members of the clan, including two women, died in the clashes before the militia agreed to lay down their arms. The clan leaders fled to Egypt by sea.[49]

After this, Hamas believed it was sufficiently strong to confront the Dughmush head on. Their area of town was surrounded and units of the Qassam brigades seized several members of the clan. The trial of strength ended with the 'Army of Islam' being compelled to surrender unconditionally. On 3 July 2007, a British journalist, Alan Johnston, was freed after 112 days of captivity: this was a success for Hamas where Muhammad

Dahlan and Fatah had been unable to act. The militias disappeared from the streets of Gaza City, to the great relief of the inhabitants. On 8 July, in a symbolic gesture, Hamas compelled one of the leaders of the toughest militia group in Gaza, Faris Abu Hassanein, to return the lion which was the pride of the Gaza City zoo. The anecdote of the reappearance of the animal in his official cage amounted to an affirmation of Hamas's new monopoly over organised violence.

The consolidation of Hamas's internal power was accompanied by the reinforcement of its control over the external frontiers. Hamas leaned heavily on those who were running the tunnels and on smugglers who were becoming too independent, which led to bloody clashes at Rafah in November 2007. The Qassam brigades suppressed the other armed groups, which were linked to Fatah, such as the Brigades of the Martyrs of al-Aqsa and the PRC, or to the PFLP and the DFLP. Hamas continued to observe a de facto truce with Israel in order not to undermine its power to impose stability within the Gaza Strip. The Qassam brigades emerged from their clandestine status, now patrolling in uniform in the streets as well as returning rocket fire at Israel when attacked. They only allowed one exception to their monopoly: in exchange for Islamic Jihad's withdrawal from the streets and the camps of the Gaza Strip, it was allowed to maintain its armed Al-Quds brigades. The skirmishes with Israel that ensued from the operations of this group were at a low level, but nonetheless brought severe reprisals from the Israeli forces. On 15 February 2008, for example, an air raid directed at the residence of an official of the Al-Quds brigades in the Bureij Camp resulted in seven deaths: the activist himself, his wife, two of their children and three other persons. In this way, however, Hamas was able to keep alive the struggle against the 'Zionist enemy', without directly engaging its own forces.

On the other hand, the suppression of all public manifestations of Fatah continued with no respite. On 11 August 2007, for example, Hamas took action against Fatah activists at a marriage ceremony in Beit Hanoun and again after Friday prayers in Abbassan. The increasing frequency of interrogation of journalists and incidents with the press was an indication that Hamas had become more sensitive to criticism. The tension mounted on occasions when competing strike calls were issued and grew worse in the run-up to the Annapolis conference. On 12 November, more than 150,000 demonstrators flooded into the streets of Gaza City to commemorate the anniversary of the death of Yasser Arafat. Stones were thrown at the Hamas police, who opened fire in response, resulting in the deaths of seven people. Mahmoud Abbas condemned what he called 'hateful crimes', which he said were committed by a 'band of rebels'.[50] Hamas arrested hundreds of those who opposed it throughout the territory, though Haniya released them only a few days later. Demonstrations against the Annapolis conference brought out tens of thousands of people, but the biggest demonstration took place on 15 December when Hamas rallied a crowd of 200,000 to celebrate the twentieth anniversary of its foundation, with a speech by Khaled Meshal transmitted live from Damascus.

Thus the two organisations that disputed control of Palestine were capable of bringing out crowds of comparable size in the streets of Gaza, with a mutual bitterness that seemed unlikely to diminish. On 31 December 2007, a gathering to commemorate the first anti-Israeli operation by Fatah was suppressed by the Hamas police, with the result that seven people lost their lives including a teenager who was shot in the head. The Haniya government reasserted its contention that Salam Fayyad's administration was illegitimate as he had never been endorsed as prime minister by the PLC, but at the same time the Haniya government was itself only able to convene a rump parliament in Gaza in which Hamas members sat alone, together with a single independent. Confronted by passive resistance from the justice system appointed by Ramallah, Hamas convened military courts to do its bidding (with the first death sentence pronounced in January 2008) and incorporated the so-called 'Islamic conciliation committees' into the system. Thirty of these committees had come into existence in the Gaza Strip, headed by the PLC member Marwan Abu Ras, which did not hand down sentences but pronounced judgements based on Islamic law that were acted on by Hamas. Judges that were resistant to Hamas's demands were forced to stand down. Last but not least, the Gaza Strip's imams were assessed according to their amenability to Hamas, and 300 of them, a quarter of the total, were forbidden to preach.[51]

As these purges were taking place, in virtually the same way and at the same time as Fatah was cleansing its own administration in the West Bank, the Sanaa declaration, signed on 23 March 2008 under the auspices of President Ali Abdullah Saleh of Yemen and calling for cooperation between Hamas and Fatah, was a dead letter from the start. In July, a series of attacks on Hamas in Gaza, with seven deaths that included five Islamist activists, prompted further arrests of Fatah supporters which went on into August. On 12 August, some 465 Fatah sympathisers were detained and 204 premises attached to Fatah were closed, for the most part permanently.[52] In November 2008, the resumption of inter-Palestinian talks in Cairo took place in a climate of mutual defiance. Egypt held Hamas responsible for the prolongation of the Gaza blockade, while Hamas accused Mubarak of partiality towards Fatah. In addition, Hamas made clear its view that when President Abbas's term of office came to an end, the Speaker of the PLC, Abdelaziz Dweik, an Islamist PLC member from Hebron, should become head of the Palestinian Authority. This argument was instantly dismissed by Ramallah, not least because Dweik had been imprisoned in Israel since August 2006, as had most of the other Hamas elected members from the West Bank.

The stand-off between Hamas and Fatah also had a media dimension. Al-Aqsa television, launched by Hamas in Gaza just before the parliamentary elections of 2006, used its satellite transmission to target the audience that had hitherto belonged to Palestine TV, set up by Arafat in 1994, which now broadcast only from Ramallah, its Gaza transmitters having been destroyed by Israel at the beginning of the second intifada. Hamas's propaganda regularly condemned what it called the 'tripartite aggression' which had been directed against it by Fatah, Israel and the United States. This was intended to be an explicit reference to the infamous 'tripartite aggression' against Egypt by Israel, France and Britain in 1956.

Hamas set up a whole series of internet sites, whose content ranged from the official pronouncements of the Haniya government to sites celebrating the Qassam brigades and their martyrs, with videos online on 'Paltube', and other sites devoted to youth, women and the welfare of Hamas prisoners. The Israeli embargo on paper enabled Hamas to monopolise the print media in Gaza, since their own presses were supplied with paper via the tunnels they controlled. Before the blockade, dozens of Arabic newspapers and magazines had been printed or distributed in the Gaza Strip, none of which now appeared.

An incidental effect of 'Cast Lead' was to cause splits in what remained of Fatah in the Gaza Strip, undermining the nationalist camp yet further in relation to Hamas. The fighters of the Al-Aqsa Martyrs' brigades, as well as the PRC, who were even more enthusiastic, gravitated towards the national consensus against the Israeli aggression. At the same time, Hamas's security imprisoned or put under house arrest more than 1,000 Fatah supporters, for fear that they would pass information to the invaders, if only inadvertently. In practice, the number of collaborators with Israel who were executed during the conflict, actual or imaginary, was estimated to have been around twenty.[53] After a crisis on this scale, no resumption of talks in Cairo between Hamas and Fatah could do much to persuade Palestinian opinion that there was any prospect of reconciliation.

At this stage, Hamas's struggle to consolidate its power in the Gaza strip took on a new dimension: rivalry to appear most committed to the jihad. The Dughmush clan had never in fact dismantled its 'Army of Islam', with which Hamas forces still occasionally became embroiled in incidents. The group known as the 'Army of the companions of God' (*jund ansar Allah*) came into being at the end of 2008 in the southern Gaza Strip under the 'spiritual' leadership of a Salafist sheikh named Abdellatif Musa. Its military leader, Khaled Banat, who liked to be known as Abu Abdullah al-Suri (literally 'the Syrian'), despite his Palestinian origins,[54] claimed to have fought the jihad in Afghanistan and in Iraq. The aggressive rhetoric of his group enabled Banat to recruit from among the ranks of the Qassam brigades, who were frustrated by the restraint imposed on them by Hamas and its military wing. In June 2009, a planned attack on Israel involving horses loaded with explosives was not carried out, but had still given Hamas real cause for concern.

Musa and Banat, far from keeping a low profile, increasingly challenged Hamas through their deliberately provocative acts. They were thought to have been responsible for numerous attacks on internet cafés and family celebrations, all deemed impious by the Salafists. On 14 August 2009, Sheikh Musa summoned his supporters to Friday prayers at the Ibn Taymiyya mosque in Rafah. In Salafist circles, a rumour was spread that the sermon would contain a vituperative attack on Ismail Haniya. Meanwhile, armed Hamas militants also came to the mosque. An officer from the Qassam brigades, who offered to parley with Sheikh Musa, was killed by a hidden sniper. The sheikh announced the establishment of an 'Islamic Emirate' in Gaza[55] and in response the Ibn Taymiyya mosque was stormed by the Hamas forces. Musa and Banat escaped but died soon afterwards when they exploded their suicide belts.[56] Their jihadist group was crushed in a matter of hours, with twenty-eight deaths, of which seven were of members of Hamas.

This outburst of violence in Rafah was the result of the irreconcilable differences between Hamas and the jihadist groups. Hamas, the 'Movement for Islamic Resistance', since its foundation by Sheikh Yassin, has always been identified with a Palestinian territory that needs to be liberated. It never abandoned its intimate focus on Palestine, while Fatah became involved in the Jordanian and subsequently the Lebanese crises, only afterwards returning to Palestine as its central preoccupation. The jihadist philosophy, however, was totally untrammelled by territorial restrictions, with global ambitions that transcended frontiers. Hamas claimed to represent the only legitimate Palestinian Authority: Osama Bin Laden and al-Qaida on the other hand accused it for this very reason of neglecting its religious duty and of allowing itself to be bound by international treaties. These charges were explicitly made by Bin Laden in December 2007 and were constantly reiterated in the accusations made against Hamas by al-Qaida and associated groups.[57] While Hamas's ambition was to consolidate its power in the only part of Palestine that was under exclusively Palestinian control, the ambition of the jihadists was to subvert this very control in order to precipitate a more apocalyptic conflict. Hamas is characterised in jihadist millenarian rhetoric as the principal enemy, and even as 'Shi'ite', and is destined to be brought low by the establishment in Gaza of a 'Caliphate' in anticipation of the universal victory of Islam.[58]

With the Ibn Taymiyya mosque massacre, Hamas believed it had at last put a stop to jihadist dissidence. It began at this point to use the expression *jaljalat* (rumblings) to designate these groups, whose numbers showed no tendency to increase. The leader of one of them, Hisham Saidni, who had been detained by Hamas, had made his escape from Gaza's central prison when it was destroyed in 'Cast Lead'. Saidni liked to call himself Abu Al-Walid al-Maqdissi and named his group of some ten followers 'Tawhid wa-l-Jihad' (Unity and Jihad), echoing the name of the militia from which the Iraqi branch of al-Qaida emerged. This jihadist group was the only one ever to have carried out a successful attack against Israel, when an Israeli soldier was killed in his jeep on 27 January 2011. Hamas re-arrested Saidni in March 2011 in Shati Camp, after he had issued a self-styled 'fatwa' justifying the murder of Christian civilians. The jihadists were believed to have been responsible for a series of attacks on the Christian community in Gaza, which had been reduced to 3,000 people, including 200 Catholics. This contrasted with the attitude of Hamas, which had included in its electoral list for Gaza a Greek Orthodox Christian, Hussam Tawil. Saidni's disciples took their vengeance on 14 April 2011 with the kidnapping of an Italian aid worker who had been in Gaza for three years, Vittorio Arrigoni, whom they hanged soon after. Arrigoni was a member of the same pro-Palestinian NGO, the International Solidarity Movement, to which Rachel Corrie and Thomas Hurndall had belonged. Hamas reacted fiercely, with at least two jihadists killed on 19 April.

After 'Cast Lead', while it took care to keep the rise of extremism in the Gaza Strip under control, Hamas also succeeded in persuading Islamic Jihad to respect its advice to exercise restraint towards Israel. This strict prohibition was strongly resented by activists of all stripes, who began to describe Hamas's front-line patrols and informants as 'drones' (*zanzanat*) in the service of Tsahal. The Haniya government in fact had more success than its predecessors in restraining rocket attacks on Israel. This somewhat surprising development, however, caused some internal stirrings of dissent within the Qassam brigades. The most belligerent of the Islamist militiamen found some relief from their frustration in the imposition of a strictly enforced moral regime on the population of Gaza. In 2010, they were apparently responsible for the destruction of two leisure centres: an UNRWA holiday centre on 23 May 2010 and an aquatic theme park on 19 September. UNRWA had been holding an annual 'summer games' in Gaza in which 250,000 young people took part, while Hamas attempted to compete with the United Nations agency in providing entertainment for the young. Embarrassed by these incidents, however, Hamas undertook to restore the facilities that had been destroyed but did not identify or attach blame to any named culprit.

The marked tendency to promote adherence to Islamic norms that had emerged in 2008 became more noticeable after 'Cast Lead'. Boys were banned from mixing with girls, the smoking of shisha pipes was forbidden and public dancing was outlawed. These prohibitions were not based on newly invented rules, though Hamas extended the definition of adultery embodied in a 1936 law from the mandate period to cover all sex outside marriage. The difference, however, was that the militant Islamists took it upon themselves, as they had not done before, to impose their vision of morality upon the public, thus resuming the intolerant intrusions which Sheikh Yassin's supporters had favoured, a quarter of a century earlier. In a region so badly overstretched by constant conflict and crippling blockade, this was experienced as an additional and unwelcome burden. On 14 December 2010, a group of social workers and local artists published a 'manifesto for Gaza's youth' on the internet. They condemned the 'nightmare within a nightmare' as they called Hamas's peremptory rule under the shadow of the Israeli occupation.[59] The Facebook page launched for the occasion soon had 20,000 'friends'.

This unprecedented level of militancy emerged in Gaza simultaneously with the revolutions in Tunisia and Egypt. On 31 January 2011, a demonstration in Gaza in support of the Egyptian Revolution was banned. The overthrow of President Mubarak on 11 February galvanised the Palestinian factions. In Gaza, the slogan 'The people wish to overthrow the regime' was adapted to read: 'The people want an end to disunity', dismissing both Hamas and Fatah in favour of the higher interests of the Palestinian people. On 14 March 2011, thousands of young people marched in Gaza City under this slogan. The next day, thousands had become tens of thousands, though parallel demonstrations were more limited in the West Bank. In Gaza, Hamas militants attempted to carry the Hamas flag, while only the Palestinian national flag was welcome at the rally.

Despite such incidents, the impetus towards national unification appeared to be laying the groundwork for at least a formal reconciliation between Hamas and Fatah. This was given further impetus by the fall of Egypt's President Mubarak, who had seemed less interested in mediation than in containing Hamas. The weakening of Bashar al-Assad's regime in Syria had the effect that the exiled Hamas leadership in Syria was obliged to pay more attention to the demands of Gaza. The Syrian uprising, which began in Deraa in mid-March 2011, gradually spread throughout the country. Ostensibly, Hamas adopted a position of neutrality between the Assad regime, which had given its hospitality to Hamas's Political Bureau, and the revolutionary coalition, which included the Muslim Brothers. Mahmoud Abbas and Khaled Meshal, who had not met since the agreement on national unity made in Mecca in 2007, met once more in Cairo to sign a further agreement. A framework of cooperation was agreed between the security services of the two sides in Ramallah and Gaza respectively. Hamas endorsed the principle that the PLO should continue the pursuit of peace negotiations with Israel: Hamas did not consider itself bound by such negotiations but declared itself ready to accept their consequences. The reactivation of the Palestinian Legislative Council that had been elected in 2006 was also agreed.

The establishment of a government soon became bogged down, however, over the issue of its leadership. Mahmoud Abbas demanded the retention of Salam Fayyad as prime minister, as he would be the only leader able to find a way round the reservations of the United States over such a government. Hamas on the other hand refused to endorse a prime minister whose position, in their eyes, lacked both legitimacy and legality. Hamas proposed instead the names of two independent businessmen who had been part of the Haniya government: Mazen Sinokrot (the economy minister, based in Ramallah) and Jawat Khodari (the communications minister and a Gaza member of the PLC).

Meanwhile, Mahmoud Abbas regained the initiative when he presented Palestine's candidature at the United Nations on 23 September 2011. Though the Palestinian Authority had been encouraged by the acceptance of Palestine as a full member of UNESCO on 5 October, the measure failed to secure the approval of the UN Security Council the following month. Hamas, who had never concealed its scepticism over the UN manoeuvre, resumed its dialogue with Fatah. On 24 November 2011, Mahmoud Abbas and Khaled Meshal met once more in Cairo to approve the holding of new elections within the space of six months. Without reneging on its attachment to the armed struggle, Hamas also committed itself to support the 'popular and peaceful' resistance advocated by the Palestinian Authority.[60] On 22 December, Abbas and Meshal found themselves yet again in Cairo, this time to discuss the inclusion of Hamas and Islamic Jihad as components of the PLO. Selim Zaanoun, the chairman of the Palestinian National Council, the PLO's 'parliament', was placed in charge of this issue. Three days later, Egypt, which was closely involved in these discussions, extended permission to Ismail Haniya to leave the Gaza Strip for the first time since Hamas had taken control of the territory, to allow him to embark on a regional tour that was intended to reinforce the 'interior' voice of Hamas as against the exiled leadership of Khaled Meshal.

After so much blood had been shed, and so many opportunities lost, the inhabitants of Gaza could hardly believe that the war of one Palestine against the other could only then come to an end.[61] A real reconciliation between Hamas and Gaza would remain the indispensable condition for the extrication of the Gaza Strip from the limbo of armed conflict to which it had been consigned since June 2007. In the final resort, the decision to take such a step was the responsibility of Mahmoud Abbas and Khaled Meshal, each of whom lived out their own daily lives far from Gaza and its preoccupations. After three distinct periods of twenty years had elapsed, a grim five-year episode that had been even more devastating for Gaza and its people than the previous eras could be about to come to an end. The vendettas of the rival militias and the duplication of Gaza's multifarious bureaucracies each represented a grave threat to any kind of durable rapprochement. The figures were remarkable. Hamas paid the salaries of 31,000 employees in the Gaza Strip while the Palestinian Authority also continued to maintain 70,000 paid officials and workers. There was also a further problem affecting trust between the two: in December 2011, Fatah claimed that fifty-three of its supporters were political prisoners in Hamas's hands in Gaza, while Hamas accused Fatah of holding 104 of its people in the West Bank. However, despite the difficulties, the rancour and the weight of past events, it would be futile to imagine that there could be a decent future and a collective destiny for the people of Gaza unless the nationalist and Islamist components of the Palestinian resistance, both of which had come into existence in the territory, were able to reach an agreement on peace between themselves.

Three generations have grown up in the Gaza Strip, as the vagaries of history have defined it. The first generation, the generation of mourning, prepared the way for second, the generation of dispossession, which in turn gave way to the generation of the intifadas. More than one and a half million men, women and children continue to pay the price for a prolonged failure to make progress which has taken many forms. In the Gaza Strip as elsewhere in Palestine, the means to escape this nightmare could be simpler than they look. They can be defined as a virtuous trio: first, the opening up of the territory; second, the development of the economy; and third, the demilitarisation of Palestinian society. Such a policy would reverse the directions that have been consistently followed for the last two decades, since the siege imposed on Gaza is only reinforcing the grip of the militias and is undermining any viable economic venture. To turn back the clock, opening up a more hopeful future, it will be necessary to return to the most promising concept that formed part of the Oslo Accords: 'Gaza First'.

It is in Gaza that the foundations of a durable peace should be laid. The issues of frontiers and settlements no longer exist in Gaza, but it was in Gaza that Israeli–Palestinian relations reached the incandescent stage of extreme violence. The Gaza Strip, the womb of the fedayin and the cradle of the intifada, lies at the heart of the nation-building of contemporary Palestine. It is vain to imagine that a territory so replete with foundational experiences can be ignored or marginalised. Peace between Israel and Palestine can assume neither meaning nor substance except in Gaza, which will be both the foundation and the keystone. Turning away from the entanglements of factitious difficulties, the history of Gaza can take a different course, and a new chapter will then be written, by and for the generation of hope.

NOTES

FOREWORD

1. French President Nicolas Sarkozy, interviewed by the Kuwaiti daily newspaper *Al-Qabas*, 11 Feb. 2009.
2. See, for example, the hagiographies of the martyrs of Hamas, such as that by Falah Salama Sudfi and A'tadal Saadallah Qanayta, *Asad al-muqawama, al-shahid duktur 'Abd al-'Aziz al-Rantissi*, Gaza: Maktab al-Jil, 2010, or Yahya Sinwar, *Al-Majd*, Gaza: Waed, 2009. A useful summary of this Islamist approach is to be found in the introduction of the Hamas publication, *Ayyâm al-Ghadab*, Gaza: Dar al-Manara, 2005, pp. 8–15.

1. THE CROSSROADS OF EMPIRES

1. Gen. 10:19.
2. Shachar, Nathan, *The Gaza Strip: Its History and Politics*, Eastbourne: Sussex Academic Press, 2010, pp. 18–19.
3. Maruéjol, Florence, *Thoutmosis III*, Paris: Pygmalion, 2007, p. 141.
4. Butt, Gerald, *Life at the Crossroads*, Nicosia: Rimal, 1995, p. 21.
5. Miroschedji, Pierre de, 'La région de Gaza, des origines à la fin de l'âge du Bronze', in Haldimann, Marc-André et al. (eds), *Gaza à la croisée des civilisations*, Neuchâtel: Chaman, 2007, p. 71.
6. http://www.imj.org.il/imagine/galleries/viewItemE.asp?case=2&itemNum= 198016 (accessed 24 Jan. 2014).
7. Hein, Irmgard, 'Gaza et l'Egypte au IIe millénaire avant Jésus-Christ', in Haldimann et al. (eds), *Gaza à la croisée des civilisations*.
8. Meyer, Martin, *History of the City of Gaza*, New York: Columbia University Press, 1907, p. 21; reprinted New Jersey: Gorgias Press, 2008.
9. Arif, Arif al-, *Tarikh Ghazza*, Jerusalem: Dar al-Aytam al-Islamiyya, 1943, pp. 16–18.

10. Judges 13:10.
11. 1 Kings 5:4.
12. 2 Kings 18:8.
13. Amos 1:7.
14. Sartre, Maurice, 'La splendeur oubliée de Gaza', *L'Histoire*, 340 (Mar. 2009), p. 11.
15. Bauzou, Thomas, 'Gaza dans l'Empire perse achéménide', in Haldimann et al. (eds), *Gaza à la croisée des civilisations*, p. 62.
16. Herodotus, *Histories*, Book 3, trans. Robin Waterfield, New York: Oxford University Press, 1998, p. 171.
17. Meyer, *History of the City of Gaza*, p. 41; Tabaa, Uthman Mustafa, *Ithaf al-'izza fi tarikh Ghazza*, Gaza: Al-Yazji, 1999, vol. 1, p. 85.
18. Sartre, 'La splendeur oubliée de Gaza', p. 12.
19. Butt, *Life at the Crossroads*, p. 54.
20. Ibid. p. 56.
21. Sartre, 'La splendeur oubliée de Gaza', p. 13.
22. 1 Maccabees 11:61–2.
23. Meyer, *History of the City of Gaza*, p. 61.
24. Sartre, 'La splendeur oubliée de Gaza', p. 13.
25. Shachar, *The Gaza Strip*, p. 23.
26. Josephus, trans. G.A. Williamson, revised by E. Mary Smallwood, *The Jewish War*, London: Penguin Books, revised edn 1981, pp. 48–9.
27. Ibid.
28. See http://commons.wikimedia.org/wiki/File:Statue_of_Zeus_dsc02611-.jpg (accessed 24 Jan. 2014). Photograph by Nevit Dilmen.
29. Shachar, *The Gaza Strip*, p. 23.
30. Sartre, 'La splendeur oubliée de Gaza', p. 14.
31. Bauzou, 'Gaza dans l'Empire perse achéménide', p. 135.
32. Ibid. p. 134.
33. The biography of St Porphyry by 'Mark the Deacon' is a major source for the history of Gaza in the fourth century AD. The text, in a translation by G.F. Hill, originally published by Oxford University at the Clarendon Press in 1913, is available at http://www.fordham.edu/halsall/basis/porphyry.asp (accessed 24 Jan. 2014). The reader is advised by this source that serious problems related to the text are discussed in the French version, edited and translated by Henri Grégoire and M.A. Kugener, entitled *Mark le Diacre, Vie de Porphyry*, Paris: Belles Lettres, 1930. A new translation by Claudia Rapp under the title, *Mark the Deacon: Life of St Porphyry of Gaza*, forms part of Thomas Head (ed.), *Medieval Hagiography: An Anthology*, New York: Garland Press, 1999.
34. Sartre, 'La splendeur oubliée de Gaza', p. 14.
35. Bauzou, 'Gaza dans l'Empire perse achéménide', p. 14.

36. Ibid. p. 136.
37. For a description of the temples destroyed at this time, see Dowling, Theodore, *Gaza: A City of Many Battles*, London: SPCK, 1913, pp. 110–14.
38. Sartre, 'La splendeur oubliée de Gaza', p. 15.
39. Downey, Glanville, *Gaza in the Early Sixth Century*, Norman: Oklahoma University Press, 1963, p. 29.
40. Saliou, Catherine, 'Gaza dans l'Antiquité tardive', in Haldimann et al. (eds), *Gaza à la croisée des civilisations*, p. 151.
41. http://www.english.imjnet.org.il/popup?c0=13127 (accessed 24 Jan. 2014).
42. Ibid. p. 144.
43. Hevelone-Harper, Jennifer Lee, *Disciples of the Desert*, Baltimore, MD: Johns Hopkins University Press, 2005, p. 17.
44. Saliou, Catherine, 'Le monachisme Gaziote', in Haldimann et al. (eds), *Gaza à la croisée des civilisations*, pp. 164–5.
45. Elter, René and Ayman Hassoune, 'Le monastère de Saint-Hilarion à Umm al-Amr', *Comptes-rendus des séances de l'Académie des inscriptions et belles-lettres*, 148, 1 (2004), pp. 359–82.
46. Hevelone-Harper, *Disciples of the Desert*, pp. 119–25.
47. Flusin, Bernard, 'Palestinian Hagiography (Fourth–Eighth Centuries)', in Efthymiadis, Stephanos (ed.), *The Ashgate Research Companion to Byzantine Hagiography*, vol. 1, Farnham: Ashgate, 2011, p. 211.
48. Saliou, 'Le monachisme Gaziote', p. 151.
49. Ibid. p. 156.

2. THE ISLAMIC ERA

1. Meyer, Martin, *History of the City of Gaza*, New York: Columbia University Press, 1907, p. 21; reprinted New Jersey: Gorgias Press, 2008.
2. Shurrab, Muhammad Hasan, *Ghazzatu Hashem*, Amman: Al-Ahliyya, 2006, p. 93.
3. Hussein, Mahmoud, *Al-Sira*, Paris: Grasset, 2005, pp. 164–5.
4. Ibid. p. 168.
5. Ibn Hicham, *Mahomet*, Paris: Fayard, 2004, p. 42.
6. Meyer, *History of the City of Gaza*, p. 74.
7. Donner, Fred M., *Muhammad and the Believers*, Cambridge, MA: Harvard University Press, 2010, pp. 53, 106; see also Prémare, Alfred-Louis de, *Les fondations de l'Islam: entre écriture et histoire*, Paris: Seuil, 2002, pp. 146–7.
8. Butt, Gerald, *Life at the Crossroads*, Nicosia: Rimal, 1995, pp. 78–9; Shachar, Nathan, *The Gaza Strip: Its History and Politics*, Eastbourne: Sussex Academic Press, 2010, p. 29.
9. Hamadani, Ibn Al-Faqih Al-, *Abrégé du 'Livre des pays'* [*Kitab al-Buldan*], ed. and trans. Massé, Henri, revised by Charles Pellat, Damascus: Institut français des études arabes de Damas (IFEAD), 1973, pp. 148–9.

10. Muqaddasi, Al-, *Ahsan at-Taqasim fi Ma'rifat al-Aqalim (La meilleure répartition pour la connaissance des provinces)*, ed. and trans. Miquel, André, Damascus: IFEAD, 1963, p. 203.

11. Ibn Hawqal, *La configuration de la terre* [Surat al-Ard], ed. and trans. J.H. Kramers and G. Wiet., Paris: Maisonneuve et Larose, 2001, vol. 1, p. 142.

12. Shurrab, *Ghazzatu Hashem*, p. 376.

13. Idrissi, Al-, *Kitab nuzhat al-mushtaq fi ikhtiraq al-afaq*, Cairo: Al-Thaqafa al-Denia, 1990, vol. 1, p. 251.

14. Dowling, Theodore, *Gaza: A City of Many Battles*, London: SPCK, 1913, p. 68.

15. Sartre, Maurice, 'La splendeur oubliée de Gaza', *L'Histoire*, 340 (Mar. 2009), p. 17.

16. Ibn Battuta, *Travels in Asia and Africa 1325–1354*, Delhi: Manohar, 2006, p. 306.

17. Abu Mustafa, Ayman, *The Trade Routes in Palestine during the Mamluk Period*, Bergen: University of Bergen, 2006, pp. 57, 75–80.

18. Shachar, Nathan, *The Gaza Strip: Its History and Politics*, Eastbourne: Sussex Academic Press, 2010, p. 35.

19. Sartre, 'La splendeur oubliée de Gaza', Eastbourne: Sussex Academic Press, 2010, p. 17.

20. Shachar, *The Gaza Strip*, p. 35.

21. Encyclopedia of Islam, 'Ghazza', II, 1056a (CD-ROM edn).

22. Cohen, Amnon and Bernard Lewis, *Populations and Revenues in the Towns of Palestine in the Sixteenth Century*, Princeton, NJ: Princeton University Press, 1978, pp. 127–8. See also Si-Salim, Issam and Zakaria Sanawar, *Liwa Ghazza fi al-asr al-'uthmani al-awwal*, Gaza: Islamic University, 2004, p. 311.

23. Si-Salim and Sanawar, *Liwa Ghazza fi al-asr al-'uthmani al-awwal*, p. 142.

24. D'Arvieux, Laurent, *Mémoires du Chevalier d'Arvieux*, Paris: Delespine, 1735, vol. 2, p. 26. Available at http://gallica.bnf.fr/ark:/12148/bpt6k104927d (accessed 24 Jan. 2014).

25. Ibid. pp. 66–7.

26. Ibid. p. 46.

27. Ibid. p. 52.

28. Arif, Arif al-, *Tarikh Ghazza*, Jerusalem: Dar al-Aytam al-Islamiyya, 1943, p. 99.

29. Shachar, *The Gaza Strip*, p. 39.

30. Krämer, Gudrun, *A History of Palestine*, Princeton, NJ: Princeton University Press, 2008, pp. 45–6.

31. Kemp, Percy, 'An Eighteenth-Century Turkish Intelligence Report', *International Journal of Middle East Studies*, 16, 4 (Nov. 1984), p. 506.

32. Ibid. p. 500.

33. Sadeq, Moain, 'Gaza durant la période islamique', in Haldimann, Marc-André et al. (eds), *Gaza à la croisée des civilisations*, Neuchâtel: Chaman, 2007, p. 102; Arif, *Tarikh Ghazza*, p. 209.

34. Manna, Adel, 'Eighteenth- and Nineteenth-Century Rebellions in Palestine', *Journal of Palestine Studies*, 24, 1 (Autumn 1994), p. 60.
35. Krämer, *A History of Palestine*, p. 44.
36. Schölch, Alexander, 'The Demographic Development of Palestine, 1850–1882', *International Journal of Middle East Studies*, 17, 4 (Nov. 1985), p. 492.
37. Ibid. p. 489.
38. Picaudou, Nadine, *Le mouvement national palestinien*, Paris: L'Harmattan, 1989, p. 31.
39. Loti, Pierre, *Le désert*, Paris: Calmann Levy, 1895, pp. 239–49, text available at http://gallica.bnf.fr/ark:/12148/bpt6k5828140t (accessed 24 Jan. 2014).
40. Shachar, *The Gaza Strip*, p. 40.
41. Tabaa, Uthman Mustafa, *Ithaf al-'izza fi tarikh Ghazza*, Gaza: Al-Yazji, 1999, vol. 2, pp. 54–5 (Bseisso), p. 183 (Radwan), pp. 255–6 (Shawa), p. 278 (Sourani).
42. Arif, *Tarikh Ghazza*, p. 100.
43. Ben Ayyash, Awda Muhammad, *Rafah, madina 'ala hudud*, Gaza: Rashid Shawa Cultural Centre, 2002, pp. 70–1.
44. Shachar, *The Gaza Strip*, p. 42.

3. THE BRITISH MANDATE

1. Grainger, John D., *The Battle for Palestine*, Woodbridge: The Boydell Press, 2008, p. 36.
2. Ibid. p. 47.
3. Ibid. p. 56.
4. Ibid. p. 67.
5. For the text, see Mackay, Ruddock F., *Balfour Intellectual Statesman*, Oxford and New York: Oxford University Press, 1985, pp. 315–16.
6. McTague, John, 'The British Military Administration in Palestine', *Journal of Palestine Studies*, 7, 3 (Spring 1978), pp. 55–76.
7. Laurens, Henry, *La question de Palestine, tome I, (1799–1922)*, Paris: Fayard, 1999, p. 273.
8. Faysal, Numan Abdelhadi, *A'lam min jil al-ruwad min Ghazzatu Hashem*, Gaza: Dar al-Duktur, 2010, pp. 405–6.
9. Butt, Gerald, *Life at the Crossroads*, Nicosia: Rimal, 1995, p. 120.
10. Krämer, Gudrun, *A History of Palestine*, Princeton, NJ: Princeton University Press, 2008, pp. 204–5, 214.
11. Laurens, Henry (ed.), *Le retour des exilés*, Paris: Robert Laffont, 1998, p. 332.
12. Mattar, Philip, *The Mufti of Jerusalem*, New York: Columbia University Press, 1988, p. 29.
13. Tabaa, Uthman Mustafa, *Ithaf al-'izza fi tarikh Ghazza*, Gaza: Al-Yazji (4 vols), 1999, vol. 2, p. 334.
14. 'Report of the District Commissioner for Gaza', 27 Mar. 1925, in *Political Diaries*

of the Arab World: Jordan and Palestine, London: Archive Editions, 1991, vol. 2, p. 160.

15. The family tree of the Husseinis of Gaza is given in Tabaa, *Ithaf al-'izza fi tarikh*, vol. 2, pp. 110–11.

16. Matthews, Weldon, 'Pan-Islam or Arab Nationalism?' *International Journal of Middle East Studies*, 35 (2003), p. 5.

17. Ibid. p. 6.

18. 'Report to the League of Nations on the Administration of Palestine and Transjordan in 1928', *Palestine and Transjordan Administrative Reports*, London: Archive Editions, 1995, vol. 2, p. 551.

19. Laurens, *La question de Palestine*, vol. 2, p. 179.

20. Ibid. p. 115.

21. Shachar, Nathan, *The Gaza Strip: Its History and Politics*, Eastbourne: Sussex Academic Press, 2010, p. 48.

22. Faysal, *A'lam min jil al-ruwad min Ghazzatu Hashem*, p. 246.

23. Guides Bleus, *Syrie–Palestine*, Paris: Hachette (Guides Bleus), 1932, pp. 622–4.

24. Matthews, 'Pan-Islam or Arab Nationalism?' p. 14.

25. Laurens, *La question de Palestine*, vol. 2, p. 234.

26. Mattar, *The Mufti of Jerusalem*, p. 64.

27. Ibid. p. 67.

28. Laurens, *La question de Palestine*, p. 308.

29. Milton-Edwards, Beverley, *Islamic Politics in Palestine*, London: I.B. Tauris, 1996, p. 39.

30. Al-Awaisi, Abd al-Fattah, *The Muslim Brothers and the Palestine Question, 1928–1947*, London: I.B. Tauris, 1999, pp. 42, 95–6.

31. Laurens, *La question de Palestine*, p. 324.

32. Mattar, *The Mufti of Jerusalem*, p. 79.

33. Ibid.

34. Resolution adopted on 10 Apr. 1937 by the Gaza Municipal Council (translator's version). See National Archives (London), CO 733/348/9–0003.

35. Porat, Yehoshua, *The Emergence of the Palestinian National Arab Movement: From Riots to Rebellion*, London: Frank Cass, 1977, p. 261.

36. Arif, *Tarikh Ghazza*, p. 98; Porat, *The Emergence of the Palestinian National Arab Movement*, p. 400.

37. 'Report by the District Commissioner for Gaza', 29 July 1939, in *Political Diaries of the Arab World: Jordan and Palestine*, vol. 4, p. 600.

38. Mattar, *The Mufti of Jerusalem*, p. 85.

39. Ibid. p. 104.

40. Achcar, Gilbert, *The Arabs and the Holocaust: The Arab–Israeli War of Narratives*, New York: Henry Holt & Co/Metropolitan, 2010, p. 146.

41. Laurens, *La question de Palestine*, vol. 2, p. 505.

42. Butt, *Life at the Crossroads*, pp. 130–1.

43. Shachar, *The Gaza Strip*, p. 50; Al-Arif, *Tarikh Ghazza*, p. 250.

44. Laurens, *La question de Palestine*, p. 491.

45. 'Report by the District Commissioner for Gaza', 17 Dec. 1942, in *Political Diaries of the Arab World: Jordan and Palestine*, vol. 7, p. 577.

46. Al-Arif, *Tarikh Ghazza*, p. 304.

47. 'Report of the Anglo-American Committee of Inquiry', 1946, in *Palestine and Transjordan Administration Reports*, London: Archive Editions, 1995, vol. 12, p. 156.

48. Khalidi, Walid, *All That Remains*, Washington, DC: Institute of Palestinian Studies, 1992, p. xxix.

49. 'Report from the District Commissioner for Gaza', 2 Feb. 1943, in *Political Diaries of the Arab World: Jordan and Palestine*, p. 175.

50. Ibid. p. 188.

51. Laurens, *La question de Palestine*, p. 495.

52. 'Report from the District Commissioner for Gaza', 15 Dec. 1944, in *Political Diaries of the Arab World: Jordan and Palestine*, vol. 7, p. 577.

53. Al-Awaisi, *The Muslim Brothers and the Palestine Question*, p. 135.

54. Faysal, *A'lam min jil al-ruwad min Ghazzatu Hashem*, p. 417; for Zafer Shawa's genealogy see Tabaa, *Ithaf al-'izza fi tarikh Ghazza*, vol. 2, pp. 255–6.

55. Al-Awaisi, *The Muslim Brothers and the Palestine Question*, p. 161.

56. Azaar, Muhammad Khaled al-, *Al-muqawama fi qita' Ghazza, 1967–1975*, Cairo: Dar al-Mustaqbal al-Arabi, 1987, p. 32.

57. Shachar, *The Gaza Strip*, p. 50.

58. 'Report from the District Commissioner for Gaza', 19 Oct. 1946, in *Political Diaries of the Arab World: Jordan and Palestine*, vol. 8, p. 599.

59. 'Report from the District Commissioner for Gaza', 3 Jan. 1947, in *Political Diaries of the Arab World: Jordan and Palestine*, vol. 8, p. 610.

60. Laurens, Henry, 'Le mufti de Jérusalem et la IVe République', *La Revue d'études palestiniennes*, 81 (autumn 2001), pp. 70–87.

61. Laurens, *La question de Palestine*, vol. 2 (1922–47), p. 571.

62. Al-Awaisi, *The Muslim Brothers and the Palestine Question*, p. 153.

63. Sherman, A.J., *Mandate Days*, New York: Thames and Hudson, 1998, p. 191.

64. 'Report from the District Commissioner for Gaza', 18 Nov. 1947, in *Political Diaries of the Arab World: Jordan and Palestine*, vol. 9, p. 478.

65. Interview with Mustafa Abdel Shafi, Gaza, 10 Nov. 2010.

66. 'Report from the District Commissioner for Gaza', 18 Nov. 1947, in *Political Diaries of the Arab World: Jordan and Palestine*, vol. 9, p. 478.

4. THE CATASTROPHE

1. Milton-Edwards, Beverley, *Islamic Politics in Palestine*, London: I.B. Tauris, 1996, pp. 39–40.
2. Morris, Benny, *The Birth of the Palestine Refugee Problem*, Cambridge: Cambridge University Press, 1987, p. 128.
3. 'Report from the District Commissioner for Gaza', 16 Dec. 1947, in *Political Diaries of the Arab World: Jordan and Palestine*, London: Archive Editions, 1991, vol. 9, p. 482.
4. 'Report from the District Commissioner for Gaza', 16 Dec. 1947, in *Political Diaries of the Arab World: Jordan and Palestine*, vol. 10, p. 216.
5. 'Telegram from British High Commissioner in Palestine', 23 Feb. 1948, National Archives (London), FP 816/116.
6. Sanbar, Elias, *1948: l'expulsion*, Paris: Les Livres de la Revue d'Etudes Palestiniennes, 1984, p. 158.
7. Khalidi, Walid, *All That Remains*, Washington, DC: Institute of Palestinian Studies, 1992, p. 96.
8. Al-Awaisi, Abd al-Fattah, *The Muslim Brothers and the Palestine Question, 1928–1947*, London: I.B. Tauris, 1999, p. 208.
9. Levenberg, Haim, *The Military Preparedness of the Arab Community in Palestine*, London: Frank Cass, 1993, p. 177.
10. Sharif, Kamal and Mustafa Sibai, *Al-Ikhwan al-Muslimun fi harb Filistin*, Cairo: Dar al-Tawzi' wa-l Nashr al-Islamiyya, 1974, pp. 89–93.
11. Ben Ayyash, Awda Muhammad, *Rafah, madina 'ala al-hudud*, Gaza: Rashid Shawa Cultural Centre, 2002, p. 93.
12. Khalidi, *All That Remains*, pp. 85, 92.
13. Azaar, Muhammad Khaled, *Al-muqawama fi qita' Ghazza, 1967–1975*, Cairo: Dar al-Mustaqbal al-Arabi, 1987, p. 37.
14. 'Telegram from the High Commissioner to the British Ambassador in Cairo', National Archives (London), OF 141/1246–0020.
15. Shlaim, Avi and Eugene Rogan, *The War for Palestine*, Cambridge: Cambridge University Press, 2001.
16. Laurens, Henry, *La question de Palestine*, vol. 3, pp. 105–6.
17. Khalidi, Walid (trans. and ed.), 'Nasser's Memoirs of the First Palestine War', *Journal of Palestine Studies*, 2 (Winter 1973), n. 4, p. 5.
18. Shlaim, Avi, *The Politics of Partition: King Abdullah, the Zionists, and Palestine 1921–1951*, New York: Oxford University Press, 1990, p. 193.
19. Heykal, Muhammad Hasanein (war correspondent for *Akhbar Al-Yawm*), *Journal of Palestine Studies*, 18, 1 (Autumn 1988), p. 118.
20. For the English translation of Nasser's account, see Khalidi, 'Nasser's Memoirs of the First Palestine War', pp. 3–32.

21. Ibid. pp. 10–12.
22. Al-Awaisi, *The Muslim Brothers and the Palestine Question*, p. 209.
23. Morris, *The Birth of the Palestine Refugee Problem*, p. 128.
24. Nasser's account in Khalidi, 'Nasser's Memoirs of the First Palestine War', p. 17.
25. O'Ballance, Edgar, *The Arab–Israel War 1948*, London: Faber and Faber, 1956, p. 137.
26. Nasser's account in Walid, 'Nasser's Memoirs of the First Palestine War', pp. 26–7.
27. *Le progrès égyptien*, 8 July 1948.
28. Al-Awaisi, *The Muslim Brothers and the Palestine Question*, p. 209.
29. O'Ballance, *The Arab–Israel War 1948*, pp. 141–2.
30. 'Palestinian Voices: The 1948 War and its Aftermath', account by Um Jaber Wisbah, *Journal of Palestine Studies*, 35, 4 (Summer 2006), p. 57.
31. O'Ballance, *The Arab–Israeli War 1948*, p. 172.
32. Shlaim, Avi, 'The Rise and Fall of the All-Palestine Government in Gaza', *Journal of Palestine Studies*, 20, 1 (Autumn 1990), p. 41.
33. Ibid. p. 43.
34. Abu Naml, Hussein, *Qita Ghazza 1948–1967: Tatawwurat Iqtisadiyya wa-Siyasiyya wa-Ljtima'iyya wa-'Askariyya*, Beirut: Center for Palestinian Research, 1979, p. 23.
35. Shlaim, 'The Rise and Fall of the All-Palestine Government in Gaza', p. 45.
36. *AFP*, Beirut, 15 Oct. 1948.
37. 'Despatch from the French embassy in Cairo', 2 October 1948, ANMO PA 425.
38. 'Despatch from Ministry of Foreign Affairs to French Embassy in Cairo', 13 Oct. 1948, ANMO PA 425.
39. Shlaim, 'The Rise and Fall of the All-Palestine Government in Gaza', p. 49.
40. Abu Naml, *Qita Ghazza 1948–1967*, p. 26.
41. Laurens, *La question de Palestine*, vol. 3, p. 170.
42. Morris, *The Birth of the Palestine Refugee Problem*, p. 220.
43. Letter for Glubb to the commander of the Arab Legion's First Brigade, quoted in Shlaim and Rogan, *The War for Palestine*, p. 99.
44. O'Ballance, *The Arab–Israel War 1948*, p. 181.
45. Morris, *The Birth of the Palestine Refugee Problem*, p. 220.
46. Cheal, Beryl, 'Refugees in the Gaza Strip', *Journal of Palestine Studies*, 18, 1 (Autumn 1988), p. 139.
47. Buji, Muhammad Bakr al- and Riyad Ali al-Ayla, *Yibna, tarikh wa dhakira*, Gaza: Matabi' Mansour, 2000, p. 89.
48. Sharif, Kamal, and Sibaï Mustafa, *Al-Ikhwan al-Muslimum fi harb Filistin*, pp. 213–17.
49. Khoury-Tadié, Arlette, *Une enfance à Gaza, 1942–1958*, Paris: Maisonneuve-Larose, 2002, p. 211.
50. Cheal, 'Refugees in the Gaza Strip', p. 143.

51. Interview with Mustafa Abdel Shafi, Gaza, 10 Nov. 2010.

52. Evidence of Um Jaber, inhabitant of Beit Affa in 1948, in *Journal of Palestine Studies*, 35, 4 (Spring 2006), p. 61.

53. Cheal, 'Refugees in the Gaza Strip', pp. 140–2.

5. REFUGEES AND FEDAYIN

1. Laurens, Henry, *La Question de Palestine*, vol. 3 (1947–67), Paris: Fayard, 2007, p. 199.

2. Shlaim, Avi, *The Politics of Partition: King Abdullah, the Zionists, and Palestine 1921–1951*, New York: Oxford University Press, 1990, p. 199.

3. Egyptian–Israeli General Armistice Agreement, 24 Feb. 1949, Article V. Text available at http://avalon.law.yale.edu/20th_century/arm01.asp (accessed 24 Jan. 2014).

4. http://unispal.un.org/UNISPAL.NSF/0/C758572B78D1CD0085256BCF00 77E51A (accessed 24 Jan. 2014).

5. Caplan, Neil, 'A Tale of Two Cities', *Journal of Palestine Studies*, 21, 3 (Spring 1992), p. 14.

6. Laurens, Henry, *La Question de Palestine*, p. 229.

7. Ibid. pp. 228–9.

8. Caplan, 'A Tale of Two Cities', p. 21.

9. Ibid. p. 22.

10. Ibid. p. 24.

11. Ibid. p. 25.

12. Al-Awaisi, Abd al-Fattah, *The Muslim Brothers and the Palestine Question, 1928–1947*, London: I.B. Tauris, 1999, p. 210.

13. Brand, Laurie, 'Nasir's Egypt and the Re-Emergence of the Palestinian National Movement', *Journal of Palestine Studies*, 17, 2 (Winter 1988), pp. 30–1.

14. *Al-Waqa'i al-flistiniyya* (Official Journal of the Gaza Strip), Cairo: Dar al-Nil, 1957, pp. 1–10.

15. Hamdan, Muhammad Said, *Siyasat Misr tijah al-Qaddiyya al-filistiniyya 1948–1956*, Amman: Al-Yazuri, 2006, p. 277.

16. Dumper, Michael, *Islam and Israel*, Washington, DC: Institute of Palestine Studies, 1994, p. 72.

17. Faysal, Numan Abdelhadi, *A'lam min jil al-ruwad min Ghazzatu Hashem*, Gaza: Dar al-Duktur, 2010, p. 456.

18. *Al-Waqa'I al-filistiniyya*, pp. 8–9.

19. Cheal, Beryl, 'Refugees in the Gaza Strip', *Journal of Palestine Studies*, 18, 1 (Autumn 1988), p. 145.

20. Ibid. p. 146.

21. Buehrig, Edward, *The UN and the Palestinian Refugees*, Bloomington, IN: Indiana University Press, 1972, p. 32.
22. Cheal, 'Refugees in the Gaza Strip', p. 151.
23. Ibid. p. 152.
24. Al-Buji and Al-Ayla, op. cit., 2000, p. 79.
25. All estimates are drawn from Hagopian, Edward and A.B. Zahlan, 'Palestine's Arab Population', *Journal of Palestine Studies*, 3, 4 (Spring 1974), pp. 51–2.
26. Feldman, Ilana, *Governing Gaza: Bureaucracy, Authority and the Work of Rule 1917–1958*, Durham, NC: Duke University Press, 2008, pp. 102–3.
27. Minutes of the fifty-second session of the UNCCP, United Nations, Geneva, 15 Feb. 1950.
28. Cheal, 'Refugees in the Gaza Strip', p. 155.
29. Quoted by Morris, Benny, *Israel's Border Wars*, Oxford: The Clarendon Press, 1993, p. 43.
30. Cheal, 'Refugees in the Gaza Strip', p. 154.
31. Morris, *Israel's Border Wars*, p. 135.
32. Ibid. p. 31.
33. Ibid. p. 188
34. Laurens, *La Question de Palestine*, pp. 298–299.
35. *New York Times*, 9 June 1950.
36. Laurens, *La Question de Palestine*, p. 300.
37. Feldman, Ilana, 'Home as a Refrain', *History and Memory*, 18, 2 (Autumn–Winter 2006), p. 45.
38. Faysal, *A'lam min jil al-ruwad min Ghazzatu Hashem*, p. 411.
39. *Al-Mussawar*, no. 1450, 14 Sep. 1951.
40. Abu Naml, Hussein, *Qita Ghazza 1948–1967: Tatawwurat Iqtisadiyya wa-Siyasiyya wa-Ijtima'iyya wa-'Askariyya*, Beirut: Center for Palestinian Research, 1979, p. 54.
41. Morris, *Israel's Border Wars*, p. 87.
42. Laurens, *La Question de Palestine*, p. 333.
43. Abu Amr, Ziad, *Islamic Fundamentalism in the West Bank and Gaza*, Bloomington, IN: Indiana University Press, 1994, p. 7.
44. Founding charter of the Jami'yyat al-Tawhid, in Sa'ati, Ahmed Muhammad, *Al-tatawwur al-thaqafi fi Ghazza*, Gaza: Islamic University, 2005, vol. 2, p. 109.
45. Milton-Edwards, Beverley, *Islamic Politics in Palestine*, London: I.B. Tauris, 1996, p. 44.
46. Ibid. p. 43.
47. Abou Iyad [Salah Khalaf], *Palestinien sans patrie: entretiens avec Eric Rouleau*, Paris: Fayolle, 1978, p. 43.
48. Tabaa, Utham Mustafa, *Ithaf al-'izza fi tarikh Ghazza*, Gaza: Al-Yazji, 1999 (4 vols), vol. 2, pp. 335–49.

49. Boltanski, Christophe and Jihane Tahri, *Les Sept Vies de Yasser Arafat*, Paris: Grasset, 1997, pp. 176–7.

50. http://www.nobelprize.org/nobel_prizes/peace/laureates/1994/arafat-bio.html (accessed 24 Jan. 2014).

51. Abou Iyad, *Palestinien sans patrie: entretiens avec Eric Rouleau*, p. 45; Balawi, Hassan, *Dans les coulisses du mouvement national palestinien*, Paris: Denoël, 2008, p. 55.

52. Abu Naml, *Qita Ghazza 1948–1967*, p. 70.

53. Gresh, Alain, 'Communistes et nationalistes au Proche-Orient', *Communisme*, 6 (1984), p. 61.

54. Abu Amr, *Islamic Fundamentalism in the West Bank and Gaza*, p. 7.

55. Abu Naml, *Qita Ghazza 1948–1967*, p. 67.

56. Sayigh, Yezid, *Armed Struggle and the Search for the State*, Oxford: Oxford University Press, 1997, pp. 81–2.

57. Abou Fakhr, Saqr, 'Genèse des organisations de la résistance palestinienne', *Revue d'études palestiniennes*, 81 (Autumn 2001), p. 50.

58. Faysal, *A'lam min jil al-ruwad min Ghazzatu Hashem*, pp. 50, 433.

59. Gresh, 'Communistes et nationalistes au Proche-Orient', p. 61.

60. Consul General of France in Jerusalem, telegram, 28 Jan. 1953, NUOI 227.

61. Haïk, Daniel, *Sharon, un destin inachevé*, Paris; L'Archipel, 2006, p. 41.

62. Theobald, Andrew, 'Watching the War and Keeping the Peace: The UNTSO in the Middle East, 1949–1956', PhD thesis, Queens University, Kingston, Ontario, 28 May 2009, p. 92.

63. Laurens, *La Question de Palestine*, vol. 3, p. 347.

64. Haïk, *Sharon, un destin inachevé*, p. 42.

65. Yassin, Abdelqadir, *'Umr fi al-manfa*, Damascus: Dar al-Wataniyya al-Jadida, 2009, p. 16.

66. Yassin, Abdelqadir, *Al-Haraka al-wataniyya al-filistiniyya*, Cairo: General Union of Palestinian Writers and Journalists, 1975, pp. 84–5.

67. Milton-Edwards, *Islamic Politics in Palestine*, p. 44.

68. Gresh, 'Communistes et nationalistes au Proche-Orient', p. 61.

69. Laurens, *La Question de Palestine*, vol. 3, p. 381.

70. Sayegh. Yazid, *Armed Struggle and the Search for the State*, pp. 61–62.

71. Consul-General of France in Jerusalem, telegram, 27 Sep. 1954, NUOI 227.

72. Morris, *Israel's Border Wars*, p. 50.

73. Laurens, *La Question de Palestine*, vol. 3, p. 406.

74. Ibid.

75. Sharon, Ariel, *Warrior*, New York: Simon and Schuster, 1989, p. 109.

76. Interview with Eyad al-Sarraj, Gaza, 6 Nov. 2010.

77. Sourani, Ghazi, *Qita Ghazza 1948–1993*, Damascus: Centre for Popular Studies, 1993, p. 14.

78. Faysal, *A'lam min jil al-ruwad min Ghazzatu Hashem*, p. 663.
79. Abou Iyad, *Palestinien sans patrie*, pp. 47–8.
80. Abu Naml, *Qita Ghazza 1948–1967*, p. 95.
81. Hamdan, *Siyasat Misr tijah al-Qadiyya al-Filistiniyya 1948–1956*, p. 347.
82. Salah Salem, Egyptian minister for national guidance, statement of 20 Mar. 1955, reported in *Manchester Guardian*, 21 Mar. 1955.
83. *The Times*, 22 Mar. 1955.
84. 'Telegram from British Ambassador in Damascus to Foreign Office', 6 Apr. 1955, National Archives, London, FO 371/115838–0010.
85. English translation in *Journal of Palestine Studies*, 2, 2 (Winter 1973), p. 6.
86. Security Council Resolution 107, adopted 30 Mar. 1955. See Theobald, 'Watching the War and Keeping the Peace', p. 111.
87. Laurens, *La Question de Palestine*, vol. 3, p. 413.
88. Telegram from Consul-General of France in Jerusalem, 19 May 1955, NUOI 227.
89. Quoted in Sourani, *Qita Ghazza 1948–1993*, Arabic text quoted in appendix. The text in English appears in the *Official Gazette* (Gaza) Special Issue, 28 Feb. 1958.
90. Telegram from Consul-General of France in Jerusalem, 19 May 1955, NUOI 227.
91. Sayigh, Yazid, *Armed Struggle and the Search for the State*, p. 63.
92. Interview with Rabah Mohanna, Gaza, 5 Nov. 2010.
93. Abou Fakhr, 'Genèse des organisations de la résistance palestinienne', p. 90.
94. Burns, E.L.M., *Between Arab and Israeli*, London: Harraps, 1962, p. 87.
95. Burns, *Between Arab and Israeli*, p. 88; Morris, *Israel's Border Wars*, p. 347.
96. Morris, *Israel's Border Wars*, p. 350.
97. Telegram from Consul-General of France in Jerusalem, 17 Sep. 1955, NUOI 227.
98. Abu Iyad, *Palestinien sans patrie*, p. 46.
99. Burns, *Between Arab and Israeli*, p. 47.
100. Interview with Misbah Saqr, Gaza, 10 Nov. 2010.
101. Bar-On, Mordechai, *The Gates of Gaza*, New York: St. Martin's Press, 1994, p. 118.
102. Burns, *Between Arab and Israeli*, pp. 140–1.
103. Morris, *Israel's Border Wars*, p. 372.
104. Ibid. p. 374.
105. Ibid. pp. 378–9.
106. Burns, *Between Arab and Israeli*, p. 148.
107. Morris, *Israel's Border Wars*, pp. 379–80.
108. Sourani, *Qita Ghazza 1948–1993*, p. 16.
109. Interview with Freih Abu Middain, Gaza, 9 Nov. 2010.

110. Interview with Misbah Saqr, Gaza, 10 Nov. 2010.
111. Abou Iyad, *Palestinien sans patrie*, p. 49.
112. Letter from Hammarsjköld to Ben Gurion, 26 Sep. 1956, quoted in Morris, *Israel's Border Wars*, p. 377.
113. Dayan, Moshe, *Diary of the Sinai Campaign*, London: Weidenfeld and Nicolson, 1966, p. 39.

6. THE FIRST OCCUPATION

1. Laurens, Henry, *La Question de Palestine*, vol. 3 (1947–67), Paris: Fayard, 2007, pp. 486–7.
2. Burns, E.L.M., *Between Arab and Israeli*, London: Harraps, 1962, pp. 486–7.
3. Interview with Intissar al-Wazir (Umm Jihad), Gaza, 4 Nov. 2010.
4. Dayan, Moshe, *Diary of the Sinai Campaign*, London: Weidenfeld and Nicolson, 1965, p. 154.
5. Morris, Benny, *Israel's Border Wars*, Oxford: The Clarendon Press, 1993, p. 408.
6. Interview with Adala Abou Sitta, Gaza, 9 Nov. 2010.
7. 'Report of the Director General of UNRWA to the General Assembly', 15 Dec. 1956, item 23, http://unispal.un.org/UNISPAL.NSF/0/6558F61D3DB6BD4 505256593006B06BE (accessed 24 Jan. 2014). For a graphic representation of the eyewitness accounts of survivors, see Sacco, Joe, *Footnotes in Gaza*, London: Jonathan Cape, 2009, pp. 92–127.
8. *Majzara qita Ghazza*, Centre d'information et de culture de l'OLP, Tunis: 1983, p. 169.
9. Sudfi, Falah Salama and Qanayta, A'tadal Saadallah, *Asad al-muqawama, al-shahid duktur 'Abd al-'Aziz al-Rantissi*, Gaza: Maktab al-Jil, 2010, p. 3.
10. Morris, *Israel's Border Wars*, pp. 407–8.
11. Interview with Moussa Saba, Gaza, 5 Nov. 2010.
12. Interview with Eyad al-Sarraj, Gaza, 6 Nov. 2010.
13. Abdel Shafi, Mustafa, *Would They Ever Learn?* Gaza: Rashad Shawa Cultural Centre, 2000, p. 559.
14. Dayan, *Diary of the Sinai Campaign*, p. 174.
15. Burns, *Between Arab and Israeli*, pp. 190–1.
16. Interview with Intissar al-Wazir (Umm Jihad), Gaza, 4 Nov. 2010.
17. See the list of the names of the thirty-six dead in *Majzara qita Ghazza*, p. 55.
18. See Sacco Joe, *Footnotes in Gaza*, pp. 212–52; 270–89; 307–34.
19. *The Times*, 18 Nov. 1956.
20. Knesset minutes, 28 Nov. 1956.
21. UNRWA director general's report to the UN General Assembly, 15 Dec. 1956, section 27. http://unispal.un.org/UNISPAL.NSF/0/6558F61D3DB6BD4505 256593006B06BE (accessed 24 Jan. 2014).

22. *Majzara qita Ghazza.*
23. Burns, *Between Arab and Israeli*, pp. 191–2.
24. Dayan, *Diary of the Sinai Campaign*, p. 175.
25. Hassouna, Issam, *23 yuliyu wa Abd al Nasir: shihadati*, Cairo, Al Ahram, 1990, pp. 75–80.
26. Abou Iyad [Salah Khalaf], *Palestinien sans patrie: entretiens avec Eric Rouleau*, Paris: Fayolle, 1978, p. 49.
27. Ibid.
28. Sourani Ghazi, *Qita Ghazza 1948–1993*, Damascus: Centre for Popular Studies, 1993, p. 20.
29. Interview with Rabah Mohanna, Gaza, 5 Nov. 2010.
30. *JTA* (Jewish Telegraphic Agency), 5 Mar. 1957.
31. Yassin, Abdelqadir, *Al-Haraka al-wataniyya al-filistiniyya*, Cairo: General Union of Palestinian Writers and Journalists, 1975, p. 32.
32. 'Documents on the Foreign Policy of Israel', Jerusalem: Israel State Archives, 2009, vol. 12, document 306.
33. Bar-On, Mordechai, *The Gates of Gaza*, New York: St. Martin's Press, 1994, p. 295.
34. 'Minutes of the Meeting between Christian Pineau and Abba Eban on 17 Feb. 1957', in *Documents on the Foreign Policy of Israel*, vol. 12, Jerusalem: Israel State Archives, document 481.
35. Interview with Mordechai Bar-On, Jerusalem, 13 Nov. 2010.
36. Interview with Moussa Saba, Gaza, 5 Nov. 2010.
37. Sourani, *Qita Ghazza 1948–1993*, p. 20.
38. Abdel Shafi, *Would They Ever Learn?* p. 576.
39. Burns, *Between Arab and Israeli*, p. 256.
40. 'Despatch from Consul-General of France in Jerusalem', 1 Apr. 1957, NUOI 250.
41. 'Telegram from the Ambassador of France in Washington', 18 Mar. 1957, NUOI 250.
42. Laurens, *La Question de Palestine*, vol. 3, p. 501.
43. *Majzara qita Ghazza*, p. 169.
44. 'Report of the Director General of UNRWA to the UN Assembly General', 15 Dec. 1956, item 33, http://unispal.un.org/UNISPAL.NSF/0/6558F61D3D B6BD4505256593006B06BE (accessed 24 Jan. 2014).
45. Interview with Intissar al-Wazir (Umm Jihad), Gaza, 4 Nov. 2010.

7. NASSER'S CHILDREN

1. Burns, E.L.M., *Between Arab and Israeli*, London: Harraps, 1962, p. 264.
2. Abdel Shafi, Mustafa, *Would They Ever Learn?* Gaza: Rashad Shawa Cultural Centre, 2000, p. 575.

3. Interview with Mustafa Abdel Shafi, Gaza, 10 Nov. 2010.

4. Interview with Misbah Saqr, Gaza, 10 Nov. 2010.

5. Sayigh, Yezid, *Armed Struggle and the Search for the State*, Oxford: Oxford University Press, 1997, p. 66.

6. Interview with Hassan Balawi, Paris, 22 Nov. 2010.

7. Abou Iyad, *Palestinien sans patrie*, pp. 51–6.

8. Interview with Rawya Shawa, Gaza, 7 Nov. 2010.

9. Laurens, *La Question de Palestine*, vol.3 p. 538.

10. Interview with Rabah Mohanna, Gaza, 5 Nov. 2010.

11. Interview with Moussa Saba, Gaza, 5 Nov. 2010.

12. Yassin, Abdelqadir, '*Umr fi al-manfa*, Damascus: Dar al-Wataniyya al-Jadida, 2009, pp. 42–3.

13. Kalfon, Pierre, *Che*, Paris: Le Seuil, 1997, pp. 267–8.

14. Interview with Mustafa Abdel Shafi, Gaza, 10 Nov. 2010.

15. Balawi, Hassan, *Dans les coulisses du mouvement national palestinien*, Paris: Denoël, 2008, p. 67.

16. Faysal, Numan Abdelhadi, *A'lam min jil al-ruwad min Ghazzatu Hashem*, Gaza: Dar al-Duktur, 2010, p. 329.

17. Laurens, *La Question de Palestine*, vol.3, p. 557.

18. Sayigh, *Armed Struggle and the Search for the State*, p. 557.

19. *Le problème des refugiés arabes de Palestine*, Cairo: Administration de l'information, 1962, p. 93.

20. For the text, see Shehadeh, Raja, *From Occupation to Interim Accords*, Leiden: Kluwer Law International, Brill, 1997, pp. 77–8.

21. Sourani, Ghazi, *Qita Ghazza 1948–1993*, Damascus: Centre for Popular Studies, 1993, p. 25.

22. Malcolm H. Kerr, *The Arab Cold War: Gamal Abd al-Nasr and his Rivals, 1958–1970*, Oxford: Oxford University Press, 1965 (3rd edn 1975).

23. Abdel Shafi, *Would They Ever Learn?* p. 632.

24. Faysal, *A'lam min jil al-ruwad min Ghazzatu Hashem*, p. 270.

25. Sourani, *Qita Ghazza 1948–1993*, p. 26.

26. Sayigh, Yezid, 'Escalation or Containment? Egypt and the Palestine Liberation Army 1964–67', *International Journal of Middle East Studies*, 30, 1 (Feb. 1998), p. 100.

27. Sourani, *Qita Ghazza 1948–1993*, p. 26.

28. Walker, Tony and Andrew Gowers, *Arafat: The Biography*, London: Virgin, 2003, p. 38.

29. Jabber, Fuad, 'The Palestinian Resistance and Inter-Arab Politics', in Quandt, William, Fuad Jabber and Ann Mosley Lesch (eds), *The Politics of Palestinian Nationalism*, Berkeley: University of California Press, 1973, p. 165.

30. Laurens, *La Question de Palestine*, p. 650.

31. Sayigh, *Armed Struggle and the Search for the State*, p. 115.
32. Ibid.
33. Shemesh, Moshe, *The Palestinian Entity, 1959–74*, London: Frank Cass, 1988, p. 82.
34. Yezid, Sayigh, 'Reconstructing the Paradox: The Arab Nationalist Movement, Armed Struggle and Palestine', *Middle East Journal*, 45, 4 (Autumn 1991), pp. 624–6.
35. Interview with Rabah Mohanna, Gaza, 5 Nov. 2010.
36. Yassin, '*Umr fi al-manfa*, pp. 57–9.
37. Milton-Edwards, Beverley, *Islamic Politics in Palestine*, London: I.B. Tauris, 1996, p. 64.
38. Tamimi, Azzam, *Hamas: Unwritten Chapters*, London: Hurst, 2007, pp. 16–17.
39. Interview with Rabah Mohanna, Gaza, 5 Nov. 2010.
40. Feldman, Ilana, *Governing Gaza: Bureaucracy, Authority and the Work of Rule 1917–1958*, Durham, NC: Duke University Press, 2008, p. 23.
41. Mubayyid, Salim, *Al-binayat al-athariyya al-islamiyya fi Ghazza*, Cairo: Al-Hayya al-Masriyya al-'Amma lil-Kitab (Egyptian General Book Organisation), 1995, p. 460.
42. Lesch, Ann Mosely, 'Gaza: History and Politics', in Lesch, Ann Mosely and Mark Tessler (eds), *Israel, Egypt and the Palestinians*, Bloomington, IN: Indiana University Press, 1989, p. 227.
43. Sourani, *Qita Ghazza 1948–1993*, p. 32.
44. Lesch, 'Gaza: History and Politics', p. 227.
45. Sayigh, *Armed Struggle and the Search for the State*, p. 44.
46. Buehrig, Edward, *The UN and the Palestinian Refugees*, Bloomington, IN: Indiana University Press, 1972, p. 130.
47. Interview with Ghazi Sourani, Gaza, 10 Nov. 2010.
48. Ben-Gal, Ely, *Mardi chez Sartre*, Paris: Flammarion, 1992, p. 290.
49. Ibid. pp. 27–8.
50. Cohen-Solal, Annie, *Sartre*, Paris: Gallimard, 1985, p. 533.
51. Interview with Mordechai Bar-On, Jerusalem, 13 Nov. 2010.
52. Sayigh, 'Escalation or Containment?' p. 110.
53. Laurens, *La Question de Palestine*, vol. 3, p. 721.
54. Sayigh, 'Escalation or Containment?' p. 110.

8. THE FOUR YEARS WAR

1. Interview with Mordechai Bar-On, Jerusalem, 13 Nov. 2010.
2. Hammel, Eric, *Six Days in June*, New York: Macmillan, 1992, p. 179.
3. Ibid. p. 215.
4. Ibid. pp. 216–17.

5. Ibid. p. 218.

6. Report of the commissioner general of UNRWA to the UN General Assembly for the period from 1 July 1967 to 30 June 1968.

7. Laurens, Henry, *La question de Palestine*, vol. 4, Paris: Fayard, 1999, p. 55.

8. Dayan, Moshe, *Histoire de ma vie*, op. cit., pp. 373–4.

9. *Jerusalem Post*, 10 July 1967.

10. Segev, Tom, *1967, Israel, and the War that transformed the Middle East*, New York: Metropolitan Books, 2005, pp. 430, 516.

11. Report of the Commissioner General of UNRWA for the period from 1 July 1967 to 30 June 1968, pp. 5–8.

12. Ben Ayyash, Awda Muhammad, *Rafah, madina 'ala al-hudud*, Gaza: Rashid Shawa Cultural Centre, 2002, pp. 287–8.

13. Interview with Adala Abou Sitta, Gaza, 9 Nov. 2010.

14. Interview with Misbah Saqr, Gaza, 10 Nov. 2010.

15. Interview with Ghazi Sourani, 10 Nov. 2010.

16. Yassin, Abdelqadir, *'Umr fi al-manfa*, Damascus: Dar al-Wataniyya al-Jadida, 2009, p. 58.

17. Tamimi, Azzam, *Hamas: Unwritten Chapters*, London: Hurst, 2007, p. 17.

18. Interview with Ghazi Sourani, Gaza, 10 Nov. 2010.

19. Quoted in Abu Amir, Adnan, *Al-haraka al-islamiyya fi Ghazza*, Cairo: Markaz ala'lam al-arabi, 2006, p. 17.

20. Yassin, *'Umr fi al-manfa*, pp. 61–2.

21. Feldman, Ilana, *Governing Gaza: Bureaucracy, Authority and the Work of Rule 1917–1958*, Durham, NC: Duke University Press, 2008, p. 34.

22. Abu Gharbiyya, Bahjat, *Min il-nakba ila al-intifada*, op. cit., 2004, p. 337.

23. Interview with Misbah Saqr, Gaza, 10 Nov. 2010.

24. Interview with Ghazi Sourani, Gaza, 10 Nov. 2010.

25. Yassin, *'Umr fi al-manfa*, p. 269.

26. Ibid. p. 65.

27. Ibid. pp. 66–7.

28. Interview with Ghazi Sourani, Gaza, 10 Nov. 2010.

29. Interview with Rabah Mohanna, Gaza, 5 Nov. 2010.

30. Interview with Ghazi Sourani, Gaza, 10 Nov. 2010.

31. Interview with Moussa Saba, Gaza, 5 Nov. 2010.

32. Faysal, Numan Abdelhadi, *A'lam min jil al-ruwad min Ghazzatu Hashem*, Gaza: Dar al-Duktur, 2010, p. 325.

33. Shlaim, Avi, *Lion of Jordan*, London: Allen Lane, 2007, p. 295.

34. Faysal, *A'lam min jil al-ruwad min Ghazzatu Hashem*, p. 113.

35. Interview with Rabah Mohanna, 5 Nov. 2010.

36. Interview with Levi Eshkol, *Newsweek*, 17 Feb. 1969.

37. Report of the Commissioner-General of UNRWA for the period from 1 July 1967 to 30 June 1968, p. 35.

38. Lesch, Ann Mosely, 'Gaza: History and Politics', in Lesch, Ann Mosely and Mark Tessler (eds), *Israel, Egypt and the Palestinians*, Bloomington, IN: Indiana University Press, 1989, p. 229.

39. Ibid.

40. Eyewitness account by Abu Hassan, in Cossali, Paul and Clive Robson, *Stateless in Gaza*, London: Zed Books, 1986, p. 64.

41. Segev, *1967, Israel, and the War that transformed the Middle East*, p. 524.

42. Ibid. pp. 520, 527–30.

43. Ibid. pp. 531–6.

44. Ibid. p. 537.

45. Lesch, Ann Mosely, 'Deportation of Palestinians from the West Bank and the Gaza Strip', *Journal of Palestine Studies*, 8, 2 (Winter 1979), p. 102.

46. Yassin, *'Umr fi al-manfa*, p. 63.

47. Report of the Commissioner-General of UNRWA for the period from 1 July 1969 to 30 June 1970, p. 41.

48. See the account by 'Abu Ali' quoted in Cossali and Robson, *Stateless in Gaza*, pp. 88–92.

49. Sourani, Ghazi, *Qita Ghazza 1948–1993*, Damascus: Centre for Popular Studies, 1993, p. 35.

50. Azaar, Muhammad Khaled, *Al-muqawama fi qita' Ghazza, 1967–1975*, Cairo: Dar al-Mustaqbal al-Arabi, 1987, pp. 146–61.

51. Faysal, *A'lam min jil al-ruwad min Ghazzatu Hashem*, p. 114.

52. See the account by 'Nabila' in Cossali and Robson, *Stateless in Gaza*, p. 125.

53. Yassin, *'Umr fi al-manfa*, p. 83.

54. Carre, Olivier, *Septembre noir*, Brussels: Complexe, 1980, p. 39.

55. Lesch, 'Deportation of Palestinians from the West Bank and Gaza', p. 104.

56. Faysal, *A'lam min jil al-ruwad min Ghazzatu Hashem*, p. 95.

57. O'Neill, Bard E., *Armed Struggle in Palestine*, Boulder, CO: Westview Press, 1978, p. 92.

58. Sourani, *Qita Ghazza 1948–1993*, p. 35.

59. Sayigh, Yezid, *Armed Struggle and the Search for the State*, Oxford: Oxford University Press, 1997, p. 287.

60. Ibid.

61. *Jerusalem Post*, 1 Jan. 1971.

62. Despatch from Consul-General of France in Jerusalem, 18 Nov. 1970, 351/AL.

63. Lesch, 'Deportation of Palestinians from the West Bank and Gaza', p. 104.

64. O'Neill, *Armed Struggle in Palestine*, p. 94.

65. Sharon, Ariel, *Warrior*, New York: Simon and Schuster, 1989, pp. 250–1.

66. O'Neill, *Armed Struggle in Palestine*, p. 94.

67. Lesch, Ann Mosely, 'Gaza: History and Politics', in Lesch, Ann Mosely and Mark Tessler (eds), *Israel, Egypt and the Palestinians*, Bloomington, IN: Indiana University Press, 1989, p. 230.

68. O'Neill, *Armed Struggle in Palestine*, p. 96.

69. Haïk, Daniel, *Sharon, un destin inachevé*, Paris; L'Archipel, 2006, p. 95.

70. Lesch, 'Deportation of Palestinians from the West Bank and Gaza', p. 104.

71. For a chronological account and the areas concerned, on the basis of reports in the Palestinian press, see Azaar, *Al-muqawama fi qita' Ghazza, 1967–1975*, pp. 162–75.

72. Interview with Eyad al-Sarraj, Gaza, 6 Nov. 2010.

73. Sayigh, *Armed Struggle and the Search for the State*, p. 287.

74. Haïk, *Sharon, un destin inachevé*, p. 95.

75. Faysal, *A'lam min jil al-ruwad min Ghazzatu Hashem*, p. 440.

76. Sayigh, Yezid, *Armed Struggle and the Search for the State*, p. 287.

77. Lesch, 'Gaza: History and Politics', p. 230.

78. Shachar, Nathan, *The Gaza Strip: Its History and Politics*, Eastbourne: Sussex Academic Press, 2010, p. 81.

79. Interview with Misbha Saqr and Ghazi Sourani, Gaza, 10 Nov. 2010.

80. *Haaretz*, 7 Jan. 1972.

81. Sharon, *Warrior*, p. 258.

82. Ibid. pp. 259–60.

83. Lesch, 'Gaza: History and Politics', p. 229.

9. THE ERA OF THE NOTABLES

1. The defence portfolio had traditionally been held by the Israeli prime minister—the only previous exception to this rule had been under the government of Moshe Sharett, from January 1954 to February 1955, when Pinhas Lavon had held the post. Ben Gurion, Israel's first prime minister, had been his own defence minister from 1948 to 1954 and from 1955 to 1963, and Eshkol had followed the same practice until the moment when he asked Dayan to step in.

2. Cramer, Richard Ben, *How Israel Lost*, New York: Simon and Schuster, 2004, p. 59.

3. Interview with Mordechai Bar-On, Jerusalem, 13 Nov. 2010.

4. Dayan, Moshe, *Story of My Life*, London: Weidenfeld and Nicolson, 1976, pp. 330–2.

5. Lesch, Ann Mosely, 'Gaza: History and Politics', in Lesch, Ann Mosely and Mark Tessler (eds), *Israel, Egypt and the Palestinians*, Bloomington, IN: Indiana University Press, 1989, p. 230.

6. Dayan, *Story of My Life*, p. 327.

7. Interview with Rawya Shawa, Gaza, 7 Nov. 2010.

8. http://www.al-monitor.com/pulse/originals/2013/02/cinema-gaza-demise.html# (accessed 24 Jan. 2014).

9. Interview with Ghazi Sourani, 10 Nov. 2010.

10. Lesch, 'Gaza: History and Politics', p. 231.

11. Shlaim, Avi, *The Iron Fist*, London: Allen Lane, The Penguin Press, 2000, pp. 255–7.

12. King Hussein, broadcasting on Amman Radio, 15 Mar. 1972: text in Lukacs, Yehuda (ed.), *The Israeli–Palestinian Conflict: A Documentary Record*, Cambridge: Cambridge University Press, 1992, p. 461.

13. Filiu, Jean-Pierre, *Mitterrand et la Palestine*, Paris: Fayard, 2005, p. 38.

14. Shlaim, Avi, *Lion of Jordan*, London: Allen Lane, the Penguin Press, 2007, pp. 348–9.

15. Ibid. pp. 343–4.

16. Shemesh, Moshe, *The Palestinian Entity 1959–1974: Arab Politics and the PLO*, London: Frank Cass, 1988, p. 263.

17. Dayan, *The Story of My Life*, p. 328.

18. Lesch, 'Gaza: History and Politics', p. 231.

19. Interview with Ghazi Sourani, Gaza, 10 Nov. 2010.

20. Lesch, 'Gaza: History and Politics', p. 232.

21. Shemesh, *The Palestinian Entity*, p. 261.

22. Interview with Misbah Saqr, Gaza, 10 Nov. 2010.

23. Shemesh, *The Palestinian Entity*, pp. 262–3.

24. Faysal, Numan Abdelhadi, *A'lam min jil al-ruwad min Ghazzatu Hashem*, Gaza: Dar al-Duktur, 2010, p. 434.

25. Lesch, Ann Mosely, 'Deportation of Palestinians from the West Bank and the Gaza Strip', *Journal of Palestine Studies*, 8, 2 (Winter 1979), p. 104.

26. Yassin, Abdelqadir, *'Umr fi al-manfa*, Damascus: Dar al-Wataniyya al-Jadida, 2009, p. 84.

27. *Palestine Lives*, Beirut: Centre for Palestinian Research, 1973, p. 78.

28. Faysal, *A'lam min jil al-ruwad min Ghazzatu Hashem*, p. 61.

29. Ibid. p. 169.

30. Hilal, Jamil, 'Class Transformation in the West Bank and Gaza', *Journal of Palestine Studies*, 5, 2 (Winter 1977), p. 172.

31. Published on 13 Aug. 1973 in *Al-Hurriyeh* (the organ of the Democratic Front for the liberation of Palestine (DFLP)), text in *Journal of Palestine Studies*, 3, 1 (Autumn 1973), pp. 187–9.

32. Yassin, Abdelqadir, *Umr fi al-manfà*, p. 84.

33. 'Political Program Adopted at the 12th Session of the Palestine National Council, Cairo, 8 June 1974, State of Palestine, Permanent Observer Mission to the United Nations', http://www.un.int/wcm/content/site/palestine/pid/12354 (accessed 24 Jan. 2014).

34. 'Seventh Arab League Summit Conference, Resolution on Palestine', Rabat, Morocco 28 Oct. 1974, http://unispal.un.org/UNISPAL.NSF/0/63D9A930E2 B428DF852572C0006D06B8 (accessed 24 Jan. 2014).

35. http://en.wikisource.org/wiki/Yasser_Arafat%27s_1974_UN_General_ Assembly_speech (accessed 24 Jan. 2014).

36. Lesch, 'Gaza: History and Politics', p. 232.

37. Tamimi, Azzam, *Hamas: Unwritten Chapters*, London: Hurst, 2007, p. 36.

38. Dumper, Michael, *Islam and Israel*, Washington, DC: Institute of Palestine Studies, 1994, p. 97.

39. Enderlin, Charles, *Le grand aveuglement*, Paris: Albin Michel, 2009, p. 53.

40. Abu Amir, Adnan, *Al-haraka al-islamiyya fi qita Ghazza*, op. cit., p. 48. *Al-Mujamma' al-islami* could also be translated as 'Islamic Centre' or 'Islamic Union'. In practice, the Arabic word *mujamma'* relates to the idea of a network as much as to a centre. It is elsewhere used to refer to a 'complex' (administrative or industrial).

41. Milton-Edwards, Beverley and Stephen Farrell, *Hamas: The Islamic Resistance Movement*, Cambridge: Polity Press, 2010, p. 40.

42. Falluji, Imad, *Ma'a al-ra'is*, Amman: Dar al-Shuruk, n.d., 2009, pp. 25–6.

43. Roy, Sara, *Hamas and Civil Society in Gaza*, Princeton, NJ: Princeton University Press, 2011, p. 74.

44. Abu Amir, Adnan, *Al-haraka al-islamiyya fi qita Ghazza*, p. 48.

45. Ibid. p. 36.

46. Ibid. p. 35.

47. Faysal, *A'lam min jil al-ruwad min Ghazzatu Hashem*, p. 398.

48. Lesch, Ann Mosely, 'Israeli Settlements in the Occupied Territories', *Journal of Palestine Studies*, 7 (Autumn 1977), pp. 26–47.

49. Sourani, Ghazi, *Qita Ghazza 1948–1993*, Damascus: Centre for Popular Studies, 1993, p. 35.

50. Hilal, 'Class Transformation in the West Bank and Gaza', p. 169.

51. Interview with Mohieddin Harara (Abu Musa), Gaza, 7 Nov. 2010.

52. Shachar, Nathan, *The Gaza Strip: Its History and Politics*, Eastbourne: Sussex Academic Press, 2010, p. 94.

10. THE ALIEN PEACE

1. 'Joint Statement by the Governments of the US and the USSR', 1 Oct. 1977, text quoted in Lukacs, Yehuda, *The Israeli–Palestinian Conflict: A Documentary Record 1967–1990*, Cambridge: Cambridge University Press, 1992, p. 16.

2. Boltanski, Christophe and Jihane Tahri, *Les Sept Vies de Yasser Arafat*, Paris: Grasset, 1997, p. 244.

3. Lesch, Ann Mosely, 'Gaza: History and Politics', in Lesch, Ann Mosely and Mark Tessler (eds), *Israel, Egypt and the Palestinians*, Bloomington, IN: Indiana University Press, 1989, p. 233.

4. Interview with Freih Abu Middain, 9 Nov. 2010.

5. Text in *Al-Ahram*, 6 July 1978.

6. Flapan, Simha, *When Enemies Dare to Talk*, London: Croom Helm, 1979, p. 83.

7. Ibid. pp. 81–2.

8. Ibid. p. 82.

9. Lukacs, *The Israeli–Palestinian Conflict*, pp. 156–8.

10. The Camp David Accords, 25 Sep. 1978, contributions by Menachem Begin to Knesset debate: see http://www.jewishvirtuallibrary.org/jsource/Politics/knesset-debatestoc.html (accessed 24 Jan. 2014).

11. English translation in *Journal of Palestine Studies*, 8, 2 (Winter 1979), p. 200.

12. Laurens, Henry, *La question de Palestine (vol. 4, 1967–1982)*, Paris: Fayard, 2011, p. 697.

13. English translation in *Journal of Palestine Studies*, 8, 4 (Summer 1979), pp. 126–7.

14. Lesch, 'Gaza: History and Politics', p. 234.

15. Interview with Rashad Shawa in the Beirut paper *Monday Morning*, 21 Jan. 1980.

16. Grimblat, François, 'La communauté chiite libanaise et le mouvement national palestinien', *Revue d'histoire des conflits contemporains* (Summer 1988), p. 80.

17. Interview with Rabah Mohanna, Gaza, 5 Nov. 2010.

18. Abu Amir, *Al-haraka al-islamiyya fi qita Ghazza*, Cairo: Markaz al-a'lam al arabi, 2006, p. 19.

19. Tamimi, Azzam, *Hamas: Unwritten Chapters*, London: Hurst, 2007, p. 41.

20. Enderlin, Charles, *Le grand aveuglement*, Paris: Albin Michel, 2009, p. 86.

21. Milton-Edwards, Beverley, *Islamic Politics in Palestine*, London: I.B. Tauris, 1996, p. 107.

22. Ibid. p. 106.

23. Ibid. p. 107.

24. Enderlin, *Le grand aveuglement*, p. 86.

25. Falluji, Imad, *Ma'a al-ra'is*, Amman: Dar al-Shuruk, n.d., 2009, p. 27.

26. Milton-Edwards Beverley, *Islamic Politics in Palestine*, London: I.B. Tauris, 1996, p. 110.

27. Mishal, Shaul and Avraham Sela, *The Palestinian Hamas*, New York: Columbia University Press, 2000, p. 20.

28. Interview with Sabha Barbari, Gaza, Nov. 2010.

29. Interview with 'Ismain' in Cossali, Paul and Clive Robson, *Stateless in Gaza*, London: Zed Books, 1986, p. 73.

30. *Yediot Aharonot*, 12 Dec. 1979.

31. Laurens, *La Question de Palestine*, vol. 4, p. 733.

32. Enderlin, *Le grand aveuglement*, p. 92.
33. Ibid. p. 79.
34. Ibid. p. 93.
35. Lesch, Ann Mosely, 'Gaza, Life Under Occupation', in Lesch, Ann Mosely and Mark Tessler (eds), *Israel, Egypt and the Palestinians*, Bloomington, IN: Indiana University Press, 1989, p. 241.
36. Doughty, Dick and Mohammad El-Aydi, *Gaza: Legacy of Occupation—A Photographer's Journey*, Hartford, CT: Kumarian Press, 1995, xxii–xxix.
37. Witness statement by 'Tariq' in Cossali and Robson, *Stateless in Gaza*, London: Zed Books, 1986, p. 81.
38. Lesch, 'Gaza: Life Under Occupation', p. 239.

11. THE NEW WAVE

1. Quoted in Filiu, Jean-Pierre, *Mitterrand et la Palestine*, Paris: Fayard, 2005, p. 101.
2. Ibid. p. 146.
3. Report of the Kahan Commission, http://www.mfa.gov.il/mfa/foreignpolicy/mfadocuments/yearbook6/pages/104%20report%20of%20the%20commission%20of%20inquiry%20into%20the%20e.aspx (accessed 24 Jan. 2014).
4. Razoux, Pierre, *Tsahal*, Paris: Tempus, 2008, p. 414.
5. Mishal, Shaul and Avraham Sela, *The Palestinian Hamas*, New York: Columbia University Press, 2000, p. 414.
6. See the eye-witness statement by Bassam (the 'bad Muslim') in Milton-Edwards, Beverley, *Islamic Politics in Palestine*, London: I.B. Tauris, 1996, pp. 113–14.
7. Abu Amr, Ziad, *Islamic Fundamentalism in the West Bank and Gaza*, Bloomington, IN: Indiana University Press, 1994, p. 43.
8. Legrain, Jean-François, 'Islamistes et lutte nationale palsestinienne dans les territoires occupées par Israël', *Revue française de science politique*, 36, 2 (1986), p. 231.
9. *Al-Hamishmar*, 27 July 1984.
10. Shikaki, Fathi, *Rihlat al-dam alladhi hazama al-seyf*, Cairo: Marzaka Yafa, 1996, p. 349.
11. Filiu, Jean-Pierre, *Apocalypse in Islam*, Berkeley (CA): University of California Press, pp. 100–101.
12. Shikaki, *Rihlat al-dam alladhi hazama al-seyf*, p. 172.
13. Enderlin, Charles, *Le grand aveuglement*, Paris: Albin Michel, 2009, p. 114.
14. Faysal, Numan Abdelhadi, *A'lam min jil al-ruwad min Ghazzatu Hashem*, Gaza: Dar al-Duktur, 2010, p. 542.
15. Hatina, Meir, *Islam and Salvation in Palestine*, Tel Aviv: Moshe Dayan Center, 2001, p. 65.
16. *Time*, 9 June 1986.

17. Milton-Edwards, *Islamic Politics in Palestine*, p. 114.
18. Hatina, *Islam and Salvation in Palestine*, p. 78.
19. Enderlin, *Le grand aveuglement*, p. 117.
20. Rantissi, Mohamed, *Survivre à Gaza*, Monaco: Koutoubia-Alphée, 2009, p. 171.
21. Abu Amir, *Al-haraka al-islamiyya fi qita Ghazza*, p. 79.
22. Mishal and Sela, *The Palestinian Hamas*, p. 24.
23. Interview with 'Sharaf' (an Islamist informer), quoted in Cossali, Paul and Clive Robson, *Stateless in Gaza*, London: Zed Books, 1986, p. 110.
24. For an account of contemporary Salafism where the Muslim Brothers are classified as 'reformist Salafists', see Rougier, Bernard, *Qu'est-ce que le salafisme*, Paris: PUF, 2008, pp. 15–19.
25. Mishal and Sela, *The Palestinian Hamas*, p. 34.
26. Sinwar, Yahya, *Al-Majd*, Gaza: Waeed, 2009, p. 455.
27. Enderlin, *Le grand aveuglement*, pp. 113–17.
28. Lesch, Ann Mosely, 'Gaza: Life Under Occupation', in Lesch, Ann Mosely and Mark Tessler (eds), *Israel, Egypt and the Palestinians*, Bloomington, IN: Indiana University Press, 1989, p. 251.
29. Filiu, Jean-Pierre, *Mitterrand et la Palestine*, Paris: Fayard, 2005, p. 243.
30. *Jewish Telegraphic Agency*, 22 Mar. 1985.
31. Interview with Rabah Mohanna, Gaza, 5 Nov. 2010.
32. Interview with Fayez Abu Rahmeh, *Journal of Palestine Studies*, 15, 1 (Autumn 1985), p. 13.
33. *Los Angeles Times*, 5 Aug. 1985.
34. Abu Amr, *Islamic Fundamentalism in the West Bank and Gaza*, p. 46; Abu Amir, *Al-haraka al-islamiyya fi qita Ghazza*, op. cit., p. 97.
35. Enderlin, *Le grand aveuglement*, p. 139.
36. Sinwar, *Al-Majd*, p. 449.
37. Mishal and Sela, *The Palestinian Hamas*, p. 34.
38. *Al-Fajr*, 13 Mar. 1987.
39. Lesch, Ann Mosely, 'Prelude to the Uprising in the Gaza Strip', *Journal of Palestine Studies*, 20, 1 (Autumn 1990), p. 17.
40. Abu Amr, *Islamic Fundamentalism in the West Bank and Gaza*, p. 48.
41. Schiff, Zeev and Ehud Yaari, *Intifada*, New York: Simon and Schuster, 1990, p. 30.
42. Interview with Rabah Mohanna, Gaza, 5 Nov. 2010.
43. Vitullo, Anita, 'Uprising in Gaza', in Lockman, Zachary and Joel Beinin (eds), *Intifada*, Boston, MA: MERIP, 2009, p. 45.
44. Lesch, 'Prelude to the Uprising in the Gaza Strip', p. 19.
45. Interview with Ahmed (Sheikh) Yassin, *Al-Fajr*, 6 Sep. 1987.
46. Lesch, 'Prelude to the Uprising in the Gaza Strip', p. 9.
47. Ibid. p. 1.

48. Abu Amr, Ziad, 'Hamas: A Historical and Political Background', *Journal of Palestine Studies*, 22, 4 (Summer 1993), p. 10.

49. Document 'Tract HMS01', French translation in Legrain, Jean-François, *Les voix du soulèvement palestinien*, Cairo: CEDEJ, 1991, p. 7.

50. Roy, Sara, 'The Gaza Strip: A Case of Economic De-Development', *Journal of Palestine Studies*, 7, 1 (Autumn 1987), p. 68.

51. Ibid. p. 70.

52. Benvenisti, Meron and Shlomo Khayat, *The West Bank and Gaza Atlas*, Boulder, CO: Westview, 1988, p. 113.

53. Roy, 'The Gaza Strip', pp. 69, 82.

12. THE REVOLT OF THE STONES

1. Document 'Tract CNUGZ', issued *c*.10 Jan. 1988, French translation in Legrain, Jean-François, *Les voix du soulèvement palestinien*, Cairo: CEDEJ, 1991, p. 13.

2. Ibid. p. 10.

3. Quoted in Legrain, *Les voix du soulèvement palestinien*, p. 257.

4. Ibid., introduction, p. 84.

5. *Associated Press*, London, 6 Jan. 1988.

6. Frachon, Alain, 'A Gaza, le lent pourrissement', *Le Monde*, 12 Jan. 1988.

7. President Mitterrand, speaking to Irish TV, 24 Feb. 1988.

8. *Time*, 13 June 1988.

9. *Uprising in Palestine: The First Year*, Chicago: Palestinian Human Rights International Committee, 1989, p. 15.

10. *Le Monde*, 19 Apr. 1988.

11. Agence France Presse, Gaza, 25 May 1988.

12. Interview with Rawya Shawa, Gaza, 7 Nov. 2010.

13. Document 'Tract HMS04', 11 Feb. 1988, French translation in Legrain, *Les voix du soulèvement palestinien*.

14. 'Hamas Charter': English translation in Mishal, Shaul and Avraham Sela, *The Palestinian Hamas*, New York: Columbia University Press, 2000, Appendix 2, pp. 176–99.

15. Ibid., Chapter 3, Article 11, p. 181. The identity of the Charter's editor remains unclear. While it is possible that he was a Gaza-based religious scholar commissioned by Sheikh Yassin to perform this task, others conjecture that the document was written by Abdelfattah Dukhan, a founder member of the Mujamma who then joined Hamas. For the former view see Hroub, Khaled, *Hamas: A Beginner's Guide*, London: Pluto Press, 2006, p. 33; for the latter see Tamimi, Azzam, *Hamas: Unwritten Chapters*, London: Hurst, 2007, p. 150.

16. 'Hamas Charter', in Mishal and Sela, *The Palestinian Hamas*, Chapter 3, Article 22, p. 189.

17. Ibid.
18. Document 'Tract CNU30', 7 Dec. 1988: French translation in Legrain, *Les voix du soulèvement palestinien*, p. 167.
19. Documents 'Tract CNU28A', 'Tract CNU28B' and 'Tract CNU28D', 30 Oct. 1988: French translations in Legrain, *Les voix du soulèvement palestinien*, pp. 203, 207 and 210.
20. Document 'Tract CNU30', 7 Dec. 1988: French translation in Legrain, *Les voix du soulèvement palestinien*, p. 229
21. Document 'Tract HMS32', 25 Nov. 1988: French translation in Legrain, *Les voix du soulèvement palestinien*, p. 227.
22. *Uprising in Palestine: The First Year*, pp. 13–21.
23. For Mabhouh's account of these two murders, see Al-Jazeera, 7 Feb. 2010, http://english.aljazeera.net/focus/2010/02/2010271441269105.html (accessed 30 Jan. 2014).
24. Tamimi, *Hamas: Unwritten Chapters*, p. 59.
25. Mishal and Sela, *The Palestinian Hamas*, p. 57.
26. Tamimi, *Hamas: Unwritten Chapters*, p. 60.
27. McGeough, Paul, *Kill Khalid*, New York: New Press, 2009, p. 116.
28. Tamimi, *Hamas: Unwritten Chapters*, p. 61.
29. For a detailed discussion of Hamas's internal administration based on various sources, see Gunning, Jeroen, *Hamas in Politics*, New York: Columbia University Press, 2009, pp. 98–103.
30. Figures from the Israeli civil administration, quoted in *Journal of Palestine Studies*, 19, 4 (Summer 1990), pp. 197–8.
31. Report of Swedish 'Save the Children', quoted in *Journal of Palestine Studies*, 19, 4 (Summer 1990), pp. 144–5.
32. Interview with Freih Abu Middain, Gaza, 9 Nov. 2010.
33. Roy, Sara, *Failing Peace*, London: Pluto Press, 2007, p. 94.
34. Tamimi, *Hamas: Unwritten Chapters*, p. 73.
35. Interview with Freih Abu Middain, Gaza, 9 Nov. 2010.
36. Roy, *Failing Peace*, pp. 43–5.
37. Hass, Amira, 'Otherwise Occupied; Access Denied', *Haaretz*, 22 Apr. 2010.
38. Israeli Ministry of Foreign Affairs, Reference Documents: http://www.mfa.gov.il/MFA/ForeignPolicy/Peace/MFADocuments/Pages/ADDRESS%20BY%20DR%20HAIDER%20ABDUL%20SHAFI-%20-%2031-Oct-91.aspx (accessed 24 Jan. 2014).
39. Ibid. p. 44.
40. For a long period of time, the brigades only had access to around twenty Swedish Carl-Gustav submachine guns. Chehab, Zaki, *Inside Hamas*, New York: Nation Books, 2007, p. 43.
41. Ibid. p. 45.

42. Milton-Edwards, Beverley and Stephen Farrell, *Hamas*, Cambridge: Polity Press, 2010, p. 119.

43. Lia, Brynjar, *A Police Force Without a State*, Reading: Ithaca Press, 2006, p. 68.

44. Chehab, *Inside Hamas*, pp. 45–9.

45. The vote took place during the transition period between the Republican administration of George H. Bush and that of the Democrat Bill Clinton, who had been elected in November but under the American constitution would not take office until January 1993.

46. *Maariv*, 5 Mar. 1993.

47. *New York Times*, 3 Mar. 1993.

48. *Al-Quds*, 10 July 1993.

49. *Yediot Aharonot*, 7 Sep. 1993.

50. http://unispal.un.org/UNISPAL.NSF/0/CF5061346A6DAEC58525610700 7825C7 (accessed 24 Jan. 2014).

51. *New York Times*, 23 Sep. 1993.

52. Chehab, *Inside Hamas*, p. 50.

53. Doughty, Richard and Muhammad El Aydi, *Gaza: Legacy of Occupation—A Photographer's Journey*, Boulder, CO: Kumarian Press, 1995, p. 191.

54. Roy, *Failing Peace*, p. 152.

13. A SHARPLY LIMITED AUTHORITY

1. Article 1 and Article 8 of the Oslo Declaration of Principles, Final Draft (19 Aug. 1993), signed in Washington, DC, 13 Sep. 1993. [This document is frequently referred to as one of the Oslo Accords together with the mutual recognition of Israel and the PLO.] See King, John, *Handshake in Washington: The Beginning of Middle East Peace*, Reading: Ithaca Press, 1994, Appendix, pp. 208–10.

2. Bucaille, Laetitia, *Gaza: la violence de la paix*, Paris: Presses de Sciences Po, 1998, p. 53.

3. Legrain, Jean-François, 'The Autonomous Palestinian Government', in Picaudou, Nadine and Isabelle Rivoal (eds), *Retours en Palestine: Trajectoires, rôle et expériences des retournées dans la société palestinienne après Oslo*, Paris: Karthala, 2006, pp. 44–117, 243–80.

4. Article 5 of the interim accord signed in Cairo on 4 May 1994 by Yasser Arafat and Yitzhak Rabin, http://www.knesset.gov.il/process/docs/cairo_agreement_eng. htm (accessed 29 Jan. 2014).

5. Boltanski, Christophe and Jihane Tahri, *Les Sept Vies de Yasser Arafat*, Paris: Grasset, 1997, pp. 55–6.

6. Almog, Doron, 'Lessons of the Gaza Security Fence for the West Bank', *Jerusalem Issue Briefs*, 4, 12 (23 Dec. 2004).

7. Quoted in *Journal of Palestine Studies*, 24, 1 (Autumn 1994), p. 165.

8. There were also some curious sidelights: for example, thousands of police uniforms donated by Japan to the Gaza police in 1994 were all too small and were ultimately given to schoolchildren!

9. Falluji, Imad, *Ma'a al-ra'is*, Amman: Dar al-Shuruk, n.d., p. 46.

10. Ibid. p. 65.

11. Bucaille, *Gaza: la violence de la paix*, p. 79.

12. Lia, Brynjar, *Building Arafat's Police*, New York: Ithaca Press, 2007, p. 170.

13. Quoted in *Journal of Palestine Studies*, 24, 4 (Summer 1995), p. 187.

14. Bucaille, *Gaza: la violence de la paix*, p. 60.

15. Ibid. p. 63.

16. Interview with Freih Abu Middain, Gaza, 9 Nov. 2010.

17. Katz, Samuel, *The Hunt for the Engineer*, New York: Fromm, 1999, pp. 242–3.

18. Falluji, *Ma'a al-Ra'is*, p. 83.

19. Gunning, Jeroen, *Hamas in Politics*, New York: Columbia University Press, 2009, pp. 110–12.

20. Bucaille, *Gaza: la violence de la paix*, p. 71.

21. Legrain, Jean-François, *La Palestine du quotidien*, Beirut: CERMOC, 1999, p. 82.

22. Ibid. p. 364

23. Ibid. p. 389.

24. Bucaille, *Gaza: la violence de la paix*, p. 71.

25. Chirac, Jacques, *Le temps présidentiel. Mémoires, tome II*, Paris: Nil, 2011, p. 186.

26. *A Comprehensive Survey of Israeli Settlements in the Gaza Strip*, Gaza: Palestinian Centre for Human Rights, 1996, pp. 58–85.

27. For the best account, see McGeough, Paul, *Kill Khalid*, New York: New Press, 2009, p. 241.

28. Ibid.

29. Bucaille, *Gaza: la violence de la paix*, p. 60.

30. *New York Times*, 17 July 1999.

31. Hass, Amira, 'Trapped in the Cage of Gaza', *Haaretz*, 14 Oct. 2000.

32. Cohen, Samy, *Tsahal and the Test of Terrorism*, Paris: Le Seuil, 2009, pp. 158–9.

14. DAYS OF FURY

1. Hass, Amira, 'Trapped in the Cage of Gaza', *Haaretz*, 14 Oct. 2000. For an English translation see 'From the Hebrew Press', *Journal of Palestine Studies*, 30, 2 (Winter 2000), pp. 98–107.

2. Cohen, Samy, *Tsahal à l'épreuve du terrorisme*, op. cit., p. 143.

3. Filiu, Jean-Pierre, *Mitterrand et la Palestine*, Paris: Fayard, 2005, pp. 133–4.

4. Almog, Doron, 'Lessons of the Gaza Security Fence for the West Bank', *Jerusalem Issue Briefs*, 4, 12 (23 Dec. 2004).

5. For a study of the relations between al-Qaida and the Muslim Brotherhood, espe-

cially Hamas, see Filiu, Jean-Pierre, 'The Brotherhood Versus Al-Qaida', *Current Trends in Islamist Ideology*, 9 (Autumn 2009).

6. *The Guardian*, 14 Sep. 2001.
7. *Washington Times*, 11 Nov. 2001.
8. *Washington Post*, 17 Dec. 2001.
9. *Maariv*, 31 Jan. 2002.
10. For the definitive account of this group, see Legrain, Jean-François, *Internet et histoire: les brigades de martyrs d'Al-Aqsa. Pages d'internet comme source de l'histoire du temps présent*, Lyon: Maison de l'Orient et de la Méditerranée, 2004, http://www.mom.fr/guides/aqsa/aqsa.htm (accessed 29 Jan. 2014).
11. *Ayyam al-ghadab* [published by Hamas], p. 26.
12. Tshahal statement of 10 Feb. 2002, quoted by Israeli Ministry of Foreign Affairs. See http://mfa.gov.il/MFA/PressRoom/2002/Pages/Palestinians%20launch%20rockets%20at%20Israel%20-%2010-Feb-200.aspx (accessed 29 Jan. 2014).
13. *New York Times*, 22 June 2002.
14. *Washington Post*, 7 Dec. 2002.
15. *Middle East Mirror*, 9 Jan. 2004.
16. *Washington Post*, 25 Jan. 2004.
17. *New York Times*, 3 Feb. 2004.
18. Hroub, Khaled, 'Hamas after Shaykh Yasin and Rantisi', *Journal of Palestine Studies*, 33, 4 (Summer 2004), pp. 35–6.
19. *Al-Rai*, 18 July 2004.
20. *Jerusalem Post*, 18 July 2004.
21. *Ayyam al-Ghadab*, pp. 55, 66, 88, 97 and 113.

15. ONE PALESTINE AGAINST ANOTHER

1. *Haaretz*, 6 Oct. 2004.
2. Qureia, Ahmed [Abu Ala], *Al-tariq ila kharitat al-tariq*, Beirut: Institute for Palestinian Studies, 2011, p. 367.
3. William Ward, evidence, Senate Foreign Relations Committee, 30 June 2005.
4. Levitt, Matthew, *Hamas: Politics, Charity and Terrorism in the Service of Jihad*, New Haven, CT: Yale University Press, 2007, p. 95.
5. *Haaretz*, 19 Dec. 2005.
6. Usher, Graham, 'The Democratic Resistance', *Journal of Palestine Studies*, 35, 3 (Spring 2006), p. 27.
7. Quartet Statement, issued in London, 30 Jan. 2006. See http://www.un.org/news/dh/infocus/middle_east/quartet-30jan2006.htm (accessed 29 Jan. 2014).
8. Interview with Ismail Haniya, *Washington Post*, 26 Feb. 2006.
9. http://unispal.un.org/UNISPAL.NSF/0/CE3ABE1B2E1502B58525717A006194CD (accessed 29 Jan. 2014).

10. Telegram from US Embassy, Tel Aviv, and US Consulate General, Jerusalem, 14 June 2006: see WikiLeaks 6 Jan. 2011.
11. Poll carried out on 6–7 July by Jerusalem Media and Communication Centre, http://www.jmcc.org/ (accessed 29 Jan. 2014).
12. Figures given in *Journal of Palestine Studies*, 36, 1 (Autumn 2006), p. 124.
13. Chirac, Jacques, *Le temps presidentiel. Mémoires, tome II*, Paris: Nil, 2011, pp. 518, 521.
14. Poll of 1,279 Gaza and West Bank inhabitants taken on 14 and 16 Sep. 2006 by the Palestine Centre for Policy and Survey Research, www.pcpsr.org (accessed 29 Jan. 2014).
15. Letter of appointment to Ismail Haniya, signed by Mahmoud Abbas, 7 Feb. 2007, http://www.alzaytouna.net/en/resources/documents/palestinian-docu-ments/109086-mecca-agreement-amp-program-of-the-palestinian-unity-govern-ment-2007.html (accessed 29 Jan. 2014).
16. Poll of 1,197 inhabitants of the West Bank and Gaza conducted between 22 and 24 Feb. 2007 by the Development Studies Programme of the University of Bir Zeit: home.birzeit.edu/dsp (accessed 29 Jan. 2014).
17. *Haaretz*, 7 June 2007.
18. Barthe, Benjamin, *Ramallah Dream*, Paris: La Découverte, 2011, p. 183.
19. Ibid.
20. Interview with Freih Abu Middain, Gaza, 9 Nov. 2010.
21. Figures cited in *Journal of Palestine Studies*, 37, 1 (Autumn 2007), p. 149.
22. Ibid.
23. *El Pais*, 20 Dec. 2010, p. 3.
24. See: 'Disengaged Occupiers: The Legal Status of Gaza', Gisha [NGO based in Israel], Jan. 2007, www.gisha.org (accessed 29 Jan. 2014).
25. Figures from the Israeli human rights organisation B'Tselem: http://www.btselem.org/statistics (accessed 29 Jan. 2014).
26. Palestinian Centre for Human Rights, annual report, 2007, www.pchrgaza.org/files/Reports/English [Ann-Rep-07-Eng.pdf] (accessed 29 Jan. 2014).

16. FIVE YEARS IN THE RUINS

1. Statement by Ehud Olmert's spokesperson, Jerusalem, 19 Sep. 2007.
2. Institut d'Etudes Palestiniennes, *Coulée de plomb*, Arles: Sinbad/Actes Sud, 2010, p. 171.
3. These figures are reported by the Israeli human rights organisation, B'Tselem: http://www.btselem.org/gaza_strip/castlead_operation (accessed 29 Jan. 2014).
4. The organisation in question is the Palestinian Committee for Human Rights (PCHR). See 'Rights Group Names 1417 Gaza War Dead', *Washington Times*, 19 Mar. 2009. PCHR report published on 12 Mar. 2009: http://www.pchrgaza.

org/portal/en/index.php?option=com_content&view=article&id=1073:confir med-figures-reveal-the-true-extent-of-the-destruction-inflicted-upon-the-gaza-strip-israels-offensive-resulted-in-1417-dead-including-926-civilians-255-police-officers-and-236-fighters&catid=36:pchrpressreleases&Itemid=194 (accessed 29 Jan. 2014).

5. http://www.jpost.com/Israel/IDF-709-of-1166-killed-in-Cast-Lead-identifed-as-Hamas-terror-operatives (accessed 29 Jan. 2014).

6. International Crisis Group, 'Gaza's Unfinished Business', Brussels, 23 Apr. 2009.

7. Issa, Ibrahim, *Al-maqalat al-ghazawiyya*, Cairo: Madbouli, 2009, p. 69.

8. Institut d'Etudes Palestiniennes, *Coulée de plomb*, pp. 213–16.

9. Harel, Amos, 'IDF in Gaza', *Haaretz*, 19 Mar. 2009.

10. http://sderotmedia.org.il/bin/content.cgi?ID=422&q=3 (accessed 29 Jan. 2014).

11. Barthe, Benjamin and Laurent Zecchini, 'Les cinq années de tractations secrètes pour libérer Gilad Shalit', *Le Monde*, 19 Oct. 2011.

12. A documentary film entitled *Rue Abu Jamil* was made in Rafah in 2009 by Alexis Monchovet and Stéphane Marchetti (broadcast by LCP in France in 2010).

13. See the weekly reports for 8 and 15 Sep. 2009 published by the United Nations Agency OCHA (Office for the Coordination of Humanitarian Affairs). OCHA: http://www.ochaopt.org/reports.aspx?id=104 (accessed 29 Jan. 2014).

14. OCHA Weekly Report, 2 July 2010, http://www.ochaopt.org/reports.aspx?id=104 (accessed 29 Jan. 2014)

15. OCHA Weekly Report, 7 Jan. 2011, http://www.ochaopt.org/reports.aspx?id=104 (accessed 29 Jan. 2014).

16. Quoted by Barthe, B. and L. Zecchini, 'Les cinq années de tractations secrètes pour libérer Gilad Shalit', *Le Monde*, 19 Oct. 2011.

17. Cohen, Yoram and Jeffrey White, *Hamas in Combat* (Policy Focus 97), Washington, DC: Washington Institute for Near East Policy, 2009.

18. Zecchini, Laurent, 'Esthète pour la cause', *Le Monde*, 3 Feb. 2010; and *passim* elsewhere, for example, the interview with Nicolas Sarkozy in the Kuwaiti newspaper *Al-Qabas*, 11 Feb. 2009, quoted at the opening of this book.

19. 'Gaza sous perfusion', *Le Devoir*, 26 June 2007.

20. Roy, Sara, *Failing Peace*, London: Pluto Press, 2007, p. 33. See also Roy, Sara, 'Gaza: The Political Economy of De-Development', Washington, DC: Institute of Palestine Studies, 1995.

21. This expression is the coinage of Benjamin Barthe: see Barthe, Benjamin, *Ramallah Dream*, Paris: La Découverte, 2011, p. 225.

22. Le More, Anne, 'Killing with Kindness: Funding the Demise of a Palestinian State', *International Affairs*, 81, 5 (2005), p. 995.

23. Amnesty International, 'Israel/Occupied Territories; Gaza Blockade—Collective Punishment', 4 July 2008. http://www.amnesty.org/en/library/info/MDE15/021/2008/en (accessed 29 Jan. 2014).

24. Roy, *Failing Peace*, p. 133.
25. Roy, Sara, *Hamas and Civil Society in Gaza*, Princeton, NJ: Princeton University Press, 2011, p. 217.
26. Zecchini Laurent, 'Dans les décombres de Gaza', *Le Monde*, 21 Mar. 2010.
27. Roy, *Hamas and Civil Society in Gaza*, p. 231.
28. Ibid. p. 233.
29. Clarens, Katia, *Une saison à Gaza*, Paris: Jean-Claude Lattès, 2011, pp. 167–8.
30. Gilbert, Mads and Erik Fosse, *Eyes in Gaza*, London: Quartet, 2010, pp. 242, 245.
31. Roy, *Hamas and Civil Society in Gaza*, p. 232.
32. See the documentary film, *Rue Abu Jamil*, referred to above.
33. Roy, *Hamas and Civil Society in Gaza*, p. 232.
34. See: http://freegaza.org (accessed 29 Jan. 2014).
35. *Wall Street Pit*, 31 May 2010, text available at http://wallstreetpit.com/30095-turkish-prime-minister-erdogan-accuses-israel-of-state-terrorism/ (accessed 29 Jan. 2014).
36. Ibid.
37. http://mfa.gov.il/MFA/HumanitarianAid/Palestinians/Lists_Controlled_Entry_Items_4-Jul-2010.htm (accessed 29 Jan. 2014).
38. 'Dashed Hopes: Continuation of the Gaza Blockade': a report published on 30 Nov. 2010 by a conference of twenty-two NGOs including the International Federation for Human Rights (FIDH), http://www.fidh.org/en/north-africa-middle-east/israel-occupied-palestinian-territories/Palestinian-Authority/DASHED-HOPES-CONTINUATION-OF-THE-GAZA-BLOCKADE/ (accessed 29 Jan. 2014).
39. Mughrabi, Nidal al-, 'Le bâtiment revit à Gaza grâce aux tunnels avec l'Egypte', Reuters, Gaza, 25 Dec. 2011.
40. Ibid. p. 8.
41. Lebhour, Karim, *Jours tranquilles à Gaza*, Paris: Riveneuve, 2010, pp. 159–9.
42. Contribution made by Christian Oberlin to a roundtable discussion on the theme of 'Childhood in Gaza', Sciences Po, Paris, 17 October 2011.
43. The United Nations OCHA has analysed authorised imports into the Gaza strip from June 2007 distinguishing 'humanitarian' from 'commercial' imports, http://www.ochaopt.org/dbs/Crossings/CommodityReports.aspx (see 'View Truckloads Data') (accessed 29 Jan. 2014).
44. Interview with Sami Abdel Shafi, Gaza, 11 Nov. 2010.
45. AFP, 23 June 2007, http://www.thisissyria.net/english/2007/06/23/arab&world/01.html (accessed 29 Jan. 2014).
46. Nabil Abu Rudeina, spokesman for the Palestinian presidency, 23 June 2007, http://www.thisissyria.net/english/2007/06/23/arab&world/01.html (accessed 29 Jan. 2014).
47. International Crisis Group, 'Inside Gaza', Brussels, 20 Dec. 2007.

48. Ibid. p. 14.

49. Ibid. p. 15.

50. AFP, Ramallah, 13 Nov. 2007.

51. International Crisis Group, 'Ruling Palestine: Gaza under Hamas', Brussels: 19 Mar. 2008.

52. Institut d'études palestiniennes, *Coulée de plomb*, p. 146.

53. International Crisis Group, 'Gaza's Unfinished Business', p. 4.

54. Fibla, Carla and Fadi Skaik, *Resistiendo in Gaza*, Barcelona: Peninsula, 2010, p. 191.

55. Muniz, Juan Miguel, 'Al Qaeda choca con Hamas in Gaza', *El Pais*, 25 Jan. 2010.

56. International Crisis Group, 'Radical Islam in Gaza', Brussels, 9 Mar. 2011, p. 13.

57. Filiu, Jean-Pierre, 'The Brotherhood Versus al-Qa'ida', *Current Trends in Islamist Ideology*, 9 (Autumn 2009).

58. See the interview with a militant jihadist in Fibla and Skaik, *Resistiendo in Gaza*, pp. 191–3.

59. A French translation was published in *Libération* on 28 Dec. 2010.

60. http://www.rfi.fr/moyen-orient/20111126-hamas-israel-le-hamas-accord-une-resistance-populaire-pacifique (accessed 29 Jan. 2014).

61. Zecchini, Laurent, 'Les Palestiniens n'attendent plus rien des contacts entre le Fatah et le Hamas', *Le Monde*, 28 Dec. 2011.

SELECT BIBLIOGRAPHY

Abdel Shafi, Mustafa, *Would They Ever Learn?* Gaza: Rashad Shawa Cultural Centre, 2000.

Abu Amir, Adnan, *Usul al-haraka al-islamiyya fi qita' Ghazza*, Cairo: Markaz al-a'lam al-arabi, 2006.

Abu Amr, Ziad, *Islamic Fundamentalism in the West Bank and Gaza*, Bloomington, IN: Indiana University Press, 1994.

Abu Naml, Hussein, *Qita' Ghazza 1948–1967*, Beirut: Center for Palestinian Research, 1979.

Abu Shaaban, Hilmi, *Tarikh Ghazza: naqd wa tahlil*, Jerusalem: Matbaa Beit al-Maqdis, 1943.

Achcar, Gilbert, *The Arabs and the Holocaust*, London: Picador, 2010.

Arif, Arif al-, *Tarikh Ghazza*, Jerusalem: Dar al-Aytam al-Islamiyya, 1943.

Ashur, Said, *Ghazzatu Hashim*, Amman: Dar al-Diya, 1988.

Atallah, Mahmud Ali, *Niyabat Ghazza fi-l 'ahd al-mamluki*, Beirut: Dar al-Afaq al-Jadida, 1986.

Azaar, Muhammad Khaled al-, *Al-muqawama fi qita' Ghazza, 1967–1975*, Cairo: Dar al-Mustaqbal al-Arabi, 1987.

Balawi, Hassan, *Dans les coulisses du mouvement national palestinien*, Paris: Denoël, 2008.

Bar-On, Mordechai, *The Gates of Gaza 1955–1957*, New York: St. Martin's Press, 1994.

Barthe, Benjamin, *Ramallah Dream*, Paris: La Découverte, 2011.

Ben Ayyash, Awda Muhammad, *Rafah, madina 'ala al-hudud*, Gaza: Rashad Shawa Cultural Centre, 2002.

Bitton-Ashkelony, Brouria and Aryeh Kofsky (eds), *Christian Gaza in Late Antiquity*, Leiden: Brill, 2004.

Boltanski, Christophe and Jihane Tahri, *Les Sept Vies de Yasser Arafat*, Paris: Grasset, 1997.

SELECT BIBLIOGRAPHY

Bseisso, Muin, *Yawmiyyat Ghazza*, Cairo: Al-Haya al-Masriyya al-'amma li-l-Talif wa-l-nashr, 1971.

Bucaille, Laetitia, *Gaza: la violence de la paix*, Paris: Presses de Sciences Po, 1998.

Buehrig, Edward, *The UN and the Palestinian Refugees*, Bloomington, IN: Indiana University Press, 1972.

Buji, Muhammad Bakr al- and Riyad Ali al-Ayla, *Yibna: tarikh wa dhakira*, Gaza: Matabi' Mansour, 2000.

Burns, E.L.M., *Between Arab and Israeli*, London: Harraps, 1962.

Butt, Gerald, *Life at the Crossroads*, Nicosia: Rimal, 1995.

Chehab, Zaki, *Inside Hamas*, New York: Nation Books, 2007.

Clarens, Katia, *Une saison à Gaza*, Paris: Jean-Claude Lattès, 2011.

Cossali, Paul and Clive Robson, *Stateless in Gaza*, London: Zed Books, 1986.

D'Arvieux, Laurent, *Mémoires du Chevalier d'Arvieux*, Paris: Delespine, 1735, text available at http://gallica.bnf.fr/ark:/12148/bpt6k104927d

Dayan, Moshe, *Diary of the Sinai Campaign*, London: Weidenfeld and Nicolson, 1966.

Doughty, Richard and Mohammad El-Aydi, *Gaza: Legacy of Occupation—A Photographer's Journey*, Boulder, CO: Kumarian Press, 1995.

Dowling, Theodore, *Gaza, a City of Many Battles*, London: SPCK, 1913.

Downey, Glanville, *Gaza in the Early Sixth Century*, Norman, OK: Oklahoma University Press, 1963.

Eisenman, Robert, *Islamic Law in Palestine and Israel*, Leiden: Brill, 1978.

El-Haddad, Leila and Maggie Smith, *The Gaza Kitchen*, Charlottesville, VA: Just World Books, 2013.

Enderlin, Charles, *Le grand aveuglement*, Paris: Albin Michel, 2009.

Falluji, Imad, *Ma'a al-ra'is*, Amman: Dar al-Shuruk, 2009.

Faysal, Numan Abdelhadi, *A'lam min jil al-ruwad min Ghazzatu Hashem*, Gaza: Dar al-Duktur, 2010.

Feldman, Ilana, *Governing Gaza: Bureaucracy, Authority and the Work of Rule, 1917–1958*, Durham, NC: Duke University Press, 2008.

Fibla, Carla and Fadi Skaik, *Resistiendo en Gaza*, Barcelona: Peninsula, 2010.

Filiu, Jean-Pierre, *The Arab Revolution: Ten Lessons from the Democratic Uprising*, London: Hurst, 2011.

Gilbert, Mads and Erik Fosse, *Eyes in Gaza*, London: Quartet, 2010.

Grainger, John D., *The Battle for Palestine 1917*, Rochester, NY: Boydell Press, 2006.

Grégoire, Henri and M.A. Kugener, *Marc le Diacre, Vie de Porphyre*, Paris: Belles Lettres, 1930.

Gunning, Jeroen, *Hamas in Politics*, New York: Columbia University Press, 2009.

Haldimann, Marc-André et al. (eds), *Gaza à la croisée des civilisations*, Neuchâtel: Chaman, 2007.

SELECT BIBLIOGRAPHY

Hamdan, Muhammad Said, *Siyasat Misr tijah al-qadiyya al-filistiniyya 1948–1956*, Amman: Al-Yazuri, 2006.

Hammel, Eric, *Six Days in June*, New York: Macmillan, 1992.

Hatina, Meir, *Islam and Salvation in Palestine*, Tel Aviv: Moshe Dayan Center, 2001.

Hassouna, Issam, *23 yuliyu wa Abd al Nasir: shihadati*, Cairo: Al Ahram, 1990.

Hevelone-Harper, Jennifer Lee, *Disciples of the Desert*, Baltimore, MD: Johns Hopkins University Press, 2005.

Hill, G.F. (trans. and ed.) *The Life of Porphyry, Bishop of Gaza, by Mark the Deacon*, Oxford: Clarendon Press, 1913 (text available at http://www.fordham.edu/halsall/basis/porphyry.asp).

Hroub, Khaled, *Hamas: A Beginner's Guide*, London: Pluto Press, 2006.

Issa, Ibrahim, *Al-maqalat al-ghazzawiyya*, Cairo: Madbouli, 2009.

Josephus, trans. G.A. Williamson, revised by E. Mary Smallwood, *The Jewish War*, London: Penguin Books (revised edn), 1981.

Katz, Samuel, *The Hunt for the Engineer*, New York: Fromm, 1999.

Kempf, Hervé and Jérôme Equer, *Gaza, la vie en cage*, Paris: Seuil, 2006.

Kerr, Malcolm H., *The Arab Cold War: Gamal Abd al-Nasir and his Rivals, 1958–1970*, London: Oxford University Press, 1965 (3rd edn 1975).

Khalidi, Rashid, *The Iron Cage*, Boston: Beacon Press, 2006.

Khalidi, Walid, *All That Remains*, Washington, DC: Institute of Palestinian Studies, 1992.

Khoury-Tadié, Arlette, *Une enfance à Gaza, 1942–1958*, Paris: Maisonneuve-Larose, 2002.

King, John, *Handshake in Washington: The Beginning of Middle East Peace*, Reading: Ithaca Press, 1994.

Krämer, Gudrun, *A History of Palestine*, Princeton, NJ: Princeton University Press, 2008.

Lang, Erica, *A Study of Women and Work in the Shati Refugee Camp*, Jerusalem: Arab Thought Forum, 1992.

Laurens, Henry, *La question de Palestine (vol. 1, 1799–1921)*, Paris: Fayard, 1999.

———— *La question de Palestine (vol. 2, 1922–1947)*, Paris: Fayard, 2002.

———— *La question de Palestine (vol. 3, 1947–1967)*, Paris: Fayard, 2007.

———— *La question de Palestine (vol. 4, 1967–1982)*, Paris: Fayard, 2011.

Lebhour, Karim, *Jours tranquilles à Gaza*, Paris: Riveneuve, 2010.

Legrain, Jean-François, *Les Palestines du quotidien. Les élections de l'autonomie, janvier 1996*, Beirut: CERMOC, 1999.

———— *Les voix du soulèvement palestinien*, Cairo: CEDEJ, 1991.

Lesch, Ann Mosely and Mark Tessler, (eds), *Israel, Egypt and the Palestinians*, Bloomington, IN: Indiana University Press, 1989.

Lia, Brynjar, *Building Arafat's Police*, Reading: Ithaca Press, 2007.

———— *A Police Force Without a State*, Reading: Ithaca Press, 2006.

SELECT BIBLIOGRAPHY

Lockman, Zachary and Joel Beinin, *Intifada*, Boston: Merip, 2009.

Loti, Pierre [pseud. Julien Viaud], *Le désert*, Paris: Calmann Lévy, 1895; text available at http://gallica.bnf.fr/ark:/12148/bpt6k5828140t

Lukacs, Yehuda (ed.) *The Israeli–Palestinian Conflict: A Documentary Record*, Cambridge: Cambridge University Press, 1992.

McGeough, Paul, *Kill Khalid*, New York: New Press, 2009.

Mattar, Philip, *The Mufti of Jerusalem*, New York: Columbia University Press, 1988.

Meyer, Martin, *History of the City of Gaza*, New York: Columbia University Press, 1907; reprinted Piscataway, NJ: Gorgias Press, 2008.

Milton-Edwards, Beverley, *Islamic Politics in Palestine*, London: I.B. Tauris, 1996.

Milton-Edwards, Beverley and Stephen Farrell, *Hamas: The Islamic Resistance Movement*, Cambridge: Polity Press, 2010.

Mishal, Shaul and Avraham Sela, *The Palestinian Hamas*, New York: Columbia University Press, 2000.

Morris, Benny, *The Birth of the Palestine Refugee Problem*, Cambridge: Cambridge University Press, 1987.

——— *Israel's Border Wars*, Oxford: The Clarendon Press, 1993.

Mubayyid, Salim, *Al-binayat al-athariyya al-islamiyya fi Ghazza*, Cairo: Al-Hayya al-Masriyya al-'Amma li-l-Kitab (Egyptian General Book Organisation), 1995.

Musallam, Manuel, *Curé à Gaza*, Paris: L'Aube, 2010.

Nasser, Jamal and Roger Heacock (eds), *Intifada: Palestine at the Crossroads*, New York: Praeger, 1990.

O'Ballance, Edgar, *The Arab–Israel War 1948*, London: Faber and Faber, 1956.

O'Neill, Bard E., *Armed Struggle in Palestine*, Boulder, CO: Westview Press, 1978.

Palestine and Transjordan Administrative Reports, London: Archive Editions, 1995.

Picaudou, Nadine, *Le mouvement national palestinien*, Paris: L'Harmattan, 1989.

Picaudou, Nadine and Isabelle Rivoal (eds), *Retours en Palestine*, Paris: Karthala, 2006.

PLO, *Majzara qita' Ghazza*, Tunis: PLO Information and Culture Centre, 1983.

Political Diaries of the Arab World: Jordan and Palestine, London: Archive Editions, 1991.

Porat, Yehoshua, *The Emergence of the Palestinian National Arab Movement: From Riots to Rebellion*, London: Frank Cass, 1977.

Qajah, Juma Ahmed, *Ghazza, khamsat alaf am khudur wa khidara*, Beirut: Dar al-Ulum al-Arabiyya, 2003.

Quandt, William, Fuad Jabber and Ann Mosley Lesch (eds), *The Politics of Palestinian Nationalism*, Berkeley: University of California Press, 1973.

Qureia, Ahmed [Abu Ala], *Al-tariq ila kharitat al-tariq*, Beirut: Institute for Palestinian Studies, 2011.

Rafiq, Abdelkarim, *Ghaza min khilal al-watha'iq al-shar'iyya*, 1980.

Rantissi, Mohamed, *Survivre à Gaza*, Monaco: Koutoubia-Alphée, 2009.

SELECT BIBLIOGRAPHY

Rashid, Harun Hashim, *Qissat madinat Ghazza*, Tunis: Alesco, 1987.

Rogan, Eugene and Avi Shlaim, *The War for Palestine*, Cambridge: Cambridge University Press, 2001.

Rougier, Bernard, *Qu'est-ce que le salafisme*, Paris: PUF, 2008.

——— *L'Oumma en fragments*, Paris: PUF, 2011.

Roy, Sara, *Failing Peace*, London: Pluto Press, 2007.

——— *Hamas and Civil Society in Gaza*, Princeton, NJ: Princeton University Press, 2011.

Saati, Ahmed Muhammad al-, *Al-tattawur al-thaqafi fi Ghazza*, Gaza: Islamic University, 2005 (3 vols).

Sacco, Joe, *Footnotes in Gaza*, London: Jonathan Cape, 2009.

Sanbar, Elias, *1948: l'expulsion*, Paris: Les Livres de la Revue d'Etudes Palestiniennes, 1984.

Sayigh, Yezid, *Armed Struggle and the Search for the State*, Oxford: Oxford University Press, 1997.

Schiff, Zeev and Ehud Yaari, *Intifada*, New York: Simon and Schuster, 1990.

Shachar, Nathan, *The Gaza Strip: Its History and Politics*, Eastbourne: Sussex Academic Press, 2010.

Sharab, Yusri Ragheb, *Qita Ghazza min ihtilal ila al-thawra*, Cairo: Mu'assassat al-Tubji, 2005.

Sharif, Kamal and Mustafa Sibai, *Al-Ikhwan al-Muslimun fi harb Filistin*, Cairo: Dar al-Tawzi' wa-l Nashr al-Islamiyya, 1974.

Shlaim, Avi, *The Iron Fist*, London: Allen Lane, The Penguin Press, 2000.

——— *Lion of Jordan*, London: Allen Lane, The Penguin Press, 2007.

——— *The Politics of Partition*, Oxford: Oxford University Press, 1990.

Shurrab, Muhammad Hasan, *Ghazzatu Hashem*, Amman: Al-Ahliyya, 2006.

Sinwar, Yahya, *Al-Majd*, Gaza: Waed, 2009.

Si-Salim, Issam and Zakaria Ibrahim Sanawar, *Liwa Ghazza fi al-asr al-'uthmani al-awwal*, Gaza: Islamic University, 2004.

Sourani, Ghazi, *Qita Ghazza 1948–1993*, Damascus: Centre for Popular Studies, 1993.

Sudfi, Falah Salama and A'tada Saadallah Qanayta, *Asad al-muqawama, al-shahid duktur 'Abd al-'Aziz al-Rantissi*, Gaza: Maktab al-Jil, 2010.

Sukayk, Ibrahim, *Shakhsiyyat araftuha wa mawaqif shadidtuha*, Gaza: Dar al-Miqdad, 2001.

Tabaa, Uthman Mustafa, *Ithaf al-'izza fi tarikh Ghazza*, Gaza: Al-Yazji (4 vols), 1999.

Tamimi, Azzam, *Hamas: Unwritten Chapters*, London: Hurst, 2007.

Theobald, Andrew, 'Watching the War and Keeping the Peace: The UNTSO in the Middle East, 1949–1956', PhD thesis, Queens University, Kingston, Ontario, 28 May 2009.

Yassin, Abdelqadir, *'Umr fi al-manfa*, Damascus: Dar al-Wataniyya al-Jadida, 2009.

CHRONOLOGY

Late Fifth Millennium BC: Earliest signs of human habitation on the site of Qatif, near the southern end of the Gaza strip.

Approx. 3100 BC: Egyptian settlement at Tell al-Sakan.

Approx. 1650 BC: Fortification of Tell al-Ajjul by the Hyksos.

Fourteenth Century BC: Foundation of the city of Gaza as capital of the Egyptian domain of Canaan.

Twelfth Century BC: Gaza becomes one of the five main cities of Philistia.

734 BC: Assyrian conquest of the city of Gaza.

601 BC: Capture of Gaza by the Babylonians.

529 BC: Gaza becomes a Persian military outpost.

332 BC: Siege and destruction of the city of Gaza by Alexander the Great.

312 BC: Gaza region becomes part of the Egyptian Kingdom of the Ptolemies.

198 BC: Gaza governed by the Seleucid dynasty from Antioch.

96 BC: The Hasmoneans introduce Judaism to Gaza.

63 BC: Gaza becomes part of the Roman province of Syria.

AD 66: Zealots attack Gaza as part of the Jewish revolt against the Romans.

AD 130: The Roman Emperor Hadrian visits the city of Gaza.

AD 291: Saint Hilarion born in the city of Gaza.

AD 332: Christian uprising in the port region of the city of Gaza, which is renamed Constantia.

CHRONOLOGY

AD 402: Destruction of the temples of the Roman deities in the city of Gaza.

AD 530–49: Mercian Bishop of Gaza.

AD 618–29: Persian occupation of Gaza region.

AD 637: Islamic conquest of Gaza.

AD 767: Birth in the city of Gaza of Imam Shafi'i (the codifier of the Shafi'i school of Islamic law).

AD 969: Foundation of the city of Cairo (*Al-Qahira*) by the Fatimids.

1099: The crusaders capture the city of Gaza.

1149: Templar citadel built in Gaza.

1187: Re-conquest of Gaza by Saladin.

1191–2: The crusader leader Richard the Lionheart in Gaza.

1244: The crusaders defeated in Gaza.

1260: Short-lived Mongol occupation of Gaza region.

1291: Gaza becomes an autonomous principality of the Mamluk Kingdom.

1387: Building of the caravanserai of Khan Yunis.

1516: Ottoman capture of Gaza.

1556–1690: Government of Gaza by the Radwan family.

1665: Nathan of Gaza proclaims Sabbatai Zvi as the Jewish messiah.

1799: Gaza captured by France's general Napoléon Bonaparte (the future French emperor).

1855: Construction of the Mosque of Hashem.

1906: The administrative frontier between the Gaza region and Egypt was defined, running through Rafah.

1908: The first motor car was introduced into Gaza.

1915 (February): The Ottoman Empire withdrew its troops from the Suez Canal to Gaza after defeat by the British army.

1917 (March–November): Fighting for control of Gaza ends with hard-won British victory.

1928 (May): Fahmi al-Husseini becomes mayor of Gaza (in office for ten years).

1929 (August): Anti-Jewish riots in Gaza.

1936 (April): Beginning of a general strike (for six months) and of the great Arab revolt in Palestine, which lasted for almost three years.

1939 (January): Rushdi Shawa becomes mayor of Gaza (in office for twelve years).

1946 (25 November): Establishment of a branch of the Muslim Brotherhood in Gaza.

1947 (29 November): The United Nations approve a plan for the partition of Palestine.

1948 (14 May): Proclamation of the State of Israel.

1948 (22 September): The All-Palestine Government proclaimed in Gaza.

1948 (15 October): Israeli counter-attack on Egyptian forces.

1948 (22 December): Renewed Israeli offensive in the Negev.

1949 (7 January): Ceasefire signed, incidentally creating the 'Gaza Strip'.

1949 (15 September): Collapse of the Israel/Palestine peace conference in Lausanne.

1951 (21 October): Israeli raid on Gaza suburbs (with many casualties).

1953 (28 August): Unit 101 (commanded by Ariel Sharon) attacks Bureij Camp.

1955 (28 February): Further raid by Unit 101 and riots in Gaza.

1955 (28 March): Gamal Abdel Nasser in Gaza.

1955 (27 August): First incursions into Israel by fedayin from Gaza.

1956 (5 April): Israeli mortar attack on the centre of Gaza.

1956 (2 November): First Israeli occupation of Gaza begins (until 7 March 1957).

1962 (5 March): New Constitution for the Gaza Strip promulgated by Egypt.

1966 (20 May): Meeting of the Palestinian National Council in Gaza.

CHRONOLOGY

1967 (6 June): Israeli invasion of Gaza.

1967 (11 June): First anti-Israeli operation in Gaza.

1967 (November): Creation of the PLF.

1968 (January): Israel dismantles resistance networks in Gaza.

1971 (Summer): Israel campaign against the PLO in Gaza.

1971 (September): Rashad Shawa becomes mayor of Gaza.

1971 (21 November): Death of Ziad al-Husseini, head of the PLF in Gaza.

1972 (September): Israel gives official recognition to Haydar Abdel Shafi's Gaza-based Palestinian Red Crescent.

1972 (22 October): Rashad Shawa deposed as mayor: Israel administers Gaza directly.

1973 (9 March): Death of Muhammad al-Aswad (the Guevara of Gaza).

1973 (7 September): Inauguration of Sheikh Ahmed Yassin's mosque.

1975 (22 October): Rashad Shawa reinstated as mayor.

1978 (16–18 October): Nationalist conference in Gaza.

1979 (1 June): Murder of Sheikh Khazandar (Fatah).

1979 (September): Israel authorises the Mujamma organisation to operate.

1980 (7 January): Islamist attack on the Palestinian Red Crescent.

1981 (1 December): Installation of Israel's 'civil administration' in Gaza.

1983 (10 March): Murder of an Israeli civilian in Gaza's market.

1984 (12 April): PFLP hijacks an Israeli bus.

1984 (13 June): Sheikh Yassin imprisoned for the first time (he was released on 30 May 1985).

1984 (9 August): Israel establishes settlement at Dugit (in the north of the Gaza Strip).

1986 (late June): Clashes between nationalists and Islamists.

1987 (2 August): Murder of an Israeli officer by Islamic Jihad.

1987 (9 December): The first Intifada begins in Gaza.

384

1987 (14 December): Foundation of Hamas.

1988 (23 March): Meeting between Shimon Peres and Mahmoud Zahar (Hamas).

1988 (18 August): Hamas Charter promulgated.

1989 (18 May): Sheikh Yassin arrested by Israel.

1990 (20 May): Murder of seven Palestinian workers from Gaza in Tel Aviv.

1991 (15 January): Israel revokes the general permission for workers to leave Gaza.

1991 (16 October): Sheikh Yassin sentenced to life imprisonment by the military tribunal of Gaza.

1991 (30 October): Haydar Abdel Shafi heads Palestinian delegation to the Madrid peace conference.

1992 (23 May): Abdel Shafi appeals for a halt to intra-Palestinian violence.

1993 (1–7 March): Israeli forces seal off Gaza strip for the first time.

1993 (23 May): Prime Minister Rabin refers to the 'Gaza First' option.

1993 (14 September): First Hamas suicide bombing in Gaza.

1993 (21 October): Murder of Assad Saftawi at Bureij Camp.

1994 (4 May): Gaza–Jericho accord signed in Cairo.

1994 (1 July): Return of Yasser Arafat to Gaza.

1994 (18 November): Palestinian police fire on Islamist demonstrators in Gaza.

1996 (5 January): Killing of Yahya Ayyash in Beit Lahya.

1996 (20 January): Election of Yasser Arafat as president of the Palestinian Authority.

1996 (24 April): Ceremony in Gaza for the official amendment of the PLO Charter.

1996 (15 July): Establishment of UNRWA headquarters in Gaza.

1996 (23 October): Visit to Gaza by France's President Jacques Chirac.

1997 (6 October): Sheikh Yassin returns to Gaza after being released by Israel.

CHRONOLOGY

1998 (14 December): US President Bill Clinton visits Gaza with his wife Hillary Clinton.

1999 (19 October): Visit to Gaza by the South African leader, Nelson Mandela.

2000 (29 September): Second intifada begins.

2000 (12 October): Israel bombs Palestinian presidency.

2001 (8 October): Riots in Gaza against the Palestinian Authority.

2002 (10 February): First rockets fired by Hamas into Israel (with no casualties).

2002 (14 February): Destruction of an Israeli tank at Netzarim.

2002 (23 July): Air raid on Gaza (seventeen dead including Hamas official Salah Shehada).

2003 (16 March): Death of the American student Rachel Corrie, crushed by an Israeli bulldozer in Rafah.

2003 (15 October): Anti-American attack at Erez: American citizens are banned from the Gaza Strip.

2004 (22 March): Death of Sheikh Ahmed Yassin in an Israeli raid.

2004 (17 April): Abdelaziz Rantissi killed in an Israeli attack.

2004 (28 June): First deaths caused in Israel by Hamas rockets.

2004 (11 November): Death of Yasser Arafat in a Paris hospital.

2005 (9 January): Mahmoud Abbas elected president of the Palestinian Authority.

2005 (19 March): Agreement by Palestinian factions to offer a truce to Israel.

2005 (22 August): Evacuation of the Israeli settlements in Gaza is completed.

2005 (15 November): US-sponsored Agreement on movement and access to Gaza (known as AMA).

2006 (25 January): Hamas victory in elections to the Palestinian parliament.

2006 (19 March): Ismail Haniya sets up Hamas government in Gaza.

2006 (28 March): First 'Grad' rocket fired from Gaza (by Islamic Jihad).

2006 (25 June): Capture of the Israeli soldier Gilad Shalit by Hamas (followed by an Israel offensive extending through the summer).

2007 (7 February): Mecca agreement between Hamas and Fatah.

2007 (14 June): Hamas expels Fatah from Gaza.

2007 (19 September): Israel declares Gaza to be 'enemy territory'.

2008 (23 January): Frontier wall between Gaza and Egypt is breached.

2008 (19 June): Truce agreement made between Israel and Hamas under Egyptian good offices.

2008 (4 November): Israel breaks truce with Hamas.

2008 (18 December): Hamas declares truce to be at an end.

2008 (27 December): Beginning of the twenty-three days of the Israeli 'Cast Lead' operation.

2009 (15 September): UN receives report of the Richard Goldstone inquiry.

2010 (31 May): Violent interception by Israel of a fleet of Turkish aid vessels destined for Gaza.

2010 (20 June): Israel partially lifts Gaza blockade.

2011 (15 March): Demonstrations in Gaza for Palestinian unity.

2011 (20 August): 'Grad' rocket fired from Gaza at Beersheba (causes Israeli deaths).

2011 (18 October): Gilad Shalit freed in exchange for 1,027 Palestinian detainees.

2011 (25 December): Ismail Haniya begins a regional tour.

POPULATION STATISTICS*

1950	288,000
1956	332,000
1967	385,000
1968	334,000
1978	434,000
1988	589,000
1993	748,000
1997	1,002,000
2007	1,417,000
2009	1,487,000

The estimate given of the population in 1967 was made by the American sociologist Janet Abu Lughod on the basis of demographic projections. In 1966, Egyptian statistics claimed to show that the population of Gaza had reached 440,000. The spectacular fall after the Israeli occupation was due to the flight of tens of thousands of inhabitants during the conflict and to the encouragement given by the Israeli authorities to the inhabitants to leave. The Israeli census of 1968 was part of a broad policy of suppression of resistance in Gaza, with the population monitored by the issue of new identity cards.

* Sources: figures for 1950 and 1956 are from Egyptian military administration, statistics office; 1968–93 are from Israel Central Bureau of Statistics; and 1997–2009 are from the Palestinian Central Bureau of Statistics (the figure for 1967 is an estimate made by the American sociologist Janet Abu Lughod).

POPULATION STATISTICS

The increase in the population of the occupied Gaza Strip between 1978 and 1988 would have been larger if demography alone had been in question. However, the Israeli–Egyptian peace process in 1982 artificially reduced the figure by cutting off part of the population of Rafah inside Egypt.

The marked increase between 1988 and 1997 arises in part from the difficulty of reconciliation between the Israeli and Palestinian statistics. (The demographer Youssef Courbage puts the extent to which Israel underestimated Gaza's population at 12 per cent.) It is also accounted for by two waves of returnees: one from the Gulf in 1991 and another when the PLO returned in 1994.

The estimation that two thirds of the population of Gaza consists of refugees (as defined by the United Nations) has remained unchanged since 1949. According to UNRWA, 67.9 per cent of the inhabitants of the Gaza Strip were refugees in 2007.

The fertility rate has remained above 5.5 per cent over the last ten years, with an annual growth in population of the order of 3.5 per cent. The proportion of 40 per cent of the population under the age of fifteen (and 57 per cent under twenty) has stayed constant over the same period.

The density of the population of the Gaza Strip overall averages more than 4,000 people per square kilometre. In Gaza City the figure is over 7,000, and it is over 5,000 for Gaza North. These are also the parts of the territory most affected by Israeli offensives that have taken place since the disengagement of 2005.

BIOGRAPHIES

MAHMOUD ABBAS (PLO name: Abu Mazen) (1935–) Place and date of birth: Galilee (Palestine, now Israel), 1935. Mahmoud Abbas fled to Syria as a refugee in 1948. He was a founder member of the then secret Fatah organisation in 1959 and took charge of liaison with Gaza under the cover of his role as an official in the Qatari Ministry of Education. He became a member of the PLO executive committee in 1980 and in 1993 he was a signatory, together with Shimon Peres, of the so-called Oslo Accords. In 1995, he became secretary-general of the PLO and was the first prime minister for the Palestinian Authority from March to September 2003. He became chairman of the PLO in November 2004 after the death of Yasser Arafat and two months later was elected president of the Palestinian Authority. At the time of writing, he has not visited Gaza since Hamas took control there in June 2007.

HAYDAR ABDEL SHAFI (1919–2007) Place and date of birth: Gaza, 1919. Haydar Abdel Shafi was the son of Sheikh Muhyeddin Abdel Shafi who represented Gaza on the Higher Islamic Council from 1930 to 1948. An advocate of Marxism, Haydar trained as a doctor at the American University in Beirut and then in the United States and from 1962 to 1964 he was president of the Legislative Council installed in Gaza by the Egyptian administration. In 1964 he joined the PLO's first executive committee. In 1969, he established Gaza's branch of the Red Crescent, recognised by Israel in 1972, which he made into a pillar of the national resistance movement. From 1973 to 1977, he represented Gaza in the clandestine leadership of the Palestinian National Front; and from 1978 to 1982 he was one of the four leaders of the national orientation committee which represented the PLO in the West Bank and Gaza. He was the head of the Palestinian delegation to the peace conference in Madrid in October 1991, a position he resigned in April 1993 in protest against the stalemate in the negotiations with Israel. He topped the poll for Gaza representatives in the elections of January 1996 for the Palestinian parliament, but resigned in October 1997, this time in protest against what he saw as Yasser Arafat's excessively authoritarian management. His final political gesture was his participation in June 2002 in the Palestinian National Initiative, which aimed to be a middle way between Fatah and Hamas.

ZIAD ABU AMR (1950–) Place and date of birth: Gaza, 1950. Ziad Abu Amr is an academic, educated in Syria and the United States, who has taught political science at the University of Bir Zeit since 1985. In January 1996, he was elected as an independent member of the Palestinian parliament, representing Gaza. Re-elected ten years later he was briefly minister of culture in the government of Mahmoud Abbas (March–September 2003), and then served as minister for foreign affairs in the government of national unity from March to June 2007.

ABU IYAD (birth name: Salah Khalaf) (1933–91) Place and date of birth: Jaffa (Palestine, now Israel), 1933. Salah Khalaf fled to Gaza as a refugee in 1948. He joined the Muslim Brotherhood while studying in Cairo in 1951. In 1952, he established a secret organisation initially named 'The Family of the Sacrifice' which then became the 'Battalion of the Revolutionary Armed Struggle'. He continued to direct small fedayin groups until 1959 when he joined Yasser Arafat in Kuwait and became a founding member of Fatah. In 1969, he played a part in the takeover of the PLO by the fedayin and then fought in the Black September conflict in Jordan. He also took an active role throughout the Lebanese crisis. He went into exile in Tunisia in 1982 and was murdered there by a Palestinian double agent in January 1991.

ABU JIHAD (birth name: Khalil al-Wazir) (1935–88) Place and date of birth: Ramla (Palestine, now Israel), 1935. Khalil al-Wazir fled to Gaza as a refugee in 1948. In 1952, he set up the 'Battalion of Justice' and threw himself into fedayin activity. He left the Gaza Strip and quit the Muslim Brotherhood to take part in 1959 in the foundation of Fatah in Kuwait. He soon assumed military leadership and retained this key role within the PLO. When he was based in Lebanon he was responsible for liaison with the occupied territories and retained this role after 1982 during his exile in Tunis. In April 1988, he was murdered in the Tunis suburb of Sidi Bou Said by Israeli commandos. His death caused an outburst of violence in Gaza, where he was regarded as the spearhead of the Palestinian resistance.

MUSA ABU MARZOUK (1951–) Place and date of birth: Rafah Camp, 1951. Musa Abu Marzouk was educated in Egypt and then in the United States as an engineer. His role in the Muslim Brotherhood was to organise external support for the Brothers in Gaza, in which he coordinated his activities with Khaled Meshal in the Gulf. In 1989, he returned to Gaza to assist Sayyid Abu Musamih to reconstruct Hamas after the arrest of Sheikh Yassin which had left it in difficulties. In 1995, he was arrested by the FBI in New York and in May 1997 he was deported to Jordan. After this, he took only a secondary role in Hamas's political bureau.

FREIH ABU MIDDAIN (1944–) Place and date of birth: Beersheba (Palestine, now Israel), 1944. Freih Abu Middain fled to Gaza as a refugee in 1948. He was a lawyer by profession and originally supported Nasser, after which he transferred his allegiance to Fatah. However, he acted as a defence lawyer for detainees of all political colours, especially the Islamists. He succeeded Fayez Abu Rahmeh as head of the Gaza Bar Association and was a member of the Palestinian delegation in the negotiations with Israel from 1991 to 1993. From 1994, he was minister of justice for the Palestinian Authority, a position to which he was reappointed in 1996 and 1998. He headed the Fatah list for Gaza Central in the parliamentary elections of 1996.

FAYEZ ABU RAHMEH (1929–) Place and date of birth: Gaza, 1929. Fayez Abu Rahmeh trained as a lawyer in Cairo. He was nicknamed the 'Lawyer for the Palestinian Revolution' when he began to defend nationalist prisoners from 1967 onward. In 1969, he was associated with Haydar Abdel Shafi in the establishment of the Red Crescent in Gaza. In 1976, he set up the Gaza Bar Association. He served as a legal adviser to UNRWA from 1982 to 1994 and was a member of the Jordanian–Palestinian joint delegation in 1985. He became the chief prosecutor for the Palestinian Authority in 1997, a post from which he resigned the following year in protest against what he saw as inappropriate actions by the Palestinian Authority.

JAMAL ABU SAMHADANA (1963–2006) Place and date of birth: Rafah, 1963. Jamal Abu Samhadana became a fighter in Fatah combat groups and was the brother of Sami Abu Samhadana, the local leader of the 'Fatah Hawks' during the first intifada. He was made colonel in the Palestinian presidential guard in 1994, but took an independent line during the second intifada when he set up the Popular Resistance Committees (PRC). This organisation, which was a coalition of different factions rather than a unified institution, succeeded in destroying an Israeli tank in February 2002. In December 2004, Jamal Abu Samhadana narrowly escaped an Israeli missile strike. In April 2006, he and his supporters jointed the 'Executive Force' set up by the Hamas government. His death in another Israeli attack two months later prompted the decision by the PRC to capture the Israeli soldier Gilad Shalit.

ISMAIL ABU SHANAB (1950–2003) Place and date of birth: Nuseirat Camp, 1950. Ismail Abu Shanab was brought up in the camp at Nuseirat and then in Shati Camp. He was educated as an engineer in Egypt and the United States. He was a close associate of Sheikh Yassin and was the first leader of the Islamic Association in 1976, also participating in the foundation of Hamas in 1987. He was imprisoned in Israel from 1989 to 1997. Until 1999, he was president of the syndicate of engineers in Gaza. From 2001, he was dean of the faculty of technology and applied science in the Islamic University of Gaza and represented the political wing of Hamas. In 2003, he was killed in an Israeli bombing raid.

KAMAL ADWAN (1935–73) Place and date of birth: Barbara (Palestine, now Israel), 1935. Kamal Adwan fled to Gaza as a refugee in 1948. In

1952, he joined the Muslim Brotherhood. He fought alongside Abu Jihad in the 'Battalion of Justice' and took part in the earliest fedayin attack on Israel in 1955. He was a founder member of Fatah in 1959, and took charge of propaganda for the organisation from 1968. He then joined the PLO where he was concerned with affairs in the occupied territories, and in particular the Gaza Strip. He was killed by Israeli commandos in Beirut in April 1973. The hospital in Beit Lahya/Jabalya Camp in the north of the Gaza Strip was named after him.

ZAKARYA AL-AGHA (1942–) Place and date of birth: Khan Yunis, 1942. Zakarya al-Agha trained as a doctor in Cairo. From 1967, he was one of the principal organisers of Fatah in the occupied Gaza Strip. He was jailed in 1975 and put under house arrest in 1988. From 1980 to 1991, he was banned from leaving the Gaza Strip. From 1985 to 1992, he headed the doctors' association in the Gaza Strip. He was a member of the Palestinian delegation in the negotiations with Israel in 1991–3 and Arafat appointed him head of Fatah in Gaza. He was minister of housing in the first Palestinian government in 1994, but resigned after being defeated in the parliamentary elections of 1996 in his seat at Khan Yunis.

IMAD AQEL (1971–93) Place and date of birth: Jabalya Camp, 1971. Imad Aqel was the first leader of the Ezzedin al-Qassam brigades. From December 1991, he was involved in many armed operations against Israel and alleged collaborators until he was killed in an ambush in November 1993.

MUSA ARAFAT (1940–2005) Place and date of birth: Jaffa (Palestine, now Israel), 1940. Musa Arafat was a cousin of Yasser Arafat. In 1994, he became head of military intelligence in Gaza. His promotion in July 2004 to the position of head of security in Gaza was vigorously challenged by members of the Fatah leadership. Ousted from the post in April 2005, he was assassinated by militiamen five months later as the Israeli forces were withdrawing from Gaza.

YASSER ARAFAT (PLO name: Abu Ammar; birth name: Yasser Abdel Raouf Arafat al-Qudwa al-Husseini) (1929–2004) Place and date of birth: Cairo (Egypt), 1929. Yasser Arafat's father was originally from Khan Yunis. He himself was brought up in Cairo and in Jerusalem. He was initially a sympathiser of the Muslim Brotherhood. In 1952, he became president of the Cairo-based General Union of Palestinian Students. In 1959, he founded Fatah, and in 1969, he became chairman of the executive committee of the PLO. He returned to Gaza in July 1994 to lead the Palestinian Authority, which had been set up under the Oslo Accords. Elected as president of the Palestinian Authority in January 1996, he mainly based himself in Ramallah, which had become the de facto capital of the Authority. From September 2002, Tsahal besieged him in his offices in Ramallah. He agreed to leave his headquarters only to be evacuated for medical treatment in France, where he died shortly afterwards in a military hospital in November 2004.

MUHAMMAD AL-ASWAD (1946–73) Place and date of birth: Shati Camp, 1946. Muhammad al-Aswad was a PFLP activist who carried out armed operations against Israel in the Gaza Strip from 1971. Known as the Guevara of Gaza for his radicalism and his reckless fighting style, he met his death in 1973 in a fierce exchange of fire after being ambushed by the Israelis.

ABDELAZIZ AL-AWDA (known as Sheikh Odeh) (1950–) Place and date of birth: Jabalya Camp, 1950. Abdelaziz al-Awda was educated in Egypt, where he was expelled from the Muslim Brotherhood in 1974. He became a teacher at the Islamic University in Gaza and imam of a mosque in Beit Lahya. He was associated with the foundation of Palestinian Islamic Jihad. He was placed under house arrest in 1983 and was the object of hostility from Sheikh Yassin's supporters. In November 1987, he was arrested, and was deported to Lebanon in April 1988. He was not permitted to return to Gaza until January 2001, when he was allowed to continue to teach Islamic law at Al-Azhar University.

FATHI BALAWI (1929–96) Place and date of birth: Tulkarem (West Bank), 1929. Fathi Balawi was born in the West Bank city of Tulkarem. He became an active Muslim Brother as a student and founded the General

Union of Palestinian Students in Cairo in 1951. As a teacher in Deir al-Balah and then in Bureij, his activity in politics and in the trade union movement led to his imprisonment in Egypt. He took part in the foundation of Fatah in 1959 and was resident in Qatar from 1962 to 1990. After four years with the PLO in Tunis, he returned to Gaza in 1994 as deputy minister of education.

MUIN BSEISSO (1927–84) Place and date of birth: Gaza, 1927. Muin Bseisso was a poet and political activist who received his education in Cairo. He was a militant communist. Jailed in Egypt from 1955 to 1957 for his part in disturbances, he was imprisoned again from 1959 to 1963. He lived an itinerant life as a poet, a revolutionary and a Marxist agitator. After living in Beirut from 1972 to 1982, he moved to Tunis when the PLO set up its headquarters in exile there. He died in London of a heart attack.

MUHAMMAD DAHLAN (PLO name Abu Fadi) (1961–) Place and date of birth: Khan Yunis Camp, 1961. Muhammad Dahlan was an organiser for Fatah and was jailed by Israel before being deported to Jordan in 1987. He was Abu Jihad's representative in the Occupied Territories and then worked for Yasser Arafat. In 1994 he became head of preventive security with the rank of colonel. In 2003, he became minister of security and then in 2005 minister for civil affairs. His role was in fact to be the enforcer for the Palestinian police, in conjunction with his loyal henchman Rashid Abu Shibak. He was elected as a member of the Palestinian legislative council for Khan Yunis in 2006 and became the principal antagonist of Hamas in Gaza, which he has not been able to visit since 2007.

MUHAMMAD DAYEF (1960–) Place and date of birth: Khan Yunis Camp, 1960. Muhammad Dayef became operational chief of the Ezzedin al-Qassam brigades in 1996. Living underground in Gaza he survived at least five Israeli attempts to kill him. He was seriously wounded in a Tsahal bombardment in 2006 and Ahmed Jabari took over as de facto head of Hamas's military wing.

IMAD FALLUJI (1962–) Place and date of birth: Jabalya Camp, 1962. Imad Falluji was educated as an engineer. He became an Islamist but left

Hamas to join Fatah in 1996. He then became the Palestinian Authority minister for telecommunications.

RAWHI FATTOUH (1949–) Place and date of birth: Rafah Camp, 1949. Rahwi Fattouh joined Fatah in Syria before moving first to Lebanon and then to Tunis when the PLO transferred its headquarters there. He returned to Gaza with Yasser Arafat in 1994. He became director general in the Palestinian presidency and was then elected as a member for Rafah in the Palestinian legislative council in 1996. In 2003 he became minister of agriculture and in 2004 he was elected Speaker of the Palestinian legislative council. He served as caretaker head of the Palestinian Authority between the death of Yasser Arafat and the accession of Mahmoud Abbas. He did not run for election in 2006.

ABDURRAHMAN HAMAD (1962–) Place and date of birth: Beit Hanoun, 1942. Abdurrahman Hamad was trained as an engineer in Egypt and the United States and taught at Baghdad University from 1976 to 1980 before taking up a post at Bir Zeit University, where he taught from 1980 to 1994. He was Fatah's representative in the collective leadership of the first intifada and was a member of the Palestinian delegation at the peace talks of 1991–3. In 1996 he was elected as a member of the Palestinian legislative council for Gaza North. He has held a number of ministerial portfolios including housing, telecommunications and transport.

ISMAIL HANIYA (1962–) Place and date of birth: Shati Camp, 1962. Ismail Haniya became a member of Sheikh Yassin's circle, first in the Mujamma and then in Hamas. He was deported to Lebanon in 1992 and rose to more senior positions in Hamas after his return to Gaza. He considered standing in the elections of 1996 but his candidacy was not supported by the Hamas leadership. He was elected as a member for Gaza in 2006 and became prime minister of the Hamas government. From that moment on, he has wielded executive power in the Gaza Strip.

FAHMI AL-HUSSEINI (1886–1940) Place and date of birth: Gaza, 1886. Fahmi al-Husseini was educated in Istanbul. A journalist by profession and a nationalist, he became mayor of Gaza in 1928. He made changes in his ten years in that post that left a lasting mark on the city. In 1938, he was detained by the British authorities, first at Sarafand and then in Acre. He was exiled to Lebanon and then permitted to return to Gaza, where he died shortly afterwards.

FAROUK AL-HUSSEINI (1929–81) Place and date of birth: Jaffa (Palestine, now Israel), 1929. Farouk al-Husseini was the eldest son of Fahmi al-Husseini, the former mayor of Gaza. Educated in Cairo, he was a lawyer by profession. As a militant nationalist, he was jailed by the Israelis in 1957. He took part in the foundation of the PLO in 1964 and helped to finance the anti-Israeli resistance in 1967. In 1974 he was a member of the first PLO delegation to go to the United Nations, under the leadership of Nabil Shaath. He then left the Gaza Strip for Cairo, where he died in 1981.

ZIAD AL-HUSSEINI (1943–71) Place and date of birth: Gaza, 1943. Ziad al-Husseini graduated from the Egyptian military academy and fought in Rafah during the Israeli invasion of 1967. With the rank of lieutenant, he became one of the first officers of the PLF in the Gaza Strip. He became commander of the PLF in 1969 and for two years succeeded in evading the Israelis until he was tracked down in 1971, when he met his death.

HASHEM KHAZANDAR (1915–79) Place and date of birth: Gaza, 1915. Sheikh Hashem Khazandar was educated at Al-Azhar University in Cairo. In 1948, he joined the Muslim Brotherhood militia in Palestine. He was a member of the Brotherhood's central committee from 1952 to 1955 but gradually drew closer to Fatah. In his position as imam of the Mosque of Umar in Gaza, he was completely converted to nationalism by the Israeli occupation of 1967. In 1972, he led the campaign against the pro-Jordanian position adopted by Rashad Shawa. He became a member of the municipal council in 1975. His assassination in 1979 is generally believed to have been the responsibility of George Habash's PFLP.

IBRAHIM MAQADMA (1950–2003) Place and date of birth: Jabalya Camp, 1950. Ibrahim Maqadma trained as a dentist in Egypt and was one of Sheikh Yassin's earliest disciples. He was imprisoned by Israel alongside the sheikh in 1984 and kept in detention until 1992. He helped to organise the Ezzedin al-Qassam brigades and was killed in an Israeli helicopter raid in March 2003 together with his three bodyguards. The mosque that was named after him in Jabalya Camp was hit by Israeli fire during operation 'Cast Lead' in January 2009.

KHALED MESHAL (1956–) Place and date of birth: Silwad (West Bank), 1956. Khaled Meshal was a member of the Muslim Brotherhood from his youth. He organised the foreign support networks for the Mujamma in Gaza, and then performed the same task for Hamas while he was resident in Kuwait and then in Jordan. In 1990 he set up and headed the Political Bureau of Hamas in Amman. In 1997, Mossad attempted to assassinate him. In 1999, he left Jordan for Syria but since 2012 he has spent much of his time in Qatar.

RABAH MOHANNA (1948–) Place and date of birth: Gaza, 1948. Rabah Mohanna trained as a doctor in Cairo, returning to Gaza in 1972. He joined the PFLP and was the target of an Islamist attack in June 1986. In 1987, he represented the PFLP in the joint leadership of the first intifada and was imprisoned by Israel. From 2000, he was a member of the leadership of the PFLP, and from 2005 he was responsible for the PFLP's operations in the Gaza Strip. Because of this, he was detained, first by the Palestinian Authority and then by the Hamas government in Gaza.

YUSUF AL-NAJJAR (1930–73) Place and date of birth: Yibna (Palestine, now Israel) 1948. Yusuf al-Najjar fled to Gaza as a refugee in 1948. As a Muslim Brotherhood activist he organised the riots of March 1955 in Gaza, and was then imprisoned in Egypt. He became a founder member of Fatah in 1959 and in 1965 he headed Fatah's armed branch, Al-Asifa (The Storm). He was murdered, together with his wife, by an Israeli commando in Beirut in April 1973.

AHMED QUREIA (PLO name: Abu Ala) (1937–) Place and date of birth: Abu Dis (Jerusalem), 1937. Ahmed Qureia began his career in international banking and became a Fatah activist in 1968, living first in Lebanon and then in Tunis. He was one of the principal architects of the so-called Oslo Accords with Israel. He was economics minister in 1994 and became a member of the legislative assembly for Jerusalem in the elections of 1996 and was elected Speaker of the parliament. In October 2003 he resigned from this post to become prime minister, a position he held until the Hamas electoral victory in January 2006.

ABDELAZIZ RANTISSI (1947–2004) Place and date of birth: Yibna (Palestine, now Israel), 1947. Abdelaziz Rantissi went to the camp at Khan Yunis as a refugee in 1948, and was educated as a doctor in Egypt. He was a disciple of Sheikh Yassin and a founder member of Hamas in 1987. In 1988, he was imprisoned by Israel and in 1992 he was deported to Lebanon. On his return, he was jailed until 1997. Having become the spokesman for Hamas, he was detained by the Palestinian Authority on four occasions. In June 2003 he escaped death in an Israeli raid on Shati Camp. In January 2004, he proposed a ten-year truce (a *hudna*) with Israel. In March 2004, he succeeded Sheikh Yassin as head of Hamas but was killed in an Israeli bombing attack the following month.

MUNIR RAYESS (1915–74) Place and date of birth: Gaza, 1915. Munir Rayess was educated in Lebanon. In 1946 he became a member of the municipal council in Gaza, of which he became the leader in 1955. In November 1956, he was asked by Israel to remain in his post but in January 1957 he was jailed until Tsahal's retreat from Gaza in March. He continued as mayor of Gaza until 1965 and was a member of the first Palestinian delegation to the United Nations in 1963. In 1967, it was at his residence that meetings were held to organise the resistance to the renewed Israeli occupation.

NAHED RAYESS (1937–) Place and date of birth: Gaza, 1937. The son of Munir Rayess, Nahed Rayess trained as a lawyer in Egypt. He was a childhood friend of Abu Jihad. In 1965, he became a volunteer officer in the PLA (Palestine Liberation Army). As a PLA officer, he participated in the formation of the PLF (Popular Liberation Forces) in Gaza in 1967. In

1968, he secretly left Gaza for Jordan. Based first in Syria and then in Lebanon, he then organised liaison between the PLO and activists in Gaza. He returned to Gaza in 1994 to sit as a judge. In 1996 he became a member of the Palestinian Legislative Council as part of the Fatah group. In 2003, he became minister of justice.

MUSA SABA (1926–) Place and date of birth: Beersheba (Palestine, now Israel), 1926. Musa Saba relocated to Gaza in 1948 and was jailed in Gaza by Israel in 1956, then in Cairo by Egypt in 1959, and once again by Israel in Gaza in 1972. He was a close ally of Haydar Abdel Shafi and from 1976 he was the head of the YMCA, which he mobilised against the Israel occupation.

ASSAD SAFTAWI (1935–93) Place and date of birth: Majdal (Palestine, now Israel), 1935. Assad Saftawi fled as a refugee to Gaza in 1948 and very soon became involved with the Muslim Brotherhood where he came to know Abu Iyad. From 1968, he was a Fatah agent in Gaza and was imprisoned by Israel from 1973 to 1978. With the approval of Abu Jihad, he assisted Sheikh Yassin in his bid to take over the Red Crescent in Gaza. Left-wing nationalists frustrated this move in 1980. He was frequently detained by Israel and in October 1993 he was murdered by masked assassins in Bureij Camp. Imad Saftawi, one of his six sons, is a well-known activist in Islamic Jihad.

MISBAH SAQR (known as the 'living martyr') (1934–) Place and date of birth: Gaza, 1934. Misbah Saqr was an activist in the Muslim Brotherhood and then transferred his allegiance to the Baath. In 1955, he went to the Egyptian Military Academy in Cairo, where in 1958 he organised a secret Palestinian 'Free Officers' movement. In 1964, he took part in the foundation of the PLA, and joined the PLF when it was established in 1967, of which he became the commander for Gaza. When Israel came close to capturing him, Yasser Arafat decided he should fake his death. Under a new identity the so-called 'living martyr' did not re-emerge in public until after the PLO had returned to Gaza in 1994. His appointment as head of preventive security was an honorary position, from which he resigned in 1996.

BIOGRAPHIES

NABIL SHAATH (1938–) Place and date of birth: Safad (Palestine, now Israel), 1938. Nabil Shaath's family was originally from Khan Yunis. In 1948, he went to Egypt as a refugee and was subsequently educated as an economist in the United States. He was a Fatah activist and in 1974 he led the first PLO delegation to the United Nations. From 1994, he was a minister in the Palestinian Authority, at various times holding the portfolios of planning, foreign affairs and culture. From 1996 to 2006 he was also a member of the Palestinian legislative council for Khan Yunis, though he lived in Ramallah. In February 2010 he became the first Fatah leader to visit the Gaza Strip since Hamas took control there.

ABDELAZIZ SHAHIN (PLO name: Abu Ali) (1939–) Place and date of birth: Bashit (Palestine, now Israel), 1939. Adelaziz Shahin fled to Rafah as a refugee in 1948. By profession he was a pharmacist. He joined Fatah in Qatar in 1963. He was arrested by Israel in 1967 and sentenced to fifteen years in prison. After his release in 1982 he was placed under house arrest, and in 1985 he was deported to Lebanon. In 1996, he was elected member of the Palestinian legislative council for Rafah and became minister for supply, a largely honorific portfolio that he held until 2003.

RAMADAN SHALLAH (1958–) Place and date of birth: Gaza, 1958. Ramadan Shallah studied in Egypt and became an economist. He played a part in founding Fathi Shikaki's Palestinian Islamic Jihad movement (PIJ). The Israeli authorities suspended him from his teaching post at the Islamic University of Gaza in 1983. In 1986, he left the Gaza Strip to go to the United Kingdom, where he took a doctorate at the University of Durham, then moving on to Kuwait and finally to the United States. In 1995 he took up residence in Damascus, succeeding Fathi Shikaki as head of the PIJ.

RASHAD SHAWA (1909–88) Place and date of birth: Gaza, 1909. Rashad Shawa was the youngest of five sons of the celebrated former mayor of Gaza, Said Shawa. Educated in Lebanon, he became the administrator (*qaimaqam*) of Haifa in 1935. In 1938, he was exiled to Jordan because of his militant nationalism but was pardoned by the British authorities in

403

1940. In January 1957 he was imprisoned by the Israelis in Gaza. A few months later he was imprisoned again, this time by the Egyptians, who jailed him in Cairo. Following this, he refrained for a long time from political involvement. In 1969, he set up the Benevolent Society and was mayor of Gaza for a year in 1971–2. He maintained his pro-Jordanian stance, as a result of which three attempts were made by nationalists to assassinate him. When he became mayor again in 1975–82, he made overtures to the PLO. He died in 1988. In 1994, his nephew and son-in-law, Aoun, became mayor, and his daughter Rawya became an independent member of the Palestinian Legislative Authority in 1996, to which she was re-elected in 2006.

RUSHDI SHAWA (1889–1965) Place and date of birth: Gaza, 1889. Rushdi Shawa was the eldest son of Said Shawa, the former mayor of Gaza. He was educated in Istanbul. He was himself mayor from 1939 to 1951. He was an advocate of the transfer to Gaza of the British base on the Suez Canal. He served once more as mayor for three months during the Israeli occupation of 1956–7. Shortly afterwards, he was imprisoned in Cairo, together with his brother Rashad, and after his release in 1958 he continued to face hostility from the Egyptians. He died in London in 1965.

SALAH SHEHADA (1952–2002) Place and date of birth: Shati Camp, 1952. Salah Shehada was one of Sheikh Yassin's staff, and was arrested with him in 1984. He refused to make any confession to his Israeli interrogators and was given two years administrative detention in place of a conviction. He was the nominal head of the 'Mujahidin of Palestine' which was in fact an inactive organisation set up to give him a position of prestige. In 1986, assisted by Yahya Sinwar, he set up the 'Majd', an internal security service for the Muslim Brotherhood in Gaza. He was a founder member of Hamas in 1987 and spent long periods in prison in Israel, but was freed in 2000. He was killed in a 'targeted' raid in Gaza in 2002, in which fifteen civilians also died.

FATHI SHIKAKI (1951–95) Place and date of birth: Shati Camp, 1951. Fathi Shikaki was brought up in the camp at Rafah. While he was studying at the University of Bir Zeit from 1969 to 1974 he was in charge of liaison between Islamist groups in Gaza and those in the West Bank. Influenced by the Iranian Revolution while he was living in Egypt, his ideas became more radical, which led him to form the Palestinian Islamic Jihad (PIJ). He returned to Gaza in 1981, but was imprisoned from 1983 to 1984 and then again in 1986. In August 1988 he was deported to Lebanon. He was assassinated by Israeli commandos in Malta in October 1995.

YAHYA SINWAR (1962–) Place and date of birth: Khan Yunis, 1962. Yahya Sinwar was an Islamist activist from his student days and assisted Salah Shehada in establishing the 'Majd', the Muslim Brotherhood's internal security service. In 1988, an Israeli court sentenced him to no less than 462 years in prison. In the event, however, he was one of the Hamas leaders who was freed in 2011 in exchange for the Israeli soldier Gilad Shalit (in whose capture in 2006 his brother had participated).

SAID SIYAM (1959–2009) Place and date of birth: Shati Camp, 1959. Said Siyam was a teacher by profession, who was one of Hamas's early recruits. He was deported to Lebanon in 1992. Shortly after his return to Gaza, he was jailed by the Palestinian Authority. In the elections of 2006, he became a member of the Palestinian Legislative Assembly, with the highest vote of any candidate in Gaza. He became minister of the interior in the Hamas government in Gaza and set up the Hamas government's 'Executive Force'. He was the only senior Hamas leader who died during the Israeli operation 'Cast Lead'.

JAMAL SOURANI (1923–2008) Place and date of birth: Gaza, 1923. Jamal Sourani was the son of Omar Sourani, who was mayor of Gaza from 1925 to his death in 1928. A lawyer by profession, he was educated in Jerusalem and Beirut. He led the nationalist militia in southern Palestine in 1947–8. He was active in opposition to the Israel occupation of 1956–7, and was elected as a member of the municipal council in Gaza in 1962. In 1964, he played a part in the foundation of the PLO.

MUSA SOURANI (1890–1972) Place and date of birth: Gaza, 1890. Musa Sourani was a well-known nationalist figure, who, together with his brother Omar Sourani (mayor from 1925 to 1928), acted as representative in Gaza for the mufti of Jerusalem, Hajj Amin al-Husseini. Musa Sourani was imprisoned by the British in 1938. He sat at the National Council of the short-lived All Palestine Government in 1948.

INTISSAR AL-WAZIR (PLO name Umm Jihad) (1941–) Place and date of birth: Gaza, 1941. As a young militant nationalist, Intissar al-Wazir married her cousin Khalil al-Wazir (Abu Jihad). On Fatah's behalf, in 1965, she played a part in the establishment of the General Union of Palestinian Women, of which she was secretary-general from 1980 to 1985. Herself wanted by Israel, she followed Abu Jihad through his various places of exile and in April 1988 was a witness to his murder. She returned to Gaza to become minister for social affairs·in 1994. In 1996, she was elected to the Palestinian Legislative Council, to which she was re-elected in 2006.

AHMED YASSIN (Sheikh Yassin) (1936–2004) Place and date of birth: Joura (close to Majdal, near the modern Israeli Ashkelon), 1936. In 1948, he fled as a refugee to Shati Camp. In 1966, he became the Muslim Brotherhood leader in the Gaza Strip. In 1973, he set up the organisation known as the Mujamma, thus extending his influence throughout the territory. Jailed by Israel in 1984–5, he founded Hamas (the Movement of Islamic Resistance) in 1987, a few days after the beginning of the first intifada. He was imprisoned by Israel in 1989 and sentenced to life imprisonment in 1991. He was freed in 1997, however, in exchange for two Mossad agents. In September 2003, he narrowly escaped an Israeli raid but died in a 'targeted' bombing raid in March 2004.

SELIM ZAANOUN (PLO name: Abu al-Adib) (1933–) Place and date of birth: Gaza, 1933. Selim Zaanoun studied to be a lawyer in Cairo and was with Abu Jihad when he went into hiding. In 1959, he took up residence in Kuwait and was involved in the foundation of Fatah. He was a PLO official in the Gulf until 1990. In 1994, he became president of the Palestinian National Council, the PLO's consultative body. He is the brother of Riyad Zaanoun, minister of health in the Palestinian Authority from 1994 to 2003.

BIOGRAPHIES

MAHMOUD ZAHAR (1945–) Place and date of birth: Gaza, 1945. Mahmoud Zahar trained as a doctor in Egypt. He assisted Sheikh Yassin in the establishment of the Mujamma in 1973 and was then a founder member of Hamas in 1987. He was deported to Lebanon in 1992 and while in exile, became one of Hamas's best-known figures. After his return to Gaza in 1994, he was received by Yasser Arafat. In 2003, he escaped an Israeli raid in which one of his sons was killed. In 2006, he was elected to be a member of the Palestinian Legislative Council. He joined the Hamas government as minister for foreign affairs. Another of his sons was killed by Tsahal in 2008.

INDEX OF ORGANISATIONS

INDEX OF ORGANISATIONS

INDEX OF ORGANISATIONS

411

INDEX OF PERSONAL NAMES

INDEX OF PERSONAL NAMES

INDEX OF PERSONAL NAMES

INDEX OF PERSONAL NAMES

INDEX OF PERSONAL NAMES